Iran Today

Iran. Cartography by Bookcomp, Inc.

Iran Today

AN ENCYCLOPEDIA OF LIFE IN THE ISLAMIC REPUBLIC

—— VOLUME ONE: A–K ——

*Edited by Mehran Kamrava
and Manochehr Dorraj*

Greenwood Press
Westport, Connecticut • London

Library of Congress Cataloging-in-Publication Data
Iran today: an encyclopedia of life in the Islamic Republic / edited by
Mehran Kamrava and Manochehr Dorraj.

   p. cm.
  Includes bibliographical references and index.
  ISBN: 978-0-313-34161-8 ((set) : alk. paper)
  ISBN: 978-0-313-34162-5 ((vol. 1) : alk. paper)
  ISBN: 978-0-313-34163-2 ((vol. 2) : alk. paper)
  1. Iran—Encyclopedias. I. Kamrava, Mehran, 1964– II. Dorraj, Manochehr.
  DS253.I69 2008
  955.05′403—dc22   2008019488

British Library Cataloging in Publication Data is available.

Library of Congress Catalog Card Number: 2008019488
ISBN: 978-0-313-34161-8 (set)
     978-0-313-34162-5 (vol. 1)
     978-0-313-34163-2 (vol. 2)

First published in 2008

Greenwood Press, 88 Post Road West, Westport, CT 06881
An imprint of Greenwood Publishing Group, Inc.
www.greenwood.com

Printed in the United States of America

∞™

The paper used in this book complies with the
Permanent Paper Standard issued by the National
Information Standards Organization (Z39.48–1984).

10 9 8 7 6 5 4 3 2 1

For
Melisa, Dilara, Kendra, Farah, Katayoun, and Maryam

Contents

✦

Alphabetical List of Entries

✦

Topical List of Entries

✦

Acknowledgments

✦

This project has been a labor of love, and we are thankful to a number of friends and colleagues for helping us along the way for the last two years or so as we have worked on its preparation. This encyclopedia would not have come about had it not been for the enthusiasm and dedication of our many contributors, and we gratefully acknowledge their collegiality, professionalism, and their patience and perseverance as they have waited and worked with us through unexpected delays in the project's fruition. Our research assistants—Louisa Anne Aviles, Vanise Castillo, and Kate Eyerman—have also been invaluable in helping us navigate through the maze of sorting out entries and getting the manuscript ready for final submission. Holta Turner deserves special thanks for her superb work and her unflappable professionalism. From the very start of work on the project, she has been our right-hand person, having been instrumental in contacting authors, liaising with the publisher, keeping track of things, and generally keeping our messy work habits in order. We also gratefully acknowledge the guidance, helpful editorial suggestions, and professionalism of Wendi Schnaufer, our editor at Greenwood. Last but not least, we are thankful to our families, especially to our wives and daughters, for cheerfully tolerating our frequent long-distance phone conversations and the many hours we each spent on the computer working on these two volumes. Without their loving care and understanding, we could not possibly have worked on this project.

Mehran Kamrava and Manochehr Dorraj

Introduction

✦

With its long history and great culture and civilization, Iran today embodies a rich, complex, and diverse mosaic that defines its national identity. Diversity is also the operative word that describes Iranian landscapes and geography, its multiple ethnic groups and their varied cultures and traditions, as well as the uneven and vastly different levels of economic and industrial development, conflicting political tendencies, and different and often contradictory social and cultural outlooks. In none of these respects is Iran exceptional. But due largely to its tumultuous political history of the recent past, it appears to encapsulate all of these internal differences and stark contrasts somewhat more distinctly than most of its immediate neighbors.

Although there is no consensus among scholars whether the revolution of 1978–1979 represented a link of continuity or a major detour from the main contours of Iranian history, there is general agreement that the revolution transformed the society and culture in fundamental ways and redefined social life. It created new institutions of governance and Islamicized the culture, education, and the legal system in an attempt to create a new society that would usher in "the reign of piety and virtue." Yet Islamization had to come to terms with the looming shadow of Iran's pre-Islamic illustrious past history and culture (Persia), as well as the realities of an interdependent, globalized world in which, as a developing country, Iran resides on the periphery. It is within the parameters of this dual impact of the past and the present that the dynamics and the complexity of social life in the Islamic Republic unfold.

In this encyclopedia, we have tried to capture this rich complexity as much as possible. We have tried to highlight the most significant aspects of life in Iran since the 1978–79 revolution—the era of the Islamic Republic so far—that we believe warrant in-depth scholarly attention. In doing so, we have relied on the expertise, knowledge, and the generous spirit of our contributing colleagues.

In broad terms, we have divided the life of the Islamic Republic into the general categories of history, politics, economics, society, and culture. While each individual entry deals with a specific topic, the themes of history, politics, economics, society, and culture inform and permeate almost all of the entries. History does not end or start with neat demarcations of time and specific dates, but rather seamlessly weaves events and developments that may on the surface appear unrelated. Although our focus here has been on life in Iran since the establishment of the Islamic Republic, some essays have elaborated on the larger historical contexts that shape and influence contemporary developments.

Perhaps no other facet of contemporary Iran has been more complex than its politics and the nuances of its political life. Difficult though this has been, we have strived to present as complete a picture of Iranian politics as possible. This has included, among other things, discussions of the country's various political institutions, its constitution, elections, political parties, the sources of political legitimacy, the criminal justice system, human rights, the travails of civil society, and the hierarchy of the Shi'a clerical establishment. We have also sought to highlight some of the most important policy pursuits and agendas in both the domestic and the international arenas. Some of the main topics covered in this respect include Iranian foreign and national security policies, Iran's relations with its neighboring states and with key international actors—the United States, the European Union, the United Nations, etc.—and its international trade and economics, especially in the field of oil and other petroleum products.

In highlighting aspects of Iran's economy, entries range from regionalism and urban development to the petroleum industry, agriculture, the banking system, issues of wealth and poverty, class structure and economic mobility, and the private sector. In a number of significant areas, economic, social, and cultural phenomena intersect, and quite a number of entries deal with these important intersections: broadcasting and communications technology, the Internet, public relations, the electronic and print media, and family planning and healthcare.

Perhaps most difficult has been capturing the richness and complexity of Iranian society, its multiple and varied facets, its expressions and outward manifestations, and its nuanced responses to political repression, instability, war, pervasive crises, and the chronic tension between modernity and tradition. Some of the entries designed to highlight these important phenomena revolve around the country's ethnic mosaic, the social role and position of women, veiling, the educational system, sports, intellectuals, the arts and artistic expression, literature, poetry, cuisine, healthcare, and the family.

Other entries deal with the nuances of the cultural life, as they cover the key role of intellectuals and their contributions to art, literature (prose and poetry), and film. These entries capture the complexities of Iranian society, including the tensions between tradition and modernity and the parochial and the global. They represent courageous endeavors under a difficult political condition to create a new artistic synthesis that is reflective of our common faith in an interdependent world, yet is uniquely Iranian in its sensibilities and temperaments. These intellectuals are the cultural gatekeepers who represent the continuity between the rich literary tradition of the past and the innovation of current Western trends. Rightly, they are revered as the artistic conscience of the society and the voice of the voiceless.

The encyclopedia offers a glimpse into an otherwise often misunderstood and complex country that is shrouded in mystery and misperception. As Iran dominates the media headlines once again and has taken center stage in U.S. and European Union strategy toward the Middle East, given the high stakes on all sides, a more nuanced understanding of Iranian society has assumed even more significance and urgency.

Although potentially a discussion of social, political, and cultural life can be contentious given ideological biases of the individuals involved, we have exhorted our contributors to maintain scientific objectivity and to put the integrity of scholarly investigation above political considerations or personal preferences. Along with our many contributors, we hope to have done our part to remedy some of the common misperceptions that often characterize the study of Iran. By presenting a multidisciplinary and textured portrayal of multifaceted dimensions of life in Iran, we believe we have made a modest start. Our hope is that other scholars in the future will carry the torch and further illuminate the complexity that is contemporary Iran. In the future, we hope to continue our collaborative efforts with one another and with colleagues across disciplinary spectrums in order to further enhance the scope, depth, and clarity of the information on Iran that is available to the public at large and to students, scholars, and policy- and opinion-molders across the world.

A Note on Transliteration

✦

This encyclopedia uses the standard transliteration for names and titles in Persian as found in the *International Journal of Middle East Studies*. Whenever possible, with the notable exceptions of *Qashqa'is* and *Shi'a*, diacritical marks have been avoided to keep the text as widely accessible as possible.

Chronology

✦

1978–1979	Islamic Revolution
January 1978	Shah Mohammad Reza Pahlavi leaves Iran, and a history of more than 2,500 years of monarchy comes to an end.
February 1978	Ayatollah Khomeini returns from France after 15 years in exile, and Mehdi Bazrgan is appointed as the head of the provisional revolutionary government.
September 1978	Khomeini is inaugurated as the Supreme leader (*Vali-i Faqih*) and is given massive supervisory power over all branches of government.
November 1978	Militant Muslim students seize the U.S. Embassy.
March 1979	Women hold demonstrations against the new government-imposed Islamic dress codes.
1980	
January	Bani Sadr is elected President.
April	United States severs relations with Iran, imposes economic and political sanctions, freezes Iranian assets, and makes an unsuccessful attempt to release the hostages.
June	Universities are shut down, and the purge of the educational system commences.
July	Mohammad Reza Shah dies and is buried in Egypt.
September	Iraq invades Iran.

1981

January   American hostages are released.

March   Bani Sadr is dismissed from presidency for his criticism that the Islamic Republic violates the human rights of its citizens. He consequently flees to France.

October   Sayyed Ali Khamenie is elected as the president, replacing Bani Sadr.

1982–1984 The campaign of Islamization of culture, education, literature, and art continues.

              The political opposition forces are crushed, and the supporters of Ayatollah Khomeini consolidate their power.

1988   Iran–Iraq War ends.

1989   Ayatollah Khomeni dies.

              Ali Akbar Hashemi Rafsanjani is elected president.

              Sayyed Ali Khamenie replaces Khomeini as the Supreme leader.

1993   Rafsanjani is reelected as president.

1997

May   Sayyed Muhammad Khatami wins a landslide victory and becomes the new president. He encourages the rule of law and reform.

              Civil organizations assume a more prominent role despite crackdown by security forces, the paramilitaries, and the vigilante groups.

              Khatami attempts to end Iran's international isolation and reaches out to Europe, the United States, and Iran's neighbors.

              Iran–U.S. rapprochement culminates in improved relations under the Clinton administration.

2001

June   Khatami wins second landslide victory and is reelected.

              Many Iranians in Tehran hold a candlelight vigil to honor the victims of the September 11 terrorist attack.

              Khatami is invited to come to New York for an interfaith dialogue.

Iran and the United States cooperate on removing their mutual foe, the Taliban, from power in Afghanistan.

2002

January   U.S. President George W. Bush declares Iran to be a part of "axis of evil."

Revelations about Iran's nuclear program become public.

Widespread disillusionment ensues with the failure of Khatami's reforms.

2004

February   In 7th Parliamentary elections, hardline conservatives retake the parliament.

The new parliament refuses to ratify the additional protocol of Paris agreement signed under Khatami's administration with the EU3.

2005

June   The election of Mahmoud Ahmadinejad consolidates the power in the hand of conservative faction in the Islamic Republic.

2006

February   The uranium enrichment temporarily halted in 2003 is resumed.

The International Atomic Energy Agency (IAEA) Board votes to report Iran to the United Nations' Security Council. UN Security Council imposes sanctions on Iran.

Khamenie appoints a bipartisan foreign policy advisory board to advise him on foreign policy.

Ahmadinejad supporters lose the elections for City Council and "the Assembly of Experts," which has supervisory powers over the executive branch and the presidency.

2007

March   The UN Security Council votes for imposing a second sanction on Iran.

IAEA declares that its inspectors have not found any evidence that Iran has a nuclear weapons program.

The U.S. National Intelligence Estimate Report (NIE), a culmination of analysis provided by some 16 U.S. government intelligence agencies, concludes that Iran has not been pursuing a nuclear weapons program since 2003.

Iran and the United States engage in several rounds of diplomatic negotiations in order to bring security and political stability to Iraq.

THE ENCYCLOPEDIA

A

✦ AGRICULTURE

Agriculture has traditionally played a significant role in Iranian economic activity. In 2004, it contributed to 14.1% of the GDP and accounted for more than 30% of employment, 26% of non-oil export, and more than 80% of food supply in the country.

Iran has a great diversity of climatic conditions, ranging from arid (central plain and southern coast) to semi-arid and Mediterranean (western and northern provinces) and very humid (Caspian Sea). Iran has considerable biodiversity, with a total number of plant species estimated to be larger than that of the whole of Europe. The diversity of the climate has supported the production of a variety of agricultural products such as wheat, barely, rice, pistachios, dates, plums, sugarcane, apples, cherries, and melons. Iran ranks first in production of pistachios, fourth in production of almonds, and eighth in production of citrus in the world.

From a total area of 165 million hectares of country, 29% are mountains or steep slopes, 21% deserts and degraded lands, 30% rangelands and marginal lands, and 2% cities, 11% agricultural lands, and 7% forest and scrublands.

Low levels of rainfall and aridity of the climate have always been major challenges to agricultural growth and productivity. Average annual precipitation is about 305 mm, varying from 125 mm in the desert to about 1,270 mm in the plains along the Caspian Sea.

According to the Ministry of Energy, average rainfall during the 2003–2004 farming year was 242.7 millimeters, showing 2% decline as compared

Women plant rice near the Caspian Sea city of Bandar-e-Anzali, 2002. The azolla plant, a floating, nitrogen-rich species, was introduced in Iran about 20 years ago as fertilizer for the rice fields. But it has spread out of control into nearby wetlands and threatens the habitats of fish and migratory birds. (AP Photo/Hasan Sarbakhshian)

with the previous farming year and a 3% decline compared with the long-term 35-year average. This may reflect the impact of recent global warming. Only 10% of the country receives adequate rainfall for agriculture. In 2005, 53% of the total country's arable land depended on the rain fall.

IRRIGATION

A system of underground water channels known as quanat was traditionally the predominant mode of irrigation. Quanat is a straight network of underground channels that bring the underground water to the surface land. There were still 60,000 quanats in operation in 1987. Currently, however, an irrigation system made up of dams, channels, and irrigation networks and the use of diesel and electric pumps have become the dominant mode of irrigation in the country. Increasing demand for underground water irrigation has resulted in significant lowering of the water tables. The improper use of modern techniques has significantly increased the salinity of the arable land in many parts of the country.

In 2004, according to the Ministry of Energy, 19 reserve dams were in operation in Iran, and a total of 142,000 hectares of land were covered by irrigation and drainage networks.

About two-thirds of the total usable surface water resources are used for agricultural irrigation and other uses, while groundwater resources are being used at their maximum safe level, with recent problems of lowering water tables. The efficiency of irrigation water use is low (in the range of 30%), representing a major bottleneck for the enhancement of production and productivity.

PRODUCTION AND TRADE

Since 1979 there has been a notable increase in areas under cultivation of a variety of crops, in particular cereals. In the case of wheat, which takes 55.6% of the total cultivated area, the area under cultivation rose by 13% or 685,222 hectares between 1979 and 1998. Production of wheat rose from 5.8 million tons in 1979 to more than 14 million tons in 2004. Between 1979 and 1998, the yield, which is an indicator of higher productivity of land and technological change, rose by 63% for wheat. The area under cultivation of rice almost doubled from 1.72 million to 2.41 million hectares, and its production and yield rose respectively by 83% and 31%. In 2005, according to the Food and Agricultural Organization of the United Nations (FAO), Iran produced 21.8 million tons of cereal, 1.65 million tons of meat, 26.6 million tons of fruits and vegetables, 695,000 tons of pulses, 11 million tons of sugar crop, 5.9 million tons of milk, and 610,000 tons of eggs.

FAO data for 2005 also show an improved agricultural picture. In 2005, Iran imported 3 million tons of agricultural imports. According to the FAO, feed grains constituted most of Iran's agricultural import in 2004, including 1.7 metric tons (Mt) of maize, 1 Mt of barley, and 0.9 Mt of milled paddy rice.

In 2005, Iran also exported 1.4 million tons of agricultural products. These exports included 138.7 Mt of pistachio valued at $555 million, 137 Mt of raisins valued at $107.8 million, 120 Mt of apples valued at $29.6 million, 51 Mt of tomato paste valued at $26 million, and 22.5 Mt of fresh fruits valued at $14.9 million. Iran also exported 105 metric tons of soya bean oil valued at $75 million. Iran's import of wheat, meanwhile, was substantially reduced to 222,000 in 2004, metric tons from a peak of 6.5 million tons in 2000.

The index of the production of food and non-food rose respectively from 56.3 and 85.4 in 1979 to 141.8 and 139.9 in 1998. Even on per capita basis the food production index rose above the pre-revolution level of 94.6 in 1978 to 115.1 in 1998. Given the fact that the Iranian population grew from 40 million in 1980 to about 70 million in 1998, this rate of growth in food production is considerable.

LIVESTOCK

Twenty-seven percent of the country's lands are pastures, making raising livestock a traditional way of life for nomadic tribes whose population has been rapidly declining since the beginning of the last century. However, there has been a significant increase in animal husbandry. Livestock production contributes about one third of the value added in the agricultural sector. Most of Iran's livestock is sheep (54 million), followed by goats (26.5 million), cattle (8.8 million), and buffalo (550,000). Livestock production amounted to 8 million tons in 2001; it is estimated that this amount will increase to 19 million by 2021. In 2003, there were 2,440,000 honeybee colonies, 598 dairy factories, 134 livestock slaughterhouses, 112 meat-processing factories, 551 pelt-, pickle-, and leather-processing firms, and 214 feedstuff factories. In 2003, Iran produced 752,000 tons of red meat, 6,316,000 tons of milk, 628,000 tons of eggs, and 29,000 tons of honey.

Increase in livestock production has significantly contributed to degradation of pastures and rangeland. These areas have had to support a significant increase in the number of grazing animals over the past several years. It is estimated that overgrazing has left only 16% of rangeland in good condition.

FISHERIES

Iran has 1,800 km of southern coast on the Persian Gulf and 900 km of coastline on the inland Caspian Sea. In addition, there are 1.5 million hectares of inland lakes and rivers. More than 200 species of fish are found in the south, which has made the southern operation increasingly more important than the northern operation. The most important catch in the Caspian Sea is the Caspian sturgeon, which is the source of roe from which famous Iranian caviar is produced. Iran's fishing industry is largely dominated by a state enterprise known as the Iranian Fisheries Corporation, or "Shillat," which operates under the Ministry of Agricultural Jihad. Shillat is in complete control of caviar production and export.

Fisheries are a large resource and fishing is a fast-growing industry; according to the Ministry of Agricultural Jihad, Iran produced 474,500 tons and exported $85 million of fish in 2005. Iran's major import partners in 2004 were, respectively, the United Arab Emirates, Brazil, and Switzerland. Iran's major export partners in 2004 were the United Arab Emirates, Germany, and Iraq. There has also been a growth in aquaculture, which started with a sturgeon breeding program in 1922. Annual fingerling production was 263 million in 1991, mostly for release as part of the government's stock rehabilitation programs.

FORESTRY

Iran's forests cover more that 7% of the area of the country. They are mostly located in the Caspian coastal area, west and southwest of the country. Commercial forestry is carried out only in the Caspian coastal area.

Forests belong to the state, and the Forest and Range Organization (FRO) is responsible for the management of the forests. Deforestation presents a significant problem in Iran. According to a World Bank report, land clearing for agriculture, firewood, and charcoal production reduced the area of forest in Iran from 17 million in 1960 to 12 million in 1990. Based on estimates for 1986–1992, the pace of deforestation is in the region of 200,000 hectares (ha) per year.

In 2004, according to FAO, Iran produced 743 metric tons of industrial round wood, 77 metric tons of wood fuel, 665 metric tons of wood-based panels, 240 tons of wood pulp, and 415 metric tons of paper and paper board.

LAND REFORM

In 1961 there was a major attempt to redistribute land to the farmers by Shah Mohammad Reza Pahlavi. About half of the country's arable land was distributed, and nearly 2 million village families received land. Although the long-term effect of the Shah's land reform is still a major point of controversy, it indeed transformed the structure of land ownership and rural society thereafter. Under the Islamic Republic there was an attempt to further redistrict the land among the landless farmers. In the period up to 1991, a total of about 1.2 million ha were redistributed among approximately 230,000 farmers' households. Creation of the new medium-sized cooperatives, or "moshaa," was promoted by the government. "Moshaa" is a mode of sharecropping in which ownership of the farm is divided among a group of farmers on the basis of equal shares. About 13,000 "moshaa" were established, grouping some 100,000 peasant families.

MARKET LIBERALIZATION REFORMS

Two distinct periods of economic policy-making can be distinguished in post-revolutionary Iran. The early post-revolutionary period was dominated by the revolutionary ideology of radical Islam and the market interventionist policies of the Prime Minister Mussavi (1979–1989). This period is characterized by mediocre growth of productivity and production in most crops, with the exception of permanent and export crops due to less government controls and international markets. A later post-market liberalization period started in 1989 and has more or less continued to the present. The significantly undervalued price of machinery and equipment resulted in rapid and perhaps over-mechanization of the Iranian agriculture in this period.

Between 1979 and 1989 the number of tractors in use jumped from 70,942 to 205,000: 189%, or an average annual growth rate of 18.9% a year. Cereal harvesting became significantly mechanized; by 1988 there were

7,155 combine harvesters, 16,455 self-propelled reapers, and 111,636 threshing machines in the country.

Failure in improving production and productivity during the 1980s initiated a series of market liberalization reforms in the early 1990s. They reflect a shift in the overall economic philosophy of the government from emphasis on price controls, farm input, and consumer subsidies and cheap credit, to recognizing the significance of market incentives, export promotion, and a better system of fertilizer distribution, research, and development. A major price reform was implemented in January of 1991. The government replaced the system of fixed prices and compulsory procurement of six strategic crops (wheat, barley, maize, sugar beet, soybeans, and sunflower seed) with that of guaranteed prices that were set below expected market prices. Starting with wheat, the guaranteed price for producers was adjusted to world price levels.

The legacy of the post-reform was as follows:

1. Shifting from inward-looking development based on agricultural development to industrial growth based on export promotion and liberal trade policies;
2. Rationalization of prices by lifting price control increase in input prices;
3. Creation of a more business-friendly environment and lowering of bureaucratic obstacles; and
4. Unification of the foreign exchange regime and de facto depreciation of the rial that in turn promoted export of agricultural products.

RURAL DEVELOPMENT

After the revolution, the state paid special attention to rural development, including health and basic needs, and rural infrastructure. Between 1990 and 1994, the Ministry of Jihad built 4,900 schools, more than 60,000 kilometers of rural roads, 320 clinics, and 2,700 mosques, and provided electricity for, and access to safe water to, 15,680 and 18,039 villages, respectively, in cooperation with local capital and organizations. By 1998, more than 37,094 villages had electricity, which is about 54% of the total number of 68,122 villages in the country. This ratio for the pre-revolutionary period was about 11%.

Crop insurance is provided for farmers by the government through the Insurance Fund for Agricultural Products (IFAP). In 2004, the IFAP insured 5,318,700 hectares of land under cultivation of farming and horticultural products against losses from natural disasters. In the same year, 4,137,000 livestock, 289.7 million poultry, and 3,423 hectares of fish- and shrimp-raising centers were covered by the Insurance Fund.

The government also provides low-interest loans to the farmers mainly through the Agricultural Bank of Iran. In 2004, the outstanding facilities extended to private farmers were 82.79 trillion rials, or about $9 billion.

According to the last Census in 1998, there were 4,410,370 rural households in Iran. An estimated 3 million of them are farm households. The typical farm is family-run: 91% of land is owner-operated. According to the World Bank report, 350 households or about 13% are commercial farmers. They owned 40% of arable land and contribute half of agricultural value added and 80% of marketed output. Subsistence farms and households generally supplement farm income from other sources.

According to a World Bank report, in spite of the recent improvement in reducing rural poverty, a fifth of farm households had less than one hectare of land, and half a million were engaged in agriculture but did not own any land in 2000.

CHALLENGES

Production and yield of industrial crops such as sugar beets, tobacco, and sugar cane has remained the most stagnant part of the agricultural sector in the post-revolutionary period. This has been mainly due to the fact that the public sector has remained the main purchaser of industrial crops.

Progress in food and agricultural production has been accompanied by increasing pressure on natural resources. Deforestation and erosion have reached alarming proportions.

Iran's agriculture remains a highly subsidized sector. In 2004, the amount of subsidy paid on major agricultural products grew by 40.9%; there was also a 13.3% increase in the guaranteed prices of wheat. This is on top of highly subsidized input prices of gasoline, electricity, natural gas, and fertilizers, which have significantly distorted relative prices in favor of the agricultural sector.

As the result of subsidies, the indiscriminate use of pesticides and fertilizers has become a major cause of environmental degradation. There are also concerns that subsidies have disproportionately favored the rural rich and middle income population at the cost of the rural and urban poor. It is estimated that 26% of the rural population live below the poverty line.

In spite of the significant amount of subsidies to the agriculture sector after twenty years, Iran ranks 14th among major producers of wheat in the world in terms of production and relies heavily on foreign supplies of animal feed. Indeed, the average yield of wheat in Iran for the three consecutive years ending with 1998 was less than 25% of Germany's and England's, less than 45% of China's, 67% of India's, and 82% of its neighbors Pakistan and Turkey.

Suggested Reading

Amuzegar, J. 1993. *Iran's economy under the Islamic Republic.* London: I.B. Tauris.

McLachlan, K. S. 1990. *The neglected garden: the politics and ecology of agriculture in Iran.* London: I.B. Tauris.

Shakoori, A. *The state and rural development in post-revolutionary Iran.* New York: Palgrave Macmillan.

MEHRDAD VALIBEIGI

✦ AHMADINEJAD, MAHMOUD, PRESIDENCY OF

The election of Mahmoud Ahmadinejad to the presidency in 2005 was surprising to many observers who had assumed Aliakbar Hashemi Rafsanjani would win. Ahmadinejad was a little-known mayor of Tehran, whereas Rafsanjani had been one of the main pillars of the clerical system. On its own, much of Ahmadinejad's rhetoric and many of his policies may initially appear illogical, but when considered as a cohesive whole within the context of the Iranian political system, a discernible logic emerges.

Iran is not a one-man dictatorship but rather an oligarchy. Elections constitute one of the main forms of struggle among individuals, factions, and subfactions. Only candidates who are trusted members of the ruling oligarchy are allowed to run for various offices. Hardliners had successfully sidelined their reformist rivals in the two previous elections: the municipal elections in 2003 and the Majles elections in 2004. Disturbed and annoyed at the political disorder and open flouting of the ideals of the revolution in dress, movies, books, and other cultural expressions, many hardline elements were determined to purge non–hardline elements from as many institutions as they could.

Despite much wrangling, the hardliners could not come up with one candidate for the 2005 presidential election. Although united against the reformists around former president Khatami and distrustful of Rafsanjani, the hardliners themselves were divided into many subfactions. The Council of Guardians approved four hardliners for the elections: Ahmadinejad, Mohammad Baqer Qalibaf, Ali Larijani, and Mohsen Rezaee. Only two days before the first round of elections, Rezaee pulled out.

Divergent class backgrounds, policy differences, and personal ambitions forced divisions to surface between these candidates both during the campaign and after the election. The hardline camp includes those from traditional conservative wealthy backgrounds in bazaars and high clerical establishments (represented best by Larijani), urban lower middle classes who have amassed great wealth and power as one of the main beneficiaries of the regime (Rezaee and Qalibaf), and the terribly poor in cities and small towns. Ahmadinejad, born into poverty, made explicit appeals to the poor, who had been mobilized by the regime during the war with Iraq and among whose ranks Basij and lower echelons of the Islamic Revolutionary Guards Corps were based. Suffering from the economic liberalization policies of Rafsanjani and Khatami, the poor voted for Ahmadinejad in large numbers. Ahmadinejad's promise to put oil money on everyone's dinner table and his harsh criticisms of the official corruption appealed to the poor.

Ahmadinejad filled his cabinet and other major posts with members of his subfaction the "Young Conservatives." Like himself, the Young Conservatives are middle-aged, survived the bloody war with Iraq and the armed struggle against domestic opponents, and have backgrounds in the military, intelligence, and security apparatuses such as IRGC, Basij, Ministry of Intelligence, and the prison system. They differ in some ways from the broader hardline faction that dominates the 7th Majles (2004–2008). This has caused friction with many traditional conservative hardline members of the Majles.

Ahmadinejad's cultural, security, economic, and foreign policies depart from those of Rafsanjani and Khatami. Called the Chinese model, Rafsanjani pursued policies to reduce tensions with the United States, substantially improve economic relations with Western Europe, liberalize the economy, increase political repression, and decrease social and cultural restrictions (regarding such issues as viewing movies and wearing the female hijab). Khatami pursued policies to improve relations with the United States, substantially improve relations with Western Europe, establish friendly relations with Sunni Arab governments, liberalize the economy, reduce political repression, and decrease social and cultural restrictions. Ahmadinejad pursues policies to improve relations with radical militant Islamic groups (Lebanese Hezbollah, Palestinian Islamic Jihad, and Palestinian Hamas), increase friendly relations with anti-American governments around the world (e.g., Chavez's Venezuela), increase populist economic policies, increase political repression, and impose stricter enforcement of social and cultural restrictions.

Ahmadinejad's government did not impose a massive crackdown as had been feared; instead, he has targeted repression. The government made pronouncements designed to intimidate the public into observing the regime's values without actually engaging in mass repression to compel them to do so. For example, the government undertook a public yet strategically nuanced action to resist satellite television programming. The government sent security personnel to destroy dishes on rooftops (worth about $20) but it did not go inside homes to confiscate or destroy the receivers (worth about $250), to avoid public resistance.

Ahmadinejad's government immediately moved to impose restrictions on the publication of books and movies it deemed as secular, liberal, and feminist. Although these measures made the middle classes and intellectuals unhappy, they brought satisfaction to the regime's conservative constituencies. The press and journalists had already been muzzled by the judiciary (under the control of hardliners) during Khatami's government, when it closed about 100 publications and prosecuted numerous journalists; therefore, Ahmadinejad's government did not have to do much except stay out of the judiciary's continued repression.

Although there were talks about imposing a much harsher enforcement on women's hijab as had been done in the 1980s, and even hardline females of the Majles talked about mandating a uniform, no visible changes occurred in the actual enforcement during the first 18 months of Ahmadinejad's government.

Although Ahmadinejad's government has specifically targeted prominent dissidents and leaders of the various mass movements for harsh repression, it has done so in a gradual, piecemeal manner with different levels of repression meted out according to different levels of activity. The government has specifically targeted leaders of labor unions, university student groups, women's organizations and teachers' syndicates, as well as prominent secular writers and intellectuals. The government has used physical attacks, imprisonment, and harsh treatment in prison, false accusations of espionage, heavy bails, and expulsion from work or school to compel them to cease activities.

Ahmadinejad attempted to deliver his campaign promises to assist the poor by providing substantial sums despite public criticisms by Majles deputies and economists that such large injections of money into the economy would have a deleterious inflationary impact. The high oil prices and the huge reserves that had been accumulated during Khatami's tenure allowed Ahmadinejad's government to inject billions of dollars into the economy. His government provided large sums of subsidized loans for newlyweds, numerous development projects in provinces, continued subsidies for basic food stuff and petroleum, reduced interest rates, and mandated an increase in minimum wage by private employers. These polices led to increased inflation as had been predicted. The decline in Tehran's stock market, capital flight, and massive reduction of foreign investments are blamed on Ahmadinejad's populist economic policies. Despite the government's stated policy to reduce unemployment, various officials have reported the official unemployment rate as 12.1% and 12.4%. Economists believe the actual rate to be closer to 20%. Ahmadinejad's economic policies have helped many poor individuals, but they also have increased both inflation and unemployment. The government received $55 billion from exports of oil and natural gas in the 2005–2006 fiscal year, in comparison to the $23 billion in the 2002–2003 fiscal year. As long as the price of oil remains high, the government can continue its policies.

Ahmadinejad's foreign policy is a return to Ayatollah Khomeini's strategic goals of exporting the Islamic revolution to the region and making the Islamic Republic the leader of the worldwide militant radical Islamic movements. Ahmadinejad's rhetoric that harshly attacked Israel and cast doubt on the Holocaust has provided his government with many benefits. These speeches made Ahmadinejad a popular figure in many Arab and Islamic countries, thus reducing the ability of their governments to side with the U.S. in its confrontation with Iran. His rhetoric has attempted to reduce the saliency of Iran's identity as a Shi'a, non-Arab power, thus enabling the Iranian government to attract militant Sunni groups to its cause in any confrontation with the United States. Such oratory has also pushed Europeans closer to the U.S. position.

Suggested Reading

Human Rights Watch. December 2005. Ministers of Murder: Iran's New Security Cabinet.

International Crisis Group. 2007. Middle East Briefing No. 21, *Iran: Ahmadi-Nejad's tumultuous presidency*. Tehran and Brussels.

Kazemzadeh, M. 2007. Ahmadinejad's foreign policy. *Comparative Studies of South Asia, Africa and the Middle East* 27, No. 2.

Samii, B. 2006. Iran: weak economy challenges populist president. http://eurasianet.org.

MASOUD KAZEMZADEH

✦ ARABS OF IRAN AND KHUZESTAN

The Arab population of the Iranian province of Khuzestan is estimated to be 3% of the more than 70 million people who inhabit Iran. This can be rounded up to almost 2,100,000. "The Arabs of Iran" refers here to the bilingual Arabic/Persian speaking people who belong to a relative majority group of Khuzestan Province of Iran. Khuzestan, one of the thirty provinces of present-day Iran, is considered to be one of the oldest settled regions of ancient Persia. In fact, the study of Iranian history should start with the study of Elamite civilization, born in the present Khuzestan area of Iran, which contributed to the birth to Achaemanid, Parthean, and Sassanid civilizations. Some modern Khuzi people—the name "Khuzestan" meaning the land Khuzis is attributed to them—do not consider themselves as Arabs, although they are born to Arabic-speaking families. They maintain that the Elamite language, left to us on the reliefs and clay tablets, was an agglutinative language different from the Arabic and Indo–European languages. They are non-Semite and non-Aryan people belonging to the ancient civilization that suffered a devastating defeat from Assyrian Assurbanipal in 640 BC and were subsequently assimilated by the Aryan Achaemanids at a later period. On the other hand, many Khuzestani Arabs refer to the names of nearly a dozen Khuzestani Arab tribes and identify themselves as belonging to them.

The Arab settlement of Iran did not come through the Islamic conquest of the land. The historical and archeological evidence proves that different tribes of Arabs had settled in different parts of Persia long before. However, with the Arab conquest of Iran, its colonization, land acquisitions, and its gradual Islamization brought about a greater influx of Arabs towards the northern and eastern regions. Before Reza Khan's coup d'etat in 1921, Khuzestan, also called Arabistan at that time, was a Sheikhdom and one of the Arab Principalities in the southwestern part of Persia—*Mamalek-e Mahruse-ye Iran*. Similar to other ethnic groups of Iran, the Arabs of Khuzestan lived in their part of the land at relative peace and were governed by local leaders.

Towards the end of the Qajar dynasty, the Sheikhdom was ruled by the Sheikh of Mohammareh, Jabir Khan, from Bani Ka'b tribe. With Reza Khan's ascendance to the throne, Jabir's powers were drastically curtailed, and he was forcibly relocated to Tehran by the government, where he later died. As mentioned earlier, the Pahlavi regime's repressive Persianization measures of ethnic peoples, although at times resulting in the assimilation of many individuals from different ethnic roots, also led to ethnic resentment and tensions among many ethnic groups. Many of the unresolved ethnic problems in Iranian society today are the legacies of the Pahlavi regime's harsh treatment of ethnic issues.

HADI SULTAN-QURRAIE

✦ ARCHITECTURE

Recent political instability and subsequent economic difficulties, as well as the radical transformation of the cultural environment, have exerted a rather negative impact on several aspects of architecture and urban planning in contemporary Iran. Under the confusing sociopolitical circumstances during the first years of the Islamic Revolution (1978–1979) and the Iran–Iraq War

Imam Mosque, Isfahan, 2007. (AP Photo/Ben Curtis)

(1980–1988), architecture in Iran became isolated from the global architectural scene. This led not only to a repudiation of architectural values imported from the West during the late Pahlavi period, but also to an abandonment of traditional architectural professionalism in a country that once created architectural masterpieces. This setback in the development of architectural design and technology was partially due to a change in curricula in architectural education. Schools of architecture tended to adopt a theoretical approach to teaching and research, a trend which upset the principal balance of theory and practice in architecture. As a consequence, the tenets of Western postmodernism were not successfully digested by Iranian architects, despite the architects' talent and potential; nor did any notable aesthetic or technical innovations occur in the architectural work of contemporary Iran.

Some of the buildings constructed during the post-revolution period aspired to compete with iconic examples evolved in Western modern architecture, but they could not go beyond the experimental stage. Driven by the Islamic spirit, a large number of the residential and governmental buildings were constructed with the intention of evoking traditional Islamic architectural forms, such as domes and arches, as well as high ornamentation, ranging from shiny glazed tile work to calligraphic decoration. Yet these buildings cannot indisputably be categorized as tours de force.

Since the 1990s, there has been an increasing concern for architectural identity in Iran, and Iranian architectural language has become genuinely eclectic. Several trends can be observed in Iranian architecture of the last decade within the framework of postmodernism. Instead of being stuck on metaphysical architectural concepts, new trends rely to a certain degree on the Iranian architectural heritage. As a telling example of the fusion of modernity and traditionalism, the Armita Tower, Tehran (1997; architect: Sharestan Consultants) is noteworthy. This 21-story steel and granite structure depends on American skyscrapers but explores the potential of indigenous Iranian architectural styles, for instance, by using the shape of a *"shamseh"* square star and a copper dome. The Sport Complex of the city of Rafsanjan in the Kerman province (2001; architect: S. Hadi Mirmiran) is a remarkable reinterpretation of pre-Islamic Iranian vernacular architecture fitting into a new architectural environment. Drawing on the typology of the traditional icehouse, the complex serves to create a fantasy of an architectural time capsule. A mature form of eclectic architecture can also be seen in the Milad Tower (due to be completed in late 2008; architect: Yadman Sazeh Co.), in the complex of the Tehran International Trade and Convention Centre (the Milad Complex). Rising to a height of 435 meters, the tower will be one of the tallest free standing structures in the world. It is a promising symbol of Iranian participation in the age of globalization. More importantly, the tower is intended to be a triumph of eclecticism, combining two different structural aspects of architecture—skyscraping high-rise construction with an Iranian-favored octagonal base. The architectural future of Iran remains unpredictable yet undoubtedly promising.

Subsequent to the Islamic Revolution, more attention was naturally given to the construction of religious buildings in search for a revolutionary identity. Although mosques were not meant to be architecture per se but were essentially built for the needs of the local community, the style of contemporary Iranian mosque architecture manifests a fascinating diversification. In general, structural and decorative clichés of Iranian mosques, such as domes, arches, courtyards, and tile work, are still predominant. But some of the contemporary mosque buildings ingeniously incorporate modern architectural concepts into their spatial organization, as can be seen in the Al-Ghadir Mosque, Tehran (architect: Jahangir Mazlum Yazdi; completed 1987). The Shrine of Ayatollah Khomeini, south of Tehran (architect: Mohammad Tehrani; completed 1991), is an impressive feat of contemporary religious architecture that acquires a postmodern ambience in terms of scale. Its gold dome towering over a high drum, together with the lavish use of glass and metal, conveys an unforgettable visual message.

Perhaps more than any other large cities in the world, Tehran struggles to cope with the city's overrunning urbanization. The demographic development, environmental problems, and chaotic traffic congestion continue to distort the cityscape of metropolitan Tehran. The life of Tehranians is threatened by poorly regulated urban planning and infrastructural systems. The network of roadways and public transportation is merely designed to connect major junctions across the ever-growing Greater Tehran. A wave of sprawling areas in the vicinity of Tehran prevents the improvement of the residential environment. Housing in Tehran has reached a crisis point, approaching the stage where homes will turn into mere shelters. In building construction, quantity has become more important than quality, and standardized pre-fabricated apartment blocks are abundantly built to sort out the issue of housing shortage. Metal and concrete are predominantly used for the purpose of speedy and economical construction. Countering the immediate negative effects of these materials, some mass-made buildings use brick cladding, giving them a traditional architectural guise. In the meantime, a gradual yet steady intervention occurs in the field of urban conservation, as reflected in the project of the Bagh-e Ferdowsi (designed by the Baft-e Shahr Consultants, Gholamreza Pasban-Hazrat and Farhad Abozzia; completed 1997; received the Agha Khan Award for Architecture in 2001). Located in the foothills of the Alborz mountains, the park is intended to create an interface between the urban population of Tehran and nature. This innovative approach to environmental design serves to add a sustainable urban feature to the city of Tehran. The park is also a notable recreation of traditional Iranian paradise gardens in contemporary times.

Iran has also recently been confronted with the issue of how to maintain a balance between urban developments and historic preservation. Like most countries in the Middle East, this dualism is a key to preserve the unique architectural heritage and cultural identity of the country. Iran is a pioneer country in the field of building conservation, not only with regard to monuments of historical importance but also concerning the issue of how to rescue non-monumental buildings and picturesque townscapes from the threat of demolition. Conservation has focused on the maintenance of the original building fabric in historic towns, primarily made of mud-baked bricks, the complex network of narrow roads and pedestrian alleys, and traditional building typologies, such as internal courtyards. Through this process, traditional craftsmanship has revived step-by-step. Attention has also been paid to the renovation of vernacular architecture, as well as the preservation of historic environments, suitable for contemporary urban requirements and the benefit of the local community. Historic cities, such as Isfahan and Yazd, for instance, have been revitalized by the careful restoration of historic buildings under the program "New Life for Old Structures" (since 1997; received the Agha Khan Award for Architecture in

2001), in collaboration with the Iranian Cultural Heritage Organization (ICHO) and the Urban Development and Revitalization Corporation (UDRC), with the result that some of the architectural ensembles in Iranian cities afford locals and visitors much enjoyment.

Suggested Reading
Archnet website: http://www.archnet.org.
Correa, C., K. Frampton, and D. Robson. 2001. *Modernity and community: architecture in the Islamic world.* London: Thames & Hudson.
Diba, D. 1991. Iran and contemporary architecture. *Mimar* 38:20–25.
Jodidio, P., ed. 2004. *Iran: architecture for changing societies.* Turin: U. Allemandi.
Micara, L. 1996. Contemporary Iranian architecture in search for a new identity. *Environmental Design: Journal of the Islamic Environmental Design Research Centre* 1:52–91.

YUKA KADOI

✦ ARMED AND SECURITY FORCES

The armed forces have always played an important role in Iran, from the Achaemenid Empire (550–330 BC) to the present Islamic Republic. They have been assigned the principal tasks of protecting the ruling family, ensuring the safety of the population, and providing for the security of the communication and economic infrastructure. They have also engaged in secondary responsibilities. As an instrument of the Empire's expansion, the armed forces were involved in diplomacy, the layout of borders, and the suppression of internal revolts and unrest. In the process of ascending to power, tribes, who have always shaped the Iranian power and its structure, were forced to abandon their traditional nomadic way of life for a more sedentary lifestyle, which introduced a new dynamic to the political and military life of the empire. One tribe's domination ended with the emergence of another tribe.

The Persian Achaemenid Empire era was one of the largest and most powerful land empires in the world, with a complex political and military system, and was celebrated for the vision of its founder, Cyrus the Great. Cyrus the Great served this civilization through his Charter (*Cylinder*), which is considered the world's first known charter of human rights. Among other things, the Charter promoted religious tolerance and freedom for the Empire's subjects. Cyrus was also known for remaining a just ruler even after acquiring tremendous military power.

Cyrus the Great's successors were less successful in their administration of the empire, mainly due to military failures. The vastness of Iran's territorial possession produced an unmanageably large state, which was one factor in the gradual demise of the dynasty. The rulers relied on European assistance in an attempt to prevent this inevitable decline.

In an attempt to reestablish Iran's diminished historical glory, Shah Abbas Safavid I (1587–1629) undertook an ambitious program to modernize his country's military forces. As his Ottoman competitors did before him, Shah Abbas dismantled the irregular army in favor of a modern force, trained by British officers who had been present in Iran since 1597. They also built an artillery factory in Isfahan. The new military capability enabled Shah Abbas to reclaim important parts of Iran's lost territory in the hands of Ottomans and Afghans.

Napoléon I of France, who was strategically interested in India, expressed a great desire to establish an alliance with Iran. In 1805 he dispatched an ambassador to Iran with a proposal: that France was ready to arm, train, reform, and reorganize Iranian military forces. This new army was to assist France in its invasion of India. However, preoccupied by other European affairs, Napoléon I decided to abandon the project regarding India and withdrew his officers from Iran. This departure created an opportunity for Britain to send a military contingent to Iran in July 1810. The British officers undid the work performed by French trainers by introducing their own assessment of the new Iranian army. Yet, frustrated by a bankrupt Iranian government incapable of building a decent artillery factory, the British officers decided to leave Iran.

Austrian officers had also been contracted by Iran to pursue its project of military reform. They created the Ministry of War and reactivated a military school founded earlier by Amir Kabir (1807–1852). All these attempts were designed to create a new strong army based on the latest European models. Nasser ed-Din Shah made a request to the Russian Emperor for the creation of a force after their Cossack unit. Russian military officers formed a brigade, a music band, barracks, hospital, and other military facilities. The work of Tsarist officers in Iran lasted for 40 years and left Iran only after the Russian Revolution. In 1911, the Iranian government decided to create a Gendarmerie force for protecting the roads and hired Swedish officers for its development.

After relative stability during the periods of the Achaemenid and Sassanid Empires, a series of successive wars resulted in territorial losses for the Iranian state. The downfall of the Persian power, which had started to accelerate under the Safavid dynasty (1501–1736, with the exception of Shah Abbas' rule), slowed down during the Qajar dynasty (1779–1925). This dynasty is considered to be the weakest, in terms of rulership, in Iranian history. Nader

Shah's military campaigns in the 1730s and 1740s to reclaim some of the loss of Persian luster in Central Asia, including Afghanistan, could not save Iran from decline.

The Iranian territory was reduced to its present dimension after successive wars with Russia. During these wars Iran lost vast territories in the Caucasus due to the Treaties of Golestan (October 1813) and Turkemanchai (February 1828). In the Treaty of Akhal (September 1881) Iran lost the last vestiges of its massive territorial possession in Central Asia to Russia. The erosion of Iranian territorial, military, and political might reached its depths in the first half of the 20th century when the country was divided into three zones: two spheres of influence controlled by Russia in the north and Britain in the south (the Anglo–Russian Convention of 1907), and a neutral buffer zone controlled by Tehran.

The triangular relationship between the Court, the armed forces, and the clergy has historically been part of Iranian political fabric. Under the 24 empires and tribes ruling over Iran up to the Pahlavi era (1925–1979), the army played a unifying role among the tribes in order to secure a large and viable political coalition on one hand and establish religious unity to support the emerging power on the other. The legitimizing function of religion has always been a source of tension between the official and the protesting religions, as well as between the society and power.

Dialectical relationships between politics, military support, and the religious justification became more prominent when religion dominated the two others.

Iran's modern military force emerged around the Persian Cossacks Brigade in November 1918 under the command of Reza Khan, the future founder of the Pahlavi dynasty. Aware of Iran's strategic importance in the European powers' rivalry in the Middle East, he started the process of purging his country's military force of European officers and mercenaries. Reza Khan had to accomplish two major tasks in order to create a truly national force. The first was to modernize an archaic and disjointed government apparatus. The second was to bring the numerous powerful tribes and their autonomous forces under the control of one coherent administration. The government introduced major reforms and infrastructure development projects that resulted in the emergence of a new Iran that was well adapted to face twentieth-century challenges.

In the field of defense and security, Reza Shah dismantled the Gendarmerie and other European forces and established a unified Iranian Army under the command of Iranian officers. This new force suppressed a series of ethno-tribal rebellions in Fars (Qashqai and Boyer Ahmadi Tribes), in Khuzestan (Arab revolt), in Azerbaijan (war against democratic forces), breaking the communist Tudeh Party, etc.

When Reza Khan became Shah in 1925, he further reformed the armed forces by imposing military conscription. This resulted in a significant rise in the number of soldiers at the state's disposal. This growth could not have happened without a considerable injection of financial resources for the purchase of new and sophisticated weaponry, as well the development of institutional infrastructure for training officers. With Reza Shah's abdication in 1941, after a massive invasion of Iran by the United Kingdom and the Soviet Union, who violated the country's declared neutrality, the Iranian army had 125,000 soldiers. Despite this impressive number, the army could not defend the country against its invaders.

When a society depends on armed forces for security, there is often a tendency among the military to influence the national agenda, whether political or economic in nature. From post-1945 Iran to the end of the Pahlavi regime, the Imperial Army officers enjoyed many privileges, such as good salaries and pensions, political nominations to the Upper House (Senate), positions in provincial governorships, and administrative responsibilities in state-owned companies.

Iran's armed forces were an important instrument of Mohammad Reza Shah Pahlavi's national security and foreign policy during his reign from 1941 to 1979, especially beginning in the 1960s and 1970s. Internally, they had to repeat the first Pahlavi's exploitation by containing all ethnic and political turmoil. Internationally, Iran's clear military advantage over Iraq imposed the terms of the 1975 Algiers Accord that favored Iranians over the Iraqis. Furthermore, a strong Iranian military force comforted the weaker pro-Western Arab regimes in the Persian Gulf region. This situation earned the Shah the title of "Gendarme of the Gulf." A significant increase in the price of oil provided the Shah with enough funds for purchasing the best military equipment available on the market.

The Islamic Revolution of 1979 put an end to 2,500 years of empires and dynastic rule over Iran by creating an Islamic order. Distrusting the powerful military and security apparatus that the Pahlavi regime has created, the Islamic Republic of Iran (IRI) both dismantled some agencies and established other new ones. The revolutionaries disbanded the Imperial Guard, the most loyal force to the Shah, and dismantled the following four intelligence services: the Organization for Intelligence and National Security (SAVAK, created in 1957), a domestic security force that performed surveillance of Iranians abroad; the 2nd Office of the Army; the Intelligence Service of Gendarmerie; and the Office of the Police Intelligence. These services spied both on each other and the rest of Iranian society but operated independently from each other by directly sending their reports to the Special Office, which was responsible only to the Shah.

In its Preamble, the Constitution of the IRI defines the nature of the armed forces as religious. It stipulates: "In the organization and equipping of the country's defense forces, there must be regard for faith and religion as their basis and rules. And so the Islamic Republic's [regular] army [*Artesh*] and the corps of Revolutionary Guards [IRI] must be organized in accordance with this aim. They have responsibility not only for the safeguarding of the frontiers, but also for a religious mission, which is Holy War (JIHAD) along the way of God, and the struggle to extend the supremacy of God's Law in the world."

Article 110 of the Constitution establishes the duties and powers of the Supreme Leader in these terms: "Assuming supreme command of the armed forces; Declaration of war and peace, and the mobilization of the armed forces; appointment, dismissal, and acceptance of resignation of the chief of the joint staff, the chief commander of the Islamic Revolution Guards Corps, the supreme commanders of the armed forces." The Supreme Leader is commander-in-chief of the armed forces, which have three main components: 1) the regular army; 2) the Islamic Revolutionary Guard Forces (IRGC/ *Pasdaran-e Enghelab-e Islami*), with its paramilitary Mobilized Resistance Force (*Basij*), founded by Ayatollah Ruhollah Khomeini in November 1979; and 3) the Law Enforcement Forces (LEF/*Nirouye* entezami, police).

According to the constitution of the Islamic Republic, the regular army is responsible for defending Iran's borders and maintaining internal order. During the Iran–Iraq War, military exigency and tight government control over the regular army leadership and activities confined the totality of the Artesh resources to the front. While the IRGC and the Basij were also committed to the front and fought alongside the regular military units, they continued monitoring the security inside Iran. After the war, the Islamic Republic authorities accelerated two policies in relation with the regular army. First, they gradually replaced the army's leadership with IRGC officers. Second, they placed a Basij watch guard in each army unit to attain a double objective: Islamicize the personnel and scrutinize their activities. While the Artesh and IRGC routinely hold joint military exercises, the regular army shows no interest in political debate inside Iran. The Artesh military exercises are mostly near Iranian border or far from cities. The IRGC and the Basij joint exercises are normally in the cities in preparation to deal with domestic unrest. Thus, whereas the regular army retains a minor internal security role, the IRGC continues to play multiple tasks.

The Law Enforcement Forces, which were created in 1991 by uniting the urban police (*Shahrbani*), rural gendarmerie (also controlling the borders against drug and merchandise trafficking), and revolutionary committees (*Komitehs*), initially assisted the IRGC and Basij in maintaining domestic order. Constitutionally, the LEF is under the Supreme Leader command. He can decide to delegate his authority to the Minister of Interior, normally responsible for the internal security.

The IRGC was established under a decree issued by Ayatollah Khomeini on May 5, 1979. The Pasdaran was formed to *guard* the revolution and to assist the ruling clerics in the daily enforcement of the government's Islamic codes and morality. It also consolidated those forces loyal to the Islamic regime into a single unit to keep effective control over the regular army, whose allegiance towards the revolution was not fully established at that time. Article 143 of the Constitution determines the responsibility of the army to guard the independence and territorial integrity of the country and establish the order of the Islamic Republic. In other words, the army is committed to Islamic ideology and must recruit individuals who have faith in the objectives of the Islamic Revolution and are devoted to the cause of realizing its goals (Article 144). The founder of the IRI prohibited any intervention by the armed forces, including IGRC, into the political sphere.

Students, workers, civil servants, and farmers constituted the core of IRGC at its conception. The Pasdaran was a political, ideological, military, and intelligence organization with three responsibilities. Politically it should defend the Islamic order against its internal and foreign enemies. A political bureau was established to publish a paper, write a political strategy for the forces, and create a section to assist foreign freedom fighters' movement. Ideologically, it promoted an Islamic direction as a practical path towards freedom. The military and security component protected the Islamic Republic through a paramilitary organized group.

These activities stipulated in Article 151 of the Constitution were harmonious with Qur'anic verse. In accordance with the noble Qur'anic verse: "Prepare against them whatever force you are able to muster, and horses ready for battle, striking fear into God's enemy and your enemy, and others beyond them unknown to you but known to God ... [8:60]," the government is obliged to provide a program of military training in such a way that all citizens will always be able to engage in the armed defense of the Islamic Republic of Iran. The possession of arms, however, requires the granting of permission by the competent authorities.

The IRI Constitution recognizes a universal responsibility for Iran to intervene on behalf of oppressed people against their oppressors. This religious solidarity explains the presence of Iranian Pasdaran in Lebanon. They provided consistent support to the Islamic group Hezbollah, who was fighting the Israeli occupation of south Lebanon on one hand, and forcing a change to Lebanese political elite for a better power-sharing among different religious groups. The Qods (Jerusalem) Force of the IRGC is responsible for extraterritorial operations.

The existence of a professional regular army with land, sea, and aviation forces did not deter the IRGC and Iranian leadership from creating a similar parallel structure for the Pasdaran. In 1986 the Pasdaran acquired limited sea and air capability.

The IRI learned a valuable lesson from the demise of the Pahlavi Regime. Although the Iranian armed forces before the revolution were very powerful in protecting the country against any foreign threat, the royal family could not count on any real internal support for their survival. The IRI found a remedy for this situation by creating a loyal force as part of the Pasdaran. The IRGC was given the mandate of organizing a large people's militia, the Mobilized Resistence Force, the *Basij*, in 1980. In his decree that ordered the creation of the Basij, Ayatollah Khomeini stated that a country that has 20 million youth should possess an army of 20 million. As an IRGC subset, the Basij was assigned to assist the Guards in preserving national security and serve as a deterrent force against foreign enemies. Basij commander Brigadier General Mohammad Hejazi estimated the number of Basij personnel at 10.3 million in March 2004 and 11 million in March 2005. On September 14, 2005, he said that the Basij had more than 11 million members across the country.

As the executors of the judiciary's decisions, the Law of Judiciary supports the Basij to confront those who disturb social peace. The Law orders all institutions in the country to collaborate with the Basij and facilitate its work. Basijis are present in all universities and schools, factories, offices, cities and districts, mosques, armed and security forces, foundations, and agencies with the main task of indoctrination of their personnel. The Basij plays a significant role in monitoring dissidents and promoting the Islamic Republic.

The Basij organization played a crucial part in preparing teenagers to launch attacks against Iraqis with their bare hands during the 1980–1988 Iraq–Iran war. In 1985, the head of the Basij forces of the Pasdaran stated that there were close to 3 million volunteers in the paramilitary force receiving training in 11,000 centers. Since then both women and men are trained to serve the revolution as Basijis.

HOUCHANG HASSAN-YARI

✦ ART

The sociopolitical turmoil generated by the Islamic Revolution in 1979 drastically changed the cultural atmosphere in Iran. Following the discouragement of avant-garde art, post-revolution Iran experienced a certain degeneration of artistic activities in various fields, from visual arts to performing arts. Representations of nudity in pictorial and sculptural forms, including women's hair, were utterly banned. Censorship was imposed on almost every aspect of Iranian art traditions—for instance, a ban on the public appearance of female singers and dancers, as well as on imported Western arts, such as film, music, and dance. The eight-year war with Iraq (1980–1988) acted as an additional barrier to art production and education in Iran. Due to the closure of art galleries, the loss of art patronage, and social stability, Iran no longer offered a creative playground. A number of prominent artists were obliged to leave the country to find freedom of expression elsewhere—thus beginning the Iranian artist diaspora in North America and Europe. Art collections associated with the previous regime were confiscated by the Foundation for the Dispossessed and the Martyrs of the Islamic Revolution, an institution that was immediately established after the revolution; some of the collections were sold and others have been kept in storage.

By international standards, Iran continued to suffer a major setback in the art movement until the liberalism of the Khatami administration began in 1997. Yet the revolution and the Iran–Iraq War did not cause the total decline of Iranian art. While the prominent media in fine arts, painting, and sculpture underwent considerable difficulty, photography and film-making enjoyed a growing popularity in Iranian society under the Islamic regime, owing to a demand for the documentation of sociopolitical changes in post-revolution times. Not only as historical records, but also as tools for self-expression, photographers and filmmakers explored the creative and artistic potentials of these two media of visual arts. Having gained international recognition, Iranian photography and cinematic production remain the major cultural exports of Iran. Celebrated contemporary Iranian photographers, both in Iran and abroad, include Abbas, Kaveh Golestan, Bahman Jalali, Jahangir Razmi, Alfred Yaqoubzadeh, and Maryam Zandi. Their photography, most of which integrates the art of camerawork into photojournalism, became important primary visual sources for understanding one of the most turbulent times in Iranian history. This art legacy is certainly passed on to the younger generation of photographers, such as Shadi Ghadirian. Similarly, Iranian films have been celebrated for their distinctive style and themes and have been awarded several prestigious prizes at international film festivals. The work of Abbas Kiarostami, an internationally acclaimed film director, typifies an intellectual movement in contemporary Iran. Dozens of Iranian film directors belong to the so-called "Iranian New Wave" engaged in creating innovative art films, for example, Bahram Bayzai, Mohsen Mahkmalbaf, Samira Makhmalbaf, and Jafar Panahi.

The revolutionary movement in the late 1970s and the war with Iraq in the 1980s led to the emergence of two powerful genres of pictorial arts—posters and murals. Through these novel media, together with other forms of public art, such as stamps and bank notes, art became a primary instrument of propaganda for visualizing Shiite political ideologies. The multiple layers of revolutionary themes—the glorification of religious devotion, the spirits of war preparedness and martyrdom, and anti-imperialistic slogans—cover the entire pictorial surfaces of posters and murals. The scenes of battle and death were imaginatively and passionately rendered in a blend of realism and surrealism. Poster makers and mural painters used their typographical ingenuity to dramatize the heroism of the revolution and the Iran–Iraq War. Such semiotic works were by no means intended to be appreciated as works of fine arts. Yet, combining the visual forces of revolution, almost equivalent to those utilized in the propaganda of the Russian Revolution, with Iranian indigenous graphic traditions, the Utopian visionary conceptualized by iconographically straightforward, somehow ultra-sentimental representations of humans and nature, serves to create unique artistic values on their own.

Such emotional aspects of art withered in the post-war period. Instead, the new generation of artists began to respond to sociopolitical conditions composedly and embarked on an inquiry into their own visual languages. Modernity has been successfully incorporated into the field of graphic design, a genre that holds much promise as yet another cultural export of Iran. Morteza Momayez was a pioneer of graphic design in Iran and received the Art and Culture Award of Excellence from the president of Iran in 2004. Momayez was largely responsible for introducing Iranian graphic design to the world. Also significant is Reza Abedini, a graphic designer distinguished for his typography in combination with subtle pictorial, poetic ambience. In 2006, Abedini was awarded the Principal Prince Claus Award.

Today, almost 30 years after the establishment of the Islamic Republic, Iranian society is gradually shifting into a new cultural era. Artists, particularly those belonging to the second generation after the revolution, search for ways to demonstrate the authenticity of their work. Asking the fundamental question of how far tradition and modernity can possibly coexist, they are in a dilemma of which they should choose or to what extent they should compromise. A majority of artists are based in Tehran, a metropolis with more than 10 million inhabitants. The Tehran Museum of Contemporary Art (TMCA; founded in 1977) has actively promoted acquisitions, exhibitions, including the Tehran Biennials, and public seminars, like the Cinemathèque for film studies. Iran still lags behind most of the world in terms of commercial galleries and needs to build up a firm commercial base for the art market so as to give artists further opportunities to publicize their artworks.

Iranian artists abroad are alert to current international and global trends but at the same time find themselves in search of their own cultural identity. Inevitably, their work reflects their exile and its resultant. As a consequence of a struggle to acculturate other cultures, they deal nostalgically and melancholically with current issues of sociopolitical orientation, gender, and religion in both their indigenous Iranian and adopted cultural spheres. Shirin Neshat, an Iranian-born and American-educated artist (received a Golden Lion at the Venice Biennale, 1999), challenges the sociopolitical and psychological dimensions of women's life in Islamic societies, by means of nihilistic black-and-white photography and video installations.

In the wake of globalization, Iran is no longer detached from the international art milieu. There have been ever-growing interests in recent works by Iranian artists, a tendency which was first visible at the beginning of the 21st century. The year of 2001 inaugurated an exhibition dedicated to the visual culture of contemporary Iran at the Barbican Centre in London. Curated by Rose Issa and Ruyin Pakbaz, the London exhibition is marked as the first of this kind. In the United States, the first loan exhibition of Iranian art since the 1979 revolution opened at the Meridian International Center in Washington, D.C. (organized in collaboration with the Tehran Museum of Contemporary Art), entitled "A Breeze from the Gardens of Persia: New Art from Iran." These events were followed by an exhibition entitled "Between Word and Image: Modern Iranian Visual Culture" organized by the Gray Art Gallery, New York University in 2002. The intriguing positions of contemporary Iranian artists continue to capture attention throughout the world (one of the most recent exhibitions on contemporary Iranian art is "Iran.com— Iranian Art Today" at the Museum für Neue Kunst, Stuttgart [2006–2007]). The boom of contemporary Iranian art exhibitions demonstrates the growth of their marketability at international auction houses. Sotheby's and Christie's, for instance, promote the sale of contemporary works by artists from the Middle East, including Iranian artists. Such a global concern for the visual culture of contemporary Iran also serves to open up a new field of study in art history and visual studies. In 2005, the Barakat Trust (UK) and the University of Oxford organized a conference, "Contemporary Iranian Art: Modernity and the Iranian Artist," intending to provide an academic framework for this new discipline and to bring together academics and artists to look into the diversity of contemporary Iranian visual cultures.

See also Art, Diaspora; Art, Visual; and Art Exhibitions.

Suggested Reading

Abedini, R., and H. Wolbers. 2006. *New visual culture of modern Iran*. Amsterdam: BIS Publishers.

Balaghi, S., and L. Gumpert, eds. 2002. *Picturing Iran: art, society and revolution*. London: I. B. Tauris.

Chelkowski, P., and H. Dabashi. 2000. *Staging a revolution: the art of persuasion in the Islamic Republic of Iran*. London: Booth-Clibborn Editions.

Issa, R., R. Pakbaz, and D. Shayegan. 2001. *Iranian contemporary art*. London: Barbican Art and Booth-Clibborn Editions.

Wijdan, A. 1989. *Contemporary art from the Islamic world*. London: Scorpion Publishing. http://www.barakat.org/iran_conf/index.html.

YUKA KADOI

✦ ART, DIASPORA

An account of the Iranian art scene abroad should be examined within the context of the turbulent historical events of the 1979 revolution. The modernist artists who left Iran valued the singular and unique styles of twentieth century art and were determined to establish an individual artistic signature. An overview of the works by the newer generation suggests the disintegration of modernist boundaries and a challenge to the idea of authorship and origin. In time, the boundaries dividing the contemporary artists outside Iran from other artists appear less essential. The work of the new generation is informed by "personal meaning," an essential factor in postmodern identity formation. Many artists create works that are related to their own personal longings and show characteristics of what postmodern theorists call a change from "grand narrative" to "local narrative." These works display personal stories of family and self, in a quest for new meanings and new visual experiences.

The art of the Iranian Diaspora encompasses the works of the trendsetters of the 1960s and 1970s, whose works were welcomed and celebrated by various intellectual communities of the time and the works of a new generation that is faced with multitudes of complexities, including the risk of being perceived as orientalizing and spiritualizing, as well as exoticizing cultural issues and differences of their background. Among different trends, a prevalent culture of political art criticism predetermined how the viewers would see and read the works of Iranian artists. Such an approach assigns a preconceived propensity to the audience in which the immigrant experience is seen as romanticized and generalized.

Nevertheless, the hum of new cultures, dislocation, assimilation, and intensity in artistic activities helped boost a process of self-examination, self-discovery, and reevaluation for the new immigrant artists and made a lasting impression on their creative expressions. Curators such as Fereshteh Daftari, Shiva Balaghi, and Rose Issa have examined how gender issues, ethnicity, and identity have been depicted in contemporary works. The generation of artists who left Iran after the revolution was deeply stirred and shaped by the currents from Iran. Many of them had already exhibited their works outside the country. This was not the case for the younger and emerging generation of immigrant artists who followed and had to struggle and compete with thousands of other artists. Their works reflect turbulence, nostalgia, and the temporal situation of their lives. The object of many became easing and evading the pain and realities of new homelands. Still others were focused on presenting idiosyncrasies and negotiating newfound identities. Encouraged by various art movements, Iranian artists explored and delved into spiritual concepts, as well as sociopolitical issues, and were able to reveal untold stories unique to them. They came to see both text and image as signs or symbols that depended on cultural conventions. They examined and read pictures as linguistic codes and created works that were commentaries on the powerful union of text and image.

Among the renowned Iranian trendsetters, Siah Armajani left Iran in 1960 and took part in many group exhibitions of Conceptual artists. Among his first exhibitions were *Art By Telephone*, at Museum of Contemporary Art, Chicago, and *Information*, at Museum of Modern Art, New York. Armajani developed a series of art objects titled *Dictionary for Building* and went on to create numerous temporary and permanent public installations. Many of Armajani's earlier works were influenced by Persian poetry. Among his famous projects are the Reading Garden No.1 in Roanoke, Virginia; Reading House in Lake Placid, New York; The Louis Kahn Lecture Room at the Samuel S. Fleisher Art Memorial in Philadelphia, Pennsylvania; and NOAA Bridges in Seattle, Washington. Armajani designed the 1996 Olympic Torch of the Centennial Olympics, in Atlanta, Georgia. His other projects include the tower and bridge at New York Staten Island, and the Round Gazebo in Nice, France.

Whereas the works of many Iranian modernists living abroad, such as Marcos Grigorian, Sirak Melkonian, Monir Farmanfarmaian, Hossein Zendehroudi, Aliasghar Masoumi, Nasser Ovissi, Jafar Rouhbakhsh, Ardeshir Mohasses, and Manouchehr Yektaii are engaged with elements such as mass, color, surface, and works in series, the works of the younger artists are at times preoccupied and characterized with theatrical elements, utilization of text and calligraphy, eclecticism, and appropriated satire. Today's Iranian art is informed by contemporary social issues that affect the artists personally.

Set apart by personal narratives, many artists challenge, revise, and question the aesthetics of traditional works and express their individual story by subverting the normative visual language. From calligraphic expressions to dislocated objects to scrutinizing social inquiries, these visual expressions bring the peculiarities of individual artist into light.

In Europe the works of Iranian-born artists such as Shirazeh Houshiary, Shirana Shahbazi, Azadeh Yavari, and Rahim Najfar followed many of the modernist tenets. Shirazeh Houshiary's paintings were originally involved with modernist issues of light, surface, biomorphic form, and texture. She later constructed surfaces using repeated words and explored many spiritual concepts found in Sufi tradition. Houshiary also produced animations that were informed by the notion of empty space and proposed a similar tension between the spiritual and the material. A graduate of Chelsea School of Art and nominated for the Turner Prize in 1994, Houshiary has exhibited at numerous venues, including the Museum of Modern Art at Oxford, England, and the Museum of Modern Art in New York. One of the artists of the 50th International Venice Bienniale of 2003 and winner of the Citigroup Photography Prize of 2002, Shirana Shahbazi, lives in Zurich, Switzerland. In her photography and installations, Shahbazi examines the contemporary face of Iran without presenting an exoticized view of the Iranian culture. Rahim Najfar, who was a student of Hannibal Alkhas, started in the Saqqa-khaneh style and went on to create abstracted landscapes that are regularly shown in Paris. Azadeh Yavari's paintings and drawings are also included in many collections and regularly exhibited in Paris. A graduate of Ecole des Beaux Arts de Paris and grand prizewinner of the First Tehran Biennale after the revolution, Yavari's paintings and drawings are poetic interplays between light and color. Many of her works focus on women in solitude, who are quietly placed in various Persian-inspired environments. The sensual effects of Yavari's visual dialogue create a stimulating narrative, which is focused on different cultural and aesthetic considerations of Iranian tradition.

In Australia, the Adelaide-based, Iranian-born Hossein Valamanesh creates sculptures that redefine the modernist tenets of the early twentieth century. Valamanesh's work is included in many collections, including the national Gallery of Victoria, Melbourne, the Art Gallery of South Australia and University of South Australia, Adelaide, University and Art Gallery of Western Australia, Perth, and the National Gallery of New Zealand. Farideh Zariv, the Canberra-based Iranian–Australian artist, was a participant in the world's longest painting project, organized by Medecins Sans Frontieres in the United Arab Emirates. The Australian Government awarded Zariv for her exhibition *Hand of Fatima* at the Canberra Museum and Art Gallery (2005), and Zariv has been the first Muslim woman artist at Iziko Bo-kaap Museum in Cape Town, South Africa. Born in Khomein, Iran and living in Singapore, Ali Esmaielipour has shown extensively in Tehran, Hong Kong, Singapore, and United States. Inspired by his simple background Esmaielipour replicates ordinary and everyday scenes of life with an unpretentious brush that speaks of his uncomplicated yet poetic eye toward his surroundings.

In the United States, a new generation of Iranian artists create works that tackle issues such as textuality and discursivity of exile, alienation, separation, fascination and identification with things "Iranian," fantasy formation, invented childhood, reconstructed memory, ethnicity, and the question of "the other." Often the final production is fantastical and individual accounts in which cultural and historical events are staged. In many the newfound imagined ethnicity could be questioned. Yet these works express a poetic consciousness toward the subjective homeland that should not be overlooked. Many delve into issues being masked behind fantasy, which pushes the boundaries of reality and results in most creative expressions. Many treat image as a process of inquiry that could bring the fundamental contradictions of each culture into the heart of discourse. The early Iranian modernist standards of artistic presentation looked at image as depiction and word as element of description. Text was seen to infiltrate a degree of nonessential explanation that could weaken the strength and transparency of expression and was often deemed decorative and supplementary. The new generation of Iranian artists can treat text differently, giving it a dual and arbitrary function. Today's artists are inclined to manipulate both the visual form of the word and the meanings attributed to the form. This recognition becomes a useful tool in their visual inquiry. In such works, text is indeed a visual language. Elements such as spatial composition, flatness, and texture bring the written word into a different artistic magnitude.

Shirin Neshat, who won the prestigious 2006 Dorothy and Lillian Gish Prize, utilized her own portrait in still photography using Persian calligraphy. Neshat's use of Persian calligraphy, which is an independent art form by itself, on her face, was among the first efforts of artists outside the country to treat text with a different perspective and in a different light. Using Persian poetry and calligraphy on a series of women, Neshat examined concepts such as martyrdom and femininity. In her early photographs known as *Women of Allah*, she depicted images of exotic veiled women who were carrying guns. Neshat's work examines the space of exile, the issues of identity, and experiences of women in Islamic societies. She questions the tension between the accepted collective identity and one's personal narrative. Neshat's installations, which coincided with the blossoming of Iranian cinema in the Western market and the popularity of sociopolitical art criticism, created heated debates about fetishization of the veil, colonial fantasies, and stereotypical characterization and exoticization of Persian culture. Among the most important works she produced were a trilogy of split-screen video installations: *Turbulent* (1998), *Rapture* (1999), and *Fervor* (2000), all poetic and yet engaged with social, cultural, and religious codes of Islamic societies. *Soliloquy* was about women unable to choose between their traditional roles and modern life. *Logic of Birds, The Last Word, Mahdokht, Zarin,* and *Tooba* are among other examples of Neshat's stylized work that deal with the concept of time, issues of relationship, and gender roles.

Y. Z. Kami diffused the concept of time and historical nostalgia into a contemporary multicultural dialogue. Using portraits as a vehicle of contrast, Kami, whose work has been extensively shown in the New York art scene, juxtaposed portraits of unnamed people against the photographs of dilapidated landscapes and buildings. His haunting portraits of people and places celebrate and acknowledge the transience of place and loss of time. In the 1990s, Kami's unsmiling and impersonal portraits of young men reminded many of the damage done by AIDS.

Nicky Nodjoumi, an established artist/educator prior to the 1979 revolution, has since exhibited his works at numerous public and private venues. Nodjoumi's main characters seem to be important and influential businessmen or religious people, engaged in vague and sometimes humorous postures. Many of Nodjoumi's figurative narratives depict political characters in satiric and surreal settings whose stances point to mischief. He captures and illustrates the moment these characters participate in the act of deceit. The participants of Nodjoumi's narratives are fragmented individuals who are displaced in imaginary spaces. These opaque and disconnected bodies occupy mysterious settings and are involved in cultural conversations burdened by upheaval and revolution. Yet, his allegorical world delegates the task of judgment to the viewer.

Shahla Arbabi's multilayered abstract vocabulary is engaged with light and space, suggesting architectural forms that can simultaneously work on the emotive inner spaces of the mind. Arbabi's playful and instinctive three-dimensional works are made of artists' materials, such as stretcher keys and frame clips. Arbabi has been able to access an expressive voice within herself that is eloquently shared with the viewer. Arbabi's work is among the permanent holdings of the Arthur M. Sackler Gallery at the Smithsonian Institute in Washington, and has been shown in many prominent venues such as the US National Academy of Sciences.

Assurbanipal Babilla, painter/playwright/actor/director, uses shocking and controversial imagery to deal with modern philosophical issues. Babilla, artistic director of Purgatorio Ink and winner of the Hellman/Hammett grant in 2005, was an avant-garde artist/director working in Tehran previous to the Islamic Revolution. He then fled to America and has since written and directed plays in Los Angeles, New York, Boston, Baltimore, Seattle, and Europe. Inspired by the Theater of the Absurd, Babilla's humorous and provoking productions feature outrageous scenes. In his paintings and sculptures, Babilla creates textural forms that similarly comment on the absurdity of human life by deliberately distorting conventions.

Seyed Alavi creates insightful site-specific installations that incorporate Iranian Sufi tradition and poetry into elements of form and composition. In many of Seyed Alavi's mystical and ethereal environments the goal is to attain spiritual insight. His works explore subtle meanings attached to word and image and evoke the poetics of language and space. The universal concept of inward journey of the self towards enlightenment constantly translates itself into Alavi's work. His public projects focus on the concept of self-realization, through a postmodern vocabulary. The presence of written words and poetry offer insight as to how our verbal and visual language constructs our reality.

In the works of artist/curator Taraneh Hemami, words function as verbal propositions seeking to draw attention to many unresolved questions in the Iranian collective psyche. Hemami's site-specific installations create ongoing records and document time, space, and people. Her community projects point to issues of displacement, preservation, and belonging. In an archive of personal photographs and narratives titled *Hall of Reflection*, Hemami explored the various experiences of the Iranian Diaspora. Exhibited through site-specific installations and virtual spaces, the archive helped construct layers of historical and cultural references. Kendal Kennedy, Roshanak Kayghobadi, Haleh Niazmand, and Yari Ostovani are among many other artist/educators who confidently take on issues of global importance and create mind provoking, cutting-edge visual ironies for their audience. The new generation of Iranian artists constantly negates, humors, questions, or blends the boundaries of demarcation between what is termed "traditional and Eastern art" with what is known as the "art of the modernized West." This approach abstains from dividing the world between the two blocks of East and West, while it taps into discussions of post-colonial theory, identity politics, feminism, fragmentation, and displacement. The new generation incorporates and teases the Middle Eastern and Western stereotypes and often questions a past which no longer exists. The younger generation redefines Iranian ethnicity, and reflects intelligently and critically about tradition, gender, and global politics. Many of Niazmand's installations are satirical commentaries about Western understandings of Iranian culture, while the works of Roshanak Kayghobadi identifies and humors the misunderstandings created and publicized by the media. Sadegh Tirafkan, Amir Fallah, Sara Rahbar, and Reza Kassaii all tackle the issues of multiple selves and cosmopolitan identity, each with their unique visual vocabulary. Sara Rahbar's portrait transformations and installations evoke intellectual inquiries that go beyond linearity of capturing and reducing experiences. The photographs and conceptual works of Sadegh Tirafkan, who works and lives both in Iran and Toronto, deal with Iranian males in different traditional gestures. Many of his works examine the concept of "other" in regard to the Iranian traditional symbolism.

The satiric works of Marjane Satrapi, the author/illustrator and cartoonist who is famous for her *Persopolis Series*, must be mentioned. Satrapi's humorous and shocking autobiographical work is accompanied by her remarkable illustrations. The four-volume *Persopolis Series* was the winner of the 2003 Fernando Buesa Peace Prize (Spain), among *New York Times* Notable Books, among *Time* Magazine's Best Comic of the Year list, Library Journal's List of the Best Books of 2003, and the Library Services Association 2004 list of the Best Books for Young Adults.

In commercial art and visual design, the visionary works of Massoud Mansouri must be mentioned. Mansouri attended Tehran University's Department of Fine Arts and Illinois Institute of Technology (IIT). In 1984 Mansouri moved to New York City and worked as an art director at several ad agencies. He later designed several luxury cosmetic lines and private labels. Mansouri joined Godiva Chocolatier as the Senior Art Director in 2000 and received Godiva's North American President's Award of Excellence in 2005. In addition to contemporizing many iconic logos, globally and in the United States, Mansouri's unique contributions include numerous cutting-edge labels, lines, products, and packaging designs.

The art of Iranian contemporary artists outside the country speaks of autonomy, which is well beyond mere negation of tradition in the name of modernity. It is engaged in multiple new identities, is informed by recognition of private spaces of self and family, and is recognized by what the artists personally define as Iranian, while embracing new alternatives. The new generation of Iranian artists is engaged in personal and psychological inquiries and challenges the viewer to rethink many Iranian stereotypes. The activism present in many of the works question the orientalized narratives often engrained in mass media displays and cyberspace images. The creative expression of Iranian artists can be examined from many art historical perspectives. In addition, their visual mastery may be understood by how they create a dialogue that depicts or challenges the traditional hegemonic

narrations, which promoted and assigned an imaginary homogeneity to Iranian history and consequently Iranian artistic culture.

Suggested Reading
Ammann, J.-C. 1987. *Siah Armajani.* Exhibition Catalogue. Amsterdam: Kunsthalle
    Basel and Stedelijk Museum.
Balaghi, S., and L. Gumpert. 2003. *Picturing Iran: art, society and revolution.* London:
    I. B. Tauris.
Daftari, F., H. Bhabha, and O. Pamuk. 2006. *Without boundary.* New York: Museum of
    Modern Art.
Fouladvand, H. 2001. *Alchemy,* Exhibition Catalogue, works by Seyed Alavi, Aylene
    Fallah, Taraneh Hemami, and Haleh Niazmand. New York: Center for Iranian
    Modern Arts.
Issa, R., R. Pakbaz, and D. Shayegan. 2001. *Iranian contemporary art.* London: Barbican
    Art Center. Booth-Clibborn Editions.

HENGAMEH FOULADVAND

✦ ART, VISUAL

A critical inquiry into various styles of Iranian visual art demonstrates its developmental process from decorative and more ornamental works towards more
conceptual themes. The Contemporary Art of Iran covers modernist art, conceptual, pop, postmodern, and all other styles that are exhibited in Iran today.
Although many Iranian artists engage in traditional forms such as painting and
sculpture, more and more are increasingly engaged in making installation,
video, and environmental art, and still others have blurred the distinction
between painting and sculpture. What is referred to as "New Art" in Iran today
crosses the boundaries of medium and engages in social, gender, and ethnic
issues, as well as human rights and all matters concerning day-to-day life in Iran.

The modernist artists of the 1960s and 1970s had already reacted against
the sentimentality and historicism of the European landscape paintings and
rejected the romanticism of the more traditional styles of paintings. Iranian
modernists were celebrating experimentation, originality, the principles of
form following function, and the use of new material in their works. The early
Iranian modernists rejected ornaments on the grounds that they were superfi-
cial and signs of an unreflective society. Artists such as Ziapour, Kazemi, Shay-
bani, Sepehri, Ruhbakhsh, Bahman and Ardeshir Mohasses, Azarghin,
Javadipour, Arabshahi, Mohsen Vaziri Moghaddam, Kalantari, Barirani,
Esfandiari, Vishkaie, and Nami, and women such as Behjat Sadr, Lili Matin-
daftari, Mansoureh Hosseini, and Iran Daroudi celebrated simplicity,

Iranians look at Don Eddy's painting "Bumper Section VII" during an international exhibition at the Tehran Museum of Contemporay Art, 2005. (AP Photo/Hasan Sarbakhshian)

innovation, and purity of form, content, and order in their works. Their works were informed by many styles of presentation as used by early 20th century artists. Exclusivity and pride in introducing authentic works were prerequisites of this era. As such, these modernists became the main support and unifying factors in present day Iranian Art. The International visual language used by many of them was regarded as universally applicable and did not apply to geographical boundaries.

Despite the rapid change of art movements and styles, "modernism" still remained a style typical of pre-revolutionary Iran. Zendeh Roudi, Tabrizi, Jazeh Tabatabai, Pilaram, Saidi, Ovissi, and other "Sagha-Khaneh artists" were among the first modernists who turned to ethnicity and popular culture. These Iranian pop artists used ordinary objects and popular images and placed them in new aesthetic contexts. To evoke authenticity and communicate genuine ethnic feelings, Marcos Grigorian turned to multitudes of primitive forms and approaches, incorporating ethnic foods such as "Nan Sangak" and "Abghousht," while experimenting with earth as an original material. Grigorian was among the first who became interested in Earth Art. Grigorian later produced a series of rugs that erased the separating line between art and craft. Today's contemporary art of Iran owes a great deal to the early trendsetters of the 1960s and 1970s. Among them is Hannibal Alkhas, whose current work is influenced by the mythology and ancient history of Assyria, Babylon, and Persia. Aydin Aghdashloo invoked, employed, taught, and challenged art history and created masterful renderings that reintroduced and celebrated the postmodern concept of "appropriation." In regards to contemporary issues such as ethnicity and identity, outside of post-impressionist contexts, depicting Iranian ethnicity or identity in order to serve the traditional aesthetic values, for its own sake, for further critical examination, or as a non-decorative subject matter, was not the norm for many modernist artists.

The 1979 revolution marked the beginning of a new era in Iranian art. Many artists and art administrators turned their attention to the sociopolitical realities of the revolution. Scenes of people's everyday lives, rural landscapes, and traditional ritual scenes, which had mostly been depicted for aesthetic pleasure, were substituted by religious works. Traditional images of poverty and injustice depicted in the pre-revolutionary period of Iran, which were mostly apolitical and depicted in the realist style, did not reflect the goals and aspirations of the revolution. Even the religious paintings, originally made to express spiritual and traditional beliefs of ordinary people, did not reflect the day-to-day practices and ideological beliefs of the new revolutionary culture. Importance of "ideology and belief" substituted technique and style as distinguishing elements of this period's art. Yet this transition did not happen abruptly. Artists such as Nodjoumi, Moslemian, Shabahangi, Espahbod, Shishegaran, Hajizadeh, and Shahlapour, and many women artists such as Parvaneh Etemadi, Manijeh Mir-Emadi, Shahla Habibi, and Farideh Lashaie, who prior to the 1979 revolution were among the up and coming talents in the Iranian art scene, were faced with many hardships. These and numerous other artists were nevertheless able to survive the turbulent years of the revolution and continue with their careers.

The new religious and revolutionary works, produced in the first decade after the revolution, manifested newfound aspirations of the revolutionary artists and rejected many of the modernist tenets. Hessein Khosrojerdi, Kazem Chalipa, Nasser Palangi, Mostafa Goodarzi, Ali Vazirian, Kaykhosro Kourosh, Iraj Eskandari, and Habibollah Sadeghi were among the pioneers in what is now called the Art of Revolution. Produced in the heat of the Islamic Revolution and during the Iran–Iraq War, these works were characterized by depiction of religious and revolutionary slogans, war, martyrdom, pain, and the general culture of ordinary people. Nasser Palangi, who had spent months with soldiers during the Iran–Iraq War, created a series titled *My Memory of the War*. He later created an important body of work titled *From Siege to Freedom* on the walls of the congregational mosque of Khorramshahr. Palangi also produced a series about women suffering during the eight-year war with Iraq.

characteristics of their cutting edge web designs are simple layouts, attention to content rather than decoration, centered orientations, 3D effects, neutral backgrounds, extensive treatment of whitespace, and fluid layouts. Of importance are the works of Reza Abedini who received the Prince Claus Award in 2006. An art director and educator, Abedini has won numerous awards for his design contributions all around the world.

In sculpture, artists such as Parviz Tanavoli, Faramarz Pilaram, Shoja-eddin Shahabi, Saeed Shahlapour, and Jazeh Tabatabai had previously used simple and pure forms. Tanavoli's exotic use of ethnic crafts as artwork was among the first attempts of Iranian modernists to dissolve the lines separating art and craft. Nami's *White* series and his other three-dimensional works were among the first attempts to examine the conceptual and textural effects of color and field. Monir Farmanfarmaian and Mansoureh Hosseni were among the first women artists who used Islamic–Iranian motifs in their works. Farmanfarmaian's mirror and glass works paved the way for many future artists. She later incorporated these motifs in her boxes. After the 1979 revolution, continuing on the modernists themes, many Iranian sculptors such as Taher Sheikh al Hokamaee, Parisa Khazabi, Fatemeh Emdadian, Hossein Broojeni, Mahin Noormah, Nasser Houshmand-Vaziri, and Simin Ekrami were able to create museum quality works. The ceramic sculptures of Maryam Salour were a combination of sophistication and simplicity, and the thoughtful constructions of Reza Amir Yar-Ahmadi crossed many boundaries. Yar-Ahmadi's talent drew meaning from furniture design and architecture. His sculptures reflect the most definitive aspect of contemporary art: its indescribability. Selected for the 50th Venice Biennale, the installations of Behrooz Daresh suspended hundreds of aluminum elements in an interplay of fantasy and reality. Mahmoud Bakhshi Moakhar created fantastical metal cypresses and incorporated mirrors into his installation, so that the work became at once conceptual and poetic. Ahmad Nadalian's *River Art* project was included in the 50th Venice Biennale. The works of this environmental artist/educator are informed by the interrelationship and interdependence of the ecological system with culture, politics, and the human nature. Nadalian's carved stones, the documentations of his "*River Art*" and "*Hidden Treasure*" projects, along with his video installations have been exhibited in numerous solo and group exhibitions around the world. Bita Fayyazi's mind-provoking work, selected for the 51 Venice Biennial, further echoed the state of contemporary art of Iran: one of promise, transformation, and productivity. With her installation entitled *Chel Gis*, Mandana Moghaddam was another distinguished artist whose work (forty braids of hair) won her a selection at the 51 Venice Biennale in 2005.

In photography, trendsetters such as Hadi Shafaieh and Assad Behroozan and other renowned artists such as Bahman Jalali, Kamran Adle, and Kaveh Golestan had already set high criteria, previous to the 1979 revolution. The portraits of Maryam Zandi, of famous Iranian characters, and the collection of photographs by renowned filmmaker Abbas Kiarostami are among the best examples produced in this field. Artist/educator Nasser Vaziri translated nuances of music into his avant-garde photography. The synesthesia evoked in Vaziri's images offers the viewer equivalent meanings in two separate mediums. Other talented photographers such as Mahmoud Kalari and Seifollah Samadian later went on to produce documentaries and became involved in filmmaking. Among the new generation of Iranian photographers, Peyman Houshmandzadeh, Nader Davoodi, Kourosh Adim, Arash Hanaei, Newsha Tavakolian, Shadafarin Ghadirian, and a group of other Iranian photographers are experimenting with new media and techniques. Shokufeh Alidusti and Esmaeil Abbasi create portraits that examine family, gender, and cultural topics while Shahriar Tavakkoli's photography explores themes of Persian literature.

Many other talented artists such as Simin Keramati, Barbad Golshiri, Shahab Fotouhi, Amir Moabed, Ramin Haerizadeh and Roknedddin Haeri, Jinoos Taghizadeh, Khosrow Hassanzadeh, Farhad Moshiri and Shirin Aliabadi, Rozita Sharafjahan, Amir Ahmad Mobed, Atila Pesyani, and Roxanna Daryadanesh are working in multimedia and have included performance in their works. Among them, Golshiri's self-referential works and Taghizadeh's performance especially delve into the frustrations of this educated group of artists and create cutting-edge social, political, and environmental commentaries. Neda Razavipour and Shahab Fotouhi work individually and in collaboration. In one of their progressive collaborations, as a public art project, they installed 70 neon light boxes in the windows of a high rise under construction in Tehran. The work created a visual dialogue between the solid texture of concrete and the ephemeral and transient lights of the empty building. *A Few Centimeters Above Sea Level* and *Census* were among the most innovating of their projects. The issues of life and death were examined in one of Afshan Ketabchi's video art installations. Her visual dialogue examined the crash of an Iranian airplane, the hopes, aspirations, and despair of the travelers, the birth of her own child through C-section delivery, the various stages of her daughter's life, the reality of death, and the concept of the grave as the final resting place of human beings. In her thought-provoking video performances Simin Keramati, who won the Grand prize of the 11th Asian Art Biennale of Dhaka, 2004, relates her deep personal and philosophical inquires with the audience, questioning the intrinsic meaning and purpose of her existence. The shut-eyed characters in Keramati's earlier paintings and her *Dream* series remind the viewer of suppressed and unleashed narratives waiting to be unlocked. She persistently directs the attention to untold stories of her characters. In her recent video performances Keramati is focused on the responsibility of action to shape human destiny. In one project, the falling earth gradually buries her motionless body. While in another work the artist connotes the helpless, vulnerable, and powerless state of a person who is falling into a deep well.

In production of contemporary Iranian art, more and more special attention is given to creating critical dialogues and engaging in cultural questions. Today's new generation of artists is able to create and view art as a process of translation. To them, issues of ethics and morality, appropriation, theatricality, and publicity become valid subject matter to work with. Depicting the simplicity and goodness of Iranian rural life, traditional and decorative heritage, and institutionalized slogans, works can present a stereotypical picture of Iranian culture. A closer look will reveal an evolutionary process, which later leads to postmodern and pluralistic works by artists who are fluent synthesizers and in command of many styles. Artworks that are informed by contemporary issues and yet offer a personal narrative seem to connect on a deeper level with viewers. Nevertheless, Iranian artistic development and creative expression should be seen within its own context. Only then can one have a fair appreciation for what is produced in Iran today.

Suggested Reading
Abedini, R., and H. Wolbers. 2006. *New visual culture of modern Iran: graphic design, illustration, photography*. Mark Batty Publisher.
Goodarzi, M. 1989. *A Decade with Painters of the Islamic Revolution*. Art Center of Islamic Propagation Organization.
Mojabi, J. 1998. *Pioneers of contemporary Persian painting: first generation*. Tehran: Iranian Art Publishing.
Tavoos Bilingual Quarterly, Iranian Art Quarterly, No 1–6, Iranian Art Publishing.

HENGAMEH FOULADVAND

✦ ART EXHIBITIONS

The developments of the Iranian contemporary art scene should be examined within the context of the tumultuous and radical historical rupture of the 1979 revolution. The early religious works struggled for a separate aesthetic vocabulary to repudiate the Western and European modernist influences. Very often, a total disregard for conscious methodological analysis encouraged many officials and teachers to misuse their positions as pulpits from which to preach and praise the new institutionalized art. Thus, art administrators became apologists for deficiencies of the new revolutionary art. The lack of professional art criticism and scholarship in the field often led to unprofessional essays, write-ups, and interviews. Corresponding with the realities of the revolution while trying to keep their modernist approach elevated, renowned artists and decision makers such as Morteza Momayez, Aydin Aghdashloo, Gholamhossein Nami, and Jalal Shabahangi were faced with complex and often contradictory dilemmas at various biennales and art competitions. For others, however, the revolution provided an excuse to reject the avant-garde trends.

The most important element essential in the analysis of the Iranian visual art scene is a conscious discussion about the social and cultural context within which the art is produced. Artistic developments cannot be thoroughly examined without the broader historical and cultural patterns. However, as one looks at the Iranian operational art history, which positions the past as a justification for contemporary trends, the risk of creating a peculiar autonomous discourse may arise. Such an analysis tends to lose its historically objective tone. The artistic development of the last decade indicates traces of a subversive art tradition that is determined to defy expectation and push the boundaries as much as possible. In Tehran, similar to many cosmopolitan cities, a younger art community interested in absurdist visual tendencies and opposed to formalist standards and criteria is forming. The effect of the 1979 Islamic Revolution on the art community was nowhere more obvious than in the selection process for art exhibits. Whereas previously one could trace the flickers of a social science context in the study and selection of art works, many judges regressed to the traditional aesthetics. Artists, teachers, and other forward-looking art administrators who had just gained a semiotic and semi-objective rather than aesthetic point of view were discouraged, and their views became problematic. Such a lens, reasonably accepted by now, examines the art object with an almost anthropological method of inquiry within a sociological framework. The artist, the viewer, and the society are engaged in a social discussion. This view is thus less judgmental or passionate.

On the other hand, the risks involved are that the works are treated as artifacts rather than works of art. The traditional aesthetic-oriented art criticism did not look upon art as an empty categorical space ready to be filled with objects, activities, and whatever is found in between. However, due to the same reasons the selections were not as interesting or exciting. The

A visitor looks at "Prostitutes" by Iranian artist Khosrow Hassan Zadeh in Berlin, 2004. (AP Photo/Franka Bruns)

traditional categories are formal, fixed, and essential, perfectly fit for an aesthetic-oriented selection process. Thus, in the first decade after the revolution, the traditional art historical criteria and the safe modernist categories were the convenient tools. In other words, a modern movement based on the rejection of tradition had itself become a convenient tradition, and the distinction between elite intellectualism and mass culture had lost its precision. As a consequence, Modernism became an institutionalized trend that was no longer a revolutionary approach. In time, issues of social change, necessity of conceptual art, performance art, and nonconventional standards of form and production, now prevalent in other societies, had to be considered and gradually became accepted and dominant trends in exhibitions and biennials.

The early years of the revolution saw numerous exhibitions at the Tehran Museum of Contemporary Art, which were characterized by the curatorial decisions reflecting the governmental policies of the new republic. Inspired by traditional wind towers of Iran, the first contemporary art museum in Iran, the Tehran Museum of Contemporary Art, was designed by architect Kamran Diba before the 1979 revolution. It offers a wide range of media and presents many educational programs and events. Of the nine galleries in this museum, the permanent collection is housed in three galleries, whereas the other six hold temporary exhibits. The permanent collection has works of international artists such as Picasso, Van Gogh, Monet, Renoir, Gauguin, Warhol, Max Ernst, Pollack, Hockney, Jasper Jones, Magritte, Giacometti, and Calder. The museum owns a collection of works by Saqqa-khaneh artists, which is derived from Iranian pop culture. The museum also holds a collection of works by Qahveh-khaneh artists, which is another Iranian school influenced by traditional Persian narratives, the classical epics of kings, and mytho-historical depictions of the Iranian past. The works are visual narratives of the battles between good Persians and evil non-Persians, suggesting a nostalgic and idealized Persian splendor in the face of foreign threats and invaders. The paintings, representing a proud Persianate collective memory, were displayed in traditional coffeehouses and gatherings. Such works later became major sources of inspiration for visual narratives of the exile community, and the notion of lost pre-Islamic greatness for Iranian historiographers. The pre-Islamic mythical subject matter, which conveyed the purification and distinctiveness of Iranian culture and territory, became problematic when manifested in many exilic imaginary works that showed an idealized and homogenized picture of the Iranian nation and history.

Under the direction of Ali Reza Sami Azar, the museum organized and exhibited works of many Iranian and international artists. Through his efforts, the museum became a national leader for its cultivation of new Iranian art, promoting emerging artists and arranging various biennials and exhibitions. Sami Azar was responsible for organizing and facilitating major Biennales in painting, sculpture, photography, traditional and Islamic art, new art, and graphic arts. Curators and scholars such as Ruyin Pakbaz, Hamid Severi, and Faryar Javaherian have been instrumental in organizing major exhibitions at the museum. Today, under a new management, the museum's artistic policies have yet again shifted, and the end result of the new direction is yet to be observed.

Niavaran Cultural Center and the Artistic Creation Foundation are among many government-run organizations that provide space for artists and support artistic endeavors. The Artistic Creation Foundation is specifically focused on the development of Islamic and Persian art and is geared toward educational training and research in artistic fields. Other art organizations, such as the Art and Culture Foundation and many government-run spaces, sponsor an institutionalized agenda that is often counterproductive and discourages the creative pursuits of the younger generation. Numerous works function as political slogans geared to change or promote institutionalized ideologies, not considering that in contemporary Iranian life there are a lot of mixed origins, offsprings, and unlike parts. Today's contemporary Iran comprises many elements of cultural hybridity. The Iranian ideals of happiness, beauty, and homogeneity, which are depicted in many miniature paintings or ceremonial scenes of Nuruz, nature scenes of Mazandaran and the Caspian Sea, tribal images of women with beautiful horses in colorful dresses dancing and singing in the fields, while perfect for ads and tourism, can become irritants to analytical eyes of many viewers.

Saba International Cultural and Artistic Gallery, the Visual Arts Center, and the Institute for Promotion of Visual Arts are among organizations supporting and promoting today's contemporary art.

Among prominent galleries, Seyhoun Art Gallery, with its more than 1,200 exhibitions, has exhibited emerging and established artists in the last four decades. The founder, Masumeh Seyhoun, an artist, trendsetter, and pioneer herself, has been instrumental in promoting and supporting Iranian contemporary art. Seyhoun Gallery has held painting exhibitions, sculpture shows, installations, performance, and video art shows by established artists such as Alireza Espahbod and emerging artists such as Afshin Pirhashemi and Mohsen Khalili. Seyhoun also shows Parvin Heidarinassab, who is an expert in restoring antique Islamic calligraphy and illuminations. Her meticulous works are reminiscent of the works of Mohammad Ehsai, a modernist trendsetter and a master calligrapher, instrumental in contemporizing Persian calligraphy and incorporating it in Iranian graphic arts. Golestan Gallery is another well-established exhibition space in Tehran. For a show at Golestan Gallery, Afshan Ketabchi appropriated Andy Warhol's rendering techniques and illustrated well-known Iranian figures such as ex-President Khatami, the renowned Iranian filmmaker Kiarostami, and Iranian Nobel Peace Prize winner Shirin Ebadi. Ketabchi's whimsical portraits were a commentary on Andy Warhol's famous saying "In the future, everyone will be famous for 15 minutes." Among artists who have shown at Golestan through the years are Bahram Dabiri, Parvaneh Etemadi, Farideh Lashai, Mehran Mohajer, Rockni Haeri, and numerous other established and emerging artists. Elaheh Javaheri, who has shown prominent artists such as Hannibal Alkhas, Nicky Nodjoumi, Parviz Tanavoli, and Jazeh Tabatabai, runs Elaheh Gallery, established after the revolution. Among newer exhibition spaces, Khaak Gallery, run by Mandana Farahmand, should be mentioned. Khaak has exhibited many works including abstract paintings of Shishegaran and multimedia installations of Barbad Golshiri, Behrang Samadzadegan, Jinoos Taghizadeh, Shahab Fotouhi, and Neda Razavipour. Silkroad Gallery (Raheh Abrisham) has shown the works of talented photographers and graphic designers. Artists such as Jalali,

Momayez, Kiarostami, Mesghali, Adim, Haerizadeh, Hassanzadeh, Ghadirian, and Ave have shown their works at the Silkroad. In addition, galleries such as Barg, Aria Eghbal, Day, and Homa should be mentioned for their role in promoting Iranian contemporary artists. Shirin Ettehadieh and Ahmad Nadalian are among the artists who have exhibited at Barg and Farah Ossouli, Samila Amirebrahimi, and Simin Keramati have previously shown their works at Aria Gallery. Homa Gallery has exhibited the works of Ardeshir Mohasses, Hannibal Alkhas, and Nicky Nodjoumi. Ahmad Nadalian is the founder of the Paradise International Center for Creation and Exhibition of Art in Nature. This educational center is in Polour, north of Tehran, and serves as a resident center for national and international environmental artists. The Paradise Center holds festivals, invites land artists, documents and organizes educational programs, and implements nature-based projects.

Primary literature and standard reference texts on contemporary Iranian visual art and exhibitions are still rare. Secondary critical writings are similarly inadequate. Of importance have been writings and the art histories of Edward Lucie Smith, Jalil Ziapour, Mansour Gandriz, Ehsan Yarshater, Karim Emami, Javad Mojabi, Firouz Shirvanlou, and Daryush Shayegan. Artist/educators and scholars such as Mohammad Ehsai, Hadi Shafaieh, Morteza Momayez, Jalal Shabahangi, Irandokht Mohasses, Parviz Tanavoli, Massoud Mansouri, Ruyin Pakbaz, Aydin Aghdashloo, Sima Kouban, Habibolah Ayatollahi, Mohammad Hossein Halimi, Mehdi Hosseini, and Abdolmajid Hosseini-Rad have trained hundreds of a new generation of Iranian artists and have researched Iranian art and art history at length. Hengameh Fouladvand and Sharon Parker have focused on the younger generation and have written extensively about developmental trends of the Iranian contemporary art. They have examined how pursuit of a signature style has been substituted by exploration of variety of expressions and how multiplicity of visual language and artistic experience has formulated major themes of the Iranian art production.

Manijeh Mir-Emadi, artist/collector and publisher, has been instrumental in supporting, exhibiting, and publishing the works of prominent Iranian contemporary artists. Mir-Emadi's Iranian Art Publishing, *Tavoos Quarterly*, and *Tavoos Online* have reviewed and published the works of numerous artists including Kiarostami, Hajizadeh, Sadeghi, Aghdashloo, Shakiba, Etemadi, Nami, and Tanavoli.

In cyberspace, the founder of iranian.com, Jahanshah Javid, has presented the works of hundreds of Iranian artists on the web. As the chief editor of the most widely read magazine among the Iranian Diaspora community, Javid has been extremely active in elevating awareness about the Iranian visual art scene around the world. Among other online venues,

TehranAvenue.com, Persianmirror.com, Iranmania.com, Pendar.net, and BBC Persian regularly display and review Iranian contemporary art. TehranAvenue, with up-to-date art reviews, appeals to many contemporary artists currently living and working in Iran. The online artists, bloggers, and contributors, who are involved in Iranian visual art, seem to regard transparency as their ethics. Many function as moderators of contemporary trends and exhibition news and educators of cutting-edge art developments under difficult circumstances. In time, the young contributors of these websites have been able to come up with statements of authority, weighing various sides of issues and promoting critical inquiry, rather than mere opinions. In 2006, a series of exhibits were organized in Tehran that focused on issues of Iranian ethnicity, its marketing, and its relationship between the Western art establishment and the rest of the world. The show originated in Europe but was later brought to Tehran by curator Tirdad Zolghadr. The show's topics were widely covered by TehranAvenue online. Commenting about the new policies, biennials, competitions, artistic censorship, and new exhibitions, artist/contributor Jinoos Taghizadeh proposed alternative art strategies. Her commentaries endorsed independence for artists. These editorials and many others point to integrity of judgment and thus give a human voice to online remarks. Among the important exhibitions and biennials that have created much debate online have been the *Gardens of Iran*, *Spiritual Vision*, and *Art of Resistance*, all of which were held at the Tehran Museum of Contemporary Art and were ambitious projects to examine and promote the concept of traditional Persian garden and sacred art. Bloggers and online contributors rebut the artistic decisions of the institutionalized art establishment, and many are able to present their own critical viewpoints to the contrary.

Today, parallel with other art scenes around the world, Tehran's new art community sees no category as divine, essential, or fixed. Cutting-edge Iranian artists struggle to be against the conventional standards of art and create mind-provoking exhibitions. Iranian artists whose works are critical of certain injustices look for alternatives. These feminists, ecologists, ethnographers, and political activists consider their art as ideological and political interventions that can influence and persuade the viewer. For them, cultural problems have to be dealt with seriously. In such context many use irony and satire to express their observation. Nevertheless, in recent years, the Iranian art community has also faced a spectacle-oriented mentality, which has gradually promoted a culture of "art event." Similar to most Western models, the most problematic dilemma arises when the content of visual art loses its importance and the attention is focused on the effect of its media existence. Several questions arise as to the purpose of such exhibitions.

To what extent have these contemporary exhibitions broken down the imposed artistic criteria and conventional categories? Can the new generation of artists question the cultural patterns most Iranians feel they must comply with? Do these new art practices suggest that norms are as arbitrary as old definitions of aesthetics in art? It is clear that pluralism and works that defy formal conventions are now commonplace in the psyche of the contemporary Iranian artists. However, it is not known how and to what extent these new works challenge the existing social norms and energize the now conditioned psyche of the viewers in order to expand the society's collective conscious.

Suggested Reading

Diba, K. 1989. Iran. In *contemporary art from the Islamic world*, ed. W. Ali. London: Scorpion Publishing Ltd.

Keshmirshekan, H. 2005. Neo-traditionalism and contemporary Iranian painting. *Journal of Iranian Studies* 38.

McFadden, S. 1981. The museum and the revolution. *Art in America*.

Pakbaz, R., and Y. Emdadian. 2001. *Pioneers of Iranian modern painting*. Tehran Museum of Contemporary Art.

The taste of dreams, A look at the works presented at the Fifth Biennial of Contemporary Painting, Tehran Museum of Contemporary Art and Nazar Cultural Center. Tehran, 2000.

HENGAMEH FOULADVAND

✦ ASSEMBLY OF EXPERTS

The Assembly of Experts for the Leadership (*Majles-e Khobrgran Rahbari*) is currently a body of 86 scholars of Islamic law (*mujtahedeen*). According to the Constitution of the Islamic Republic of Iran, it is tasked with selecting (Article 107 and 111) and dismissing (Article 111) the supreme leader (*rahbar*) in case of the inability to perform constitutional duties or determination that from the beginning certain qualifications were not met. Additional responsibilities include the supervision of the rahbar's activities and promulgation of laws regarding the activities of the Assembly itself.

Article 107 of the constitution was revised substantially in 1989 to reiterate and enhance the existence and duties of the Assembly of Experts. In the 1979 constitution, the selection of the leader could be made possible through direct election or through the selection of elected experts. The experts, in case of lack of consensus regarding a qualified leader, could also select a leadership council of three to five people. The 1989 amendment eliminated direct election of the leader and the leadership council. The elected Assembly of Experts became the sole body in charge of selecting a qualified supreme leader.

In case of a rahbar's dismissal or death, the Assembly is expected to choose and introduce a new leader as soon as possible (Article 111). The task is to select a jurist (*faqih*) who is well versed in Islamic jurisprudence, is just and pious, has "correct political and social judgment," and is endowed with sufficient "prudence, courage, management capabilities, and power" (Article 109). In case there are many candidates who have these qualifications, the one with stronger juridical and political judgment shall be chosen (Article 109).

Currently, members of the Assembly of Experts are elected by a direct public vote for eight-year terms from thirty electoral constituencies. The Assembly must meet at least once a year for a one-week session whose minutes are kept confidential. Up to now, its sessions have been mostly held in Tehran out of convenience. However, the secretariat of the Assembly is based in Qom. Members of the Assembly of Experts do not face any restrictions concerning their engagement in other occupations, such as membership of parliament or holding government positions. As a result, a good number of leading officials in the Islamic republic have been and are members of the Assembly of Experts. Organizationally, the Assembly consists of a leadership and six committees. The leadership is elected by a secret ballot for two years and consists of the Assembly's chair, two vice-chairs, two secretaries, and two assistants.

The idea of an assembly of experts was born out of the immediate postrevolutionary debates regarding the nature of a constituent assembly. Ultimately, those who promoted the idea of a full constituent assembly from all over the country lost to those who called for the smaller, expert-based, Assembly of Experts for the Drafting of the Constitution. With the drafting and subsequent ratification of the constitution on December 2, 1979, this first Assembly of Experts was disbanded.

In December 1982, as specified by Article 108 of the constitution, the law for the creation of an 83-member body was passed by the Guardian Council and approved by Ayatollah Khomeini. The Assembly of Experts in its current version began work in 1983. Subsequent Assembly of Experts elections have been held in 1991, 1999, and 2006. Since the constitution leaves the assembly itself in charge of further changes in the eligibility criteria and process for the Assembly of Experts, these issues have been hotly contested, in 1990 causing an all-out confrontation among Iran's various political factions.

The initial criteria for eligibility passed by the Guardian Council was that candidates had to be "fully versed with the basis of *ijtihad* and educated at prominent religious schools in order to be able to discern the competency of candidates for *marja'iat* and leadership." They were also expected to have the support of three well-known teachers in religious schools, unless they were candidates whose ijtihad was either explicitly or implicitly acknowledged by the supreme leader or recognized in religious circles. The 1990 changes in the Assembly of Experts' procedural laws required eligible candidates to have ijtihad "to the degree of being able to infer in issues of fiqh" and be religiously competent enough to choose the supreme leader who no longer needed to be a *marja'* (source of emulation). More controversially, the new changes designated clerics on the Guardian Council as the source of assertion for the eligibility of candidates. Only candidates implicitly or explicitly approved by the supreme leader were spared Guardian Council approval. Furthermore, a written and oral competency test of religious laws was established to help the Guardian Council in its decision.

These changes created uproar and were seen as a move by conservative clerics and the supreme leader to assure their continued dominance over the Council of Experts. The opponents of the new law called the move unconstitutional and the role of Guardian Council interference in the election process rather than the constitutionally sanctioned supervision or observation. More importantly, the new changes brought forth serious questions about the indirect role the rahbar ends up playing in their own selection and supervision process.

In the initial established set of criteria for eligible candidates, the electorate could exert indirect influence over the selection, dismissal, and conduct of the rahbar through the election of Assembly of Experts candidates who were qualified on the basis of their competency and publicly established expertise. With the new changes, rahbar, who according to Section 6, Article 110 of the constitution has the authority to "appoint, dismiss, and accept the resignation of the clerics in the Guardian Council," exerts indirect influence in the vetting of the candidates for a body that is responsible for his own selection and conduct. Despite the serious questions that were raised about the impact of this circular vetting process on the ability and independence of the Assembly of Experts to supervise the conduct of the rahbar, the changes were ultimately approved, tens of candidates were disqualified, and many prominent clerics refused to submit applications, a practice that continues to the present.

More significantly, the changes initiated for the 1991 Assembly of Experts election turned out to be critical since they led a clarification regarding the vetting process in all elections. Clarifying the electoral supervisory role given to it by Article 99 of the constitution, the Guardian Council announced that its supervisory role was one of "approval supervision" (*nezarat-e estesvabi*), which meant the need for Guardian Council approval regardless of approval by the ministry of interior.

Controversy regarding the activities of the Assembly of Experts has not been limited to the 1991 changes. During the First Assembly of Experts (1983–1991), eight regular yearly sessions were complemented with three special sessions. In the first special session in 1985, Grand Ayatollah Hossein Ali Montazeri was chosen as the designated successor to Ayatollah Ruhollah Khomeni, the Founder of the Islamic Republic. He was later stripped of his position. In the second extraordinary session, held immediately after Ayatollah Khomeini's death in 1989, the Assembly quickly chose Hojjatoleslam Ali Khamenei, himself a member of the Assembly, as the next rahbar of the Islamic republic. Finally, the third special session was held after the amendments to the constitution were approved by the voters in 1989. In this session, the Assembly reconfirmed the designation of Ali Khamenei as Iran's new rahbar. Since his initial designation had occurred prior to the constitution being amended and when the criteria of being a *marja'* (source of emulation) as a necessary qualification for becoming rahbar was still in place, the reconfirmation was deemed necessary to placate doubts about Khamenei's leadership.

The Second Assembly of Experts (1991–99) began with the disqualification controversy generated out of new vetting powers assumed by the Guardian Council. Extensive disqualification and withdrawal of prominent approved candidates led to very few eligible candidates and the decision on the part various political groups not to offer a list of candidates. A huge drop in voter turnout from 77% in 1983 to 37% in 1991 reflected both voter unease about the vetting process and a drop in voter enthusiasm for key institutions of the Islamic Republic. During this session, very little was done and the Assembly was unable to complete its own internal regulations. However, it added the new practice of issuing statements regarding various domestic and international events that seem to have little to do with the limited mandate of the Assembly of Experts regarding the selection of rahbar.

Elections for the Third Assembly of Experts in 1999 occurred after the reformist Mohammad Khatami had won the presidency. This victory energized various reformist groups to try to limit the vetting process exercised by the Guardian Council. Ultimately, however, the efforts failed and only one reformist group, *Kargozaran-e Sazandegi* (Servants of Construction), officially participated in the election by offering a list of candidates. Close to 46% of eligible voters participated in this election. The noteworthy developments during the election were the candidacy of several non-clerics, even if all of them were eventually disqualified, and the candidacy of all members of the Guardian Council, the body in charge of vetting candidates for the Assembly of Experts. The Guardian Council rejected the charge of conflict of interest and was unmoved by the criticism of its extensive disqualification which astonishingly confirmed the eligibility of only one candidate for the city of Qom, the center of religious teachings in Iran. During this session, in which there were two meetings each year, the reformists continued to criticize the Assembly of Experts for being monopolized by the clerics, not making public its proceedings, and becoming involved in issues that are outside its mandate. They also continued to call for the abolishing of the Guardian Council's vetting process.

The election for the Fourth Assembly of Experts also occurred amidst controversy in 2006. This election took place after the conservative Mahmoud Ahmadinejad had become the president of Iran. It, as predicted, did not substantially affect the assembly's political makeup. Nonetheless, the election was controversial because of the attempt by Ahmadinejad's supporters to unseat former president Ali Akbar Hashemi Rafsanjani and increase the presence of the supporters of a rival cleric, Ayatollah Taqi Mesbah Yazdi. Having routed Rafsanjani in the presidential contest, Ahmadinejad appeared to be signaling his intent to push him out of the political scene once and for all; the president's supporters in effect turned the poll into a referendum on Rafsanjani. They did not get the answer they wanted. The people of Tehran, voting in higher numbers than the previous two elections, elected Rafsanjani with a high margin in Tehran and handed Ahmadinejad supporters a defeat throughout Iran. Another noteworthy development in this election was the affirmation by the Guardian Council that women and non-clerics could conceivably stand for the Assembly, even if none of the clerics and women who took the written exam were deemed eligible during this particular election.

The events associated with the last election highlight the fact that the Assembly of Experts has not been immune to the intense political competition that has characterized the Islamic republic since its inception. Like in other political institutions of the Islamic Republic, attempts at controlling electoral competition through a vetting process and more stringent eligibility requirements have limited the political participation of various groups. Successive elections have also reduced the number of high-standing clerics who have shown interest in the Assembly. The First Assembly included a number of sources emulation. This is no longer the case and is in all likelihood reflective of the dissatisfaction a number of high ranking clerics have with the politicization of the electoral process through the Guardian Council's vetting process.

Suggested Reading
Assembly of Experts official website: http://www.khobregan.ir.
Center for Iranian Studies, *Understanding Iran's Assembly of Experts*. Policy Brief #1.
    http://www.dur.ac.uk/resources/iranian.studies/Policy%20Brief%201.pdf.

Chirazi, A. 1997. *The Constitution of Iran: politics and the state in the Islamic Republic.* London: I.B. Tauris.

Constitution of the Islamic Republic of Iran. http://www.oefre.unibe.ch/law/icl/ir00t___. html.

Moslem, M. 2003. *Factional politics in post-Khomeini Iran.* Syracuse; Syracuse University Press.

FARIDEH FARHI

✦ AUTHORITARIANISM

The Iranian regime after the Islamic Revolution of 1979 is an authoritarian regime for many different reasons. This regime grants wide and unlimited powers to law enforcement agencies; there are almost no checks and balances in the Islamic Republic of Iran. Laws are routinely ignored and government actions follow the judgments or whims of unelected officials; and criticizing the leader often results in the imprisonments of writers, political activists, and journalists. It also imposes the moral and religious values of the majority over matters of private life. According to Articles 5 and 110 of the IRI Constitution, the Leader is above the law, unaccountable, and is not restricted by a constitution, laws, or opposition; he has lifelong tenure and cannot be replaced by any elections. Iranian citizens cannot choose their leader freely among various competitors in elections. No freely elected body is allowed to monitor or question the Leader. Political power in Iran is concentrated in the hands of the Leader and a small group of clerics who are not constitutionally responsible to those governed.

There has been an aggressive attitude toward individuals or groups disliked by authorities. The media puts an excessive emphasis on socially advocated ego qualities of the Leader. Iranians are rewarded or punished based on whether they obey or disobey social conventions and the rules of authority figures. They are expected to submit to authorities and authority figures. Nobody is allowed to publicly criticize the Leader. The freedom to create opposition political parties or other alternative political groupings with which to compete for power with the ruling group is either limited or is nonexistent. On occasion, the state has raided people's houses in order to confiscate satellite dishes and receivers, to stop people from having private parties, or to curtail the practicing of a religion somehow different from the official one, even if it falls within the framework of Islam and Shi'ism. The Iranian state also commonly censors books, scripts, playwrights, lyrics, and artworks, filters Internet sites, and monopolizes electronic media.

The Islamic regime is founded on the principle of the rule of a jurist who has absolute power. Initially, the Supreme Leader was supposed to be a source of emulation in religious matters also. This requirement was later dropped when the Constitution was revised. According to Article 5 of the Constitution, "during the occultation of the *vali-e 'asr* (hidden Imam), the leadership of the *ummah* (Islamic nation) devolve upon the just and pious person, who is fully aware of the circumstances of his age, courageous, resourceful, and possessed of administrative ability, will assume the responsibilities of this office in accordance with Article 107." This article submits the power of appointing the leader to the Expert Assembly. These experts are supposed to be elected by popular vote, but various formal and informal limitations ensure the continued dominance of the same clerical elites and their continued doctrinal conformity. Article 99 of the Constitution, for example, hands the supervision of elections to the Guardian Council; according to this article, the Guardian Council has the responsibility of supervising the elections of the Assembly of Experts for Leadership, the President of the Republic, the Islamic Consultative Assembly, and the direct recourse to popular opinion and referenda. The Guardian Council has interpreted this supervision to be approbatory (*nezarat-e estesvābi*). Candidates for elections to the presidency, the parliament, and the Assembly of Experts are vetted for moral purity as well as for their belief in and dedication to the political system and especially the leader.

Article 117 of the Constitution transfers the authority to appoint the Leader to a few individuals who are indirectly appointed by the previous Leader, having already passed the filter of the Guardian Council. They are also given the constitutional power to monitor the existing Leader, although questioning the Leader runs the risk of being disqualified by the Guardian Council in the next election. The second section of Article 117, which states, "the Leader is equal with the rest of the people of the country in the eyes of law," is, therefore, contradictory.

Because the leader is not really accountable to any elected body, he has enormous powers. According to the dominant reading of the Constitution, Article 110 recounts some of these powers:

1) Delineation of the general policies of the Islamic Republic of Iran after consultation with the Nation's Expediency Council; 2) Supervision over the proper execution of the general policies of the system; 3) Issuing decrees for national referenda; 4) Assuming supreme command of the Armed Forces; 5) Declaration of war and peace and the mobilization of the Armed Forces; 6) Appointment, dismissal, and resignation of the Islamic jurists on the Guardian Council, the supreme judicial authority of the country, the head of the radio and television network of the Islamic Republic of Iran, the chief

of the joint staff, the chief commander of the Islamic Revolutionary Guards Corps, and the supreme commanders of the Armed Forces; 7) Resolving differences between the three wings of the Armed Forces and regulation of their relations; 8) Resolving the problems which cannot be solved by conventional methods, through the Nation's Expediency Council; 9) Signing the decree formalizing the election of the President of the Republic by the people. The suitability of candidates for the Presidency of the Republic, with respect to the qualifications specified in the Constitution must be confirmed before the elections by the Guardian Council, and, in the case of the first term of a President, by the Leader; 10) Dismissal of the President of the Republic, with due regard for the interests of the country, after the Supreme Court holds him guilty of the violation of his constitutional duties, or after a vote of the Islamic Consultative Assembly testifying to his incompetence on the basis of Article 89; 11) Pardoning or reducing the sentences of convicts, within the framework of Islamic criteria, on a recommendation from the Head of judicial power.

In reality, the Leader acts as if he is above the law—in many instances, he is the law.

Iranian post-revolutionary authoritarian regime asks for strict obedience to the politico-religious authority. This authority does not stop in the political sphere and extends itself to social and cultural realms to maintain and enforce social control. Ideological social control is pursued through the use of oppressive measures. In the Iranian Islamic authoritarian state, citizens are subject to state authority in every aspect of their lives, including many private issues like sexual life, which even other authoritarian political philosophies and ideologies would see as matters of personal choice and privacy.

Although the Islamic regime has been changing during its three decades of development, the authoritarian face has been a constant feature. The revolution of 1979 was a transition from neo-patrimonial authoritarianism to revolutionary charismatic authoritarianism and later hierocratic authoritarianism. With promulgation of the absolute guardianship of jurist in the late Khomeini period (1987), built into the revised constitution of 1989, the nature of the regime gradually turned into a "sultanistic" one.

The role of ideological appeals in sustaining authoritarianism has been prominent in the whole twentieth century, from nationalism to populism, and from developmentalism to Islamism. All these ideologies have served the interests of the ruling caste: nationalism for Europe-educated intelligentsia, populism for revolutionaries, developmentalism for technocrats, and, for now, Islamism for clerics.

Suggested Reading

Bāzargān, M. 1998. *Be'that va Ideology* (*Prophetic mission and ideology*, written in 1964), Tehran: Enteshār.

Chehabi, H. E. 2001. The political regime of the Islamic Republic of Iran in comparative perspective. *An International Journal of Comparative Politics* 36, No 1.

Khomeini, R. 1991. *Sahifeh-ye Nur* (*Scroll of Light*), Tehran: Sāzmān-e Madārek-e Farhangi-ye Enqelāb-e Eslāmi.

Linz, J. J. 2000. *Totalitarian and authoritarian regimes*, London: Boulder.

Mohammadi, M. 1999. *Civil society: Iranian style*. Tehran: Markaz.

Mohammadi, M. 2000. *Political reforms quandary in Iran today*. Tehran: Jame'eh ye Iranian.

Shari'ati, A. 2000. *Ommat va Emāmat* (*Islamic nation and its leadership*), Collected Works, Vol. 26, 10th print.

MAJID MOHAMMADI

✦ AZERI TURKS AND AZERBAIJAN

It is estimated that there are approximately 23 million Azeri Turkish speakers in Iran today. Iranian Azerbaijan covers Turkish-speaking northwestern provinces of Iran. Human habitation of Azerbaijan began around 6000 BC. During the Achaemenid period, Azerbaijan was part of the satrapy of Media. After the Achaemenid Empire collapsed, Atropates, the Persian satrap of Media, claimed the independence of his region in 321 BC. He managed to maintain good terms with Alexander. A successor to Atropates, known to us from Greek sources, is Artabazanes who later submitted his power to Seleucid suzerainty. During the Sassanid period, it appears the land was officially named Atropatene/Aturpatakan and its inhabitants were subdued by Sassanid rule. During the early Islamic caliphate, Azerbaijan formed a separate province administering the low lands between the western shores of the Caspian Sea and Araxes River. Two cities, Ardabil and Maragha, have been mentioned to be major centers during that time. Arabic sources mention Azerbaijan as the birthplace of Zoroaster. Azerbaijan fell to Arabs during Omar's caliphate. The Babak Khorramdin movement against the caliphate, which lasted more than 20 years, manifested the continuing loyalty of Azerbaijanis to local ancestral feeling. Seljuk Turks—Oguz Turkmen expelled from Khorasan by Sultan Mahmud—arrived in Azerbaijan around 1029. After the decline of the Seljuk Empire, Hulegu put an end to the caliphate of Baghdad in 1258 and made Maraga his capital.

In 1501, Shah Esmail made Tabriz his capital. During the Qajar dynasty, Tabriz remained as the second city of Iran and the seat of Valiahd—the crown prince. Tabriz played a leading role in the periods of storm and stress starting with the Constitutional movement of 1906. After WWI, Sheikh Muhammad Khiabani rose to prominence in 1920, proclaimed Azerbaijan to be Azadistan, disputing the central government's power over Azerbaijan. In September of 1941, the Allied forces pressured Reza Shah Pahlavi out of office. During the 16 years of Reza Shah's rule, Azerbaijanis felt comparatively neglected and the use of Azeri Turkish was forbidden in the favor of the Persian language. Reza Shah's repressive measures to consolidate heterogeneous tribal, religious, and ethnic forces in order to create a unified nation had left the government in Tehran much more vulnerable. As a result of his forced abdication, the central government lost virtually all its control over the country. Azerbaijanis took the opportunity to write and publish newspapers in their native Azeri Turkish language and asserted their identity through a number of social and political moves. Being supported by the occupation forces in 1945, the Democratic party of Azerbaijan was established, and Ja'far Pishavari, a highly educated nationalist, was elected premier of the autonomous Azerbaijan by the national assembly. During the one-year rule of the Democratic Party of Azerbaijan, Pisahavari instituted land reform and undertook major developmental and infrastructural works. Azeri Turkish was recognized as the administrative language, and school children were able to learn their mother tongue.

With the withdrawal of the Soviet army from Iran under UN pressure and U.S. "impatience," central government forces from Tehran toppled the autonomous government of Azerbaijan, executing party members and killing a number of others. Some key members of the Democratic Party of Azerbaijan fled to Soviet Azerbaijan.

In the modern era, Azerbaijan covers the main Turkic-speaking area of Iran, encompassing Western and Eastern Azerbaijan, Aardabil—Arasbaran— and Zanjan provinces. There are very small pockets of Tati and Harzani speakers in Eastern Azerbaijan. After the Pahlavi state's repressive Persianization of Iran and its suppression of ethnic languages and cultures, Azerbaijanis have found themselves disenfranchised and neglected. For some Azerbaijanis, the sense of "otherness" has been sharpened by the past-Pahlavi regime's misinterpretation of nationhood, which is still overshadowing the policies and mindsets governing Iran. The Khiyabani movement of 1920 and Pishavari's autonomous Azerbaijan of 1945–1946 were moves to rebel against Azerbaijan's disenfranchisement and deprivation. The summer of 2006 witnessed street protests all over major cities of Azeri Turkish speaking regions. A number of people were killed, and many were arrested, with some still in prison. Unlike other Iranian ethnic groups, a good number of Azerbaijanis are scattered all over Iran, many of them living in Tehran. Turkic dynasties' many centuries of rule over Persia has left Azerbaijanis with a sense of attachment to all parts of Iran, and, as a result, many of them have been assimilated into the Persian culture.

HADI SULTAN-QURRAIE

B

✦ BAHAIS

The Babi religion began with a group of young people in nineteenth-century Iran as a reform movement within Islam and eventually led to the formation of the Bahai religion, with the ultimate ambition of establishing the "unity of mankind," the coming together of all races, nations, and religions in understanding and unity of purpose in a just society. It is the story of the Bab and Bahaullah, both in their twenties, leading figures such as Mullah Husayn Bushrui (Babulbab), Muhammad Ali Barfurushi (Quddus), and Zarrin-Taj Ghazvini (Tahirih). As with the start of most new religious movements, the government of the time characterized the Babi–Bahai movement as a political revolt. Nevertheless, for the believers their religion was a new revelation from God, and the Bab and Bahaullah—its "twin manifestation" (Prophets)—sent as redeemers of mankind. Bahaullah wrote that "the world's equilibrium has been upset through the vibrating influence of this most great, this new World Order. Mankind's ordered life has been revolutionized through the agency of this unique, this wondrous System—the like of which mortal eyes have never witnessed."

Basic Principles and Beliefs

Bahais believe the purpose of life is to know and worship God, serve humanity, and to grow spiritually and morally. God cannot be encompassed by the human mind and is unknowable in his essence. He reveals his attributes and will through a dynamic "progressive revelation," communicated by a neverending sequence of universal Prophets or "Manifestations of God," according to the needs of a given time and place. The Bahai religion recognizes both Abrahamic and non-Abrahamic religions and considers each of the following to be Manifestations of God: Abraham, Moses, Krishna, Buddha, Zoroaster, Jesus, Muhammad, and most recently, the "Twin Manifestations" of the Bab and Bahaullah.

Bahaullah explained that the concept of the equality of station of the holy Prophets, first proclaimed by Muhammad, proceeds indefinitely. Bahaullah is the latest but not the last of these Prophets. This is a fundamental departure from and a point of contention with the Islamic belief that Muhammad was the final Prophet with no other Prophet succeeding him until the "Day of Resurrection." Bahaullah explained that the coming of each new Prophet serves as the "Day of Resurrection" for the believers of the previous religion whereby their belief will be tested. Bahais believe in the independent investigation of truth, which means that each individual should investigate the truth of the claims of the Bab and Bahaullah and compare them to other claims independently based on his/her own knowledge and learning before accepting the religion.

Other tenets of the faith include the essential harmony of science and religion, universal compulsory education, a spiritual solution to economic problems, equality of rights for men and women, universal peace upheld by a world federation, and the practice of prayer, pilgrimage, and fasting. While many may consider some of these principles as givens for the modern world, the full significance of Bahaullah's message and its impact on the world over the past century can be understood only in light of the times and cultural context in which the principles were put forth.

CENTRAL FIGURES

On May 23, 1844, 25-year-old Siyyid Ali-Muhammad—known as *the Bab* (Gate)—in Shiraz, Iran, announced that he had come in fulfillment of Islamic prophecies, to establish a new religion, and to prepare the way for the next Prophet who would usher in a new age of world peace and unity. The advent of the Bab and his teachings threatened the position of the Muslim clergy, and he faced intense opposition. After suffering repeated persecutions during his six-year ministry, he was publicly executed in Tabriz on July 9, 1850. Mirza Husayn Ali Nuri, entitled *Bahaullah* (Glory of God), was an Iranian nobleman and son of Mirza Abbas Nuri, a minister of State in the Qajar dynasty. He was a 27-year-old man living in Tehran in 1844 when the news of the Babi religion reached him through the Bab's first disciple. Bahaullah readily accepted the message though he had never met the Bab himself. He immediately began to promulgate Bab's teachings and shared in the sufferings of its followers. His possessions were confiscated and he was thrown into an underground dungeon called Siyah Chal. Thereafter, he suffered many years of imprisonment and banishment. In 1863, while exiled in Baghdad, he proclaimed his revelation that his mission was a universal one and that he had brought teachings for the betterment of the world and the establishment of universal peace and justice. Bahaullah spent the rest of his life in exile and died in 1892 in Akka in modern-day Israel. After the passing of Bahaullah, his son Abbas succeeded him (1892–1921), who is known by the title *Abdul-Baha* (servant of Baha), and traveled and promulgated the new religion in the West in the latter part of his life. After Abdul-Baha, his eldest grandson *Shoghi Effendi* became the leader of the faith, serving as its guardian from 1921–1957. Shoghi Effendi implemented the foundations of the faith's administrative system.

Administration

Among the features of the governance structure proposed by the new religion was elimination of the role of professional clergy. This model, novel in an Islamic environment, posed a threat to the position of the Muslim clergy in its country of origin and is one of the root causes of persecution of Bahais there. The religion is governed by democratically elected international, national, and local councils, each composed of nine members. The *Universal House of Justice* is the international council and supreme administrative body of the religion and is headquartered in Haifa, Israel near the resting places of the Bab and Bahaullah. The affairs of the religion in every country are managed by a National Spiritual Assembly (NSA) and in every locality with nine or more Bahais; the Bahais elect a Local Spiritual Assembly (LSA) to administer the local affairs of the religion. All electoral processes are conducted without nomination or campaigning and voting is through secret ballot.

Key Statistics

The Bahai Faith is an independent world religion with members in more than 235 countries and territories; its literature has been translated into some 800 languages. More than 2,000 native tribes are associated with the religion, and its adherents are people of all ages, ethnicities, and religious backgrounds. It originated in Iran in 1844 and has its own sacred scriptures, laws, calendar, and holy days. There are some 5 million Bahais worldwide with about 300,000 living in Iran, where the religion has never been officially recognized. There are over 180 NSAs and over 10,000 LSAs throughout the world. Shortly after the Islamic revolution, the Iranian government forced the Iranian Bahais to dissolve their administration.

HISTORICAL RESTRICTIONS

The Bahai Faith has been subject to persecution in its birthplace since its inception. The execution of the Bab in 1850 halted neither the spread of his teachings nor the determination of his disciples, who defended themselves against attacks by clergy and government. A campaign of extermination in the early 1850s killed thousands of Babis. As their numbers and influence increased they came under demagogic attacks. In moments of national distress or revolution, foreign invasions, or epidemics, Bahais could always be blamed. In 1896, a pan-Islamic group attempted to assassinate Nasir'd-Din (Shah of Iran); Bahais were immediately accused of the act. In 1903 more than 100 Bahais were massacred in Yazd. During the 1906 revolution there were new attacks on Bahais all over Iran. During the 1930s, all civil rights such as recognition of marriage, publication of literature, gatherings, and Bahai schools were prohibited. A large-scale attack was launched in 1955 during which a mullah publicly denounced the Bahai Faith as a "false religion" and urged attacks against its adherents. On May 17 of that year, parliament banned the "Bahai Sect." What followed was a severe campaign of persecution of Bahais, including the destruction of the dome of the Bahai National Center in Tehran, as well as the desecration and damage to the House of the Bab in Shiraz, a holy site. With the creation of the fundamentalist Islamic organization named *Hojjatiyeh* in 1950s, which identified one of its central goals to be eradicating the Bahai Faith, the persecution of Bahais intensified.

ISLAMIC REVOLUTION

After the Islamic revolution of 1979, there has been a new surge in persecution of the Bahais in Iran. These included the arrest and execution of hundreds of innocent Bahai men and women for not recanting their faith, banning of Bahai administrative institutions, deprivation from government jobs, denial of access to education, and the demolition of their holy places. The House of the Bab in Shiraz, the most holy place in Iran for Bahais, was demolished on March 24, 1980. The Shiraz local government participated in the demolition and later turned the site into to a public thoroughfare, and a new mosque was built on the site. Authorities destroyed other holy places such as the gravesite of early Babi leader Quddus in Babol, the house of Mirza Buzurg Nuri, father of Bahaullah, which was also a historic treasure. Bahai cemeteries in Tehran and other cities have been bulldozed in many towns, most recently in Najafabad.

Today, Bahais in Iran continue to face restrictions on official employment and university admissions. In the 1990s, due in part to international pressure, Bahai students were allowed to enter primary and secondary schools.

tends to legitimize the acceptance of Islam in Baluchi genealogy. The history of present Baluchistan of Iran is closely tied to the history of Southern Afghanistan and parts of modern Pakistan. Baluch identity formation burgeoned with the acquisition of power by the local leaders in Kalat, dating back to 1666, by establishing the succession of a dynastic tradition. By the rise of Baluch Khans during later years, Baluchis consolidated their power base in Southern Afghanistan and Quetta (Pakistan), extending their domain to Kerman and Persian Golf coastal areas. After the assassination of Nader Shah in 1747, the Baluch khan, Ahmad Shah Abdali of Kalat and Gandahar, became the heir to Nadir's authority and established an organized state allocating lands to the tribes according to the number of their fighting men. Establishing their authority in the later period, the British decided to rule them through the proxy of local leaders. Over the more than 100 years of British domination of the area (1839–1947), a huge bulk of information became available in the form of published gazetteers. British colonization of India laid the Baluch territory open to systematic British dominance. In March 1924, the control of the Sarhadd district tribe formally was handed over to the Iraniahn government. After Kalat became an integral part of Pakistan, Afghanistan's Hilmand river development schemes and Pashtunistan policy affected Baluch life in the region drastically. In Iran also, the Pahlavi regime tried to neutralize Baluch leaders' powers and to suppress any activity that could lead to Baluch consciousness. The systematic suppression of the Baluch people's ethnic consciousness in the Pakistani province of Baluchistan and the Iranian province of Sistan o Baluchistan, and the neglect of the people inhabiting the neighboring corner of Afghanistan, have made the Baluch people leave their homeland and settle in other places. Baluchistan of Iran is the least populated area of the country. The government of the Islamic Republic has encouraged people from other parts of the country to settle in the province of Sistan o Baluchitan, which has caused a good deal of resentment among the native Baluch people. According to the preliminary results of the 2006 Iranian census, Sistan o Baluchestan had the third highest population growth in Iran, trailing only Southern Khorasan and Bushehr provinces. According to the same head count, the population of Sistan o Baluchestan is 2,400,000. The census does not specify the ratio of Baluch and non-Baluch residents. Considering the attempts of the Iranian government to populate the province by people from other parts of the country, the exact number of the native Baluchis is much more difficult to determine. On the Pakistani side of the border, the same policy is carried out by the Pashtunization of the Baluch territory.

As with other ethnic groups in Iran, the Pahlavi regime's suppression of ethnic aspirations became an established policy, which continues to guide the Islamic Republic's policies in dealing with the various Iranian ethnic groups.

The heightened ethnic awareness in an information age and the collapse of the former Soviet Union have provided ample means and reasons for ethnic resentment and demands for human and national rights equal to those of the dominant group. Recently, ethnic resentments have turned to be very violent both in Pakistan as well as Iran. The Pakistani army bombed the hideout of Nawab Akbar Bugti, killing the Oxford-educated Baluch leader of Pakistan, resulting in violent protests. On the Iranian side of the border, there have been numerous bloody clashes between Iranian security forces and followers of Abdumalek Rigi, a Sunni Baluch leader.

HADI SULTAN-QURRAIE

✦ BANISADR, ABOLHASSAN (1933–)

Born on March 22, 1933, in Hamadan, Persia, Abolhassan Banisadr served as President of Iran immediately following the Iranian Revolution of 1979, from February of 1980 to June of 1981. He is the son of Ayatollah Sayed Nas-rollah Bani-Sadr and is married to Ozra Bani-Sadr. He has studied at the University of Tehran as well as at the Sorbonne in Paris. As the first President of Iran elected to lead the new Islamic republic, Banisadr began his political career as early as the 1960s by protesting the dictatorship of 38-year leader, Shah Mohammad Reza Pahlavi.

Mohammad Reza Pahlavi, the Shah of Iran who rose to power in 1941 at the age of 22 as leader of Iran's constitutional monarchy, faced widespread opposition from Iranians, particularly during the 1960s and 1970s. Factions of Iranian opponents objected to the Shah's dictatorship and carried out riots and demonstrations against his government for a variety of reasons, ranging from advocacy of a greater role of Islam in the Iranian government to interest in promoting a more liberal constitutional democracy. Many Iranians objected to the Shah's strict policies of censorship, brutal treatment, and imprisonment of political activists. Some insisted that the Shah was overly concerned with emulating Western ideals and catering excessively to the United States and Israel.

Abolhassan Banisadr participated in political protests and riots in the early 1960s, during which he was once wounded and twice imprisoned. Banisadr subsequently fled to France, where he pursued studies in economics and sociology at the Sorbonne, in Paris. While abroad, Banisadr became affiliated with the Iranian resistance movement led by Ayatollah Ruhollah Khomeini, an Islamic fundamentalist likewise seeking asylum in France. In fact, Banisadr returned to Iran with Ayatollah Khomeini in 1979, at the start of the

Iranian Revolution; however, he was not an Islamic cleric. In those early days of the revolution, Khomeini maintained that clerics were not to run for positions within the government.

Upon his return to Iran, Abolhassan Banisadr served as Iranian Minister of Economy and Finance, from 1979 to 1980. Also during 1979, he briefly served as the acting Foreign Minister. During an eventful two years in his homeland, Banisadr also survived two helicopter accidents at the Iran–Iraq border line in western parts of Iran.

The Iranian Revolution of 1979 saw the overthrow of Shah Mohammad Reza Pahlavi in January of 1979 and the introduction of the current Islamic republic, led by Ayatollah Ruhollah Khomeini. Banisadr was elected to the presidency in January 1980. The election was very competitive and included nine other candidates.

During his presidency, Abolhassan Banisadr faced several challenges involving economic, military, and foreign relations. Most of the obstacles that Banisadr faced involved the mediating of tensions over the direction of the new Islamic Republic of Iran in the face of the threat of a developing war with Iraq.

One such hindrance can be observed when Banisadr was faced with the failed Nojeh coup. This incident involved an alleged collusion between Zbigniew Brzezinski, the U.S. national security advisor, and King Hussein of Jordan. Allegedly, the two met in July 1980 in the Jordanian city of Amman to arrange the overthrow of Ayatollah Khomeini's regime by Iraqi forces under President Saddam Hussein. In fact, the intervention was to be passed off as a response to a request for support from Iranian loyalist officers under Shapour Bakhtiar, who were planning their own revolt against the Iranian government. However, Khomeini quickly learned of this plot through various intelligence channels, and President Banisadr covertly captured approximately 600 officers, many of whom were subsequently ordered to be executed, effectively curtailing the coup. On September 22, 1980, Iraqi President Saddam Hussein proceeded with the invasion of Iran, thus initiating the war between Iran and Iraq.

Eventually, rising tensions between Banisadr and Ayatollah Khomeini led the Ayatollah to instigate the impeachment of Abolhassan Banisadr. Banisadr was impeached for several reasons, including his outright objection to the Ayatollah's policy of executing political dissenters and his discontent of the leadership role taken on by the Ayatollah, which he feared was becoming more and more like a dictatorship. Finally, as Banisadr's popularity increased significantly due to his successful management of the conflict with Iraq, Khomeini and his administration feared that Banisadr would become too powerful, and sought to depose him. Before the official impeachment papers were signed, the Pasdaran (the Iranian Revolutionary Guard) also seized the Presidential buildings and gardens as well as arrested newspaper writers who were closely linked to Banisadr.

Abolhassan Banisadr was impeached from the presidency on June 21, 1981, substantiating his ideological and political differences from Khomeini and the Ayatollah's administration. Banisadr was reported to have had conflicts with the clerics in power, particularly Mohammad Beheshti, who was the head of the judicial system at the time. Some Iranian forces under Khomeini, the Pasdaran, executed several allies of Banisadr, including Hossein Navab, Rashid Sadrolhefazi, and Manouchehr Massoudi. Banisadr himself narrowly escaped execution by Khomeini's orders and fled Iran in 1981, once again seeking asylum in France. He was succeeded as President of Iran by Mohammad Ali Rajai.

Banisadr stated that he offered a letter of resignation to Khomeini; however, the Ayatullah declined to accept and publish that letter. As an alternative, Banisadr was subsequently impeached as well as banished and outlawed from the country. He claims that if he had been able to resign as opposed to being impeached that he would have posed a very dangerous influence. The former president adamantly proclaimed that he had no intention of relinquishing his title and the ensuing responsibilities associated with his position.

Finally, during the ongoing tumultuous times, Banisadr decided to leave the country. Banisadr thought he had several reasons for his decision, including the fact that far too many of his supporters were wasting their time in an effort to protect him. He also thought his dramatic escape in a military aircraft from a military base would validate the belief of a substantial amount of resistance to his impeachment.

When Banisadr arrived in Paris, he was greeted by admirers. Numerous Iranian supporters were waiting for the former president. As a result, Banisadr believed that the chance of his resistance movement becoming successful was extremely high, especially since there was an increasing opposition to Khomeini. One of his goals upon arriving in France was to see mass demonstrations occur in Iran similar to those that were effective in overcoming the Shah.

Although Abolhassan Banisadr successfully arrived in France aboard a hijacked Iranian plane on July 29, 1981, and was given political asylum by the French Foreign Ministry, French authorities insisted that this refuge was contingent upon Banisadr's agreement to refrain from participation in any political activity while within French territory. Indeed, Banisadr expressed his intentions to remain in political asylum until Iran successfully implemented a democratic government. Former President Banisadr's wife, Ozra Banisadr, reported that she was imprisoned and threatened with execution while attempting to flee from Iran to Paris with their son Ali, then eight years old. Massoud Rajavi, a leader of the Mojahedin, fled from Iran to France in 1981, along with the Banisadr family. Rajavi, born in Tabas in 1948, had joined the Mojahedin in 1966 and declared himself the leader of this cult by 1981. Upon escaping to Paris in 1981, Abolhassan Banisadr joined Rajavi in founding the National Council of Resistance of Iran. His daughter, Firouzeh Banisadr, was married in 1982 to Massoud Rajavi. The couple divorced in 1984, however, after a falling out between Abolhassan Banisadr and Rajavi.

Banisadr remained politically active during his years of political exile in France, openly discussing the Iran–Iraq War, the Iranian Revolution, and emerging controversies, including the hostage crisis of 1980, between the United States and Iran. Observing the Iran–Iraq War from his place in political asylum, Banisadr openly condemned the Iranian offensive actions against Iraq. He criticized the war in general, claiming that the conflict would result in lowering profits from oil in the Middle East and would thus have negative effects upon the Iranian economy and Iraq. Rather, he indicated that the United States and Israel stood to gain the most from the conflict.

Banisadr also addressed the controversial debate over secret negotiations between Iran and the United States to delay the release of American hostages in Iran. In fact, Banisadr, who served as President of Iran during much of the 444 day hostage incident, claimed that the Reagan administration had in fact engaged in secret negotiations pertaining to the release of these hostages.

In addition to speaking out on political issues relevant to Iran and Iranian foreign relations in particular, Banisadr published various articles and several books since his relocation to France. Today he is considered an expert on the subject of the Iranian Revolution and the Iranian war with Iraq, although it appears that Banisadr has lost his political suitability as a possible alternative if the situation in Iran were to deteriorate and necessitate new leadership. His website (http://www.banisadr.com.fr) in the Persian language contains an archive of his analysis and writings. His activities are very much limited to his analysis of the most current political issues of Iran and the region at large. They are written in Persian and seem to be primarily directed toward the Iranian community in France. He continues to publish an Internet version of his once widely read journal *Enghelab Eslami*, which now bears the name *Enghelab Eslami in Exile* (http://enghelabe-eslami.com).

Bani-Sadr's literary contributions include: *Complot des ayatollahs* (La Decouverte, 1989); *Le Coran et le pouvoir* (Imago, 1993); and *My Turn to Speak: Iran, The Revolution and Secret Deals with the U.S.* (Br MacMillan, 1991).

JALIL ROSHANDEL

✦ BANKING, ISLAMIC

After the revolution of 1979, the banking industry was nationalized and all banks came under government control. From a total of 36 banks (7 specialized banks, 26 commercial banks, and 3 provincial banks), 9 commercial and specialized state-owned banks were born. In addition, in each province a provincial bank was created and the whole banking system came under state ownership. In 2003, four private banks were licensed.

The Koran prohibits payment and receipt of interest. In 1979, in order to claim that there was an Islamic economic system distinguished from established economic doctrine, the new leadership quickly changed the banking system to Islamic banking. To make Iran's banking system Islamic, the Council of Money and Credit (CMC) temporarily changed the term "interest" to "service fee" and "guaranteed profit." Many argue that this is a semantic replacement of the term "interest" by the term "profit." Under the Islamic Banking system, the banks are business partners with their customers rather than lenders. In 1983, the Majles passed the Interest Free Islamic Banking Law, which determined the activities in which the banks may participate using their financial resources. These activities are as follows:

1. Interest-Free Loans: Cooperatives, small businesses, and farmers who suffered from a natural disaster may obtain interest free loans of which the maximum amount is 5,000,000 Rials (about $600) with a maturity of up to 5 years; a 1.5% service fee will be charged.
2. Civil Participation: Banks may enter into a partnership for a particular project, which will end with completion of the project. The minimum and maximum return for the bank's investment is determined by the CMC. The maximum amount of investment by the bank is 80% of total capital needed.
3. Legal Participation: Banks may provide some capital for a new firm or buy some shares of an existing firm to a maximum of 49% of a new firm's total capital and 20% of an existing firm's total capital.
4. Direct Investment: Banks may directly invest in production projects by incorporating a new firm. The minimum expected rate of return is determined by the CMC.
5. Arbitrage: Banks can buy the products from the producers in advance with cash at a specific price and resell them after they are delivered.
6. Cash Capital: Banks provide the cash, the second party uses the money, and they share the profit. The bank has to recover its capital and expected profit in one year. The profit rate for the bank is set by

the CMC. Banks can not engage in this type of contract for importing products within the private sector.

7. Working Capital: Banks may buy raw material, spare parts, and tools for business entities and sell it on credit. The profit for the bank is set by the CMC, and the bank has to receive and clear the account in one year.

8. Selling Fixed Assets on Credit: Banks may buy any fixed asset with a useful life of more than a year and sell it on credit to the applicant. The length of time of this credit can not exceed the useful life of the asset. The selling price is based on a cost-plus-profit pricing method. The profit rate is set by the CMC.

9. Housing: Banks may invest in residential construction and sell the housing units to people with mortgage loans. The selling price is based on a cost-plus-profit pricing method.

10. Lease Purchase: Banks may buy any asset that has a minimum of two years useful life and lease it to the applicant. The leaser has to pay 20% of the price of the asset in advance and at the end of contract becomes the owner.

11. Contracting: Banks may sign an agreement with a second party to perform a specific task for a specific fee as a contractor, or contract out a specific task.

12. Sharecropping: If banks own agricultural land, they may give the right to a second party to utilize the land and share the crop or the profit. The contract is for one year, which may be renewed.

So far Iranian banks have largely failed to contribute to the economic growth and development of the country as they are legally obligated. One of the major roles that banks play in financing development projects includes the utilization of funds in financing various projects. Another role is mobilizing and channeling funds into productive activities. Banks, by joining entrepreneurs who lack funds for investment, can increase the production capacity of the country and provide greatly needed new employment opportunities. When Islamic banks enter into joint investment activities with real or legal entities, banks have to complete a feasibility and profitability study of the projects they finance. Since these projects contribute to the gross national product of Iran, they can reduce inflationary pressures. Banks cannot perform this task unless they finance commodity-producing projects and serve as an instrument of growth as prescribed by banking law and the Constitution.

Financing priorities of the banking system under Islamic Banking are directed primarily toward trade and short-term financing, which is an easier and more profitable route of investing bank funds. Banks lack experience in financing industrial and other productive projects. Banks have invested in longer-term development projects in the public sector, which have been pre-scribed and mandated by the government. Long-term direct investment and partnerships with the private sector have constituted a small percentage of total banking system operations. This is due to the banks' heavy use of short-term deposits and the lack of private sector interest in investing in long-term projects due to misleading government policies. Even if the banks had more discretionary power in allocation of their resources and could commit funds for these types of projects, given the political and legal systems' uncertainties, the private sector is less motivated to undertake and invest in long-term proj-ects. Also, the government's own financial needs have preempted the use of deposits for long-term investment. The transformation from the conventional interest-bearing basis to the interest-free Islamic system has not been produc-tive. As a result of the difficulty of creating non-interest bearing instruments to finance government deficits, the central bank has become a well known printing press, monetizing the public debt at no cost to the government. Also, the government has borrowed billions of dollars from foreign sources, has paid and still pays interest, and violates the same Islamic rule that is imposed on Iran's economy and banking system. In 2005, the government paid $1,166 million interest for external debt.

The average economic growth from 1960–1977 was 9.8%. From 1977–1988, due to the revolution, Islamic banking, and the Iran–Iraq War, the country experienced a declining economy and the average growth for this pe-riod was negative, −2.4%. The average growth rate for 1989–2002 was 4.7%. Total Factor Productivity (TFP), before the revolution, from 1960–1976, was 3.2%, but from 1977–1988 and from 1989–2002 it was negative, −9.6% and −1.8%, respectively. The ratio of average investment divided by GDP for 1962–2002 is 30.5%, highest amongst the six high-growth Asian Economies, but Iran has the lowest average growth of 4.6% in comparison with these countries. The GDP growth rate for Iran has been 50% lower. Growth in Iran has resulted from investment, but not efficient use of resources.

The banking industry in Iran is underdeveloped and is faced with several weaknesses. A number of these structural factors are related to the ownership of banks by the government. The allocation of credit and rate of return is set by the government annually. Lack of competition, weak supervision, ineffi-ciency, mismanagement, corruption, and Islamic banking principles, which are very rigid and incapable of providing services and products needed for the modern economy, are some of these weaknesses. The banking industry is undercapitalized; the risk-weighted capital adequacy of the banking system is 7.2% for private banks and 5.5% for state-owned commercial banks, compared with 8% international standards. Return on assets for state-owned commercial banks it is 0.6% and return on equity for the banking system is 20%. Islamic banking experience in Iran shows that its importance lies in symbolism, political power, and cultural meaning, and not as its viability as a modern banking system. It cannot integrate with global banking. Also, the Central Bank as a supervisory agency for the banking system is not independent and is focused on compliance with government directives rather than risk assessment. The Central Bank has failed to provide the public with the banks' financial statements. Except for recent years, there are nonblank credit cooperatives and "Qarzul-Hasanah Fund" institutions that are not subject to supervision. Because people have difficulty obtaining credit from the banking system and have to wait for a long time in order to get credit, if any, they may obtain credit only from Qarzul-Hasanah Funds, which charge more than 40% in interest.

ECONOMIC PROBLEMS

After the revolution of 1979, Iran experienced high levels of inflation, high unemployment, and a decline in economic growth. By 1980, there was a 20% decline in industrial output, and private sector investment in machinery has declined to 23% of the 1977 level. Except for agriculture, all major economic activities declined during the 1980s. Between 1984 and 1988, total investment declined by 56% and investment in machinery decreased by 70%. Between 1977 and 1988, per capita national income declined about 50% and urban unemployment increased from 4.4% to 18.9%. Private sector investment in 1987 through 1990 was about half of what it was in 1977, and state investment was about 25% of the 1977 level. Inefficiencies had occurred throughout the economy, including the banking industry. Iran has a command economy, and 85% of the economy is under government control—more than China, which is about 50%. The government sector is very inefficient and an employee in the government sector is providing only 20 minutes of useful and productive work per day. In other words, one person is working and 24 people are getting paid without providing any service. There are several factors which are the root of economic problems in Iran, namely, the legal system, political uncertainty, corruption, mismanagement, brain drain, and the Islamic banking system as it is explained in this entry.

The nationalization and conversion to the Islamic banking system has contributed to the decline in economic activity in Iran. The financing priorities of the banking system under Islamic Banking are mandated by the government and directed primarily toward trade and short term financing, which are easier and more profitable routes of investing the banks funds. Long-term direct investment and partnerships with the private sector in long-term projects have constituted a small percentage of total banking system operations. The lack of experience of banks in financing industrial and other productive projects is another weakness of the system. The government has used the banking system to prop-up inefficient, mismanaged, and money-losing state-owned enterprises to achieve political objectives. This policy has crowded-out the private sector, causing a decline in economic activity and raising unemployment and inflation. Given the political and legal systems' uncertainties, the private sector is less motivated to undertake and invest in long-term projects.

Suggested Reading

Amuzegar, J. 1997. *Iran's Economy under the Islamic Republic.* I.B. Tauris, London.

Goldsmith, R. W. 1969. *Financial structure and development.* New Haven, CT: Yale University Press, pp. 48–49.

International Monetary Fund, *Country Report, No. 06/129*, April 2006.

International Monetary Fund, *Country Report, No. 04/306*, September 2004.

SIAVASH ABGHARI

✦ BAZARGAN, MEHDI (1907–1995)

Mehdi Bazargan was an engineer and a prominent Iranian politician, particularly throughout the Iranian Revolution of 1979, and one of the few pioneers of a new interpretation of Islam. Bazargan was primarily known for his liberal political perspectives and revolutionary interpretations of the Muslim religion as they pertained to the nascent Republic of Iran. In fact, Bazargan was recognized as a central architect of a new political paradigm for the formation and development of the government of the post-revolutionary Iranian Republic that placed Islam in the greater context of a complex sociopolitical environment emerging in the Republic.

As the first Prime Minister to serve the Islamic Republic of Iran following the Iranian revolution, Mehdi Bazargan was associated with a liberal stance regarding the direction of the Iranian government and strong opposition to the radical Islamist clerics he feared were undermining the democratization of the Iranian government in its formative years. Bazargan was furthermore recognized as a devout advocate of democracy in the new Islamic Republic of Iran.

Prime Minister Medhi Bazargan, 1979. (AP Photo/Bob Dear)

Mehdi Bazargan was born in September of 1907 into a family of merchants in Tehran, Iran. His father, Hajj 'Abbasqoli Tabrizi (d. 1954), was a successful merchant and devoutly religious. He received an admirable education, first attending secondary school at the prestigious, notoriously modern Dar Al-Mu'allimin (The Teacher's College). From there, at 19 years of age, Bazargan went on to study engineering and thermodynamics at École Centrale des Arts et Manufactures in Paris, France, for which he received funding from the Iranian government. Bazargan was known for his pro-democracy activism and voluntarily entered the French Army while studying in France to fight against Nazi Germany.

Though he was not formally trained as a cleric or religious teacher, Bazargan was deeply involved in the study and lay interpretation of Islam. In fact, in addition to his political involvement, liberal political views, and advocacy of the democratization of the Iranian national government, Bazargan is defined by his theological perspective and analysis of the Muslim religion and his avant-garde interpretation of the Quran. Among his more notable interpretations of Islam, Bazargan reasoned that because God created nature, religious laws effectively served the dual purpose of guiding religion and regulating nature. It was due to this reasoning that he arrived at his belief in natural law. The controversial role of the prophets and the nature of their mission in leading the people represent another vital issue that Bazargan addressed in his interpretation of Islam.

In 1936, Bazargan returned to Iran where he initially became involved in government service. He subsequently taught as a professor of thermodynamics, and later headed the first Department of Engineering at Tehran University during the late 1940s.

With the rising popularity of political tolerance as a topic of much attention and debate in Iran in the 1940s and early 1950s, Mehdi Bazargan became more involved in the political sphere. Among his first significant political achievements, Bazargan contributed to a mosque association, namely Qānūn-e Eslām, as well as the Islamic Association of Students, and helped to found and administer the Engineers' Union. He then became involved in the Iran party, and subsequently in the National Front Party in Iran. Bazargan was thereafter delegated by Prime Minister Mohammad Mosaddeq to oversee the nationalization of the Iranian oil industry, a momentous event for the government of Iran, which effectively transferred the industry from British to Iranian control. In fact, Bazargan served as the head of the National Iranian Oil Company, founded under Mossadegh in 1951. Thus, he became the first Iranian to hold this position. Also in the 1950s, Bazargan served as deputy Prime Minister of Iran, representing the nationalist party.

Bazargan's role as a leader in the revolutionary Iranian democratic and liberal movements changed following the 1953 coup in Iran, which ended the dictatorship of 38-year leader Shah Mohammad Reza Pahlavi. The Shah, who rose to power in 1941 at the age of 22 as leader of Iran's constitutional monarchy, faced widespread opposition from Iranians, particularly during the 1960s and 1970s. Mehdi Bazargan became highly involved in the National Resistance Movement following the coup, serving as executive secretary of the movement for several years. During this time he was jailed twice: once in 1955 and again in 1957.

In the 1960s, his dual interests in political and religious reform were underscored by his participation, during the liberalization movement, in both the Second National Front and the clerical reform movement, which was intended to establish a new code of religious leadership following the death of Ayatollah Hosein Borujerdi. During this period, he joined Ayatollah Mahmud Taleqani and his followers in a movement to democratize the Shi'i clerical organization.

Mehdi Bazargan should also be credited as the founder of the Freedom Movement of Iran (FMI) in 1961 (also known as the Liberation Movement of Iran, or *Nehzat-e Asdi- Iran), a* short-lived resistance movement protesting the

White Revolution of the Shah. Though the effectiveness of this movement was curtailed by the Iranian government, leadership of the Freedom Movement of Iran arguably represented Bazargan's greatest political achievement. As leader of the FMI, Bazargan first articulated the necessity of Islam in Iranian society, insisting that the people of Iran adhere more to the "Islamic" than an "Iranian" identity. Moreover, he inspired a new outlook regarding the nexus of Islam and politics, essentially advocating constitutionalism and democracy in Iranian government. The FMI was essentially disbanded due to the imprisonment of several key members for protesting against the Shah and his administration. Throughout the 1960s and 1970s, Bazargan was imprisoned on several occasions for his opposition to Shah Mohammad Reza Pahlavi through nonviolent protests and activities of such groups. As the political and ideological leader of the Freedom Movement of Iran, Bazargan was sentenced to ten years imprisonment, but received a royal pardon after having served three years.

During his trial in 1963, Bazargan's religious perspective with respect to the interpretation of Islam began to examine in greater detail the notions of the freedom of man and the resulting necessity of democratic government. His theory of the freedom of man was rooted in his interpretation of the Quran with respect to the story of the creation of man. Based upon his reading, Bazargan theorized that man is unique in his capacity for possession of knowledge and freedom of choice. The inherent freedom of man, he concluded, required individuals to exercise choice and discretion in the institution of a democratically elected government.

Following his imprisonment for political rebellion, Bazargan intentionally adopted a less public political stance and minimized his position in political activity in general, participating mainly in intellectual movements, including discussions with religious clerics on the topics of Marxism, the meaning of government, and refinement of religious theory pertaining to Islam. In 1977, Mehdi Bazargan cofounded the Iranian Human Rights Association, or Society for the Defence of Human Rights, thus reentering the political sphere in Iran. While Ayatollah Khomeini arose as the leader of the Iranian Revolution in the late 1970s, Mehdi Bazaran was gaining recognition as a principal activist in the revolutions of nationalism and the redefinition of Islamic discourse in Iran.

For this reason, along with the overthrow of Shah in 1979, Bazargan was appointed to the post of provisional Prime Minister of the new Islamic Republic of Iran on February 5, 1979, by its leader, Ayatollah Ruhollah Khomeini. Bazargan resigned from this position within one year citing that certain radical clerics were undermining his government; however, he did continue to serve in the Iranian parliament for several years. Additionally, Mehdi Bazargan served as a member of the original Iranian Parliament, or *Majles*, in the wake of the Iranian Revolution. Despite continual harassment and enduring conflict with his radical Islamic clerics, Bazargan continued to serve on the Iranian Parliament for several years.

However, Bazargan increasingly came into conflict with religious clerics, including Ayatollah Khomeini, who advocated a greater role of Islam in Iranian government. As a leader of the democratic and liberal movements in Iran at this time, Bazargan disagreed with the Ayatollah and clerics on political issues involving the role of Islam. For instance, Bazargan objected to the establishment of the Assembly of Experts for the Leadership of Iran (also known as the Assembly of Experts), a congress of 86 publicly elected high level clerics charged with electing the Supreme Leader and overseeing his decision-making and executive activities. Moreover, he disapproved of the title "Islamic Republic" for the government of Iran.

Bazargan repeatedly warned against the dangers of tyranny, among which he cited the destruction of individual morality as the primary hazard to social disorder. In his consideration of authoritarian rule and tyranny, Bazargan posited that the resultant chasm between the ruling and the ruled presented an obstacle to the social order and challenged the freedom of the ruled to participate in government.

Bazargan decided to resign from his post along with his cabinet on November 5, 1979. His resignation was allegedly a protest against the U.S. Embassy takeover and hostage-taking crisis, which occurred on November 4, 1979. However, Bazargan's resignation may also be perceived as a consequence of the rapidly intensifying revolutionary movement in Iran, and particularly his ongoing disagreement with radical Islamic clerics, who he claimed thwarted the progress of democratization of the Iranian government. Most likely, the U.S. Embassy takeover and hostage-taking crisis underscored his frustration with the radical Islamic clerics of the Iranian administration and provoked his resignation.

He was preceded as Prime Minister by Shapour Bakhtiar and succeeded by Mohammad Ali Rajai.

During the last eight years of his life, the religious and intellectual analytical interpretations of Mehdi Bazargan began to represent a marked digression from his earlier theory. Whereas he previously interpreted the mission of the prophets in the Muslim religion, a vital issue of controversy among interpreters of Islam, as a duty to guide the people in their conduct of government and life, he came to question the role of the prophets in advising the people in their conduct of worldly affairs. In his later interpretation of Islam with respect to the mission of the prophets, he adopted the theological perspective that these religious figures primarily represented a duty to inform human beings of the way of God and the existence of the afterlife. Regarding the institution and conduct of government, he claimed that the people should refer to the examples of science and philosophy, rather than religion, in determining the proper means of governance. He solidified this theory in the early 1990s, expressing his interpretation of the role of the prophets as depicted in the Quran as a mission to inform and guide human beings with respect to the way of God and the afterlife. In 1992, Bazargan spoke of a new theological opinion of the purpose of the mission of the prophets. His newfound opinion was met with several different reactions ranging from complete disbelief to acceptance as well as expansion.

Living in a sort of political limbo during the last years of his life and continually harassed by opponents, Bazargan was deemed a barely tolerable representation of opposition to the radical elements of the Islamic government. In the years before his death, Bazargan became one of the most persistent critics of the Islamic government. He spoke of the extreme political suppression that existed and also of the substantial amount of corruption that persisted at the heart of the judiciary system. He also spoke harshly on the government's effort to close newspapers, quiet protestors, and destroy the work being accomplished on the long-suffering human rights crisis.

While traveling from Tehran, Iran to Zurich, Switzerland, Bazargan died of a heart attack on January 20, 1995 at the age of 93. He is remembered for his liberal political advocacy and support of democratic governance in the new Republic of Iran and for his revolutionary lay interpretations of Islam.

Suggested Reading
Barzin, S. 1994. Constitutionalism and democracy in the religious ideology of Mehdi Bazargan. *British Journal of Middle Eastern Studies* 21:85–101.

JALIL ROSHANDEL

✦ BROADCASTING

Broadcasting in Iran has had a tumultuous history. In the face of various challenges, however, it has developed into a formidable operation under the Islamic Republic of Iran. Although radio and television have experienced periods of growth and stagnation throughout their history, the largest expansion of broadcasting has occurred under the Islamic Republic of Iran. Radio had its origins in military applications when the Germans established a long-wave radio connection between Isfahan in central Iran and Neon in Germany in 1915. Radio sets were introduced in the early 1930s. As early as 1938, nightly radio programs by the British Broadcasting Corporation (BBC) were being listed in an Iranian newspaper. The beginning of radio broadcast in Persian was in the broadcast of a short daily program from Ankara in Turkey. As World War II started, Berlin and London began their broadcasts to Iran, to be followed by Moscow, Rome, New Delhi, and Baku. An early form of radio reception in Iran before 1940 entailed receiving programs by foreign broadcasters from the Soviet Union, BBC, Germany, and France. In this military context, and in the context of the state's early use of radio as a means of political hegemony, the Iranian experience with this medium marked it as a tool of propaganda.

Iran started operating its first radio station in 1940. Radio Tehran, which operated in short-wave and medium-wave bands, broadcast programs in Persian and in other languages (English, French, German, Arabic, and Turkish). By 1965, the number of radio receivers was estimated at 2 million with an audience of 20 million, reaching 45% of the population. According to some estimates, by 1992 there would be at least one radio receiver for each family in Iran.

Unlike radio, television started as a commercial venture by entrepreneurs in 1958. As a monopoly concession, this venture not only entailed a five-year monopoly to operate television transmitters, it also offered exclusive rights to the proprietor to import television sets during the same time period. Two stations were set up in Tehran and Abadan, a city in the oil-rich region province of Khuzestan. Thus, Television Iran (ITV) was born. The content of television at this stage was mostly entertainment based on American imports and genres (dubbed American films and locally produced variety and quiz shows). Recognizing the importance of the medium, the Pahlavi regime established a state-owned second network, National Iranian television (NITV) in 1967. To expand production activities and to control the means of popular communication, a single structure was set up by the Pahlavi government in 1971 that incorporated the existing broadcasting outlets to form a public broadcasting monopoly, National Iranian Radio and Television (NIRT). By the end of the decade, television had become an enormously popular medium.

In the immediate aftermath of the revolution in 1979, NIRT was subject to a process of "cleansing" (*Pak-sazi*), which entailed removal of staff, content, and all symbols assumed to be associated with the monarchy. These events started the project of "Islamization" of Iranian media by the state. NIRT was renamed Voice and Vision of the Islamic Republic shortly after. The ambivalent or dismissive attitudes of the state and many religious authorities toward specific media and cultural forms (e.g., broadcasting, cinema, music) were transformed by Ayatollah Khomeini's positive statements of acceptance of modern media as tools of education and Islamization projects. Khomeini even advocated the independence of broadcasting to preserve its credibility in order to make sure the masses did not turn to foreign sources for their news.

During the Iran–Iraq War (1980–1988), the broadcasting outlets were used as instruments of mass mobilization to support the war efforts. More important, the state restricted content to either local productions or to content that would not violate Islamic tenets as defined by the Islamic Republic. In early years after the revolution, improvisation and a "make it up as we go along" spirit defined the programming strategy of the Iranian television. The programming lineup was a mixture of news and public affairs, religious programming and sermons, and educational programs. It also included a limited range of entertainment, which consisted of occasional serials such as *Tanzavaran* (*The Satirists*), *Baad Banha* (*Sails*), and *Doorbin Makhfee*, the Iranian rendition of *Candid Camera*. Other entertainment programs included films and episodic television imports from the Soviet Union, Eastern Europe, Asia, and the Third World, a list that demonstrates the Islamic Republic's attempt to remove Western cultural influence from television and popular culture. Toward the end of the decade, *Oshin*, a Japanese television serial, became one of the most popular television shows. The appearance of the American *Little House on the Prairie* and the British *One by One,* as family-oriented programs, on the Iranian television during this period indicates what forms of Western programs the Islamic Republic deemed acceptable. It also demonstrates that it is the content and not the communication technology that is the subject of concern with the Islamic Republic.

Local broadcasting productions expanded in the early 1990s. The two main radio networks broadcast 49,124 hours of programming in 1990. The main genres and contents in radio programming include cultural and social, news and public affairs, arts and literature, sports, instructional programs, discussions in history, Friday prayers, music, Islamic education, entertainment, Quran and call to prayer, economy, politics, and defense. At this point, there were three radio stations devoted to recitations of the Quran. What was particularly notable about radio programming at this time was the absence of Western popular music and female solo singers of any background (though female announcers and on-air personalities were present). Television in the same period similarly experienced growth and Islamization of its content. Television broadcasting hours in 1990 totaled to 12,262. By 1991, 85.3% of television programs were produced in Iran. This is in sharp contrast to the pre-revolution domestic production level of only 30%. Some scholars have included the imported television contents, some of which were said to be entirely alien to the local cultural and religious traditions, among the contributing factors to the alienation of the Iranian masses that led to the revolution of 1979.

Broadcasting in Iran today is a vast operation and covers a wide range of activities in production and distribution. The Islamic Republic of Iran Broadcasting (IRIB) operates several radio and television networks inside and outside the Iranian borders. IRIB has an impressive Internet presence and operation as well. The main terrestrial television networks include Channel 1, Channel 2, Channel 3, Channel 4, Tehran Channel (*Shabakeh Tehran*), News Channel (*Shabakeh Khabar*), and Education Channel (*Shabakeh Amoozesh*). Jam-e-Jam Networks (IRIB1, IRIB2, and IRIB3) are among the nonterrestrial television services offered by IRIB. These networks are a part of external programming offered by IRIB, available via satellite and streaming live via Internet on IRIB's website. Receiving these programs entails purchasing a satellite dish, without any further subscription fee. For those who live in North America, for example, a satellite dish costing around $250 pointed at Telstar 5 satellite would enable one to receive, among other channels, IRIB2 and News Channel from Iran. Other external networks include Sahar TV (*Shabakeh Sahar*) in several languages, and Alalam TV (*Shabakeh Alalam*) and Alkawthar TV (*Shabakeh Alkowsar*), both in Arabic. Quran TV (*Shabakeh Qurane* or *Seemaye Quran*) is devoted to the recitations of the holy book. Labbaik, listed as "Labbaik Internet television network" (*Shabakeh Televezioni Interneti Labbik*) on IRIB's website, is devoted to Mecca and other holy sites in Saudi Arabia. This network offers a form of virtual pilgrimage and a spiritual journey in cyberspace to all, and especially those who might not be in a position to make the physical journey. IRIB operates an active film production unit, Sima Film. IRIB also operates radio and television stations in provinces outside of Tehran. It operates 26 broadcasting centers in provinces across the country, with 32 public relations entities associated with the various broadcasting outlets.

IRIB's radio operation is equally impressive. It operates national and provincial networks, as well as foreign language services directed at the audiences outside of Iranian borders in 27 languages. The national radio networks include Nationwide Radio (*Radio Sarasaree*), Quran Radio (*Shabakeh Quran*), Culture Radio (*Shabakeh Farhang*), Education Radio (*Shabakeh Moaref*), Youth Radio (*Shabakeh Javan*), and Sports Radio (*Shabakeh Varzesh*). Provincial channels broadcast programming in Persian and various local dialects across the country. IRIB's World Services 1 through 6 (*Radio Boroon Marzi*) are among the outlets that broadcast programs in various languages. Other networks available to the outside world include Message Radio (*Radio Payam*),

Radio Dari, and Friendly Voice Radio (*Radio Seda-ye Ashena*). The majority of these networks are available via Internet. IRIB has a significant Internet presence (http://www.irib.ir). Many of Iranian television and radio offerings are available via Internet. IRIB's website includes access to many of its publications and reports, mostly in Persian. IRIB has an associated college (*Dansehskadeh seda va sima*), a research center (*Markaz-e Tahgheeghat*), and is quite active in public opinion research regarding its programs (*Nazar sanjee barname-e*).

According to IRIB's annual report for 2005–2006 (year 1384 in the Persian calendar), IRIB produced 60,764 hours of television programming, and broadcast 175,756 hours of programming. During this year, 73% of this broadcasting was internal, and 27% was external. IRIB produced 204,615 hours of radio programming and broadcast 268,373 hours of programs. Eighty percent of this broadcasting was internal, and 20% was external. The report announced 4% annual growth in television broadcasting and 5% growth in radio broadcasting compared to the previous year.

The Islamic Republic of Iran has been successful in expanding broadcasting operations and in offering a wide range of programming and production activities. Although this expansion started during the second term of the presidency of Rafsenjani, the pace accelerated notably during the second half of the last decade. Any examination of recent annual reports by IRIB would demonstrate that in terms of volume of media production it surpasses many of the European broadcasting entities. These developments have been noteworthy, although at times some media observers' ideological prejudices against the Iranian government have prevented them from acknowledging such developments in terms of quantity and quality of programming. It is important to note a few factors regarding broadcasting developments and their larger cultural and sociopolitical implications. First, by restricting access to its television (and film) market, the Iranian state has facilitated the growth of the local production and distribution mechanisms structurally, which has further entailed fostering indigenous technical and artistic talents and capabilities. In the age of globalized television markets, which often works to the advantage of Western/Northern multinational media companies, state restrictions have led to greater self-sufficiency. Second, it is true that broadcasting in Iran is under the control of the conservative elements of the state, as broadcasting is under the direct control of the office of the Supreme Leader by law. However, IRIB is far from a monolith in the field of cultural production. Working within the constraints of the "Islamic" media and Iranian political system, producers, directors, and artists have developed aesthetic and professional codes that are culturally dynamic and socially relevant. It is unclear how else the enormous popularity of some of the programs in entrainment with audiences inside and outside Iran produced by the creative personnel in IRIB could be explained. Here descriptive data should be separated from normative claims. Third, the broadcasting does not exist in isolation from other audio-visual media (e.g., video, cinema, popular music, all of which have had productive relationships with broadcasting). More importantly, the Internet and satellite television keep the more limiting aspects of broadcasting in check, as they are part of a cultural geography that does not coincide with the borders of the nation and its state. Fourth, those factors that give broadcasting its relevance and cultural legitimacy are often parts of larger, if contested, cultural traditions and norms whose origins are outside of the broadcasting codes and regulations. Viewed in this light, broadcasting in Iran is, even in the face of state restrictions, part of a dynamic popular culture that remains creative and vital.

See also Broadcasting, Historical Evolution of.

Suggested Reading
Banani, A. 1971. The role of the mass media. In *Iran faces the seventies*, ed. E. Yar-Shater. New York: Praeger.
Malek, A., and M. Mohsenian-Rad. 1994. Iran. In *Mass media in the Middle East: A comprehensive handbook*, eds. Y.R. Kamalipour & H. Mowlana. London: Greenwood Press.
Mowlana, H. 1989. The Islamization of Iranian television. *Intermedia* 17:35–39.
Semati, M. 2008. *Media, culture and society in Iran: living with globalization and the Islamic state*. London: Routledge.
Semati, M. 2007. Media, the state, and the pro-democracy movement in Iran. In *Globalization and media transformation in new and emerging democracies*, eds. I. A. Blankson & P. D. Murphy. Albany, NY: SUNY Press.
Sreberny-Mohammadi, A., and A. Mohammadi. 1994. *Small media, big revolution: communication, culture, and the Iranian revolution*. Minneapolis: University of Minnesota Press.

MEHDI SEMATI

✦ BROADCASTING, HISTORICAL EVOLUTION OF

The Iranian Ministry of War purchased and installed a Russian-made wireless telegraph system in 1925, at Qajar Palace in Tehran. The 120-meter transmission tower is still standing and serves as a testimonial to the beginning of telecommunications in Iran. Six years later, in 1931, two low-power (20 kilowatt) shortwave radio transmitters became operational but, according to the

Ministry of Post, Telegraph and Telephone, private importation, sale, and ownership of telecommunication devices (telephone and telegraph) were still forbidden. Exempting the new wireless media (the music box and later the radio) and "talking movies," the road was paved for the development of radio and cinema in Iran. In terms of programming, most broadcasting consisted of music, hence the term, "music box." Radio Tehran was inaugurated in 1940 and, subsequently, the first regularly programmed and operated Amplitude Modulation (AM) radio stations (network) in Iran went on the air in Tehran, Tabriz, Mashhad, Kerman, Khoramshahr, and gradually expanded to other cities.

The first Iranian television stations, established in 1959, were funded by private entrepreneurs in Tehran and Abadan, located in the southwestern part of Iran. At the beginning, due to both a shortage of professional programmers, engineers, personnel, and studios and production facilities, the broadcast hours were limited to 4 hours per weekday (6:00 PM to 10:00 PM). Both stations, called "Iran TV," used low power tansmitters, hence their signals were limited to a small number of people who owned TV sets. An outcome of this limitation was that during the broadcast hours many Iranian families would visit their neighbors' who owned TV sets and huddle around the "magic box" to view their favorite programs.

Shortly after the arrival of broadcasting in Iran, training courses and programs were established to fulfill the technical and programming needs of both radio and television. The Institute of Journalism, supported by Kayhan (one of the major daily newspapers), was established in 1964 at the University of Tehran. The name was later changed to the Institute for Communication Research. Gradually, the Institute increased its course and program offerings to include journalism, cinematography, photography, public relations, and translation. In addition, the College of Television and Cinema, which was associated with the Iranian National Radio and Television, was established in Tehran to offer two-year training programs in broadcasting.

Less than a decade after the establishment of television in Iran, the acquisition of advanced broadcast technologies and skilled personnel, as well as improved administrative and legal matters, resulted in the formation of a national television network in 1966. The early privately owned commercial stations were purchased by the government. Therefore, in 1967, the newly formed Iranian National Television (INTV) network began its trial programming under direct government supervision. Simultaneously, the numer of programs, hours of broadcasts, and areas of network coverage increased.

In 1967, the Shah and Shahbano (King and Queen), Mohammad Reza and Farah Pahlavi, respectively, formally inaugurated the new national television network which was planned and developed by a French group. The French had developed their own television standard (SECAM: System En Coleur Avec Memoire), which was subsequently employed by Iranian television as well. However, in 1998, the standard was changed from the SECAM to the PAL (Phase Alternate Line) system of broadcasting which was developed in Germay and also used in the United Kingdom. The American system is NTSC (National Television Standards Committee), which is incompatible with other standards and vice-versa.

Shortly after 1967, the Iranian National Radio merged with the Iranian National Television, creating the National Iranian Radio and Television (NIRT). The broadcast network was governed by the General Department of Publications and Broadcasting, which was a government authority responsible for broadcasting and broadcast regulations in Iran. However, the actual production, transmission, and the technical matters were carried out by NIRT, under direct supervision of the government.

By 1977, the black-and-white television system was replaced by a color system, and broadcast studios were equipped with advanced technologies. At that time, 93% of cities and 45% of rural areas were able to pick up the television signals of Channel One and Channel Two. Two other channels, Educational TV and International TV, were also operational—the first aired instructional programs, and the second, programs in English. One of the radio broadcasts was also devoted to international programming in English. The first live satellite broadcast, aired on the national Iranian television network, took place in October 1969, when the late Mohammad Reza Shah met with the U.S. president Richard Nixon, and the next live broadcast was the landing of the first Apollo on the moon.

After the 1979 Iranian Revolution, the name of the broadcast regulatory system was changed to Islamic Republic of Iran Broadcasting, or IRIB (Sazeman-e Seda va Sima-ye Jomhuri-ye Eslami-ye Iran), which is also commonly known as Seda va Sima (Sound and Sight). According to Article 175 of the Iranian constitution, private broadcasting is forbidden.

Furthermore, it was decided that the IRIB's domestic and external broadcast signals must be expanded to cover all parts of the country and include international programs aimed at many nations. Hence, during the 8-year Iran–Iraq War (1980–1988) and the imposition of economic sanctions on Iran by the United Sates, domestic production of radio and television sets and broadcast transmitters became a priority. One of the challenges facing the establishment of complete broadcast coverage in Iran was its vast territory and mountainous areas. To overcome these obstacles, broadcast translators were installed and communication satellites were utilized to not only achieve almost total AM-FM radio and TV coverage in Iran, but also to transmit radio and TV programs to other parts of the world.

Based on 2006 data, the IRIB radio and television networks employ 300,000 personnel throughout the country and, via satellite transmission, are accessible to the entire population (over 75 million). It also broadcasts programs in nearly 30 languages through its world services. As of 2007, IRIB broadcasts six national channels, one international news channel (Khabar "News"), four satellite channels for international viewers (IRIB2 or Jam-e-Jam, Al-Alam, Al-kowthar, and Sahar), and approximately thirty provincial channels—one per province or "Ostaan." All international channels are accessible throughout the world via satellite: IRIB2 broadcasts programs in Persian which are intended for expatriate Iranians; Al-Alam and Al-Kowthar broadcast in Arabic; and Sahar airs programs in Arabic, English, French, Kurdish, and Azari languages. The IRIB provides eight major radio stations, including four national channels. Most of the radio and television channels are also accessible via the Internet.

In many ways, IRIB is the most powerful media, cultural, and educational corporation in Iran—similar to TimeWarner in the United States. It is an independent organization, aligned with the Supreme Leader, which, in addition to owning and operating the broadcast media in Iran, owns the Sima Film production company; organizes film, music, and arts festivals; publishes books, newspapers, magazines; and even operates its own College of Sound and Sight (Daneshkedeh Seda va Sima). IRIB has established bureaus around the world, including Tajikistan, Syria, North America, Latin America, Afghanistan, Turkey, Iraq, Azerbaijan, Bosnia, England, Paris, Germany, India, Lebanon, Malaysia, Pakistan, and Russia.

See also Broadcasting.

Suggested Reading

Kamalipour, Y., and H. Mowlana, eds. 1994. *Mass media in the Middle East: A comprehensive handbook*. Westport, Connecticut: Greenwood Press.

Mohsenian-Rad, M. 2006. *Iran in four communication galaxies*. 3 volumes in Persian Press.

Islamic Republic of Iran Broadcasting website: http://irib.ir.

YAHYA KAMALIPOUR

C

✦ CARPETS

Despite a rapid modernization in Iranian lifestyle, the carpet remains an essential part of Iranian culture. This thick woolen fabric is an extremely durable and versatile piece of soft furniture which still occupies a prominent space in various Iranian residential environments. At home it functions as a visually attractive multipurpose fitting comparable to tables, chairs, and beds. The carpet is also highly esteemed as an important family inheritance transferred from generation to generation. In addition to such unique cultural connotations, the carpet-weaving tradition in Iran is closely associated with socioeconomic conditions, as well as with the layers of traditional and modern society. Floor coverings are customarily woven by nomadic tribes intended primarily for personal use but are eventually sold at domestic and international markets, whereas the commercial production of carpets plays a critical role in both national and regional development schemes.

Like other major art productions, the carpet industry was seriously affected by the Islamic Revolution in 1979. Having been regarded as "bourgeois," the production of good carpets was significantly discouraged. Equally, the austere atmosphere during the Iran–Iraq War did not provide a favorable environment for the recovery of productivity in carpets of fine craftsmanship and beautiful design. The economic climate in post-war Iran, characterized by a centralized economy and a high rate of inflation, was disadvantageous to the promotion of the carpet industry. A high exchange rate of the Iranian rial to the U.S. dollar fixed in the early 1980s did raise the price of exported Iranian

An Iranian man drinks tea as he sits on his carpets in a Jomeh Bazaar (Friday Market) in Tehran, 2008. The famous Jomeh Bazaar is held every Friday to display mostly bric-a-brac, traditional dress, and handicrafts, on three floors of a multistory car park in central Tehran. (AP Photo/Vahid Salemi)

carpets an exceptional amount. This prompted foreign importers to buy carpets from other countries. Consequently, Iran could not hold its dominant position in the global carpet industry, and its market share significantly fell from approximately 40% down to approximately 15%. The Iranian government was forced to make a drastic change in foreign trade policies, intending to regain the economic benefits of the rug trade, yet the Iranian carpet industry was nearly plunged into the depths of degeneration. As the U.S. dollar became weaker in 1985, however, Iranian carpet exports began to increase again. By 1995, the Iranian carpet industry had managed to regain a nearly 30% market share.

Since early times, the carpet has been a major asset to Iranian society. As the term "Persian" may be synonymous with a luxurious silky carpet with a smooth surface and skin-like texture, the carpet is of great importance as a cultural export of Iran. Carpets not only feed the well-established European market, but they are also now exported to the newly growing markets of Asia and South America. Today, the European Union is the largest single market for weaving products; therefore, the EU imports a large amount of carpets and rugs from Iran. Despite the official embargo on Iranian imports, it seems that Iranian carpets continue to be sold in the United States through third parties in order to circumvent import restrictions. While the foreign supply of carpets provides crucial resources for Iran, the growth of the carpet market causes a change in the practice of Iranian carpet-making, both positively and negatively.

It is perhaps inevitable that carpet production has been mechanized for mass production in modern times, although handwoven carpets are still widely produced in urban and village workshops. The handknotted carpet is highly regarded as an object of value at home and abroad. Yet due to the devaluation of the Iranian currency, Iranian carpets are becoming cheaper for foreign buyers. The lower the price is set for Iranian carpets, the lower the value is applied for the laborious handwork of weavers. A tendency to underrate Iranian products at the rug market does not help to promote their technical and stylistic innovations on their own and makes carpets mere customer-oriented products. In order to meet the demands of customers, the size and shape of Iranian carpets intended for export tend to be designed for fitting their living environments, such as rooms with hard furniture and stairs. The design is often standard, ranging from flamboyant floral patterns, medallions, and geometric schemes to a variety of other Western-style designs. It is crucial for the development of the Iranian carpet business to encourage joint ventures with foreign counterparts, thus raising the profile of Iranian products in international markets and in turn to promote the creation of individual carpets with innovative designs, so as to stay ahead of the competition with China and other rivals.

The carpet industry in Iran is subject to the unstable political and economic situation in Iran, as well as to frequent changes in Iranian trade laws. Yet the current state of the carpet industry somehow remains in an optimistic condition. The production of carpets is largely divided into two strands, commercial and tribal, and carpet-making centers are extended over a wide geographical area in Iran.

Carpet styles vary according to regions and tribal groups. Many rugs are produced among nomads in the Khorasan province in the northeast, and small pile rugs of the Baluchs are particularly notable for their bold designs and vivid colours. Among tribal carpets produced in the south, the Kilims of the Qashqa'i, a nomadic tribe living in the Fars province, and those produced in the Khamseh confederacy, are the best known in the carpet market. Central Iran is famous not only for its classical carpets produced in Kashan and Isfahan but also for its rich heritage of tribal rugs, such as those made by the Kashgais. West Iran is also an important carpet-producing area. Some of the carpets of outstanding quality come from the town of Saruq, north of Arak, and the village workshop of the Bakhtiaris. Finally, in the Azerbaijan province, the Shahsavan tribe has been making various types of weaving products, including floor covers, household bags, horse covers, and panels for cradles. Rugs produced in the small town of Heriz and its surrounding villages are characteristic of the use of geometrically composed medallions with pendants.

Whereas some traders promote the mass production of carpets economically woven by using synthetic fibres with stale, identical designs, others deal in authentic "Persian" carpets with professional ethics and great enthusiasm for the revival of the art of the loom in the country. Several firms have dedicated themselves to the revitalization of handmade Iranian carpet traditions. Their professional philosophy and connoisseurship lies in the meticulous research on weaving techniques and designs, the use of locally produced handspun pure wool and natural dyes, and more importantly, the appreciation of ancient craftsmanship cultivated by the hands of knotters for many centuries. In pursuing quality rather than quantity and contributing to the rejuvenation of traditional craft techniques, their weaving products deserve special attention.

Suggested Reading
GHEREH website: http://www.ghereh.org.
HALI website: http://www.hali.com.

YUKA KADOI

✦ CASPIAN SEA REGIMES

The Caspian Sea is the largest entirely enclosed body of salt water in the world. It is located in northwest Asia where Azerbaijan, Iran, Russia, Turkmenistan, and Kazakhstan share the Caspian Basin. It represents an extremely fragile ecosystem. There are immense fishery resources in this area that produce 90% of the world's supply of sturgeon. Additionally, there are considerable oil and gas deposits in the subsoil. This area has been a noted leader in the petroleum and gas industry. Even in the mid-nineteenth century, the region was producing half of the world's total crude oil. However, in the mid-1950s there was a significant reduction of Caspian oil production. Exploratory efforts were reduced and, as a result, production decreased as well.

The sea itself is approximately 700 miles extending from north to south and approximately 250 miles across. It is also connected to the Black Sea by the Volga and Don rivers, and the Sea of Azov, which is a branch of the Black Sea. The area is extremely complex and has diverse people, nations, and languages. The entire population of individuals within this area does not exceed 30 million, and their culture and heritage date back further than many European nations.

The history behind the Caspian Sea region is extensive and has proven to have many dealings with the subject of oil. The collection of oil has been noted in very early records with many viewing it as a "magic potion" of sorts. After waging war on Persia to gain control of Baku, the Caspian Sea eventually came under Tsarist Russian control. Although there has been a long history of oil within this region, it was only been recognized as a major symbol of the region's potential since 1991. For a great deal of time during the Soviet period, the Caspian Basin was closed to the world's oil industry. Both Iran and the Soviets were reluctant to enter into an open conflict because of the fear that it may bring back the old hostilities of post-WWII.

Iranian President Mahmoud Ahmadinejad delivers speech during the Caspian Sea leaders' summit in Tehran, 2007. (AP Photo/Vahid Salemi)

After the collapse of the Soviets, the basin was subsequently opened and emerged as a vast natural gas and oil resource. The amount of oil within this area is expected to be the largest outside of the Persian Gulf. An advantage for the Caspian Sea in economic development is that it is far more stable than the Persian Gulf region with similar abundances of resources, thus explaining why many oil companies have been rushing to this area ready to invest billions to tap into the largely untouched resources. A major disadvantage of the Caspian Sea, however, is its lack of transportation routes to the market and consumer centers.

The Caspian Sea is often viewed as a difficult place to work. There is a great deal of tacit ethnic tension within the area, and many conflicts have erupted either within the area or can potentially break out in a relatively short period of time. In order for others to exploit the oil reserves in this delicate area, there are three main difficulties that must first be addressed. The first is the issue of legal confusion over the definition of the Caspian Sea's legal status. There also exists the inability to gain agreement from the five coastal states. There is also disagreement over the jurisdiction of the region as well as control over its economic sectors. A second obstacle is that of the regional rivalries in the area. Oil and gas transportation from the sea evokes strong reactions from actors within the area, especially those of Russia, Turkey, and Iran. Finally, there are serious concerns over ecological and environmental issues. Along with this is the fear of ruining the precious ecosystem that currently exists in this area.

With the fall of the Soviet Union in 1991 came a significant opportunity for the United States to enhance its commercial interests and energy security. Because the Caspian region was closed to foreign investment during Soviet rule, it was subsequently opened and many opportunities were presented. The United States, as the largest consumer and number one importer of oil, supported nation building with the region and realized that by opening up trade with the Caspian region it would reduce not only their dependence on the Persian Gulf but also the world's. The United States opposed the Russian monopoly over the oil and oil pipelines, but also had placed sanctions against Iran that eventually extended to the Caspian. The U.S. policy in the Caspian was aimed at encouraging Turkey to play a frontline role in developing an energy infrastructure.

The Caspian Sea as an important transportation route can bridge Europe and Central Asia. The five coastal states that each file varying legal claims are Russia, Iran, Azerbaijan, Kazakhstan, and Turkmenistan. Because this region is so unique, it raises many legal issues. These issues touch upon many international law concepts, including the law of treaties, law of the sea, environmental law, and state succession, to name a few. The difficulties surrounding these issues are not simply about politics but also involve economic issues, which only compound the overall complexity.

The Soviet–Iranian treaties that were signed in the early twentieth century, as well as other treaties signed by the Tsarist Russia in the eighteenth and nineteenth centuries, are often cited as the source of current legal status of the Caspian Sea. The first of such treaties was the Treaty of Resht in 1792, which provided for the freedom of commerce and navigation. This treaty was signed between Russia and the Persian empires. The second and third treaties were the Golestan Treaty in 1813 and the Turkomanchai treaty in 1828. The latter allowed for Russia to have the sole privilege of having a naval fleet in the Caspian Sea. The Soviet government eventually drew up a new arrangement with Persia that declared all past agreements between the two obsolete. The foundation for bilateral relations between Persia and the Russian Socialist Federal Soviet Republic (RSFSR) came from the Treaty of Friendship in 1921. Even this treaty, however, did not specifically address the legal regime of the

Caspian Sea. Natural resources in this area were also not specifically addressed but instead were only mentioned with their relation to fishery agreements.

An attempt to establish a legal framework began in the 1930s. In regards to navigational issues, there were two treaties that dealt with this issue. The first was the Treaty of Establishment, Commerce, and Navigation in 1935. This treaty was between Iran and the Union of Soviet Socialist Republics (USSR) and was later replaced by the Treaty of Commerce and Navigation in 1940. Both of the aforementioned treaties excluded any third parties from the Caspian Sea region and went on to restrict the rights of ship passage from other states. Both treaties did allow for both states to fish in all areas of the sea with the exception of a ten-mile zone along the coast.

However, coastal states have not yet been able to settle the boundary line issue in the Caspian Sea. The only treaty to make even a vague reference to this notion is the 1940 treaty, which included an Exchange of Notes that mentioned that the Caspian Sea is "regarded by both contracting parties as a Soviet and Iranian Sea." While this interpretation held for quite some time, it was later questioned by the three other Caspian states after the dissolution of the USSR. Although this treaty was questioned in several different arenas, it was upheld because the treaty with the former USSR was legally binding on the newly independent states.

Another difficult question that emerges is how to classify the Caspian Sea. This is important because the rules of international law depend on how the body of water is defined. Additionally, the manner in which the sea will be regulated also depends on the classification. For example, if the area is defined as a sea, the United Nations Convention on the Law of the Sea would be applicable. With this definition, each littoral state would have a territorial sea in addition to an economic zone and a continental shelf. In geographic terms the Caspian Sea cannot be classified as a sea. However, the alternative classification is as a lake, and if this were the case, customary international law concerning border lakes would be in effect. If classified as a lake, it would be considered a transboundary lake. An international lake is one that is completely surrounded by the territory of several states. The foremost argument for the classification to be that of a lake is the history on its delimitation. The problem that comes up next is that the body of water does not fit nicely into either classification. There are obviously numerous arguments and reasons for wanting the area to be classified one way or the other. Each classification has benefits and disadvantages for the individual regions, and this contributes largely to why the issue over classification has been so intense.

While the history of the Caspian Sea has included numerous negotiations over the legal status, those between Iran and Russia both argued in favor of the sea being governed by a condominium regime. However, the treaties in effect and the current international legal status do not support this stance. Moreover, international law is not in accordance with supporting a condominium regime. All in all, the body of water does not appear to fit into the definition of a sea nor that of a lake. Additionally, the information does not support the decision of a condominium regime. This obviously begs the question of what to do with this body of water.

The legal status of the Caspian Sea has yet to be resolved, and after more than sixteen years the bordering states still view this issue as contentious. A part of the problem is that energy resources have not been distributed evenly, allowing for some areas to receive smaller portions of the Sea. If all states agreed to the process of division by a median line, the problem of where to draw the line emerges. All actors want at least an equal share of the sea, if not more. Even with representatives from all five littoral states meeting regularly, a consensus has yet to be reached. Some of the most recent issues that have been debated were what seabed resources Iran, Turkmenistan, and Azerbaijan would claim and the specifications for how the line would be drawn. There are still many issues that have yet to be even discussed, let alone decided upon. A few of these topics include transboundary pollution issues, issues of regional military activity, and issues of ship transit procedures, to name just a few. In the meantime and in the absence of a legal regime an environmental degradation of the sea is imminent.

Generally speaking, at the outset, the United States paid very little attention to the former Soviet republics with the possible exception of Kazakhstan. The reason for not disregarding this particular area was due to the tremendous concentration of former Soviet Union nuclear weapons. The myths about the enormous quantity of oil within the Caspian region have grown exponentially over the years. The United States quickly identified this region as one of strategic significance. The U.S. Department of State even declared that the potential within this area could be estimated to be as high as 200 million barrels of oil. Various company representatives seized on the notion that exporting oil and gas to international markets was actually in existence. While there were many pipeline variations offered, the United States supported the alternative of many pipelines being in existence.

Bill Clinton's presidency placed an emphasis on aiming policies for the Caspian Basin to ensure the independence and prosperity of post-Soviet states. Because of the recent nature of the United States' relation with this region, most of the U.S. policies geared toward this area have been those created by President Bill Clinton. Russians perceived U.S. policies as if there were a political will to weaken the Russian influence throughout the region. One aspect that did not change was the U.S. policy of energy diplomacy. The goal was to make major reforms within the Caspian Basin, and therefore the United States and Russia, in addition to Kazakhstan, supported the Caspian Pipeline Consortium. While many American citizens would be unable to give any information about this region, it remains of great importance to the U.S. government because of its oil and gas. Although the state of affairs between the two regions are unlikely to change anytime in the near future, the interest of the United States is relatively modest when compared to the interest other countries have for the Caspian region. To the United States this region is poor, militarily insignificant, sparsely populated, and extremely distant. It appears that the initial interest in economic reform has waned in recent years.

The United States has an enormous stake in the region, although many have argued that they have also largely neglected the Caspian Basin because of the ongoing fascinations that exist elsewhere, particularly in Russia and in the Persian Gulf region. While the United States seeks stability and independence of the Caspian Sea states, they are also driven by significant need for oil and natural gas. Even with this notion in mind, the Caspian region has greater degrees of stability compared to other areas. The region expects the United States to have a genuine desire to encourage peaceful resolutions for conflicts and also promote regional security arrangements. Nevertheless, the region is suffering from an intrinsic sovereignty crisis, and therefore U.S. support for stability will indirectly be seen as support for the sovereignty for the area.

Suggested Reading

Bahgat, G. 2003. *American oil diplomacy in the Persian Gulf and the Caspian Sea*. Gainesville, Florida: University Press of Florida.

Barnes, J. 2002. *Energy in the caspian region*. New York: Palgrave.

Crandall, M. S. 2006. *Energy, economics, and politics in the Caspian region*. Westport, Connecticut: Praeger Security International.

Gokay, B., ed. 2001. *The Politics of Caspian oil*. Great Britain: Palgrave.

Janusz, B. 2005. The Caspian Sea: legal status and regime problems. *Russia and Eurasia Programme*. Berlin: Wissenschaft, Stiftun, & Politik.

JALIL ROSHANDEL

✦ CHINA–IRAN RELATIONS

Sino–Iranian relations have an enduring history dating back more than 20 centuries. The ebb and flow of these interactions are reflected in both countries' shared historical perceptions and national ambitions. Initial contact between Han China and the Parthian empire of Persia began in 139 BC when a Chinese envoy, Zhang Qian, traveled west along the Oxus River in search of allies. Although Zhang Qian did not reach Parthia, he obtained detailed information about Parthia which he conveyed back to the Han capital at Chang-gan. Diplomatic and commercial relations between the Han and Parthian empires began linking the two empires via the Silk Road. A second drive took place during the Tang Dynasty (618–907) when the Silk Road further connected the commerce and culture of East and West. During this period, Sassanian Persia sought the assistance of Tang emperor Gao-tsung in resisting the Arab conquest of Iran. Following the Mongol conquest of both countries, exchanges blossomed again in the thirteenth century as Persian and Chinese officers served in their respective Mongol dominion. Here, diplomatic missions enabled a deeper appreciation for their mutual history and culture.

Contemporary relations expanded during the Mao and Pahlavi governments. Mohammad Reza Shah had ambitions of extending Iran's regional power throughout the Persian Gulf. In order to achieve such preponderance, the Shah needed the support of the non-regional powers, including China. Through this opening of political support for the Pahlavi government, Sino–Iranian relations developed along mutual concerns for Soviet expansionism. Both countries sought to contain Soviet influence in Egypt, India, and Iraq. Their interests further converged as Beijing and Tehran worked to protect their common entente with Pakistan. Encouraged by Sino–American rapprochement, diplomatic relations were officially normalized between Tehran and Beijing in August, 1971. Iran officially recognized the People's Republic of China (PRC) as the "sole legal government of China," and China supported Iran "in its struggle to protect its natural resources." Iran also reaffirmed Beijing's claim to Taiwan.

The resumption of official relations between the Tehran and Beijing commenced a series of diplomatic exchanges. Queen Farah and Princesses Ashraf and Fatemeh were among the first to signal the importance of Sino–Iranian relations on their visits to China. Chinese diplomats also returned similar sentiments on visits to Tehran. Sino–Iranian relations remained steady despite the deaths of Zhou and Mao Zedong in 1976. The last exchange between Pahlavi Iran and the PRC was a visit by Foreign Minister Huang Hua in 1978. Hua's visit occurred in the wake of anti-Shah revolutionary activity. This would be the last official diplomatic visit before the Islamic revolution.

The new Islamic Republic of Iran formed by Ayatollah Khomeini in 1979 proclaimed a foreign policy of "neither East nor West." The theocratic government sought to distance itself from the dependent commercial and diplomatic policies of the monarchy. In theory, Tehran sought a policy of isolation and independence. Moreover, the Iranian perception of China was largely hostile due to Beijing's relations with the Pahlavi government. Iran was forced to assume more pragmatic relations, though, due to its revolutionary ideology, U.S. sanctions resulting from the hostage crisis, and regional isolation resulting from the outbreak of the Iran–Iraq War. Through repeated diplomatic exchanges and a realistic posture, Iran found itself on common ground with China. On its face, the ties that bind Iran and China are commercial in nature, but they quickly become intertwined as strategic considerations for both nations demonstrated the triumph of a growing strategic partnership.

Iran's initial contact with China was ideologically cautious but economically motivated. In desperate need to access economic markets, Beijing provided Tehran with weapons and commercial trade. These initial transactions during the first decade of the revolution facilitated further cooperation at the military, energy, and nuclear level. The death of Khomeini in 1989 led to a shift in Iran's foreign policy orientation. No longer bound to the Ayatollah's ideological predilections, Tehran sought a strategic shift towards overt Sino–Iranian cooperation. Indeed, in the aftermath of Beijing's 1989 Tiananmen Square massacre, both countries shared common interests in opposing western penetration into their societies. The 1991 Gulf War extended their collaboration as neither supported the prospect of U.S. military expansion in the region. Moreover, Beijing was a useful ally for Tehran, often supporting the Iranian regime at the United Nations Security Council (UNSC). Such support however was contingent on balancing its newfound Iranian relationship against its American one.

Interestingly, the first high-level diplomatic visit to China was led by then Majlis member (and future President and Supreme Leader) Seyed Mohammad Ali Hossein Khamenei in February 1981. Ali Akbar Velayati and Hashemi Rafsanjani also made trips to China in 1984 and 1985, when they discussed the common interests of Sino–Iranian relations and nuclear and economic cooperation. In 1989, Khamenei traveled to China as President, the first visit to the country by an Iranian head of state. China took advantage of this opening to distribute military hardware denied by the west.

By 1982, Beijing was accused by Washington of accounting for 40% of Iran's arms supplies. Five years later, Iran's military imports from China had doubled. For Tehran, Beijing provided an important role as Iran's seminal weapons supplier during the eight-year war. Repeated deals were made throughout the 1990s, such that China became Iran's leading supplier of weaponry after Russia. Purchases included Chinese Silkworm anti-ship missiles and C-802 anti-ship missiles, among others which could threaten the growing American presence in the Persian Gulf. Contributions were also made to Iran's ballistic missile program where Chinese experts assisted their Iranian counterparts in matching their own technology. The Zelzal and Shahab missiles, while also incorporating outside guidance, resemble indigenous Chinese models. Additionally, Beijing assisted Tehran in developing dual use chemical weapons capabilities.

Among Beijing's main concerns has been weighing its Iranian relationship against U.S. pressure. Under coercion from the Clinton Administration, Beijing promised to halt sales of cruise missiles as well as refrain from upgrading dated Iranian missile technology. Needless to say, U.S. attempts at restraining China's proliferation penchants have been challenging. Repeatedly and most recently, the U.S. Treasury Department has targeted a number of Chinese companies with sanctions for violating their national export laws with ongoing exports to Tehran.

Economic relations with Beijing also commenced during the decade of the 1980s. Iranian international isolation drew Tehran east in search of new trading partners. Bilateral trade agreements were signed in 1982, solidifying the Sino–Iranian commercial relationship. The end of the Iran–Iraq War led to increased economic cooperation as Beijing contributed to Tehran's post-war reconstruction efforts. Chinese loans were issued to help refurbish factories and refineries. Chinese ventures have assisted Iran in developing its mining and metallurgy resources. In joint cooperation, Chinese corporations constructed the Tehran metro system. Housing construction was another early area of cooperation, as was modernization of Iran's transportation system linking the Iranian and Central Asian railways. These agreements provided mutual benefits for both countries. Iran needed the internal reconstruction and development as well as the technical training of its labor market while the Chinese profited from monopolizing the Iranian enterprises including the energy market. By 2004, trade between China and Iran hit a record $7 billion, a 42% increase from bilateral trade in 2003 of $4 billion. Non-oil trade was at a record high of $1 billion for 2004 and double for 2005. By 2008, trade is expected to be a record $8 billion. Over 250 Chinese investments are percolating in Iran. This remarkable economic synergy is serving Iran in the wake of the international uproar over its nuclear program.

China's appetite for energy increased voraciously in the early 1990s, and it became a net importer of oil in 1993, hungrily searching for markets. Iran was one of those markets with the fourth largest reserves of oil and second largest of natural gas. Moreover, its strategic proximity and increasing economic and political impact on the cusp of the Caspian Sea and Persian Gulf only enhanced its viability. The delicate cultivation of Sino–Iranian relations conveniently benefited both countries' commercial needs. Iran was in need of technical assistance in developing its oil and gas resources while China sought to quench its thirst for energy supplies. Again, this investment relationship has brought Beijing into conflict with the United States, which seeks to restrict all possible speculation in the Islamic Republic. For the Chinese leadership, walking the tightrope between their growing domestic energy imperatives and their fragile relations with the George W. Bush administration is ever important. Iran underscores the convergence and divergence of Sino–American interests.

Recently highlighting this Sino–Iranian dynamic percolating in the form of commercial energy ties is a liquefied natural gas (LNG) contract worth $100 billion and signed with the Chinese company Sinopec, allowing them to develop the Yadavaran oil field in exchange for the purchase of 10 million tons of LNG a year for the next quarter of a century. Once Yadavaran becomes operational, Tehran has committed to sell its Chinese comrades 150,000 barrels per day (bdd) of crude oil at market prices. For both China and Iran, this deal is a commercial and political coup, providing each with their respective energy and security requisites. Throughout 2005, Iran was China's third largest supplier of oil. However, by January 2007 Tehran had trumped Riyadh as Beijing's number one energy provider. A second phase of the Iran–China strategic energy cooperation agreement will involve expanding Iran's oil and gas pipeline facilities, which have been obstructed through U.S. opposition. Attempting to facilitate greater access to Middle Eastern and Central Asian energy resources, Beijing has plans to construct a pipeline in Iran to take oil about 620 miles to the Caspian Sea and connect it with the planned pipeline from Kazakhstan to China.

Support for Iran's nuclear program was a key element of Sino–Iranian relations from 1985 to 1997. All western countries had withdrawn their assistance for Iran's nascent nuclear program in the aftermath of the Islamic Revolution. For Tehran, China's willingness to assume nuclear cooperation in spite of U.S. opposition signaled the durability of Sino–Iranian relations. Commencing with Hashemi Rafsanjani's visit to Beijing in 1985, negotiations were finalized such that China became Iran's most valuable nuclear partner. The agreement established the parameters for Chinese assistance to develop the Esfahan Nuclear Research Center, which was not declared to the International Atomic Energy Agency until 1992. Beijing supplied Tehran with four teaching and research reactors for ENRC and supplied the fissile material for all four reactor cores. These reactors were later approved and inspected under the International Atomic Energy Agency (IAEA) safeguards. While none of the reactors were considered a threat due to the insignificant levels of plutonium production, for Tehran the immediate gain came from the technical training of Iranian scientists who could apply these models to build superior reactors. Tehran continued to send engineers and technicians for advanced training in China. In 1991, China sold Iran 1.8 metric tons of uranium materials that were not reported to the IAEA until 2003. In September 1992, President Rafsanjani returned to China where he negotiated another contract for the design, construction, and operation of nuclear power plants, among other issues. Under the agreement China was to assist in the construction of four 300 megawatt nuclear power stations modeled after those existing in China. Throughout this period, Tehran also received assistance with atomic laser technology, nuclear fusion research technology, and a uranium conversion plant. The latter, which was disclosed to the IAEA, caused much consternation from the United States. Indeed, by 1997 through significant American pressure, China withdrew its support for Iran's nuclear program.

Despite Beijing's nuclear disengagement, Tehran's nuclear program continued to benefit through measures of diplomatic support. Most recently evidenced in the rounds of circular diplomacy, Beijing, along with Moscow, has obstructed efforts to sanction Iran against pressure from Washington. In August 2002, Iran's clandestine nuclear activities were revealed by the Iranian opposition group the Mujahedin-e-Khalq. The exposure of two undeclared enrichment facilities and a plutonium production facility opened the Iranian dossier first at the IAEA and then the United Nations Security Council. Ultimately, amidst their economic interests, China has sought to avoid any Security Council opening reminiscent of the Iraq War that would lead to a military encounter with Iran. Thus far, it has tactically toed the line against economic sanctions, following its Russian counterpart.

The emergence of Shanghai Cooperation Organization (SCO), an intergovernmental body founded by China, Russia, Kazakhstan, Kyrgystan, Tajikistan, and Uzbekistan in 2001, has provided regional countries with a forum for cooperation on security and economic issues. In 2005, Iran, Pakistan, and India also joined as observer nations, hoping to eventually convert their status to full member nations. Some have suggested that the SCO could eventually threaten the west as "an OPEC with bombs." The significance of the SCO is indeed a merger of security and energy interests that could pose a challenge to U.S. interests in the Caspian and South Asian region. Needless to say, despite the warming of Russo–Chinese relations and the invitation of Iranian President Ahmadinejad to the June 2006 SCO summit in Beijing, Iran's status has yet to be elevated, although it does actively seek membership. For Tehran, this convention provides a unique opportunity to interface with its regional and strategic allies.

China's Muslim communities provide yet another layer to the dynamic of Sino–Iranian relations. Residing primarily in Xingjiang province, the 8.4 million Uighurs and the 9.8 million Hui have been targeted by Beijing for their grievances against the central government and their separatist aims of establishing an Islamic Republic of East Turkestan. Often the Islamic Republic of Iran has clashed with the People's Republic of China over its repressive policies towards its Muslim population. With a direct policy of exporting the revolution, Xingjiang received Iranian funding to construct mosques and religious schools. Repeatedly, Chinese diplomats warned their counterparts to cease these coercive measures in Chinese territory. However, Tehran continued to go so far as to recruit Chinese Muslims to study in Iran's seminaries. Ironically, in this situation, Beijing has cooperated with Washington's war on terror, linking its own Muslim problem with the global conflict. This has enabled the Chinese government to crack down domestically against the ethnic minority. Beijing has also used its relations with Iran as a soothing mechanism. In 1992, Former President Rafsanjani visited Urumqi and Kashgar, even attending afternoon prayers in the Kashgar mosque. Former President Khatami toured Xingjiang province, suggesting the region could bridge the divide between the China and the Middle East. Beijing facilitated these visits to prevent further Iranian interference in Chinese Muslim affairs.

Iran and China share mutual historical appreciation, and through their historical foreign relations they have evolved to respect the ideological concerns of contemporary states. This relationship that grew out of commercial necessity for Tehran to one where Beijing assisted Tehran with economic, military, energy, and nuclear development bears strategic importance for both countries. Iran has profited from this relationship not only on the economic plane but also through the balanced diplomatic assistance offered by Beijing.

Suggested Reading
Garver, J. 2006. *Iran and China: ancient partners in a post imperial world.* Seattle: University of Washington Press.

SANAM VAKIL

✦ CINEMA

Western readers who are used to seeing images of Iran as a "theocratic" or "fundamentalist" society may find it surprising that Iranian cinema is recognized as one of the most innovative national cinemas in the world today.

Giants of world cinema, such as Jean-Luc Godard, Akira Kurosawa, and Werner Herzog, have lavishly praised Iranian filmmakers. Film festivals the world over have recognized Iranian cinema by rewarding Iranian films and filmmakers. When the Islamic revolution ushered in sweeping changes in 1979, no one would have predicted this fate for cinema under the Islamic Republic. During the revolution and its immediate aftermath, Iranian media were subject to "cleansing" (*pak-sazi*) of all symbols of monarchy and perceived "un-Islamic" and corrupting Western influence. As tangible objects that could be easily identified and located, movie theaters became a favorite target for the revolutionary fervor. A report by the Research Center of Iranian Parliament (*Markaz pajoheshhaye majlis shoraye Islami*) claims 31 movie theaters in Tehran and 89 movie theaters in other cities were destroyed (although other researchers claim a higher number). Moreover, scores of creative personnel from the film industry fled the country or were forced out of the industry. All the signs from this period pointed to a bleak future for cinema in Iran under the Islamic Republic.

However, fortunes of Iranian cinema began to change shortly after the arrival of Ayatollah Khomeini, the leader of the Iranian revolution and the founder of the Islamic Republic, from exile. Against those who might see modern media and their essence as a corrupting Western influence, Ayatollah Khomeini expressed a view that had a transformative effect. He stated, "We are not opposed to cinema, or radio, or to television." He characterized the cinema as "a modern invention that ought to be used for the sake of educating the people, but as you know, it was used instead to corrupt our youth." Moreover, he insisted, "it is the misuse of cinema that we are opposed to, a misuse caused by the treacherous policies of our rulers." Although a notable film culture existed before the revolution, Ayatollah Khomeini's words transformed a context of blind hostility and prejudice to a context in which institutional efforts would attempt producing an "Islamic" cinema.

Institutional support and state investment in cinema before the revolution was provided through state-controlled entities and bodies such as National Iranian Television and Radio, the Ministry of Culture and Art, The Institute for Intellectual Development of Children and Young Adults, Film Industry Development Company, and Telfilm. These efforts led to the creation of the New Wave movement in Iranian cinema that produced important films such as Dariush Mehrjui's *Gav* (*The Cow*, 1969), Masoud Kimiai's *Qaisar* (1969), Bahram Baizaie's *Ragbar* (*Downpour*, 1970), Mehrjui's *Postchi* (*The Postman*, 1970), and Amir Naderi's *Saz Dahani* (*Harmonica*, 1973). Other efforts outside of the realm of state activities included film schools, the New Film Group, Free Cinema, and collaborative projects between independent filmmakers and writers. Among films created by these efforts were Sohrab Shahid Saless' *Tabiate bejan* (*Still Life*, 1975) and Baizaie's *Gharibeh va meh* (*Stranger and the Fog*, 1975). The production of such artistically challenging films, however, was no match for misguided policies (e.g., import laws, taxes) and the adverse economic conditions (e.g., inflation, interest rates, expensive raw material) that the film industry faced until the 1979 revolution.

Following the "cleansing" of cinema in the immediate aftermath of the revolution, there was a period of uncertainty regarding the direction for the film industry based on an insufficient number of films deemed appropriate. This period saw a sharp rise in the number of imported films, including films that stirred revolutionary ardor (e.g., *Battle of Algiers*, *Z*, *State of Siege*). The uncertainty was partially settled as the industry entered a period of rationalization, which entailed legislations regulating exhibition by the Ministry of Culture and Islamic Guidance. Other entities that helped usher in an "Islamic cinema" include The Foundation for the Disinherited (*Bonyad Mostazafan*), the Ministry of Reconstruction Jehad, and the Islamic Propagation Organization. The establishment of Farabi Cinema Foundation in 1983 was a significant step. According to its website, it was charged to cover all aspects of film industry: produce films, give low-interest loans, lend equipment and provide post-production resources, produce publications on cinema, sponsor film festivals, engage in coproduction projects, and get involved in promoting and marketing Iranian films throughout the world.

These steps and favorable economic policies led to a marked increase in film production (from 23 in 1983 to 57 in 1986). As the industry entered the 1990s, a commercially viable cinema began to appear, as the stability of the industry encouraged banks to offer loans to producers during a period of "reconstruction" in the aftermath of Iran–Iraq War. Introducing Iranian films in international film festivals was well underway at this time. The landslide election of Mohammad Khatami as president in 1997, on a platform that advocated civil society, rule of law, democratic institutions, as well as greater freedom for the media, ushered in the "reform" era. Khatami's plans for privatization of the economy, building on initiatives undertaken during the reconstruction era under president Rafsanjani, entailed a smaller role for the state in various aspects of the film industry.

Current research and new reports provide a picture of mixed results. A 2007 report of a comprehensive study of the film industry by the Research Center for the Iranian Parliament documents "challenges and prospects" for Iranian cinema. The study covered developments and trends over a period of 15 years from 1991 to 2005 (in the Persian calendar from 1370 to 1384, which corresponds to the period of March 1991 to February 2006). Some of their findings are reported here. Although the number of theaters went up from 272 in 1991 to 274 in 2005, the population explosion renders that number a negative growth rate. Overall, the average annual growth rate for the number of movie theaters per 100,000 moviegoers, the number of seats per 1,000 moviegoers, and number of moviegoers were −1.4, −2.7, and −8.9, respectively. Movie attendance had a dismal negative growth rate. Whereas 66 million bodies attended movie theaters in 1991, only 18 million did so in 2005. It is helpful to note a few well known reasons for this drop, as the report points to a number of these. Worn out theaters, old and outdated facilities and equipment (to a point that families do not see theaters as an appropriate place to spend their leisure time), and lack of availability of theaters in many parts of the country and for all sectors of society are some the reasons for this drop in attendance. Other reasons include cinematic productions that are "far from audiences' tastes and needs," rapid expansion of information technologies and audiences' access to formidable films from around the world, competition from satellite television, DVD, and video, and a "lack of sophisticated filmmaking techniques." The number of distributed titles on video rose from 97 in 1993 (the first year for which data was available) to 1249 in 2005.

Other quantitative measures included the following. The number of feature films made in 1991 was 40. That number for 2002, 2003, 2004, and 2005 were 54, 77, 62, and 75, respectively. The number of films exhibited dropped from 388 in 1991 to 335 in 2005. The average price of tickets rose from 225 Rials in 1991 to 11,000 Rilas in 2005. While the average costs for making a feature film in 1991 was 275,000,000 Rials, it reached 1,820,000,000 Rials (about $200,000.00 using today's currency rates) in 2005.

Another important growth area was participation in international film festivals. Both the number of Iranian films and the number of times Iranian films entered international film festivals rose. The number of films entering international film festivals rose from 35 in 1991 to 95 in 2005. Similarly, the number of film festivals held in Iran rose from 9 to 22 in the same time period. A growth area that reflects a notable film culture and a strong interest in filmmaking is the number of private (vocational, non-degree granting) film schools and academies (reaching 158 in 2005). The number of non-governmental film production companies rose only modestly for the period from 20 to 25, reflecting the difficulties of privatization of the film industry in Iran. The formation of various non-governmental associations, which rose from 47 to 99 by 2005, is an interesting and encouraging development. However, the non-governmental industry guild, House of Cinema (*Khaneh Cinema*), is effectively a liaison between these newly formed associations and the Ministry of Culture and Islamic Guidance.

It is clear that the most pressing issues facing Iranian cinema are crumbling infrastructure and deficiencies in the distribution and exhibition of film. The state has spent considerable energy and resources on monitoring content and establishing censorship regimes at the expense of sound policymaking, especially in the area of privatization, infrastructures, equipment and facilities, and physical space for establishing modern and accessible exhibition outlets near residential areas, shopping centers, and business districts. The lack of vision in management and policymaking has effectively led to a "parallel market" in which unauthorized goods and services thrive. Despite these difficulties, and thanks to the sheer fecundity of its talents, Iranian cinema continues to be dynamic, engaging various genres and subject matters. The top five films at the box office in 2006–2007 (1385 in the Persian calendar) reflect this reality. These were *Cease Fire* (*Atash bas*), *M as in Mother* (*Meem mesl-e madar*), *Wedding Supper* (*sham-e aroosi*), *Under the Peach Tree* (*Zir-e derakht-e holoo*), and Trap (*Taleh*). *The Outcasts* (*Ekhrajiha*), a release in 2008 (1386), is believed to be the box office champion in the history of Iranian cinema thus far. This controversial film takes the subject of Iran–Iraq War as a source for "dark comedy." The war genre, also known as the "holy defense cinema," has been a staple of postrevolutionary cinematic productions. Its appropriation for generic makeover is a positive sign. *Cease Fire*, a story of love, marriage, and divorce, a film with a relatively critical outlook, was written and directed by Tahmineh Milani. Milani is one of the growing numbers of female directors in Iranian cinema. The strong presence of women behind and in front of the camera is a welcome development. That presence is a positive byproduct of attempts to produce an "Islamic cinema." As some feminists have pointed out, Islamization has entailed mobility for women by "cleansing" those public spaces that previously had been associated with "sin" or simply "inappropriate" for women. Observing *hijab* (and other Islamic codes) in the film industry and the participation by Islamist women legitimized cinema and public spaces such as movie theaters for traditionalists and many with religious orientation.

The institutionalization of cinema over the last two decades, a strong film culture already established, the international demand for Iranian films, and a seemingly endless supply of new talent will keep Iranian cinema viable for the time being. However, it is recognized that sound economic and management policies as much as new infrastructure are needed to maintain this important national cinema. The latter requires much-needed investment from the private sector. Major investment, however, will not be forthcoming in the absence of a wider context of economic and political stability.

Suggested Reading

Dabashi, H. 2001. *Close up: Iranian cinema, past, present and future*. London: Verso.

Iranian cinema: challenges and prospects. A report by Research Center of Iranian Parliament on the status of art in Iran 1991–2005. 2007. *Bonnie Film* 1010:25–27.

Issa, R., and S. Whitaker, eds. 1999. *Life and art: the new Iranian cinema*. London: National Film Theatre.

Issari, M. A. 1989. *Cinema in Iran, 1900–1979*. Lanham, Md: Scarecrow Press.

Naficy, H. 2001. Islamizing film culture in Iran: A post-Khatami update. In Tapper, R., ed. *The new Iranian cinema: politics, representation and identity*. London: I. B. Tuaris.

Naficy, H. 2008. Iranian émigré cinema as a component of Iranian national cinema. In Semati, M., ed. *Media, culture, and society in Iran: living with globalization and the Islamic state*. London: Routledge.

Sadr, H. R. 2006. *Iranian cinema: a political history*. London: I. B. Tuaris.

MEHDI SEMATI

✦ CIVIL SOCIETY

Since the 1990s, the debate surrounding civil society has brought the discussion of the common standards of moral decency to Iran's domestic forefront. More specifically, since the election of President Mohammad Khatami in May 1997, Iran took a momentous step toward the creation of a vibrant civil society. The Khatami administration (1997–2005) changed the terms of debate over governance and democracy. In keeping with the rule of law, the civil society discourse has fostered the idea of reconciling cultural and religious customs with the emerging standards of international legitimacy. There has emerged sharp disagreement among the ruling elite as to how to respond to the civil society's growing demands on the political regime, with the conservatives favoring the all-too familiar mode of social control and reformists calling for an open society.

REFORM IN THE POST-KHOMEINI ERA

Khomeini's death and the rise of President Aliakbar Hashemi Rafsanjani (1989–1997) left Iran a "theocracy without a chief theocrat," in which the populist fervor of the early years of the Islamic revolution—with its street demonstrations and popular display of support—was gone. In the aftermath of Khomeini's death, factional dispute and competition increased. A national referendum abolished the post of prime minister and replaced it with a popularly elected president as head of the government who did not need to be approved by the Majlis (parliament). This also meant that the *velayat-e-faqih* (rule by jurist-consult or the supreme leader) would no longer dominate the political sphere. The president, therefore, emerged as the most powerful figure in the state. This transformation, experts noted, marked the "the transition from the consolidation phase to the reconstruction phase of the Islamic Revolution."

Although the Majlis was important in promoting popular sovereignty in the post-Khomeini era, it failed to provide genuinely broad political participation. Parliamentary elections were manipulated by oversight committees that controlled access to the Majlis. Interfactional disputes continued to present problems for the executive branch. The radicals, led by Ali Akbar Mohtashemi, advocated the nationalization of foreign trade, major industries, and services and sought land reform and progressive taxation. They turned the Majlis into a populist forum and questioned the qualifications of Ali Khamenei as the *velayat-e-faqih* and then of President Rafsanjani's reform initiatives. The radicals, however, lost their majority in the Majlis in the April and May 1992 elections.

The victory of the pragmatists demonstrated that Iran's devastated economy and practical needs had replaced vague political and ideological slogans. Rafsanjani's liberalization program (1989–1997) encountered many setbacks, including low levels of private investment, low growth rates, budget bottlenecks, and mounting foreign debt. Corruption and mismanagement of resources also complicated the state's liberalization programs.

KHATAMI'S ERA: TOWARD BUILDING A CIVIL SOCIETY

Khatami's landslide victory in 1997—he received almost 70% of the popular vote—was a firm rebuke to hardline clerics who had dominated Iranian politics since the 1978–1979 revolution that toppled the pro-U.S. shah. Khatami's supporters—mainly youth, women, intellectuals, and ethnic minorities—demanded greater social and political freedom and more political pluralism.

Khatami brought greater freedom and tolerance not just to the political regime but to the society as well. As a direct result of his policies, freedom of the press was reasonably upheld and people spoke more openly about public policies and their shortcomings. Khatami bolstered women's freedom in some areas and appointed several female deputy vice presidents for technical affairs and sports. Female students started to compete equally with male students for university seats in all engineering fields previously reserved solely for males.

Khatami greatly contributed to the growth of civil society in Iran by opening up the political climate, by espousing the formation of different political parties by civil groups, and by supporting the rule of law. He laid the groundwork for introducing transparency into the political texture of society via the institutionalization of law and multiparty system. Support for the rule of law was widely regarded as the key to the formation and the expansion of civil society. Some experts observed that the establishment of parties from below or by civil groups was a direct threat to clerical control and was difficult to reconcile with theocracy, which is based on the theory of divine legitimacy of the regime.

Khatami abolished the president's slush fund, spoke favorably of all aspects of a civil society, and mentioned both the negative and positive achievements of Western civilization. He frequently referred to the "dialogue among civilizations and cultures" as the most effective way to achieve global détente. Under his regime, Iran accepted the Chemical Weapons Convention, and many restrictions were placed on religious vigilantes and militia who spied on people's private lives to enforce Islamic social codes—that is, codes of dress and behavior.

THE OPPONENTS OF CIVIL SOCIETY

The expansion of modern Islamic civil society, including the growth of professional associations and trade organizations, has been a sign of new setbacks for Iran's hardline clergy, whose failure to restrict that growth and whose theocratic vision and narrow definition of loyalty to the Islamic Republic have alienated large segments of Iranian society.

The Assembly of Experts, dominated by conservative clerics and responsible for the selection of the Supreme Leader, reasserted its conservative composition again in elections of October 23, 1998, in which the conservatives gained 54 out of the 86 seats and Khatami's supporters won only 13 seats; 16 seats went to independents.

Threatened by reform and the expansion of civil society, the radical vigilantes changed tactics, expanding their strategy of *defamation* in dealing with internal reformists who operate within Islamic legal bounds, to include *disappearance* and *murder*—a violent approach reminiscent of killings of Iranian dissidents abroad. The defamation tactics included calculated attacks on major political and religious figures. These included casting by parliament of a vote of no confidence against the former Minister of Interior Abdollah Nouri, who criticized the judiciary's "arbitrary" actions; putting on trial and in jail the former Tehran mayor, Gholam-Hussein Karabaschi, whose newspaper, *Hamshahri*, had boosted Khatami's presidential campaign, on charges of mismanagement and malfeasance; and placing under house confinement Grand Ayatollah Hussein-Ali Montazari, who appealed for "greater political pluralism and more respect for human rights." Ayatollah Montazari criticized the Supreme Leader, Ayatollah Ali Khameni, for his unbridled intervention in the country's political affairs, demanding further authority to the elected president from the delegation.

The defamation attacks continued by vigilante groups, known as *Ansar-e Hezbollah* (the Partisans of the Party of God), who would "serve as enforcers for conservative clerics." Such assaults took the form of verbal and physical attacks on certain media and their closure, frequent and violent disruptions and the cancellation of public lectures by the philosopher Abdol-Karim Soroush, vandalizing the offices of the opposing media and organizations and beating up their leaders.

The serial killings in the country, which led to the slayings in late 1998 of five prominent secular critics of the Islamic government's conservative faction, renewed the fears of a long-anticipated ideological turmoil and political schisms with the possibility of inciting further violence throughout the country. The killing of Dariush Foruhar, former labor minister in the Bazargan government, and his wife, Parvaneh Eskandari, who belonged to National Iranian People's Party—an outlawed but tolerated opposition party—and who lived under house arrest, sent shock tremors up the reformists' spines.

In the following weeks, the kidnapping and slayings of Jafar Pouyandeh and Mohammad Mokhtari, writers who were determined to form a secular writers' association, and Majid Sharif, an outspoken social critic of the conservative clerical establishment, fueled fears of a broader violence. Reza Alijani, the editor of *Iran-e Farda* (Tomorrow's Iran), a monthly political and economic review, was threatened with death should he give interviews to the foreign press.

CITY COUNCIL ELECTIONS

In the municipal elections on February 26, 1999, in which almost 60% of the qualified voters participated, voters picked 111,000 council members in 720 cities, 240 towns, and almost 34,000 villages in the first municipal elections. These elections became a new battleground between reformers and conservatives. For the most part, Iranians voted for reform, as reform candidates made a clean sweep in the Tehran City Council elections and appeared to have won significantly in the 28 provincial capitals. Abdollah Nuri, known for his reformist policies, and also former interior minister who was dismissed in fall 1998 by the Majlis, received nearly 42% of the 1,408,275 votes cast in Tehran. Saeed Hajarian, another reformer, came in a distant second with 27% of the votes. Third place went to Jamileh Kadiver, a journalist with reformist credentials. All three candidates were among those whom the Conservatives failed to bar from the ballot prior to the elections. The 4,000 female candidates were another success story as they won all the seats in four cities.

These elections—the first in the history of Iran—were critical because the newly elected councils forced the establishment to transfer some power to the people. The elected city and village council people in turn elected

720 local mayors. Each council operated like a local parliament, with functions ranging from observing to impeaching local authorities. The councils' other responsibilities included running socioeconomic and development projects, as well as participating in political and cultural affairs in ways that are compatible with the local communities' needs and demands. The reformists viewed these elections as perhaps the most important move toward implementing Khatami's key pledge, namely, the imperative of establishing the institutions of civil society en route to democratization.

Sixteen reformist political groups formed a political alliance that brought under one umbrella a formidable force to endorse a single slate of candidates in the city council elections. This new electoral alliance, which supported President Khatami's reform efforts, embraced several key organizations, including the Militant Clerics Society (*Majma-e Ruhaniyun-e Mobarez*), the clerical group that has endorsed government subsidies on basic goods, the Servants of Construction (*Khedmatgozaran-e Sazandegi*), a pro–free economy party, the Islamic Iran's Partnership Party (IIPP), the Mujahedin of the Islamic Revolution (MOIR) headed by Behzad Nabavi, who negotiated the release of the American hostages in 1981, the Majlis Hezbollah Assembly, which consists of Rafsanjaniite deputies in the parliament, the Society of the Forces Following the Imam's Line, whose leaders were responsible for the 1979 takeover of the U.S. embassy, and the Office for Fostering Unity, which was the nation's largest pro-Khatami student organization.

The other organizations in the electoral alliance represented professional groups, such as engineers, teachers, doctors, and laborers, as well as the Islamic Iran Solidarity Party and the Society of Majlis Deputies from Various Terms. Of the 15 new Tehran councilors, 13 were reformist and two were conservative. The dramatic changes in the post-Cold War world presented opportunities to build bridges between the Iranian people and global civil society and international human rights movements. Younger Iranians openly questioned the state's practices and policies. Many individuals and groups routinely castigated the government publicly for its restrictions on basic civil and political liberties.

A low turnout in Iran's sham parliamentary elections of 2004 returned the country to the religious dictatorship reminiscent of the early years of the Islamic Republic. A widespread national apathy and an active resistance by reformist groups, who boycotted these parliamentary elections, along with the wave of resignations by Iranian political officials, placed Iran's parliament in the hands of conservatives. Parliament became a rubber stamp for Iran's highest religious authority: Ayatollah Sayed Ali Khameni. Many saw these developments as a blow to Iran's reform movement.

In July 2005, Mahmoud Ahmadinejad, Tehran's mayor, became the nation's new president. During his tenure as mayor, Ahmadinejad reversed many of the changes transpired by previous moderate and reformist mayors, putting serious religious emphasis on the activities of the cultural centers founded by previous mayors. Ahmadinejad was also known for his separation of elevators for men and women in the municipality offices. Hardliners under President Ahmadinejad insisted on enforcing Iran's strict Islamic dress code, which obliged Iranian women to wear proper *hijab*. There have been some reports of imposing a single university dress code on women, while not allowing perfumes and cosmetics to be used on university campuses. Ahmadinejad and his Minister of Justice have vowed that "improperly veiled women" will be treated as in un-Islamic dress.

Ahmadinejad, however, appointed a woman as Vice President. Fatemeh Javadi was appointed as Vice President and Head of the Environment Protection Organization. Javadi's appointment indicated that President Ahmadinejad was following the footsteps of his predecessor. Javadi who held a doctorate in geology, was expected to be the only female in the Iranian cabinet and would replace Massoumeh Ebtekar, who was the only female in the cabinet of President Khatami.

Ahmadinejad banned Western music from Iran's radio and television stations. As the head of Iran's Supreme Cultural Revolutionary Council, Ahmadinejad promised to confront the Western cultural invasion and to promote Islamic values. Ahmadinejad's ban on media has also included censorship of the content of films. A ban on foreign movies could be a harbinger of many cultural restrictions to come. The banning of Western music was the beginning of yet another wave of cultural war at a time when Western music and films were widely available on DVDs on the black market.

There are more than 3 million homes that have satellite televisions. Many Iranians listen to Voice of America and watch CNN and BBC world news. There are between 3 and 5 million internet users in Iran. An underground culture continues to dominate Iran's social and cultural life in the face of government-imposed restrictions. Modernization and technology have radically altered the cultural life of many Iranians. Closing the borders in the name of reverting to the cultural revolution of the early years of the revolution is bound to be untenable.

Iran faces many structural obstacles en route to building a civil society. For these setbacks to be removed there needs to be a balance between civil society and state organizations. Such a balance requires the existence of an independent judiciary, separation of powers, and a free press. The absence of these conditions in Iran is further confounded by the fact that ideological loyalties and commitments continue to determine the shape of political groups and the degree to which they can function within a safe environment.

The gap between Iranian politics and society is still noticeable. Although Iranian society has been exposed to modern ideas and constructions, Iranian politics has straddled autocratic and democratic tendencies. The result has been an intensified power struggle between two factions of the clerical regime with masses of ordinary people, secularists, and Islamic revisionists caught in the middle. A highly evolving and complex process, Iranian politics continues to grapple with the reality of civil society and the rule of law—elements without which no democratic system can function. Iranian society, on the other hand, is thoroughly impregnated with modern ideas such as civil society and internationally recognized human rights.

Islamic moderates can play an important part in shaping the future. Change is going to be slow, gradual, and orderly. The fact remains that civil society needs not be of necessity anti-statist. Civil society is most likely to expand its political significance in the wake of a gradual change by the political regime. It is now a matter of time before democratic forces, both Islamic and secular, prevail over reactionary forces. Until then, the expansion of civil society is one of the means by which to safeguard and promote the individual's dignity, liberty, and autonomy *vis-à-vis* the absolutist tendencies of a theocracy.

Suggested Reading

Bill, J. A. 1993. The challenge of institutionalization: revolutionary Iran. *Iranian Studies* 26:403–406.

Fairbanks, S. C. 1998. Theocracy versus democracy: Iran considers political parties. *Middle East Journal.* 53:17–31.

Kazemi, F. 1995. Models of Iranian politics, the road to the Islamic Revolution, and the challenge of civil society. *World Politic.* 47:575–605.

Limbert, J. W. 1995. Islamic republic of Iran, in David E. Long and Bernard Reich, eds. *The governments and politics of the Middle East and North Africa*, 3rd ed. Boulder, Colo.: Westview Press;41–61.

Mahmood Monshipouri, Mahmood. 1995. *Democratization, liberalization, and human rights in the third world*. Boulder, Colo.: Lynne Rienner Publishers.

Milani, M. M. 1993. Power shifts in revolutionary Iran. *Iranian Studies.* 26:359–374.

Norton, A. R. 1993. Future of civil society in the Middle East. *The Middle East Journal.* 47:205–216.

Wright, R. 1996. Dateline Tehran: a revolution implodes. *Foreign Policy.* 103:161–174.

MAHMOOD MONSHIPOURI

✦ CLASS SYSTEM AND SOCIAL STRATIFICATION

Discussing how the 1979 revolution and the post-revolutionary conditions affected Iran's class configuration requires a theoretical–empirical framework for reclassifying the population data into social classes, as well as a study of changes in the class structure in the socioeconomic context of the period.

Social stratification is about the distribution of power. Differentiated advantages (disadvantages) that people may enjoy are aspects of their socioeconomic power. Economic resources that people possess are an important source of power. If class structures are linked to socioeconomic inequalities in terms of what people possess and the power relations that exist among various social groups, then we must explain the economic bases for these asymmetrical relations.

On an abstract level, class structure of a market economic system is based on an asymmetrical relationship between employers and employees. This is true, despite the peculiarities of each economy in their differentiated level of development, and the variation in the role of the state in the reproduction of economic and political activities. In modern market economic systems, this asymmetrical relationship has given rise to three dimensions for the identification of relational class structure. The identification of the location of individuals in relation to each other in the process of economic activities are based on the three interrelated axes of (1) ownership of economic property (physical and financial capital), (2) possession of scarce skills/credentials, and (3) organizational assets/authority.

The position of members on these three axes defines their class structure. The state—as employer of part of the workforce and the regulator and controller of the reproduction of the existing order—mediates this asymmetrical relation of classes. In this sense, class structure can be identified as relations of ownership because those who own scarce economic resources enter into an asymmetric relationship with those who do not. This relationship gives rise to class locations in economic structures and determines the class interest of their occupants.

Within the above theoretical context, Iran's class structure could be approximated by interlacing three matrices of occupational status—economic activities, occupational status-major occupational groups, and major occupational groups—economic activities in three decennial censuses of population and housing in 1976, 1986, and 1996. The result reflects the impact of the revolution and the post-revolutionary economic crisis on the class structure of Iran.

The transient post-revolutionary period in Iran has two distinct periods with distinctly different characteristics. First is the retrenching of capital in response to the overwhelming expression of antagonism toward the existing economic order, in the course of the revolutionary upheaval and the post-revolutionary turmoil. This resulted in the shriveling of capitalist relations of production, and an elaboration of the maze of entangled market networks conducive to the growth of petty-commodity production. We call this degenerative process "structural involution," which is characterized by widespread disruptions in production and capital accumulation (investment), resulting in deproletarianization of the urban economy, peasantization of agriculture, and a significant increase in small-scale service activities. The reversal of this trend, in a move toward economic restructuring and liberalization, may be noted as a "de-involutionary process." This reversal trend is characterized by revitalization of capitalist relations of production, reconstitution of market institutions, proletarianization of the workforce, and depeasantization of the rural economy.

These important changes created new politico-socio-economic opportunities for some and limited the opportunities for others. Some activities expanded, others contracted; certain occupations thrived, whereas others deteriorated; some social groups gained proximity to the centers of power and decision-making, while others became more distant and less privileged. These changes affect the distribution of employment, as well as the pattern of employment status and occupational positions. In "normal" circumstances, these changes are generally effected in a long-run trend in response to technological, demographic, or socioeconomic changes. In the transitional process in the post-revolutionary conditions, changes in the occupational pattern of the workforce are abrupt and unstable.

Table 1 depicts the class composition of the employed workforce in Iran in these three years. The demarcation of the two phases of post-revolutionary period in "involutionary" and "de-involutionary" phases below (i.e., 1979–1989 and 1990–present) closely corresponds to the timing of three decennial censuses, 1976, 1986, and 1996 (the results of the 2006 census will be published in 2008). It is evident that the empirical verification of the class nature of the Iranian workforce in 1976–1996 is a preliminary, though essential, step toward an analysis of social classes and the dynamics of its change in the Iranian society. Such an analysis requires both objective and subjective interaction of classes in concrete circumstances.

1. Capitalists are the owners of physical and financial means of economic activities, and employ workers. We divide the capitalists into modern and traditional occupational categories. By modern subcategories of occupations we mean capitalists whose occupational locations are

managerial-administrative or professional-technical. These are the occupational locations of capitalists in the modern firms of the more advanced
industrial economies. Traditional capitalists are those whose occupational
position is in clerical, sales and services, agricultural, or production.

2. Petty bourgeoisie are self-employed persons who do not hire any paid
   worker but may rely on the work of unpaid family labor. They consist
   of modern and traditional categories, similar to capitalists. Inasmuch as
   they (and small capitalists) rely on unpaid family workers, frequently
   young male and female adults, and because family labor is not considered a distinct class location, unpaid family workers are effectively a
   part of the self-employed petty bourgeoisie.

3. The middle class are employees of the state or the private sector, in
   administrative-managerial and professional-technical positions. They
   exercise some authority and enjoy relative autonomy. In this category
   are those employed in economic activities and social services of the
   state. Those employed in the political apparatus of the state as high-
   level professional-manager-administrators, and the rank and file of the
   political functionaries, including the military and paramilitary forces,
   are part of an ambiguous class location that we call "political
   functionaries," and we group them in a distinct category separate
   from the middle and working classes.

4. The working class are those who do not own the means of economic activity and do not benefit from the authority, and autonomy of those in
   the "middle class." They are employees of the state or the private sector.
   Those who work at the lower ranks of the political apparatus of the state,
   but have little autonomy or expertise, constitute the rank and file of
   "political functionaries." They are not included in the working class.

In 1976, nearly one-third of the Iranian employed workforce were self-
employed petty bourgeois, 99% of whom were in a traditional occupational
positions (such as farmers, textile/rug makers, carpenters, grocers, and truck
or taxi driver-owners). Among the capitalists, the large majority owned small
enterprises, with two or three workers, and were in traditional occupational
positions. About 40% of the Iranian employed workforce was in the working
class, about half of whom worked in enterprises larger than 50 workers. The
middle class was tiny (5%), and less than one-third of them worked for the
private sector (Table 1).

The 1979 revolution was a social rupture, egalitarian in character, and
openly antagonist toward large capital and capitalists, especially those affiliated
with foreign enterprises. Soon after the revolutionary surge, the government

Table 1   Class Composition: 1976, 1986, and 1996

	1976		1986		1996	
	1,000	%*	1,000	%*	1,000	%*
Capitalists	**182**	**2.1**	**341**	**3.1**	**528**	**3.6**
Modern	23	12.8	22	6.5	75	14.1
Traditional	159	87.2	319	93.5	453	85.9
Agriculture	36	19.5	113	33.1	124	23.5
Production	66	36.5	138	40.5	223	42.2
Middle class	**477**	**5.4**	**774**	**7.0**	**1,493**	**10.2**
Private sector employees	102	21.3	64	8.3	219	14.6
State employees: economic and social	376	78.7	710	91.7	1,274	85.4
Petty bourgeoisie	**2,810**	**31.9**	**4,390**	**39.9**	**5,199**	**35.7**
Modern	34	1.2	48	1.1	164	3.2
Traditional	2,776	98.8	4,343	98.9	5,035	96.8
Agriculture	1,704	60.7	2,333	53.1	2,199	42.3
Production	592	21.1	1,310	29.8	1,803	34.7
Unpaid family workers	**1,021**	**11.6**	**484**	**4.4**	**797**	**5.5**
Working class	**3,536**	**40.2**	**2,702**	**24.6**	**4,533**	**31.1**
Private sector employees	2,970	84.0	1,810	67.0	3,109	68.6
Agriculture	614	17.4	294	10.9	416	9.2
Production	1,919	54.3	1,271	47.0	2,151	47.4
State employees: economic and social	566	16.0	892	33.0	1,424	31.4
Political functionaries	**731**	**8.3**	**1,851**	**16.8**	**1,560**	**10.7**
Administrative and managerial	9	1.2	11	0.6	39	2.5
Professional and technical	51	6.9	192	10.4	205	13.2
Rank and file	672	91.9	1,647	89.0	1,315	84.3
Military and paramilitary forces**	386	52.7	1,197	64.7	881	56.5
Unspecified	**41**	**0.5**	**458**	**4.2**	**463**	**3.2**
Total	8,799	100.0	11,002	100.0	14,572	100.0

* Percentages of major categories add up to 100 for total employed labor force. Subcategories add up to 100 within each category.
** Already included in the subcategories of "political functionaries."
SOURCE: Nomani and Behdad 2006.

nationalized large manufacturing and financial enterprises. Revolutionary Islamic Courts confiscated property of those who were found "Corrupt on Earth." Land-hungry peasants took over rural land. The urban poor occupied vacant apartments, and workers' councils captured the control of many enterprises. The revolution disrupted the "normal" functioning of the society. Most significantly, it jeopardized the sanctity of property rights and safety of capital, weakening capitalist relations of production, and entangling the elaborate maze of the market networks, extending the ownership of the Islamic state and Islamic foundations in economic activities.

The absence of a clear revolutionary program with a definition of the economic order that was expected to replace what existed and was disrupted prolonged the crisis. The war with Iraq, the international economic sanctions, and the oil price collapse in 1985 and 1986 only accentuated the economic crisis. These important changes created new politico-socioeconomic opportunities for some and limited the opportunities for others—some activities expanded, while others contracted. Some social groups gained proximity to the centers of power and decision-making, others became more distant and less privileged.

These changes affected the distribution of employment and the pattern of employment status and occupational positions, and resulted in the growth of petty-commodity production and small-scale capitalist activities. This deviation from "normal" evolution is called "structural involution." The Islamic state amplified the involutionary trend with its populist policies, at times even inciting anti-capitalist tendencies and encouraging small-scale activities. The resulting changes in the economic structure affected the class composition of the Iranian workforce. It is expected that the outcome of these changes are deproletarianization of the urban economy, peasantization of agriculture, and a significant increase in small-scale service activities.

By 1986, the number of the self-employed (petty bourgeoisie) had grown by more than double the rate of growth of the workforce (nearly all in traditional positions), and the working class (employed by the state and private sector) had shrunk by a quarter. The number of small capitalists almost doubled since the last census. The average number of wage earners per capitalist employer (concentration ratio) fell from 16 in 1976 to 5.3 in 1986. The first post-revolutionary decade was a setback for the bourgeoisie and capitalist relations of production. In the same period, the middle class employees in the private sector decreased to half of what it was in 1976. Obviously, the smaller, more traditional enterprises needed fewer managers and professional workers. At the same time, the middle-class employees of the state increased by almost 90%. Between 1976 and 1986 more than one million workers were added to the rank of government functionaries, 800,000 of whom were added to the armed forces. Women's employment decreased not only relatively, but also absolutely.

The Islamic state faced a dire economic situation with the disrupted economy, its presence in a costly war, and the enforcement of suffocating sanctions amidst a rapidly growing population. By the late 1980s, the state realized that its claim for establishing the rule of the "disinherited" and its plan for the recognition of an Islamic economy came to a dead end. With the death of Ayatollah Khomeini in 1989, the time for change arrived. By 1992, the liberalization policy of the government of Hashemi-Rafsanjani was underway for reconstructing and rejuvenating the market and its institutions.

Yet it did not take long before the liberalization policy of Hashemi-Rafsanjani came under popular criticism because of high inflation, high unemployment, bankruptcy of many small capitalists and petty bourgeois producers, and the decline of real income of many wage earners. For the first time, during the Rafsanjani presidency, the Islamic Republic found it necessary to include open political unrest as a constraint in its public policy formulation. Thus, Hashemi-Rafsanjani pursued a zig-zag policy of economic liberalization. Despite the limited advances of economic liberalization in the 1990s, continuing into the Khatami presidency, the involutionary trend of the Khomeini decade was reversed substantially. The foreign exchange rate was realigned, price controls were mostly lifted, some subsidies were reduced, and others were eliminated. The increase in oil prices in these years, allowing for continued inflow of imports, made the timid liberalization policy somewhat acceptable.

However, if a post-revolutionary crisis lingers because of the continuation of negotiations and struggles among the ruling political factions and contending social forces vying to promote their interests and the establishment of a new economic order, this phase of the post-revolutionary period can be noted as a "de-involutionary process." Thus, in spite of change in the major aspects of the orientation of state's socioeconomic policies, the characteristic of de-involutionary process is not the end of the post-revolutionary crisis.

Although the process of deinvolution was not complete by 1996, its manifestation on the class nature of the workforce is amply present in that year's census, the move toward revitalization of capitalist relations of production and reconstitution of market institutions has given rise to proletarianization of the workforce, and in turn, depeasantization of the rural economy can be expected in this phase. Thus, by 1996 the impact of this rejuvenation in the capitalist relations of production on the class nature of the employed workforce can be seen. The working and middle classes (employed by the private sector and the state) grew; the concentration ratio (wage earners per capitalist employer) increased (albeit marginally), and the number and share of capitalists, mostly owner-managers of small-scale enterprises, and self-employed petty bourgeoisie in modern occupations increased; and women gained increased access to employment opportunities.

Meanwhile, the traditional petty bourgeoisie, in urban and rural areas, suffered a relative setback. A large segment of the population found itself vulnerable to a decline in real income in the face of intermittent spells of high inflation. In the June 2005 presidential elections, Ahmadinejad attracted part of the traditional petty bourgeoisie and the less privileged and poor urban and rural population to vote for his populist social justice, anti-corruption, and the redistribution of oil income promises. The vote for Ahmadinejad, for a large segment of his supporters, was, above all, a vote against Hashemi-Rafsanjani and his economic liberalization policy. This implies a continued resistance toward full rejuvenation and reconstruction of capitalist relations of production in Iran, by a considerably large class of traditional petty bourgeoisie, in alliance with the unemployed youth, the poor, and the disenfranchised. As of 2007, except for out-of-budget handouts to selected provinces, partisan redistribution of money to mosques and factional followers, massive replacement of former administrators and managers of state apparatus and economic establishments by the people close to the new government, suppressive measures against the press, unions, and students, the balance of socioeconomic balance of power was left unchanged. Different factions of the ruling elites are still bitterly negotiating amongst themselves. Thus, the Islamic Republic has not succeeded in overcoming its post-revolutionary crisis.

Suggested Reading

Nomani, F., and S. Behdad. 2006. *Class and labor in Iran: did the revolution matter?* Syracuse, NY: Syracuse University Press.

Wright, E. O. 1997. *Class counts: comparative studies in class analysis.* Cambridge: Cambridge University Press.

FARHAD NOMANI AND SOHRAB BEHDAD

✦ CONSTITUTION

The constitution and a constitutional form of government came to Iran at the peak of its modernization process at the turn of the century in 1906 and as the result of the Constitutional Revolution (1905–1911). The latter was a popular revolution that included all social classes, proposed a constitution, and, in agreement with the age-old Iranian political tradition, established the Shah as its guardian on December 30, 1906. Following his signature on the constitution, a telegram was sent to all Iranian embassies declaring that henceforth, Iran "has joined the constitutional countries." This was a prophetic statement in that, ever since, the word "constitution" has become part of the vocabulary of the political discourse in Iran, so much so that the Pahlavi autocrats and even the radical revolutionaries who demanded the establishment of Islamic government felt they could not do without it.

The original document borrowed heavily from the Belgian constitution of 1831 and provided for the establishment of a parliament composed of all social classes, including especially the aristocracy, the religious class, the merchants, and the new class, for now called the subjects (ro'aya). It was a short document that was approved by the national assembly and set into motion the Iranian constitutional monarchy that began operation in October 1906. It was decided that there should be amendments to the constitution, known as "the Supplement to the Constitution," that reflect the specific Iranian polity and culture. For example, Article 35 of the amendments declared monarchy as "a trust that with the gift of God is given to the person of the king by the people." This is both preserving an old tradition and creating a new revolutionary position in that people can take kingship away from the person at any time, thus there is no longer any sacred right of the king. Furthermore, there was an explicit discussion during the proceedings that the "parliament is the creator of the law," secularizing the legal system. In short, the new constitution was to establish the universal application of the rule of law. It is true that in its final formulation, Article Two of the Supplement established a council of grand religious jurists in order to oversee and ensure that no law violated Islamic principles. It should be noted that this was very different from the claims post-1979 that religious provisions should positively dictate all laws. The 1906 constitution would have been sufficient, had it not been used as an instrument for "the rule by law," instead of "the rule of law," by the subsequent ruling Pahlavi dynasty. Indeed, the revision of the constitution in 1959 gave absolute power to the king to dissolve the parliament anytime he desired it, and in fact turned the parliament into a rubber stamp institution for the king. This may, in fact, be one of the causes of the 1979 revolution that asked for freedom, independence, and equality of all citizens.

The debate over a new constitution began before the monarchy fell and during Ayatollah Khomeini's stay in Paris (October 1978 to February 1979). It was during this time when a group of concerned Iranians formulated a republican constitution and presented it to Khomeini. Khomeini is said to have liked the draft constitution, and the only change he added, in the form of a note on the document's margin, related to the office of the president. He added the phrase "az rejal bashad" (should be a male) to the document.

This initial draft did not become the new republic's basic law. The real debate on the constitution took place in Iran after the establishment of Islamic rule. This debate, by the Assembly for the Final Debates on the Constitution, led to the drafting of a completely different document, this time reflecting the Islamic sensibilities of the victors of the revolution. Although it claims that the future government is an Islamic Republic, in reality, the political system created is a bicephalous (two headed) government machinery, with the Leader in charge of the Islamic dimension and the President in charge of the republican dimension, with the republican dimension having less content and weight. The head of the government is an elected president, who in turn nominates a prime minister and a council of ministers, who will have to secure final approval from the elected members of the assembly (the office of the PM has since been abolished). There is a judicial branch with a Minister of Justice, yet the chief justice and most judges are selected and gain their final approval from the Leader, who is the supreme power in the country.

Indeed, the office of the Leader is the embodiment of the idea of the supreme authority of the jurist as elaborated in Ayatollah Khomeini's manifesto of an Islamic state. According to his formulation, the ultimate arbiter in all public decisions in Iran should be a jurist who is the representative of the Shi'i Imams, the last of which is said to still be alive and will return to Earth to establish justice and good governance. He is the highest authority and the head of the Islamic dimension of the Islamic Republic of Iran. This idea was incorporated into articles 2, 5, and 110 of the new constitution. Article 2 stipulates that continual independent reasoning by qualified jurists constitutes the main principle of the Islamic system of government. Article 5 grants rights to a qualified jurist or a council of jurists to act as the leader of the Islamic republic for the duration of the occultation of the absent Imam, and Article 110 enumerates the various areas that the authority of the leader extends. He is the absolute power in the country, holds the supreme commands of the armed forces, and can dismiss the president if necessary. To make sure that Islamic principles are observed, the constitution also stipulates the creation of a powerful twelve-member council called "the Council of Guardians" (*Showra-ye Negahban*). Articles 91, 96, 98, 99, and 118 of the constitution elaborate on the Council's duties. Their task is similar to that of the council of supreme religious leaders described in article 2 of the amendments to the 1906 constitution, i.e., to make sure that no law passes that might contradict Islamic principles. However, their authority is broader and much more extensive. It ranges from interpretation of the constitution to supervision of presidential and parliamentary elections, as well as referendums. In practice, however, they have taken the supervision to its greatest extent. For example, it is the body that eliminates candidates and bars them from participation in the electoral process in the name of purity and religiosity. In fact, both offices of the Leader and that of the Council of Guardians have become the hotbed of conservatism, even though as long as Khomeini was alive and acted as the leader, that office was more neutral.

For the most part, it was the conservatism of the Council of Guardians that created many obstacles for the government for implementing its duties. As a result, in 1988 the three branches of the government inquired from Khomeini whether the concept of "interest" (*maslaha*), a notion rather common in Sunni political thought but not in political thought of Shi'ism, could be invoked to trump those decisions that are blocked by the Council of Guardians. In a response on February 2, 1988, Khomeini ordered the formation of "the Council for Ascertaining the Interest of the Ruling System" to do precisely that, with the comment that "the interest of the ruling system belongs to the issues that transcend everything else." This council has now become a permanent feature of the Islamic Republic, and the leader extended its mandate by incorporating it in the revised constitution in 1989.

Established in the summer of 1989, the Assembly for Revising the Constitution was charged with making the government more efficient. This was a 20-member Assembly appointed by Khomeini in April 25 that presented a revised constitution for the referendum of July 28, 1989. In the new constitution, the office of the Prime Minister was eliminated altogether, the Council for Ascertaining the Interest of the Ruling System found a place in the new constitution, the office of the president became stronger, and more importantly, the office of the leader became the absolute ruler in the country. For example, note the following changes with regard to the office of the leadership. (1) Whereas the first constitution stipulated for a leader or a council of leaders, the new one eliminated the possibility of a council altogether. Article 111 of the revised constitution states that when there is a need to select a new leader: a "council, consisting of the President, the Head of the Judiciary, and one of the *foqaha* of the Assembly of Experts, will perform the leader's responsibilities. This council, which must be controlled by the ulama will lead the country until the Assembly of Experts selects a new leader." (2) To be a leader, according to the first constitution, one had to have reached to the highest level of Shi'i hierarchy, namely Marja' (the source of emulation). The revised version removed this condition. Article 109 limited the quality to being well informed about jurisprudence (*fiqh*), and well versed with sociopolitical problems. (3) The power of the leader is extended to deciding the "general policies of the Islamic Republic," according to article 110. (4)

Although the Council for Ascertaining the Interest of the Ruling System found a place in Article 112 of the new constitution, it is still under the leader's authority. As the article states, it is the leader who sets its function in motion and it is he who decides "the permanent and changeable members of the Council." For example, on March 18, 1997, the leader Ayatollah Seyed Ali Khamenei appointed 27 new members for five years and made Hojjat as-Islam Ali Akbar Hashemi Rafsanjani as its chair.

Suggested Reading

Mallat, C. 1993. *Renewal of Islamic law: Muhammad Baqer as-Sadr, Najaf, and the Shi'i International*. New York: Cambridge University Press.

Schirazi, A. 1997. *The constitution of Iran: politics and the state in the Islamic republic*. Translated from German by John O'Kane. New York: I. B. Tauris.

Surat-e Mashruh-e Mozakerat-e Majles-e Barrasi-ye Neha'i-ye Qanun-e Asasi-ye Iran (Proceedings of the Assembly for the Final Debates on the Constitution of Iran). 1985. Tehran: Majlie-s Shoray-e Eslami.

Surat-e Mashruh-e Mozakerat-e Shoray-e Baznegari-e Qanun-e Asasi-ye Iran (Proceedings of the Council for the Revision of the Constitution of Iran). 1990. Tehran: Majlie-s Shuray-e Eslami, 3 volumes.

FARHANG RAJAEE

✦ CRIMINAL JUSTICE SYSTEM

Iran's criminal justice system was overhauled after the overthrow of the monarchy and the establishment of the Islamic Republic in 1979. Iran's constitution has entrusted supreme power in the hands of the Supreme Jurisconsult (*velayat-e faqih*). Article 5 of the constitution states that in the absence of the Twelfth Imam, all political and legal power emanates from the *velayat-e faqih*. Both Ayatollah Khomeini and his successor Ayatollah Khamenei have issued rulings that have impacted the nature of the country's criminal justice system and laws governing judicial decisions. In addition, Articles 4 and 170 of Iran's constitution have placed a ban on all laws deemed to be un-Islamic by proper religious and judicial authorities of the country. In the early years of the Islamic Republic, the shortage of qualified judges who could authoritatively interpret Shi'a legal principles had forced the country to rely on the judicial rulings, or *fatwas*, of Ayatollah Khomeini as their guide in rendering decisions in courts. Consequently, vastly different standards were applied to similar cases, depending on the particular judge's interpretation of Khomeini's *fatwas*. As a result, it was common in the early stages of the post-revolutionary period for individuals convicted of committing the same type of transgression, but living in different parts of Iran, to have received vastly different sentences. It was not until the centralization of functions of the Islamic judges under the Supreme Judicial Council that some degree of uniformity was established in the administration of justice in the country.

The Islamic Republic's criminal justice system operates under Islamic law, or the *shari`a*, as interpreted by the Ja'fari school of Shi'a jurisprudence. Within this framework, punishment for certain categories of crime is deemed to be non-negotiable by many religious judges in Iran. The concept of Islamic criminal law differs from the prevailing notion of the law in secular societies in the West. This is partly due to the heavy influence of the *shari`a*, and partly because in many instances the subject of the law is not the person but his/her family. For example, murder is viewed not simply as an offense against society but first and foremost as a crime against the victim's family. Therefore, the punishment for murder is designed to not only deter crime but also to compensate the family of the victim. Hence, retribution and blood money have been an integral part of the Islamic punishment for murder. This is similar to the concept of *wergeld*, which was practiced by many European nations from the fifth century to the advent of feudalism in the ninth century. Unlike its European version, the Islamic criminal justice system provided exceptions for minors and the mentally ill when it came to handing down harsh punishment for criminal transgressions. On the other hand, Islamic criminal law remained unchanged whereas Western law evolved over time and incorporated safeguards and guarantees for the protection of the accused and adapted itself to reflect changes in societal values and mores.

The Qur'an specifies punishment for only a few categories of crime. These transgressions include adultery, consumption of alcohol, fornication, theft, brigandage, and lewdness. According to the dominant school of Shi'a jurisprudence, apostasy and rebellion against a righteous Islamic government also fall into the category of crimes with Qur'anic punishments, which may range from flogging to execution. Islamic Iran's penal code has divided crimes into four categories of *hudud, qisas, ta'zir,* and *diyat. Hudud* crimes are acts prohibited by God and punished by mandatory penalties defined by the Qur'an. The Iranian penal code considers the following as *hudud* offenses: theft, adultery, apostasy, consumption of alcoholic beverages, and rebellion against Islam as interpreted and defined by the religious authorities and jurists in the country. Since the punishment for *hudud* crimes are religiously mandated, the judge exercises minimal discretion as to the type of punishment imposed.

Qisas crimes include murder, manslaughter, battery, and mutilation. Iran's criminal code regards such offenses as acts against the victim and his/her family. As a result, the decision to inflict retribution on the culprit rests with the victim and the victim's family in case of murder. Although retribution in kind and vendettas are allowed under the *qisas* crimes and punishment, it is worth noting that both the Qur'an and the Iranian penal code recommend forgiveness because the act of forgiving pleases God. The practice of *qisas* had its origin in pre-Islamic Arabia where acts of vengeance and blood feuds were accepted practices in settling intra- and intertribal conflicts.

Ta'zir offenses are those for which no specific penalties are mentioned in the Qur'an or the Prophet Mohammad's sayings and tradition (*hadith*). Therefore, the punishment of *ta'zir* crimes is left to the discretion of the judge. In Iran, judges' discretionary power in this regard has been circumscribed because the law has now codified the range of allowable punishments for *ta'zir* crimes. They may range from admonition, to fines, to the confiscation of property, or even flogging for "immoral behavior." *Diyat* is not strictly a separate category of punishment under the Iranian penal code. It refers to a form of compensation which is to be paid to the victim or his/her family as reparation for an injury or murder. In other words, *diyat* becomes a form of punishment if a victim or his/her family (in case of unintentional manslaughter) chooses not to ask for retribution under *qisas* and instead demands blood money from the perpetrator of the crime. The Iranian penal code has extensively codified the nature of *diyat* for various types of crime and the modalities of monetary payment to the victims.

The Islamic Republic has established several types of criminal courts. The *Komiteh* Courts were among the earliest such courts. These were ad hoc neighborhood courts that came into existence in the immediate aftermath of the disintegration of the monarchical government. They exercised quasi-independent judicial authority and interfered with the country's legally instituted judicial organs. The *Komiteh* courts were eventually absorbed into the other judicial organs and gradually withered away. The Islamic Revolutionary Courts, which started as temporary courts for speedy trials of officials of the deposed Pahlavi monarchy, eventually became the most powerful courts in the country. These courts now have jurisdiction over the following offenses: all crimes against Iran's security, waging war on God, which is an undefined transgression in the country's penal code, narcotics smuggling, plunder of the public treasury, profiteering, and acts that are designed to undermine the Islamic Republic.

Suggested Reading

Asli, M. R. 2006. Iranian criminal justice system in light of international standards relating to victims. *European Journal of Crime, Criminal Law and Criminal Justice* 14:185–2007.

Dahlen, A. 2003. *Islamic law, epistemology and modernity: legal philosophy in contemporary Iran*. New York: Routledge, 2003.

Rezaei, H. 2002. The Iranian criminal justice under the Islamization project. *European Journal of Crime, Criminal Law and Criminal Justice* 10:54–69.

Tabataba'i, H.-M. 1984. *An introduction to Shi'i law: a bibliographical study*. London: Ithaca Press.

NADER ENTESSAR

✦ CUISINE

The cuisine of Iran in its delicacy and intricacy resembles her other great arts: carpet weaving, miniature painting, and poetry. This cuisine, which has been perfected through centuries of refinement, can hold its place with the most sophisticated cuisines of the world, such as the Chinese and the French. Iranian cuisine, in its present form, has its origin in the Safavid period (1501–1722) when Shi'i Islam was declared the official religion.

The origin of Iranian cuisine lies in its ancient empires, particularly that of the Sassanids (226–651 AD), who ruled over most of the present day Middle East. As the empire expanded, major developments took place in the culture of food and cooking. The court cuisine reflected the grandeur and extravagances which were partially responsible for the downfall of the empire. Many of the prerequisites of a great cuisine existed in Sassanid society. The cuisines of the various conquered regions were brought together, along with ingredients from far off lands. The desire for luxury and the love of all pleasures including good food was present at the court.

After the Muslim conquest of Persia (636 AD) this lifestyle and cuisine was inherited and revived by the 'Abbasid caliphs (750–1258) who emulated most things Persian. The banquets of the caliphs were renowned for their extravagance, variety, and lavishness. According to the Sassanid tradition, a court gentleman was expected to have a practical and literary acquaintance with cooking, in addition to his other accomplishments.

Erudition and the art of poetry and conversation were essential elements of the royal banquet.

The cooking was cosmopolitan, the ingredients rare and expensive from distant lands, and the procedure complex and lengthy. The names of many of the dishes and the flavorings in Iran, such as rose water from Fars and saffron from Isfahan, bear witness to the fact that their origin is Persian.

The end of the 'Abbasid era (1258) brought about a change in the class of people interested in cooking. It was no longer the game of princes, but the realm of scholars, who were interested in preserving the posterity the foods they liked. Thus, almost all the recipes which survive date back to the thirteenth century.

There is a lacuna in our knowledge of Iranian cuisine from the fall of the caliphate at the hands of the Mongols in 1258 and the rise of the Safavids in 1501. Amongst many other things, the advent of the Mongols and their subsequent conquest of Persia resulted in an interruption in the tradition of writing books of recipes. Consequently, we do not have any exact descriptions of the cuisine prevalent in Persia during that period, although there are detailed descriptions of the ingredients available in geography books, travel accounts, and other writings of the time. Because of their mobile nomadic nature, the Mongols did not possess a *haute cuisine*. Their cuisine consisted of horse meat and fermented milk. They possessed only one cooking utensil: a pot. Because of the meager sources available for the cuisine during this period, the Mongols not only failed to influence the Iranian cuisine but rather adopted it and subsequently imported it to India. Only one dish from the Mongol period, *shula*, based on rice, still exists in Iranian cuisine. In the Safavid cookbooks discussed below, there are fifteen types of *shula*, but the most prevalent in Iran today is *shulazard*, a type of sweet rice pudding with saffron. The fact that the Turko–Mongolian pastoral nomads roaming Persia in the Middle Ages did not possess an *haute cuisine* is further verified by the travel account of Ruy Gonzales de Clavijo, ambassador of Henry III of Castile to the court of Taymur in 1403. He describes many meals served en route by the local tribal notables or vassals of Taymur as well as feasts given by Taymur. According to his account, the principal meal of the élite was meat. More specifically, it consisted of both horse and sheep, either roasted or boiled, and a whole roasted horse with its head was considered the fanciest meal. The food of the poorer members of the population also originated from their pastoral nomadic existence. It included a preserved dairy product, which appears to be a cross between cheese and yogurt and which can be kept for long periods.

Knowledge of the cuisine of the settled Iranian population in the Timurid period comes from the unexpected quarter of the fifteenth century poet Bushaq (Abu Ishaq) At`ima (d. 1423–1427?). His *Divan* (collected poems) is the only complete source available on the subject for the period under discussion and contains numerous culinary terms of Iranian cuisine up to Bushaq's own time. This text includes a wide variety of information including the names of various foods and ingredients, but also the festive occasions associated with them, the eating habits of people, and some brief recipes.

The *Divan* consists of seven different parts. Its longest and most informative section for culinary purposes is the first part *Kanz al-Ishtiha* (Treasury of Appetite). It starts with an introductory section in prose followed by ten chapters in poetry. The sections are categorized according to different types of food, and it includes sections on ready made food available in the bazaar, ingredients available in the grocery shop, and food appropriate for the poor. This work further reveals that Iranian cuisine had either not disappeared during the 150 years of upheaval in the history of Persia or once again found its way back into Persia.

The renaissance of Iranian society after centuries of conquest and rule by numerous scattered dynasties took place under the Safavids (1501–1722). There are few historical manuals of cooking in Persian, but two manuals dating from the Safavid period have recently been published. The first, called *Karnama,* was written in 1523 by a cook named Muhammad ʿAli Bavarchi who worked for an unknown aristocrat during the reign of Shah Ismaʿil (1501–1524). The second, called *Maddat al-Hayat,* was written 76 years later in 1599 by Nuralla who was cook to Shah ʿAbbas (1588–1629).

A comparison of the two manuals sheds a considerable amount of light on the development of cooking during the Safavid period. Bavarchi, the earlier cook, mentions 26 different kinds of *pilaw* (rice cooked in the Persian manner containing various other ingredients) and 18 kinds of *ash* (a thick soup containing herbs, cereals, and rice). By the time we get to Nuralla's manual there are 54 kinds of *pilaw* and 32 types of *ash.* The variety has almost doubled. Bavarchi does not give any recipes for *dolma* (stuffed vegetables or stuffed vine leaves), whereas Nuralla gives two *dolma* recipes. They both mention only one type of *kuku* (an egg-based dish, a cross between a quiche and an omelette).

Another cooking manual in Persian has come down from the Qajar period (1796–1925). It is called *Sufra-yi Atʿima* and was written in 1883 by Mirza ʿAli Akbar Khan Ashpaz Bashi, cook to Nasir al-Din Shah Qajar (1848–1896). A comparison of the three manuals is most illuminating. The recipes from the Qajar period are much more elaborate, refined, and time consuming, and include dishes which did not exist in the Safavid period. A particular feature of Safavid cooking in common with that of the ʿAbbasid and the Timurid periods is one-pot cooking. Even the cooking of rice (*pilaw*), which reaches the height of its refinement during the Qajar period, went through a one-pot process during the Safavids. In contrast, Mirza ʿAli Akbar Khan, the Qajar cook, describes in detail the fourfold process of washing, soaking, boiling, and baking which goes into the final production of the rice. A particular feature of Iranian cuisine, the finely chopped herbs which go into many dishes, is absent in the Safavid recipes, although there is evidence that they were in existence in that period. In point of fact, aside from the preponderance of the many rice dishes, the Safavid cuisine resembles more of the ʿAbbasid and the Timurid periods in Persia than the Qajars.

Iranian cuisine as it is practiced and consumed today is distinguished from other cuisines in general, and that of the neighboring countries in particular, by certain principles governing the combination of ingredients that produce a delicate blend of flavors. These combinations lend themselves to an endless variety. The cuisine is neither hot nor spicy. Two specific and distinctive ingredients of Iranian cuisine are the indigenous saffron and the Indian lemon. They are both fragrant and give the food a special type of piquancy and a beautiful color. Another distinguishing mark of Iranian cuisine is the blend of meat or chicken with nuts and fruit. However, the highlight and perhaps the most unique feature of Iranian cuisine is the preparation of rice, which is unparalleled anywhere in the world. This fluffy rice, each grain of which remains fully cooked but separated from the rest, forms the basis of Iranian cuisine. The rice is prepared either plain (*chilaw*) or with ingredients (*pilaw*). The plain rice is eaten with various ragouts (*khurisht*) consisting of meat or chicken stewed with various fruits, vegetables, or fresh herbs. This method of eating rice is one of the original features of Iranian cuisine. The *pilaw* contains the same ingredients as the ragouts but in a dry form. There are many different kinds of thick soups, *ash* usually eaten in the winter and numerous other side dishes both vegetarian and otherwise. One dish, a pot-au-feu of meat, pulses, and potatoes, *abgusht*, is the daily lunch of laborers.

This delicate cuisine is both labor-intensive and time-consuming. Fresh herbs, which need to be cleaned and chopped very finely, are used in many dishes along with chopped, braised, onions. All the stews and thick soups have to simmer for many hours whilst the soups must be stirred constantly. There is no dish which can be produced on the spur of the moment except for a sweet version of an omelette known as *khagina* and an onion soup with coriander known as *ishkana*. All the dishes require many hours of preparation followed by multiple cooking processes ranging from braising, frying, to boiling. In spite of this, the cuisine as it evolved during the Qajar period has survived to this day and is prepared in homes all over Iran and in the houses of Iranians in exile.

Suggested Reading
Ghanoonparvar, M. R. 1982. *Persian cuisine* (2 vols). Lexington, KY: Mazda Publishers.
Mahdavi, S. 2005. Bavarchi, Nurralla in Alice Arndt, ed., *Culinary biographies*. Houston, Texas: Yes Press.
Shaida, M. 1992. *The legendary cuisine of Persia*. London: Leiuse Publications.

SHIREEN MAHDAVI

E

✦ EBADI, SHIRIN (1947–)

Shirin Ebadi is an Iranian lawyer, human rights and peace advocate, teacher, and writer who received the Nobel Peace Prize in 2003 for her pioneering efforts to promote democracy and human rights, especially for women and children. She is the first Iranian and the first Muslim woman to receive the Nobel Prize. Thanks to her significant contributions to the causes of human rights, peace, justice, and democracy during her pre- and post-Nobel years of activism at national and international levels, Ebadi has become one of the most prominent and resolute voices of justice and human rights in Iran and beyond.

PERSONAL AND PUBLIC LIFE

Ebadi was born on June 21, 1947, in the city of Hamadan in central western Iran. When she was one year old, her family moved to Tehran, where she continues to reside. Ebadi was raised in a middle-class, educated, and cultured Muslim family filled with love. Her mother dedicated herself to her four children. Her father, Mohammad-Ali Ebadi, was the city's chief notary public and one of the pioneers of the modern Census and Recording (*Sabt-e Asnad*) of the city of Hamadan, and also one of the first instructors of commercial law, who had written several books prior to his death in 1995. Ebadi grew up with two sisters and a brother, all of whom, like herself, achieved degrees in higher education.

Ebadi attended *Firooz Koohi* elementary school and continued her high school education first at *Anooshiravan Dadgar* and then at *Reza-Shah Kabir*,

Author Shirin Ebadi poses with the German copy of her latest book *Iran Awakening: A Memoir of Revolution and Hope* during a media conference in Berlin, 2006. (AP Photo/Jan Bauer)

where she received her diploma. In 1966 she was admitted to the University of Tehran, where she began her studies in Law. She received her Bachelor's degree in three and a half years and immediately took part in the Judicial Training program, and after a six-month internship period she officially began her career as a judge in March 1970. In the meantime, she continued her studies, and in 1971 received her Master's degree with Honors from the University of Tehran.

Following her various posts in the Judiciary branch of government, Ebadi advanced to the rank of the District Chief Judge of the 24th precinct in 1975. She was the first woman in Iranian history to achieve Chief Judicial status. But after the 1979 revolution and the inception of the Islamic Republic of Iran, Ebadi, along with other female judges, was dismissed from her position. This was due to the new government's interpretation of Islam, which considered women too emotional and hence unfit for judgeship. Ebadi was demoted to a secretary position at the branch where she previously presided. She and her female colleagues protested their demotions and were subsequently given somewhat higher positions as Legal Advisors. Nonetheless, Ebadi found her situation intolerable and took early retirement in 1984.

Since the independent Lawyers Association had been out of commission for years and law licenses were placed under the supervision of the Judiciary branch of the Islamic government, Ebadi's application for a law license was repeatedly rejected. This made her in effect homebound for several years, during which Ebadi used her free time to write books and articles for various journals and publications. Her writings, boldly critical of the *Shari'a*-based ruling law, earned her renown. In 1992, Ebadi was finally allowed to obtain a license to practice as an attorney, soon turning her law office into a major advocacy center for civil and human rights.

Ebadi married Javad Tavassolian, an electrical engineer, in 1975. Their two daughters have followed their mother's path: Negar, born in 1980, received her MS degree in telecommunications engineering from Canada's McGill University, and Nargess, born in 1983, graduated from the law school of the University of Tehran and is studying for a Master's degree in law at McGill University.

SOCIAL INFLUENCE AND CONTRIBUTIONS

Through her writings and practice, Ebadi soon emerged as a leading advocate of human and civil rights in Iran. As an attorney as well as a writer, she defended many cases concerning children and women's rights and freedom of expression, thus challenging the religious authorities' interpretation of Islam while demonstrating the need for an overall reform of the Iranian religious courts and justice system. While practicing law, she also directed and assisted several UNICEF research projects concerning children's rights and well-being in Iran. As a part-time lecturer, she also taught law at the University of Tehran, mentoring international students in human rights internship programs. During the 1990s, she was among the academics and intellectuals who paved the way for the reform movement, manifested later in the May 1997 landslide presidential election of the reformist Mohammad Khatami.

Ebadi's own introduction to politics was as a six-year-old child when she found all the adults around her, including her parents and grandmother, "in a terrible mood sitting huddled around the battery-operated radio, closer than usual, listening to the trembling voice that announced the fall of Mossadegh" (Ebadi 2006, 4). She later learned that after four days of turmoil in Tehran, the popular and democratically elected Prime Minister Mohammad Mossadegh (a secular nationalist) had been toppled in a coup d'etat supported by the United States Central Intelligence Agency and the British Intelligence Service. As reflected in her memoir, this sad turning point in Iran's modern history left a lasting impact on Ebadi's political views. As a secular yet devoted Muslim, her feminist perspectives became intertwined with her nationalist and anti-imperialist tendencies rooted in the Iranian people's years of struggles and aspiration for an independent and progressive modern nation since the Constitutional Revolution of 1905–1911.

Along with other activists and lawyers, Ebadi has founded two important non-governmental organizations: the Society for Protecting the Rights of the Child (SPRC), also known as the Association for Support of Children's Rights in Iran, and the Defenders of Human Rights Center (DHRC). The SPRC, founded in 1994, focuses on children, raises awareness, and lobbies the Majlis (Islamic parliament) to introduce legal reforms in accordance with the United Nations Convention on the Rights of the Child. One of the cases of child abuse and violence that Ebadi represented was the case of Arian Goleshani, an eight-year-old boy whose mother was not given custody of her child and thus witnessed his death due to abuse from his stepmother. This blatant case of child abuse caused wide national and some international outrage against the unjust nature of the law. Subsequently, the text of a bill against physical abuse of children, originally drafted by Ebadi, was passed by the Iranian parliament in 2002.

Among the many victims of human rights violations Ebadi has defended in court, many were cases of prominence at the national level. For instance, in 1998, Ebadi was the defense lawyer for the families of the victims of political assassinations (known as the *Chain Murders*) of dissident intellectuals: writers and activists such as Dariush Forouhar and Parvaneh Eskanadri Forouhar (a prominent couple found stabbed to death at their home). The Chain Murders were part of a terrorizing attempt by the extremist hardliners determined to end the more liberal climate fostered by the reform movement and election of President Khatami. The murders were solicited by a team of the agents of the Iranian Ministry of Intelligence led by Saeed Emami who alegedly committed suicide in jail before being brought to the court of justice.

Ebadi also represented the family of a young man, Ezzat Ebrahimnezhad, who was murdered during the attack on the Tehran University dormitory in July 1999. His case was the only officially accepted case of murder in the widespread Iranian student protests of 1999. Antagonized by Ebadi's resolute and vocal style of defense of the victimized students, the Iranian Islamist judiciary arrested her in June 2000. She was accused of producing and distributing a videotape that allegedly "disturbs public opinion." This was the videotaped confessions of Amir Frashad Ebarahimi, a former member of one of the main suppressive vigilante groups known as *Ansar-e Hezbollah*. In the confession, Ebarahimi implicated certain senior officials and high-level conservative authorities who ordered the group to attack supporters of the reform movement and commit atrocities against the reform-minded members of President Khatami's cabinet. Ebadi argued that she had only videotaped Amir Farshad Ebrahimi's confessions in order to present them to the court, as she had already deposited the tape to President Khatami and the head of the Islamic judiciary. But, in order to discredit this videotaped deposition, hardliners controlling the judiciary system named the case as "Tape Makers" (*Navar Sazan*) and arrested Ebadi and her colleague Rohami. They were tried in a closed court and sentenced to five years in jail and suspension of their law licenses. However, a court of appeal overturned these sentences and Ebadi was released from the jail after three weeks of solitary confinement.

Ebadi has also defended various cases concerning freedom of press and freedom of expression in relation to the banning of newspapers and periodicals, including the cases of Habibollah Peyman, Abbas Marufi, and Fraj Sarkouhi. To better coordinate and strengthen the defense of the victims of human rights violations, Ebadi, along with other prominent lawyers such as Fatollah Soltani, Mohammad Seifzadeh, and Mohammad-Ali Dadkhah, and Farideh Gheirat, founded the DHRC (her second NGO) in 2001.

In recognition of Ebadi's resolute and sustained struggle for human rights and democracy, especially the rights of women and children, she has received many awards and honors. One of her books, *The Rights of the Child: A Study on the Legal Status of Children's Rights in Iran,* 1987 (which was later translated into English and published by UNICEF in 1994) was selected as the Outstanding Book of the Year by, ironically, the Iranian Ministry of Islamic Culture and Guidance. She received the Human Rights Watch award in 1996 and the Rafto Human Rights Award from Norway in 2001. Then on December 10, 2003, Ebadi was awarded the Nobel Peace Prize for that year.

IMPACT OF THE NOBEL PRIZE

When on October 11, 2003, the Norwegian Nobel Committee announced Shirin Ebadi as the recipient of the Nobel Peace Prize for her courageous efforts for democracy and human rights, especially for the rights of women and children, the news filled Iranians all over the world with pride and joy. Except for the ruling conservatives, people in Tehran started congratulating each other in the streets. Taxi drivers flashed their lights, beeping and distributing pastries while weeping with joy (*Haera*). The timing and choice of this Nobel Prize illuminated the state of human rights in Iran and thereby affected the politics of Iran's international relations.

Honoring a feminist Muslim woman with the Nobel Prize has highlighted the issue of women's rights in Islamic societies in general and in the Islamist regime of Iran in particular. It has provided more legitimacy and credence to the cause of the women's movement in Iran led by many activists and feminist lawyers for over 100 years now. As evident in the growing activism and expanding networking of women activists in Iran since 2004, the Nobel Prize seems to have galvanized the women's rights movement. Unlike Western pressures threatening military attacks, the Nobel Prize has symbolized a constructive international intervention as it has boosted the self-esteem or self-confidence of feminist activists in Iran. In the current women's campaigns to illegalize and stop violent practices such as stoning ("Petition") and especially the "One Million Signature Campaign for Equal Rights," one can detect positive impact, whether direct or indirect, of the Nobel Prize and Ebadi's national and international efforts.

Sample of Women's Press and Growing
Feminist Activities in Iran
✦

http://www.zanan.co.ir/archive.html

http://herlandmag.info

http://www.irwomen.net

http://www.meydaan.com/English/default.aspx

http://www.irwomen.net/news_en.php

http://hastiandish.net

While thousands of jubilant women (along with many men) wearing white scarves and holding red roses rushed to the airport in Tehran to welcome back Shirin Ebadi after her reception of the Nobel Prize in December 2003, conservatives and fundamentalists were either silent or offended, calling the award a political game. Iranian state media waited hours to report the Nobel committee's decision—and then only as the last item on the radio news update. Even the moderate President Khatami downplayed the historic significance of the Prize by stating that although the scientific Nobels are important, the Peace Prize "is political and not important." Khatami's words raised objections in the general public and among many reformers as well; some viewed it as a sign of jealousy since he was a Nobel Prize nominee for his *Dialogue among Civilizations* proposal in 2001.

At the international level, the decision of the Nobel committee surprised some observers. In the face of other prominent candidates such as Pope John Paul II, some viewed Ebadi's selection as a calculated and political one, along the lines of the selection of Lech Walesa of Poland and Mikhail Gorbachev of the former Soviet Union. Other observers have perceived the selection of Ebadi by the Norwegian Nobel committee to represent an implicit criticism of U.S. policy in the Middle East, particularly the 2003 invasion of Iraq and potential military targeting of Iran, a member of the "axis of evil" as designated by President George W. Bush.

Ebadi herself has repeatedly and explicitly rejected military intervention in Iran. At a press conference shortly after the Peace Prize announcement and in many subsequent media appearances and lecture presentations at different universities, Ebadi has stated that "the fight for human rights is conducted in Iran by the Iranian people, one cannot import democracy through cluster bombs."

POST-NOBEL ACTIVITIES AND CONTRIBUTIONS

Utilizing her high profile as a Nobel Laureate, Ebadi has tried to garner more global awareness and international support for the women's rights movement and the pro-democracy and human rights activists in Iran. Yet like many other feminists and pro-democracy activists in Iran, she seeks social transformation from within, through generating cultural, ideological, and political changes. One of the main obstacles to change, Ebadi claims, is the misuse of religion, "an incorrect and fundamentalist interpretation of Islam," which is reinforced by the paternalistic culture and patriarchal political structure in Iran and the rest of the Middle East. Ebadi believes Islam can and must be interpreted differently in order to adapt to modern realities and the universal declaration of human rights.

Another serious problem in Iran today, Ebadi argues, is the lack of an independent judiciary system; judges must be independent of the Islamic government. She stresses the fact that women in Iran are becoming better educated than men as they make up over 60% of the university enrollments and are playing increasingly more active role in socioeconomic and cultural life. Yet the legal and overall sociopolitical status, individual freedoms, and choices of women have actually regressed since the Islamic Revolution instead of progressing in accord with women's social achievements.

Some Iranian dissidents inside Iran, but increasingly outside Iran, have criticized Ebadi for her avoidance of a confrontational stand against the Islamic Iranian regime. They argue that Ebadi has not capitalized on the Nobel Prize to mobilize opposition to the repressive regime. Opponents argue that the state of human rights in Iran has deteriorated under President Ahmadinejad, while Ebadi is still using a reformist and compromising approach and rejecting the Western military intervention in Iran.

Ebadi, however, has retained a sense of humility, arguing that she is a "simple defense lawyer who unfortunately has no golden key to enable [her] to open the doors of the prisons in order to free all the prisoners of conscience." Despite Ebadi's increased fame since receiving the Nobel Prize, she warns against the danger of personality cults and maintains that she has no desire to be a spokesperson or role model for Iran's 70 million citizens. She does not consider herself as the leader of the opposition nor would she desire any partisan role or governmental position. Ebadi wants to remain "a simple lawyer," committed to the pursuit of peace, justice, and human rights.

Ebadi has remained as courageous a defense lawyer as the Nobel selection committee praised her to be, not "heeding the threat to her own safety." So far, she has been among the most active Nobel laureates at national and especially international scenes. She has continued representing prisoners of conscience and victims of human rights violations mostly on a *pro bono* basis, including some of national and international significance. In November 2003, for example, she represented the family of a Canadian–Iranian freelance photographer Zahra Kazemi, who was murdered while in jail in Iran. In the summer of 2006, during the prolonged hunger strike of Akbar Ganji, Ebadi continued legal representation of a prominent investigative journalist imprisoned for six years despite the authorities' threats and intimidations against her. On May 17, 2007, Ebadi announced that she would defend the Iranian–American scholar Haleh Esfandiari, who has been jailed in Tehran since early May 2007. Ebadi and her colleagues have also provided sustained legal representations to more than 50 women activists in Iran arrested during 2006 and 2007 because of their participation in peaceful demonstrations or in the "One Million Signature Campaign for Equal Rights."

In addition to sustained efforts in representing victims of human rights violations inside Iran, Ebadi has been in great demand for speaking engagements internationally. She frequently appears in the media; travels extensively in order to present lectures or deliver the commencement addresses at several major universities; and consults with research institutions, think-tanks, human and women's rights organizations, and the U.N. agencies in Asia, Africa, North America, and Europe.

Ebadi has received over a dozen honorary doctorate degrees from major universities in the United States and Europe and has been awarded several new human rights prizes, including the *Légion d'honneur* from the French President Jacques Chirac in the Elysee Palace in Paris in November 2006; the Lipentz Freedom of Expression Prize from German Reporters; Lila's Prize for the Most Courageous Woman from German Readers; and the Best Women's Writers Prize from Al-Zahra University in Iran. In 2005, Ebadi was voted the world's twelfth leading public intellectual in "The 2005 Global Intellectuals Poll" by *Prospect Magazine* (U.K.).

Ebadi's latest book *Iran Awakening: A Memoir of Revolution and Hope* (with Azadeh Moaveni) was published in several languages in 2006 and has been well received internationally. A reading of *Iran Awakening* was serialized as BBC Radio 4's *Book of the Week* in September 2006. Ebadi's memoir would have not passed the censorship office in Iran to receive a permit for publishing in her home country Iran. It was therefore crafted mainly for an international audience. Ironically she was also faced with restrictions in the United States due to the Department of Treasury's trade laws that included prohibitions on writers from embargoed countries. Supported by some other writers, Ebadi sued the Department of Treasury in 2004 arguing that the law infringes on the first amendment. After a long legal battle, Ebadi was finally able to publish her book in the United States with Random House in 2006.

Without shying away from the term "feminism," Ebadi identifies herself as a Muslim feminist, an identity that may sound like an oxymoron to the ears of some puritanical secularists as well as anti-feminist Muslim fundamentalists and traditionalists. But Ebadi represents the creativity in women's ways of fighting patriarchy, the multiplicity of women's voices, and the diversity in the women's movement and feminism in Iran as in many other societies living under religious laws and traditionalist rules. Ebadi indeed symbolizes the paradoxical status of Iranian women and a growing women's rights movement and feminist consciousness in the Middle East. As a staunch advocate of universality of human rights, Ebadi debunks cultural relativism. She boldly criticizes not only the retrogressive laws and repressive state policies in Iran, but also the patriarchal and chauvinistic foundations of Iran's culture and traditions.

Along with five other women Nobel Peace Laureates: Jody Williams (United States), Wangari Maathai (Kenya), Rigoberta Menchú Tum (Guatemala), and Betty Williams and Mairead Corrigan Maguire (Ireland), Ebadi initiated the formation of a transnational NGO, called the "Nobel Women Initiative for Peace, Justice and Equality." Registered in Canada and inaugurated in April 2006 at the headquarters of the Feminist Majority Foundation in Los Angeles, this new organization aims at spotlighting and promoting the efforts of women's rights activists, researchers, and organizations working to advance peace, justice, and equality ("Nobel Women Initiative"). NWI has been pursuing the release of Daw Aung San Suu Kyi (Burma), the only imprisoned Nobel Peace Prize Laureate, who remains under house arrest in Burma. The NWI's First International Women's Conference ("Women Redefining Peace in the Middle East & Beyond") took place in Galway, Ireland from May 29–31, 2007. More than 80 leading women activists and researchers from 37 countries participated in this conference, during which Ebadi and other women Nobel Peace Prize laureates pledged to become "a global voice in tackling violence against women and in peace advocacy."

Publications of Shirin Ebadi

✦

BOOKS

Penal Codes (written under Professor Abdolhassan Ali Abadi). Tehran: Meli Bank Publishing, 1972.

Medical Laws. Tehran: Zavar Publishing, 1988.

Young Workers. Tehran: Roshangaran Publishing, 1989.

Laws of Literature and Arts. Tehran: Roshangaran Publishing, 1989.

Architectural Laws. Tehran: Roshangaran Publishing, 1991.

Refugees Rights. Tehran: Ganj-e Danesh Publishing, 1993.

History and Documentation of Human Rights in Iran. Tehran: Roshangar Publishing, 1993.

The Rights of the Child: A Study of the Legal Aspects of Children's Rights in Iran (Translated into English by Mohammad Zamiran). Tehran: UNICEF, 1994.

With Zamiran Mohammad. *Tradition and Modernity.* Tehran: Ganj-e Danesh Publishing, 1995.

Comparative Children's Rights (Translated into English by Hamid Marashi). Tehran: Kanoon Publishing, 1997.

Women's Rights. Tehran: Ganj-e Danesh Publishing, 2002.

With Kim, Uichol, and Aasen, Henriette Sinding, eds. *Democracy, Human Rights, and Islam in Modern Iran: Psychological, Social, and Cultural Perspectives.* Bergen, Norway: Fagbokforlaget, 2003.

Iran Awakening: A Memoir of Revolution and Hope (with Azadeh Moaveni). New York: Random House, 2006.

ARTICLES

1. "Children and Families Laws," a series of articles within the *Encyclopedia Iranica,* Columbia University Press.
2. "Parental Rights," *CNRS Catalogue; Humanities and Social Sciences* CNRS press, France.
3. "Women and Legal Violence in Iran," *Bonyade Iran Journal.* Paris, France.
4. More than 70 articles dedicated to various aspects of human rights, some of which were presented in the UNICEF CRS seminars in 1997.
5. Numerous articles in weekly magazines such as *Fekr-e No, Zanan, Iran Farda,* and more recently in Internet journals such as *Roozonline* on women's or human rights issues.

Suggested Reading

Ebadi, S. 2006. *Iran awakening: a memoir of revolution and hope* (with Azadeh Moaveni). New York: Random House.

Haeri, S. 2003. Iranians celebrated with joy Ebadi's Nobel Peace Prize. *Iran Press Service.* October 10. http://www.iran-press-service.com/articles_2003/Oct2003/ebadi_wins_nobel_peace_101003.html.

Khoshnoudi, B. *Shirin Ebadi: a simple lawyer* (film). http://www.frif.com/new2005/shir.html.

Nobel Women's Initiative: http://www.nobelwomensinitiative.org/home.php.

Omestad, T. 2007. Iran's 'illegal' jailing of an American scholar. *Newsweek.* May 17. http://www.usnews.com/usnews/blogs/news_blog/070517/irans_illegal_jailing_of_an_am.htm.

One Million Signature Campaign. http://we-change.org/english.
Petition to Eradicate the Law of Stoning. http://www.meydaan.com/English/default.
aspx.

NAYEREH TOHIDI

✦ ECONOMY, EMPIRICAL ASSESSMENT OF

Since the revolution of 1979, many obstacles, both internal and external, have hindered the stability and growth of Iran's economy. While impediments to economic recovery and prosperity accompany revolutions in general (such as those which occurred in Algeria and Cuba, for example), they typically emerge with a uniqueness that is characteristic of the country and reflect the constellation of political, demographic, social, and economic factors coming into play at the time.

The case of Iran presents a prime example of how the sometimes self-inflicted internal and external economic and political conditions have impeded attempts to emerge from a form of colonialism. It experiences internal rebellion and external sanctions and aggression as it attempts to achieve economic and political independence within a global political economy. Taken separately, each of the many hurdles to Iran's economic recovery would be somewhat daunting; taken together, they are formidable. Included among the major external factors are the following:

- The Eight Year War between Iran and Iraq, which brought extraordinary calamity to the Iraqis and the Iranians, resulted in approximately one million casualties and caused tens of billions of dollars in physical damage;
- An economic embargo placed upon Iran by the United States;
- What might be described as less than favorable treatment of the country by other advanced industrial nations in regard to intermediate and long term loans and so-called dual use technologies;
- Massive immigration of refugees from Iraq and Afghanistan; and
- An oil price collapse in the mid-1980s, which cut Iran's oil revenues by more than 50%.

Equally formidable internal strife and economic mismanagement have accompanied the external obstacles just outlined. The major problematic factors that have been generated internally are enumerated as follows:

- Confiscation and nationalization of properties that, according to the revolutionary courts, had been illegitimately acquired by their owners;
- Forced sale of some agricultural lands to the people who worked the land;
- Nationalization of banks and establishment of Islamic banking in 1983 to 1984;
- Monetization of the government deficits;
- A foreign exchange rate system characterized by too many new initiatives and policy reversals;
- A sudden and frequent economic policy reversals in general;
- An absence of the uniform application of laws and regulations;
- Widespread corruption, rampant throughout the country; and
- A dwindling share of Iran in international trade (exports and imports).

POPULATION GROWTH

The population of Iran rose from 18.95 million to 68.8 million between 1956 and 2004 (see Figure 1). During the 20-year period between 1956 and 1976, the population growth rate was approximately 3.0% to 3.6% per year, while during the decade of 1976 to 1986 the growth rate jumped to almost 5% per year. However, during the early years of the 1990s, the average rate of growth declined to just over 1.5%. That rate continued its decline to below

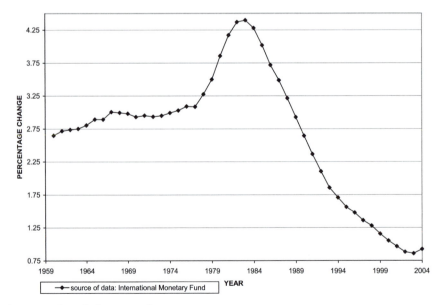

Figure 1   Population growth.

1% in the first half of the new millennium. This population trend means less than half of the population is 30 years old or younger and is in need of education, vocational skills, and jobs.

DISTRIBUTION OF POPULATION

Similar to other countries, there has been a consistent migration of the population within Iran from rural to urban areas. Even though the rural population increased in actual numbers from 13 million in 1956 to 22.8 million in 2005, there was actually a decline in rural residents as a proportion of the nation's population (see Table 2).

Typically, urban migration places tremendous pressure upon a country's social service system, due to the higher visibility and concentration of urban problems. Also, rural populations have traditionally been relatively self sufficient in terms of food production and consumption. Migration to the cities changes their status from producers/consumers of foodstuffs to that of consumers only. Both of these have led to higher imports of foodstuffs and poverty.

Table 2 **Urban and Rural Distribution of Population (in millions)**

Year	1956	1966	1976	1986	1991	1995	2001	2002	2003	2004	2005
Total	18.95	25.79	33.71	49.45	55.8	60.05	64.5	65.5	66.9	67.5	68.5
Urban	5.9	9.8	15.9	26.8	31.8	36.8	41.8	44.2	44.7	44.8	45.7
Rural	13.0	15.9	17.8	22.3	23.6	23.0	22.7	22.3	22.3	22.7	22.8
Percentage rural	68.6	61.6	52.8	45.0	42.2	38.3	35.2	34.0	33.3	33.6	33.3

SOURCE: Iran Statistical Yearbooks.

PRODUCTION (GDP)

After the revolution, during a period spanning approximately ten years, the production of goods and services in real terms fell as long as the Iran–Iraq War continued. After the war, in 1989, production began to rise. However, Iran's growth rate has not been large enough to spur a significant increase in per capita income to reach and surpass the pre-revolution estimates. In the first half of 1990s, a modest upward trend had resulted in an increase in the measure. However, it stagnated for the rest of the decade. The measure has had a positive trend in this millennium mostly due to higher oil prices.

One could identify several factors leading to the decline in income. One obvious factor, justifiably, was the country's preoccupation with its war efforts.

Another reason for the economy's lackluster performance was the collapse of oil prices in the mid-1980s. This was considered a strategy of Iraq's allies to defeat Iran in the war. That is, by denying Iran revenues from oil, it was

Figure 2   Oil and gas as a percentage of GDP.

assumed, Iran would try to cut its losses and surrender or at least agree to a ceasefire. The price of Iranian light oil fell an estimated 55%, from $28.00/pb in 1986 to as low as $12.75 in 1989. Iran's oil revenues took a tumble and fell to $9.673 billion in 1988.

However, arguably, the most important factor in this regard is the low levels of investment, public and private, which is itself a result of uncertainty about the socioeconomic-political position of the country in which Iranian potential investors/entrepreneurs find themselves.

One interesting development in economic context has been the decline in the share of gas and oil as a percentage of GDP (Figure 2). This has been due to increase in the non-oil GDP rather than decline in oil and gas income. This could be hailed as a good omen for Iran's economic and therefore political security. However, one should not lose sight of the fact that most of Iran's imports are still paid for by Iran's exports of oil and gas.

INVESTMENT

Even though there might be several reasons for the "sick" state of the Iranian economy, one could pinpoint and shorten the list by looking at one of the most important factors. The investment picture of post-revolutionary years has not been promising. The volatile rate of investment explains the slow capital formation and low growth rate of the GDP (Figure 3). The low and volatile investment rates have not been limited to the private sector. It has also been a characteristic of the public investment as well (Figure 4).

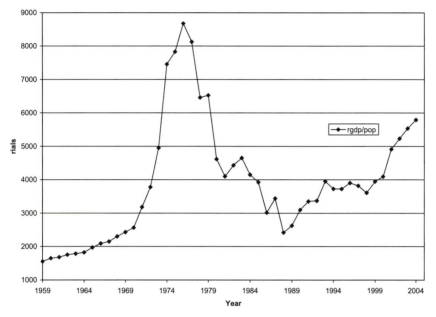

Figure 3   Per capita real GDP.

Both public and private sectors have been investing lower percentages of the GDP in construction and machinery every year. In 1990, private investment in machinery and construction, as a percentage of the GDP, was 7.9%. The same scenario is true for government investment, which dropped to 7.9% as well. These figures are low by any standard, whether it is that of industrially advanced countries or of newly industrialized countries. Investment on the part of both the private and government sectors has been higher in the area of construction relative to the resources going toward machinery.

These low levels of investment have alarming implications for the country's industrial capacity to maintain and expand production as well as to contain inflation. There is no doubt that these levels will not lead to a higher standard of living or to the prospect of a high-enough growth rate for the economy to absorb current open and disguised unemployment as well as the estimated 1 million new entrants into the job market every year. The question then becomes, why such a low investment? The answer is the same. When there is uncertainty, there is limited or no investment in long-term projects. People will invest only in very liquid businesses so that they can cash in their holdings on short notice to avoid being caught with their wealth tied down in illiquid assets. Uncertainty due to social factors such as unrest, lawlessness, and lack of a protective civil society diminish the willingness of investors and frighten potential long-term investors; hence the flight of

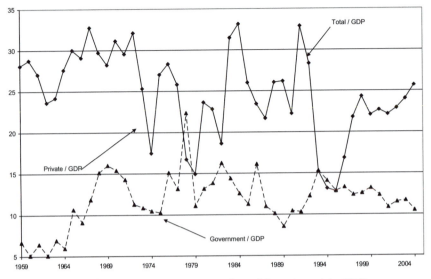

Figure 4 Ratios of private, government, and total investment to GDP.

capital to a safe haven and avoidance of long term commitment to any investment strategy.

Inflation

Figure 5 shows annual inflation rates. These rates could be grouped into four different time periods. The first grouping covers the early years before the oil price rise. The second time period includes the years after the oil price increase and up to the revolution. The third period covers the post-revolutionary years, most of which were taken up by the Iran–Iraq War. Finally, the fourth period reflects the post-war and "post-Khomeini" era. As it shows, prior to the oil price rise (1963–1972), inflation in Iran was rather tame, with an average rate approximating 2.4% per year. However, this does not hold true for the subsequent three time periods.

Budgetary constraints became almost irrelevant to Iran's economic planning, at least for a short while when huge oil revenues accrued due to the spiraling oil prices triggered by the Arab oil embargo in 1973. Prior to that year, the availability of foreign exchange dictated the government's project selection, and therefore imported inflation (i.e., inflation due to higher imported goods prices, monetization of foreign reserves by the central banks, and higher demand for exportable goods) was not a problem. However, the tremendous increase in the price of oil gave the government an opportunity to engage in grandiose nationwide projects that were beyond the absorption capacity of the country. Iran's infrastructure was too limited to accommodate these new projects, and inflationary pressure started to mount.

In pursuit of rapid economic development, the government, on one hand, used the oil revenues to finance almost all of the old and new projects. This contributed to an increase in the monetary base and money supply and therefore in aggregate demand. On the other hand, due to the limited capacity, the higher aggregate demand could not be satisfied internally, hence goods had to be ordered from abroad. Due to the universal inflationary situation of the 1970s, all of the ordered materials carried with them an inflationary premium. Regardless of this, however, the open door policy was ineffective because of the inability of importers to bring their merchandise into the country due to inadequate port and transportation facilities. There was a waiting period of more than six months for ships to unload their cargo in the port cities of the Persian Gulf, and when they did unload, they were unable to transfer the merchandise to its final destination. Since there were no storage facilities, the imported goods could not be safely stored in these port cities. As a result, the imported items were stored in open facilities located around the outskirts of the port cities, a practice which resulted in their ruin. Therefore, the inflationary pressure could not be eased by a greater volume of imports.

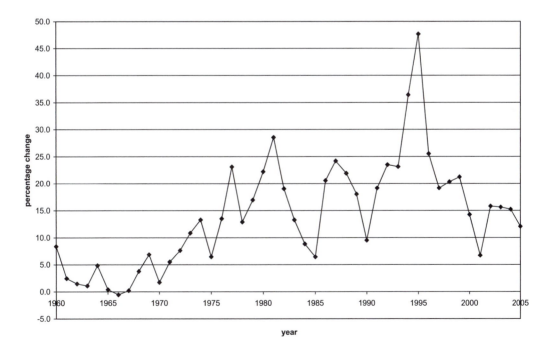

Figure 5   Annual inflation rates.

Another factor contributing to the inflationary build-up prior to the revolution was the higher per capita income. As purchasing power trickled down to the masses, demand for goods and services increased, which in turn increased the intensity of inflation. Pre-revolutionary Iran provided a classic example of a country in which there were too many dollars chasing too few goods.

However, the revolution added a new dimension to the already festering inflationary problem. Besides fiscal and monetary policy mismanagement, many other conditions that tended to exacerbate Iran's inflationary problems can be identified: the eight-year Iran–Iraq War and its ramifications, the exodus of the managerial and industrial leadership strata of the country, the foreign embargo imposed by the United States along with unfavorable economic treatment by other nations, and a decline in oil revenues were among the major contributors to the problem.

In general, for each of the time periods specified above, the average yearly inflation rate was growing. The sudden rise in inflation immediately after the jump in oil prices jolted the economic system because people were not used to that magnitude of instability. However, the years following the revolution were not any better. Although inflation rates reported by official sources are high, unofficial anecdotal estimates are at much higher levels.

The official estimates include all of the prices that are controlled by the government directly or through its agencies, companies, and bonyads (religious foundations). These goods and services, such as electricity, water, bread, tobacco and tobacco products, tea, and sugar, are subject to government mandated price controls. Even so, they continue to be included in the calculation of price indexes, upon which they have a biasing effect due to their combined magnitude. Therefore, when the controlled prices of these commodities are combined with the prices of other free market goods, the results are much more moderate official inflation rates.

OBSERVATIONS

Among the self-inflicted and self-destructive wounds is the insecurity of individual citizens. Human rights violations are repeatedly acknowledged by officials of the United Nations and independent researchers and are highlighted by the media with a troublesome frequency. One could refer to the student unrest and the arrests and imprisonment of prominent figures, as well as serial killings, from 1997 to 1999. The second reason for the ills of Iran is the ease and frequency with which laws and regulations are revoked and modified. Third, one might not be able to depend, with certainty, on the laws of the land as the guiding principles. These laws may or may not stand the test of time and may be dismissed as un-Islamic or against the interest of Islam.

A fourth related problem, which would possibly explain the faltering private investment, is lack of uniformity in the application of the laws of the land and uncertainty due to political instability, and the sense of individual insecurity which these conditions instill. Court decisions as well as other official rulings depend on who one is, where one is, and with whom one is acquainted. In Iran, individual government officials could and would interpret the law to suit the person and not the situation. For example, one person could obtain a permit to open a business while the next person with the same qualifications might be denied the permit. It is commonly known and believed that in Iran nothing is impossible if one knows the right people and is ready to pay the price (bribe).

The fifth area of concern has to do with Iran's international relationships. The revolutionary zeal and fervor, which understandably were present at the beginning of the revolution, gave way to a more rational decision-making process. However, Iran's leadership has persistently clung to many tenets of the revolution, refusing to engage in rapprochement with the country's international adversaries and underestimating their willingness and ability to cause damage directly or through roundabout methods. The controversial positions taken by Iran in regard to various issues have often resulted in negative opinion within and throughout the international community. The direct damage of the eight-year Iran–Iraq War and the freezing of Iranian assets by the United States are self-evident and need little elaboration.

However, since the revolution Iran has been paying for its political leanings in other less quantifiable ways. An example of this has to do with the "containment" policy, by which Iran has been penalized persistently in at least three important and long-lasting ways. One punitive aspect, promoted by the United States, is the unwritten and circuitous international prohibition of the transfer of technology, which might be considered as capable of serving dual purposes by the United States. Even though, on the surface, other countries do not directly subscribe to or participate in this prohibition, they have conducted business with Iran with a watchful eye on these transactions. This means that Iran cannot openly buy what it needs without a great deal of European and Japanese governmental "red tape." This red tape and watchfulness is, of course, to protect the images of these countries as perceived by the international community. Japan and the European nations do not want to be accused of supporting or arming a "rogue" nation. The second way that Iran is penalized by the "containment policy" is that trading countries have raised the overall price of doing business. In the financial markets, Iran's credit rating is far lower than what a country like Iran should receive. There is not one instance in which Iran has failed to pay its debt, even during the chaotic days of the hostage crisis and frozen Iranian assets. Yet Iran must pay higher interest rates due to, among other things, low credit ratings and high country risk. Other examples abound. Iran has not been able to buy oil technology in a competitive way. The Conoco example, even though it is unique in its circumstances, is not an isolated one. Third, the "containment" strategy keeps foreign investors away. Even though Iran has been trying to lure businesses to invest in the country proper or in the Free Trade Zone areas, the attempts have been less than successful.

It is well established that Iran is a marginal country in exports and imports (total trade) relative to the world total trade. But Iran's absence from international arenas denies it a forum to defend and protect its interests. One such example is the WTO. Being a member of WTO means participation in the decision-making process. The WTO's decision-making is based, in general, on the GATT practice of decision-making by consensus. This means that a decision is finalized not necessarily because all of the present members agree with it. Rather, a decision may be made because those countries that are present may not object strongly enough to the matter to block the passage of a given motion. By definition, in an organization that operates by consensus, presence means having the ability to protect one's interest. Those who are not present at the table do not have a voice and their interest may be infringed upon. Given Iran's faltering trade situation, she might badly be in need of trade partners and of becoming a part of the multilateral trade.

The impact of openness on the economy of a member state is another factor. Openness imposes the tyranny of the global market. The country is no longer allowed to plunder its scarce resources in the production of commodities that do not have clear international comparative advantage. International competition forces each country to be much more judicious and a great deal less cavalier in its choices of what and how much to produce.

Finally, from the discussion of output (GDP), faltering investment in machinery and in construction, and spiraling inflation, it is apparent that monetary policy has not been effective in stimulating real economic activities, nor has it been used successfully to control the value of the currency. It has been employed in an on-again off-again manner rather than as a tool for proactive decision-making.

See also Economy, Historical Background of; Economy, Informal Sector; Economy, Private Sector; and Economy, Structural Analysis of.

Suggested Reading

Amirahmadi, H. 1992. Economic cost of the war and reconstruction in Iran. In *Modern Capitalism and Islamic Ideology in Iran*, ed. C Bina and H Zangeneh. New York: St. Martin's Press, 257–282.

Amirahmadi, H., and H Zangeneh. 1997. An analysis of the Iranian government budgets. *Public Budgeting and Financial Management.* Vol 9.

Bakhash, S. 1998. The politics of land, law, social justice in Iran. *Middle East Journal.*
43:186–201.

Bina, C., and H. Zangeneh, eds. 1992 *Modern capitalism and Islamic ideology in Iran.*
New York: St. Martin's Press.

Cooper, R. 1968. National economic policy in an interdependent world. In Richard
Cooper, *The economics of interdependence: economic policy in the Atlantic community.*
New York: McGraw-Hill.

Dadkhah, K. M. 1985. The inflationary process of the Iranian economy, 1970–1980.
International Journal of Middle East Studies. 17:365–381.

Ghasimi, M. R. 1992. The Iranian economy after the revolution: an economic
appraisal of the five-year plan. *International Journal of Middle East Studies.* 24:599–614.

Zangeneh, H. 1997. International trade in Iran: an appraisal. *Research in Middle East
Economics.* Vol 2.

Zangeneh, H. 1997. The Iranian economy and the globalization process. In *Iran encountering globalization,* ed. A. Mohammadi. London: Routledge/Curzon, 107–134.

Zangeneh, H. 1999. Economic consequences of student unrest. *Journal of Iranian
Research and Analysis.* 15:132–141.

Zangeneh, H., and J. M. Moore. 1994. Economic development and growth in Iran. In *Islam,
Iran, and World Stability,* ed. H. Zangeneh. New York: St. Martin's Press, 201–216.

HAMID ZANGENEH

✦ ECONOMY, HISTORICAL BACKGROUND OF

Modern Iran is essentially a corollary of conditions and struggles that led
to the Constitutional Revolution (1906–1911) and materialization of a two-
fold objective, namely, the establishment of democracy and eradication of
foreign domination. These goals, however, have yet to be realized. Modernity, and with it modern economic thinking, therefore, had obtained an indigenous context for those Iranians who have engaged in a long, passionate,
and forthright struggle for these twin goals up to the present time. Thus, any
holistic examination of Iran's economy considers continuity and change, and
thus the accumulating material foundations upon which these struggles
found cross-sectional political expression. The 1979 February insurrection,
dubbed the "Iranian Revolution," is an instance of such sociopolitical erup-
tions that have obtained a place in history.

The economy of Iran has gone through three transformative episodes
since the Constitutional Revolution. The first period is known as "primary
accumulation," a pre-capitalist stage in which separation of the producer
from means of production generates an unlimited reservoir of wage labor that

in turn lays the cornerstone of capitalism proper. This stage gained strength through the Constitutional Revolution and continued halfway through the Reza Shah period (1925–1941) for a significant part of the country. Reza Shah understood that the key to modernization of Iran lies in the replacement of traditional and religious institutions with their twentieth-century modern counterparts. But he himself, alien to the very first tenet of the Constitutional Revolution, was the front man in a British coup d'état (1921) which eventually established him as an absolute monarch until his exit in 1941. Centralization of state structure was the precondition for centralization of economy. The most important development project in Reza Shah's era was the construction of Trans–Persian Railway. Construction of modern manufacturing plants and light industry was also significant, culminating in some 350 modern plants by 1941.

The second period is the transition to what is known as the capitalist mode of production. This period extends beyond World War II, including the Mossadegh period (1951–1953) and through to the so-called White Revolution, a series of reform programs, the chief exponent of which was the land reform. The primary concern of the land reform program, although concealed as the petty ownership of agricultural land, was class polarization and incursion of the world market into the Iranian countryside. This was a universal strategy by the Kennedy administration not only for Iran but also for a number of developing countries within the U.S. orbit. In this period, creation of *internal market* was accomplished through a multi-phased land reform program, which in turn cleared the way for *import-substitution* industrialization strategy in Iran. Aside from the unsettled dispute over the efficacies or inefficacies of these programs, land reform in Iran has in effect led to eradication of vestiges of the pre-capitalist self-sufficient communities that once stood between wage-labor and the increasing penetration of the world market and transnational capital. Finally, after the 1960s reforms, Iran's economy had become a *de facto* component of the world market. Subsequent events, which led to globalization of the oil sector in the early 1970s, also completed the task of integration within the global economy beyond the Shah's regime. Notwithstanding the obstruction of U.S. sanctions, Iran's economy today is much more in tune with the global economy than at any time in its previous history.

The strategy of "development planning" in Iran (not unlike its "Third World" counterparts) started with U.S. initiative in 1947, under Mohammad Reza Shah. The newly found Plan Organization oversaw planning and implementation of the first seven-year economic development plan in March 21, 1949, the beginning of Persian calendar. The primary focus of development projects was to build the infrastructure and then to assess the development of industry. The First Economic Development Plan (1949–1955) was a dismal failure in all its principal aspects, yet the alien practice of planning had begun to take hold within Iran's development thinking. The Second Economic Development Plan (1956–1962) coincided with stark sociopolitical realities of post-1953 CIA coup d'état that overthrew Premier Mossadegh and brought Mohammad Reza Shah back to power. The overthrow of Mossadegh was equivalent to denationalization of Iranian oil and the return of Iran's national oil deposits to a front consortium that represented the International Petroleum Cartel. The Second Economic Development Plan was funded with growing oil revenue (80%) and foreign loans (20%), showcasing the construction of a number of projects, such as building reservoir dams on the Dez, Karaj, and Safid Rivers. This was the time of overspending and credit expansion that led *inter alia* to reevaluation of foreign exchange assets and nearly depleted all foreign currency reserves between 1955 and 1960. By 1959 the post-coup binge had to grapple with severe inflation.

The Third Economic Development Plan (1963–1967), shortened to a five-year plan hence, to some extent reflected the tenet of the "White Revolution." The latter is a reference to a series of reform programs that was packaged in Washington and, despite the Shah's unwillingness, marketed along with the newly devised "Alliance for Progress" strategy by the Kennedy administration. This was a response to stagnant socioeconomic structure, over-centralized bureaucracy, and prevailing economic crisis in Iran. However, the universal significance of this package will be misplaced if one fails to recognize its very response with respect to the unfolding political crisis and social instability that ramified the ambiance of the post-coup period in Iran. The land reform was the centerpiece of all this for two objectives: (1) to eradicate the peasant agriculture and to destroy the remnants of the pre-capitalist past, and (2) to put an end to self-sufficient production in farming communities.

The distribution of land in its immediate aftermath had indeed led to the creation of a substratum of petty landowners. Yet given the size and condition of their land, these landowners ultimately had to lose their land and reluctantly join the growing ranks of the wage laborers in the countryside and in urban centers in Iran. A small number of fortunate owners, who had enough to add to the size of their holdings and were able to produce, still had to compete in the open market for their products. Hence, from its very inception, the land reform program must be viewed as a vehicle for class polarization and thus creation of wage labor, not the production of the petty landowner for its own sake. In a nutshell, Iran's land reform program in its most holistic contextual framework was a perplexing story of (latent) "primary accumulation." This was a preamble to the transformation of rural class structure toward the establishment of commercial and corporate agriculture and the massive migration of surplus labor to urban areas. In the meantime, oil revenue became the pivot for both the government budget as well as any real or imaginary economic development projects ever since. Hence, *rentier state,* a term that aptly connects the institution of state, dynamics of capital accumulation, and entire economic structure to a single commodity, has become an enduring feature of Iranian state-society relations.

The Fourth Economic Development Plan (1968–1973) accelerated the eradication of pre-capitalist vestiges and stepped up the transformation of the countryside, in tune with a kind of development that catered to international capital and facilitated the penetration of the world market across the economy. The GDP averaged at 11.8% but distribution of income worsened significantly at this time. The leading sectors were industry, petroleum, transportation, and communication. The focus of development was the urban areas. The Fifth Economic Development Plan (1973–1977) allocated some $37 billion, two-thirds of which was allocated to investment in housing, manufacturing, mining, oil and gas, and communication and transportation in the same period. The total plan allocation was increased by 92% as a result of sudden rise in oil revenues. In the meantime, the Shah ignored some of the major priorities of the Fifth Plan and instead focused assiduously on the development of the military industrial complex and the procurement of sophisticated weaponry. This meant that the lion's share of the rising oil revenue was solely under the direction and discretion of this absolute monarch. Given the four-fold increase in the price of oil, Iran's oil export revenue increased from $3.6 billion in 1972 to nearly $21 billion in 1974. "Uneven development" though is indeed a mild description of this sort of politically motivated spontaneous expansion, which was neither in accord with the socioeconomic welfare and expectation of the majority nor in tune with the sociopolitical aspiration of a sovereign and self-reliant Iran. Oil revenues declined slightly in 1975, and then increased to $22.9 billion and $23.6 billion, respectively, in 1976 and 1977, before declining again to $21.7 billion and $19.2 billion, in 1978 and 1979, when the "Iranian Revolution" was in full swing.

In addition to doubling investment figures, the Shah went on the binge buying the most sophisticated military hardware that have ever been allowed to be purchased by a "Third World" country, with the blessing of the Nixon administration. In authoritarian regimes, political reforms meant to extend the life of the system often have the opposite effect, instead expediting revolutions. Yet, at the same time, by not giving up to reform and reconciliation, such regimes would almost always shortchange themselves and jeopardize the chances for their survival. The Shah's conundrum was not unique. There are plenty of examples in contemporary world history. Somoza in Nicaragua, Marcos in the Philippines, and Suharto in Indonesia are three notorious examples. That's why, for regimes such as these, it is always too late to reconcile, and it is always too soon to give up power. To put it in Hegelian terms, the Shah's predicament (and predicament of the Carter administration in respect to keeping him in power) was the chronicle of perpetual resolution of contradictions at the higher level. Simply put, the day of reckoning for the survival of the Shah's regime was really some twenty-odd years too late. Therefore, neither Carter's human rights policy was to blame nor should Brzezinski's saving-the-Shah proposition be taken seriously.

The Shah's ostentatious, post-oil crisis programs and the Nixon Doctrine in the Persian Gulf obtained their unity of purpose and unanimity in oil revenues. Consequently, the oil crisis was a boon to programs that went much further than the ambition for development and modernization of Iran. Indeed, some observers conclude that the Shah, as an indispensable pillar of the *Pax Americana*, subsidized the U.S. foreign policy with Iranian (domestic) wealth and from Iranian national treasury. This amounts to double jeopardy against the Iranian people. Massive military expenditures, on the one hand, and limitless imports necessitated by the expansion of credit and conspicuous consumption, on the other, had almost immediately led to inflationary spiral fittingly feeding upon the rising oil revenues. In addition, the oil boom of the 1970s led to further class polarization and income inequality across the board. The profound economic crisis and the combination of a decade-long intense political repression and despotic rule had soon put the country on an irreversible course. The Shah's rentier state was in deep trouble. This time, unlike the summer of 1953, even the most unsophisticated Iranians were able to read Washington's hand. At long last, in February 1979 in a massive, spontaneous, and revolutionary insurrection the monarchy was overthrown.

See also Economy, Empirical Assessment of; Economy, Informal Sector; Economy, Private Sector; and Economy, Structural Analysis of.

Suggested Reading

Amuzegar, J., and M. A. Fekrat. 1971. *Iran: economic development under dualistic conditions*. Chicago: University of Chicago Press.

Baldwin, G. B. 1967. *Planning and development in Iran*. Baltimore: Johns Hopkins University Press.

Bina, C. 2005. Mossadegh, the oil crisis, and price of independence." In *The Mossadegh experience and the future of Iran*, eds. H. Keshavarz-Sadr, and H. Akbari. Bethesda, Md: Ibex Publishers (in Persian): 71–138.

Bina, C., and B. Yaghmaian. 1988. Import substitution and export promotion within the context of the internationalization of capital. *Review of Radical Political Economics*. Vol 20.

Bina, C., and B. Yaghmaian. 1991. Postwar global accumulation and the transnationalization of capital." *Capital & Class*. No. 43.

Chakravarty, S. 1987. *Development planning: the Iranian experience*. London: Oxford University Press.

Fitzgerald, F. 1974. Giving the Shah everything he wants. *Harper's Magazine*.

Karshenas, M. 1990. *Oil, state and industrialization in Iran*. Cambridge: Cambridge University Press.

Katouzian, H. 1981. *The political economy of Iran*. New York: New York University Press.

Mahdavy, H. 1970. The patterns and problems of economic development in rentier states: the case of Iran. In *Studies in the economic history of the Middle East*, ed. M. A. Cooke. London: Oxford University Press; 428–467.

Najmabadi, A. 1987. *Land reform and social change in Iran*. Salt Lake City: University of Utah Press.

National Security Archive, Electronic Briefing No. 28, *The secret CIA history of Iran 1953 coup*. Washington, DC: George Washington University. http://www.gwu.edu/ ~nsarchiv/NSAEBB/NSAEBB28/index.html#documents (retrieved: 3/9/ 2007).

Pesaran, M. H. 1976. Income distribution and its major determinants in Iran. In *Iran: past, present and future*, ed. J. W. Jacqz. New York: Aspen Institute for Humanistic Studies; 267–286.

United States Congress, House of Representatives, Committee on Government Operations, *Hearing Before a Subcommittee on U.S. Aid Operations in Iran*, 84th Cong., 2nd Sess., May 2, 31, June 1, 5, 8, 11–13, 18–19, 25–27, 29, July 16, 1956.

United States Congress, House of Representatives, Committee on International Relations, Special Subcommittee on Investigations, *The Persian Gulf 1975: The Continuing Debate on Arms Sales*, 94th Cong., 1st Sess., June 10, 18, 28, July 29, 1975.

CYRUS BINA

✦ ECONOMY, INFORMAL SECTOR

Accurate information about the informal sector of Iran is almost impossible to gather, but the sector is huge and is growing throughout much of the developing world, including in Iran. The United Nations Country Assessment in 2003 reported that 65% of Iran's GNP is generated by the informal sector. The same report points out that due to the nature of the informal sector, accurate information is impossible to collect. Nevertheless, estimates indicate that approximately one quarter to half of total employment is in this sector of the economy. An internal Iranian government report estimates that up to 27% of employment in agriculture, hunting, fishing, and forestry; 19% in manufacturing; 14% in sales; 7.3% in transportation; and 1% in real estate are in the informal sector. In terms of GDP, the same report shows that the informal sector constituted 13.7% of production in agriculture, hunting, and forestry; 15% in manufacturing; 15.6% in sales; 6.4% in transportation; and 13.5% in real state (based on 1997 national census). It should be noted that the report measures only legal activities and that the black market and underground economy are not included. Clearly, the size of the country's underground economy, both legal and illicit—especially in smuggled goods— is quite significant.

Throughout the developing world, many states use the informal sector to generate employment as part of their poverty alleviation strategy. In the case of Iran, this sector started to grow during the years of the Iran–Iraq War (1980–1988) and continued to expand during the post-war period. During President Rafsanjani's reconstruction period (1989–1997), the state policy to increase employment amplified the expansion of this sector. Generally, throughout developing countries, the relationship between the state and the informal sector is far from straightforward. This is true in Iran, which recognizes that for the urban peasants the informal sector may be the only source of employment. On the other hand, the informal sector does not generate taxes and for a country which wants to move away from dependency on oil revenue, taxes are a critical source of state funds. This was apparent in our fieldwork where the city sometimes imposed tight controls on street peddling but other times, such as close to the New Year, the city's control was lax.

The informal sector has been growing exponentially because of three major factors. First, as the literature on the topic indicates, there is a direct correlation between urbanization and growth in the informal sector: the sector is becoming an urban phenomenon. Compared to the Iran of a few decades ago, Iran today is primarily an urban society in which the informal economy tends to expand. Second, Iran has absorbed the largest refugee population in the world, constituted mainly of Afghans. Currently, 4% of the population in Iran is Afghan refugees (U.N., 2003), and to this number we may have to add refugees from the war in Iraq. Third, Iran is suffering the consequences of unemployment. The informal sector of the economy is much more labor-elastic than the formal sector, and therefore rising unemployment has a direct impact on the growth of the informal sector.

There have been several studies of the informal sector, one of the notable being that by Jomehpoor (2003). The study was based in a middle-income neighborhood in Sayyed Khandan, and the data showed that average income of workers in the informal sector ranged between 50 and 100 dollars per month. Out of a sample of 50 respondents, more than 80% in the informal sector were migrants to the capital from rural or smaller cities, and 20% were foreign nationals, mostly of Afghan origin. Most of those in the informal sector were employed in the informal economy because they could not find jobs in the formal labor market. Some choose this sector because of lack of capital. More than 42% of the respondents did not like to work in this sector.

By and large, most research on the topic has not been gender disaggregate. But in a country with strict gender segregation codes, it is imperative to have gender disaggregated data. While gender segregation in the job market is a world phenomenon (women tend to occupy "unskilled" and poorly paid jobs while men tend to occupy well-paid jobs), in the case of Iran and some other Muslim countries it is two-fold. Gender segregation in the work place is typically to the disadvantage of women; however, in the case of Muslim countries in general and Iran in particular, the issue is more nuanced. Studies focused on women's employment in the informal sector present an unexpected picture. Women of high- and middle-income classes tend to choose the informal sector because they are free from imposed dress codes. Field study in Iran indicates that many women prefer to work at home, where they are free from dress codes. This applies to the elite and the middle class who do not want to wear the hijab. In the aftermath of the revolution, many women from elite and middle-class backgrounds were forced to leave their jobs because of their association with the previous regime or their unwillingness to wear the hijab. Some of these women started to work from their homes in fields such as fashion design, accounting, translation, and tutoring. Many women of high- and middle-income background are in fact very satisfied to be in the informal sector because it gives them space to dress as they wish and they are free from male harassment. There are many highly educated female laborers in this sector. However, at the other end of the scale, for women of low-income households, the informal economy is an important source of income and employment where they can rely on their extended family network, friends, and community for their startup capital as well as their market.

By and large the informal sector throughout the developing world suffers from a lack of documentation. This is indeed the case with Iran. It means that those employed in this sector are easily forgotten and ignored, are absent from social policies, and remain unprotected. Considering that the informal sector is a source of employment for the poor, those who are engaged in this sector and belong to low-income classes remain in precarious working conditions and are in dire need of labor protection.

See also Economy, Empirical Assessment of; Economy, Historical Background of; Economy, Private Sector; and Economy, Structural Analysis of.

Suggested Reading

Bageri, F, A.-A. Maziar Yazdy, A. A. Banoie, and H. Varmiyar. 2003. *Ravesh andezeh giry bakhsh gher e rasmi dar Iran* (Measuring the informal sector in Iran). Tehran: Groheh pajohesh maryayeh eghtesadi (Centre for Research on Economic Statistics in Iran).

Bahrmaitash, R. 2007. Iranian women of low income households as "the other": the subaltern women and the informal economy and micro credit. Paper presented at Engaging Islam, at University of Boston, September 12–16.

Daza, J. L. 2005. Informal economy, undeclared work and labour administration. Geneva: ILO.

Kazemipour, S., and R. Bahramitash. 2007. *Women's role in the informal sector*. Tehran: Center for Population Studies and Research on Asia and the Pacfic.

Poour, M. J. 2003. *Mashaghe gere rasmi be onvaneh ney masaleh shary va abad ejtemai va eghtesady an: baresi moredy dar poul sayyd khadan*. [Looking at the informal sector as an urban socio-economic problem: the case of Sayyd Khadan]. Tehran: Fasnameh Olome Ejtemai (Allmeh Tabbatano University Quarterly).

United Nations Common Country Assessment of the Islamic Republic of Iran (2003). Tehran: United Nations.

ROKSANA BAHRAMITASH AND SHAHLA KAZEMIPOUR

✦ ECONOMY, PRIVATE SECTOR

During the eighteenth and nineteenth centuries the traditional Iranian private sector comprised artisans, craftsmen, merchants, and small farmers, and retailers whose locus of activities was the Bazaar. Under the Reza Shah, the founder of the Pahlavi dynasty, substantial effort was made to modernize the economy and the country. As a result, a modern segment of the Iranian private sector emerged, with origins in the landowning classes, tribal chief's families, and the royal family. In the early 1960s, the Shah's so-called White Revolution by and large transformed the structure of land ownership in the agricultural sector, by transferring a significant amount of land to the peasants, and created the foundation of growth of small land-owning farmers in the rural areas. In spite of the considerable growth during the reign of the Palahvis, a healthy growth of the private sector was checked by cronyism, favoritism, and concentration of wealth in the hands of the royal families and their associates. This is argued to be one of the contributing factors to the overthrowing of the Pahlavi dynasty and the establishment of the Islamic Republic system in 1979.

The advent of the Islamic Revolution introduced significant changes to the structure and operation of the private sector. This was particularly the case in the first decade of post-revolutionary economic policy-making after

Iranians shop at Tehran's main bazaar.
(AP Photo/Vahid Salemi)

the revolution. According to analysts, two major factors have significantly influenced the scope and pattern of the private sector's role in the economy after the revolution. First, it has been the incoherent economic policies and the existing ambiguities of the institution of private property and the economic role of the state. Continuous struggles between the radical and liberal factions of the clerical establishment during the fist decade of the revolution, in particular in the areas of land reform, labor laws, foreign trade, development strategies, and planning, practically undermined the formation of coherent development strategies and planning during the first decade after the revolution. Second, it has been the expanded size of the public sector in favor of the private sector. As a revolutionary measure and to undermine the royalists economic power, the Revolutionary Council nationalized more than a thousand factories, banks, and financial industries that constituted the backbone of the modern industrial private sector of Iran. Subsequently, section 44 of the Constitution of the Islamic Republic subsumed the role of the modern private sector under the role of the public and cooperative sectors of the Iranian economy. Consequently, pragmatism and expediency has emerged as the main venue to encourage and promote private activities and investment under the Islamic Republic.

POST-REVOLUTIONARY REFORMS

Beginning in early 1990s as the result of early revolutionary failures in economic policy formation, there appeared a strong desire by the reformists and the pragmatic factions of the ruling establishment to amend the Constitution in favor of a more prominent role for the private sector. Market liberalization reforms that were initiated after the election of pragmatic president Rafsanjani in the early 1990s continued more effectively under the presidency of the reform-minded Khatami and his reformist allies in the Sixth parliament. Among such reforms were the unification of the exchange rate, reform of the taxation laws, banking, and finance, establishment of the Oil Reserve Fund, unification of the exchange rate, financial reforms such as the licensing of three new private banks, removal of tax exemption status of the Revolutionary Foundations or "Bonayds," continued progress in the creation of the National Taxation Office, introduction of trade liberalization measures such as removal of quantitative restrictions in favor of tariffs and Value Added Tax, revitalization of Tehran Exchange Market, and creation of free trade zone in Qeshm island in the Persian Gulf. Passage of the reform bills proved to be a daunting task for the reformists who had to face stiff opposition from the well-entrenched conservatives in the Council of Guardians, a conservative body that can overrule legislation by the parliament, or Majles, on the basis of non-conformity with the Islamic Law.

FIVE-YEAR DEVELOPMENT PLANS

During the presidency of the pragmatic Akbar-Hashemi Rafsanjani in 1994, the Islamic Republic implemented its First Five-Year Development Plan. Although the first two development plans laid the foundation of more significant economic plans to revitalize the economy and encourage the participation of the private sector, it was only during the Third Five-Year Plan (2001–2005) that the domain of state control of the economy was reduced in favor of more sustained, less restrictive, and transparent private economic activities. During this period the Iranian economy experienced a continuous and relatively respectable 5% annual rate of growth in the non-oil sector. One of the objectives of the current Fourth Five-Year Plan (2005–2010) is to consolidate the achievement of the previous plan and improve income distribution and regional development disparities.

In 2004, under the directive of the Expediency Council, Iran prepared a so-called Vision Plan that outlines the major policies and objectives of the economic policy-making in the course of the next 20 years.

PRIVATIZATION

In October 2004, The Expediency Council passed a law that rescinds articles 43 and 44 of the Constitution, both of which restrain the domain of private activities. As the law states, "to bring about economic development and prevent further losses to the national economy, the government is authorized to cede large industries and those mentioned in articles 43 and 44 of the Constitution to the cooperatives and private sectors except for downstream oil and gas industries." Various areas of the economy, including the postal service, airlines, shipping, telecommunication, power generation, foreign trade, banking, insurance, and railway, were selected to be privatized.

In 2007, Supreme Leader Ayatollah Khamenei called for an expedited privatization process outlined in the amendment of Article 44 and enhancing enforcement of private property rights and contracts by the special courts set up by the Justice Ministry. In theory, the process starts with an initial public offering of 5%, which would set a market price for the remaining shares. In 2005, the government planned to sell $2.5 billion worth of public enterprise to the public but could only divest $800 million. In that year the executive bylaw of the "Expansion of Small and Medium Enterprises" was also approved in order to promote private activities in these areas.

According to analysts, one of the major problems with the privatization drive has been a lack of ability of the private sector to purchase large share blocks of public stocks. Instead, banks, insurance companies, and pension funds, which are themselves public entities, have been buying the share of state enterprises. The privatization drive is planed to be completed by the end of the Fifth Five-Year Development Plan in 2014/2015.

THE PRIVATE SECTOR'S OUTPUT, EXPENDITURE, AND INVESTMENT

In contrast to the industrial sector, where large public enterprises produce more than 60% of the value-added, the role of the private sector in small industries, construction, retail, and services is quite prominent. For example, 93% of Iran's industrial units are privately owned small companies. Private sector share of agricultural production that is dominated by small farmers amounted to 85.9% of the total in 2004. The service sector that was responsible for 49.5% of GDP in 2004 is also predominantly owned and operated by private individuals and firms. In the construction sector, private firms were responsible for the construction of 283,072 buildings, which constituted 5.6% of the GDP in this year. More recently, the establishment of six private banks, among them Kar-Afrin Bank and Parsian Bank, has paved the way for more prominent private activities in the financial sector of the economy. In 2006, the market share of private banks' lending rose from 10.5% to 15%.

In 1984 the government passed a law that monopolized exploration of the large mines in the hands of the government. However, in 1998, after significant setbacks due to uneconomic operation of the public mines, a new mining law was enacted that allowed private mining activities. In 2004, there were 3,125 mines in the country from which the private sector accounted for 43% of the total value added. Private companies are responsible for 90% of the new explorations in the mining sector. In 2004, private consumption expenditure accounted for more than 52% of the total consumption expenditure compared to 11.4% public sector's expenditure consumption in this year.

On the investment side, in 2003, the private sector's investment in machinery and construction, respectively, accounted for 42.9% and 18.7% of the total gross fixed capital formation in the economy. In that year, the share of private sector investment in machinery was 420% of the public sector's investment in this area. In spite of the significant amount of the public sector's investment in construction, the private sector's fixed capital formation in this area was only 10% less than the public sector. The revitalization of Tehran Stock Exchange market in 1991 has significantly promoted private capital formation in all sectors of the economy. From March 1999 to March 2003, the TSE price index (TEPIX) jumped from 2,206 to 11,400 and trading increased from 1.7 billion shares to 7.9 billion shares. The exchange hit a high of 13,836 in December 2004. Faced with political uncertainty, as the result of new presidential election and escalation of Iran confrontation with the West on the nuclear issue, the TEPIX index fell by 21.9% in 2005 relative to the year before.

THE NEW LAW OF FOREIGN DIRECT INVESTMENT

In 2002, Foreign Investment and Protection Act (FIPA) law was enacted to encourage foreign direct investment. One hundred percent of foreign ownership is allowed under the new law as long as the value ratio of goods and services produced by aggregate of foreign investments does not exceed 25% in each economic sector and 35% in each subsector. Ownership of land of any type and to any extent in the name of foreign investors is not permitted. Repatriation of capital is allowed under FIPA as long as the foreign currency earned is the result of export of goods or services produced or services by the foreign company.

According to the Ministry of Industries and Mines in 2004/2005, a total of $3,697.9 million worth of joint foreign investment under the FIPA was approved.

LABOR LAWS

Shortly after the revolution and under the radical revolutionary environment various labor committees emerged in the factories, significantly tilting the balance of power in favor of labor, *vis-à-vis* the management. To control the rising turmoil and confusion, the government immediately established the Islamic Workers Councils and the Worker's House, which also ensured the state's control over labor and movements within a politically acceptable domain. Although forming unions is legal, in practice no union system exists in the country. Guild unions that operate locally do not have much power to represent the organized labor.

The first Labor Law under the Islamic Republic was enacted in 1993. It is generally regarded as an employee-friendly law. Under the current law an employee may only be dismissed upon the approval of the Islamic Labor Council or the Labor Discretionary Board. In theory, businesses with more than five employees cannot fire an employee if she or he has been working for more than six months. An employment contract can only be terminated if the employee becomes totally disabled, retires, resigns, dies, or the project is completed in task-specific contracts. The Labor Law recognizes oral, written, temporary, and indefinite employment contracts. Membership in the Social Security System for all employees is mandatory. Different economic activities have a national minimum wage rate that is established by the Supreme Labor Council. The lowest minimum wage in 2005 was set at $120 a month. There have been recent attempts by the Parliament to amend the existing Labor Law to increase productivity, encourage innovation, promote investment, and in particular to eliminate some of the obstacles the Law has presented in the new drive towards privatization.

CHALLENGES

In spite of various efforts and policies, and relative to other developing countries, the private sector remains significantly subsumed under the control of the state, which subjugates the interest of this sector under its immediate or long-term political objectives. As a result of the bloated public sector, cronyism, bribery, black market activities, and corruption have become rampant in the economy. Corruption is perceived as widespread. Iran ranks 88th out of 158 countries in Transparency International's Corruption Perceptions Index for 2005.

Relative to international standards, doing business in Iran both for domestic and foreign companies continues to remain a challenging task. Although there have been some improvements in the areas of property rights and contacts, the national regulatory environment and a lack of total independence of the judicial body from political influence continue to present major obstacles to the overall health of a free-enterprise economy. According to the Economist Intelligence Unit (EIU), with regards to risk of investment, Iran's overall risk rating was a D on an A through E scale in 2004. EIU ranked Iran last for doing business among 60 countries. In 2004, the World Bank ranked Iran in the bottom 24% in voice and accountability, the bottom 9% in regulatory quality, and the bottom 27% in government effectiveness, among other indicators of governance.

In 2007, the Heritage Foundation index of Economic Freedom found the Iranian economy 43.1% free and ranked Iran as the 150th freest economy in the world and 16th among 17 countries in the Middle East/North Africa region.

Another major obstacle confronting a healthy growth of the private sector is Iran's international isolation and U.S. economic sanctions. In March 2007, in response to Iran's defiance of the international community's call to monitor and regulate its nuclear program, the Security Council banned Iran's arms exports and imposed a freeze on the financial assets of 28 individuals and entities. U.S. economic sanctions on Iran, imposed after 1986, and the subsequent imposition of the Iran–Libya Sanctions Act (ILSA, 1996), have had a significant impact on various sectors of the economy that were previously dependent on the imports from the United States as well as U.S. markets and technical know-how. Although substitution of the United States by other emerging economic powers such as China, India, and South Korea has reduced the impact of the U.S. sanctions, the sanctions have strategically impacted the structure and operation of certain areas of private economic activities such as the traditional carpet industry and pistachio production.

There are also signs of the revival of radical economic Islamic thinking under President Ahmadinejad. In the beginning of his presidency he pledged to "put the oil money on everyone's dinner table" by slowing down indiscriminate privatization of the state enterprises, distributing "Justice shares" to the masses, substantially reorganizing the oil ministry, and offering low-interest marriage loans to working young couples. As the result of his expansionary fiscal policies, there were two supplemental budgets in 2006 that increased the size of government expenditure by 27% relative to 2005. At the same time, due to the new rising unfavorable conditions for foreign investment, there was 9.1% reduction in joint foreign investment in the country.

See also Economy, Empirical Assessment of; Economy, Historical Background of; Economy, Informal Sector; and Economy, Structural Analysis of.

Suggested Reading
Amuzegar, J. 1993. *Iran's economy under the Islamic republic.* New York: I.B. Tauris & Co Ltd.
Bakhash, S. 1990. *The reign of the Ayatollahs, Iran and the Islamic revolution.* New York: Basic Books.
Nomani, F., and S. Behdad. 2006. *Class and labor in Iran: did the revolution matter?* Syracuse, NY: Syracuse University Press.
Central Bank of Iran: http://www.cbi.ir.
Statistical Center of Iran: http://eamar.sci.org.ir.
Iran Trade Point: http://www.irtp.com.

MEHRDAD VALIBEIGI

✦ ECONOMY, STRUCTURAL ANALYSIS OF

The present-day economy of Iran, as with any other developing economy, is a reflection of cumulative evolution and social conditions that have been articulated and reinforced into a social whole. Modern Iran essentially and distinctively has its roots in the Constitutional Revolution (1906–1911).

Modernity, and with it modern economic thinking, is therefore an outcome of well over a century of passionate, self-propelling, and forthright struggle that placed Iran at the threshold of the new century today. Therefore, it would be simple-minded, if not entirely obtuse, to judge this country merely by the appearance of its Islamic camouflage. A balanced analysis of the socio-economic institutions and the economy of Iran must thus avoid reductionism, which often leads us to overly simplistic and prejudiced accounts, as have been exhibited by the captive U.S. media and the George W. Bush administration. Moreover, one has to look at the preponderance of historical evidence that predates the present and that implicates the United States in more than a few occasions since the CIA coup d'état in 1953. Despite their turbulent past, the majority of Iranians preferred to make their own history and fighting their own fight along their twin goals of the previous century. Iranian economy thus cannot remain immune from the impact of either its predisposed history or its pre-given institutions.

By February 1979, the Iranian economy had already been at a standstill when oil production—which was slacking off due to persistent strikes by oil workers and personnel—came to a halt, along the remaining sectors (public and private) which suddenly folded like a giant house of cards. Yet it had taken nearly a year of bloody struggle, a stage-managed (U.S.) Embassy take-over, and an imposed imperialist war (via U.S.-backed Saddam Hussein) to eventually turn the tides against the major constituents of the February insurrection. This kept Ayatollah Khomeini in control and led his bloody and forceful consolidation of power under the Islamic Republic. Aside from these cumulative political repercussions, the economic consequences of both the U.S. Embassy takeover (1979–1981) and the Iran–Iraq War (1980–1988) have been immense. The former resulted in an initial round of hefty economic sanctions that amounted to freezing more than $14 billion in Iranian assets, which essentially were lost by Iranians to U.S. government and U.S. private banks in sheer retaliation. In retrospect, this by itself may easily acquire the title of "most clever highway robbery of the twentieth century," a de facto pillage of a wounded and desperate "Third-World" nation that dared to engage in revolution. The new regime established itself not without enormous economic and political costs on the part of Iranian people—save for incalculable loss of human lives—both in the process of internal struggle and in the course of an eight-year war with Saddam Hussein of Iraq.

Iran, a country with an area equal to those of France, Germany, Italy, Britain, the Netherlands, and Belgium combined, and with a population just over 70 million, ranked 19th in GDP and 4th in production of oil worldwide. Under the Islamic Republic, the evolution of Iranian economy can be divided into four distinct periods: (1) wartime economy (1980–1988); (2) economic reform and postwar reconstruction (1989–1996); (3) political reform and high expectation (1997–2004); and (4) political uncertainty and economic strangulation (2005–the present).

WARTIME ECONOMY (1980–1988)

The aspiration that brought down the Shah's regime was three-fold: (1) to gain political and economic sovereignty, (2) to share economic wealth of the country with all citizens, and (3) to include all Iranians in economic and political decision-making. However, both internally and externally, all these hopes were quickly dashed. Internally, the conservative wing of the clergy opted for monopolizing power against the rest of the political opposition and insurrectionary forces. Externally, sudden invasion of the country by Saddam Hussein, and his continued material and moral support by the Reagan administration, not only destroyed much of the economic infrastructure of an already disrupted country but also threatened the very sovereignty and territorial integrity of Iran. Hence, from the outset, Iran's economy was already between the pincers of internal revolutionary upheaval and the external force of devastation. In summary, one may portray the contour of this period as having enormous capital flight, massive "brain drain," unimpeded population growth, unreliable sources of foreign exchange, a sizeable budget (and balance of payment) deficit, rampant inflation, considerable unemployment (some 1.8 million persons or about 14.5% of labor force in mid-1986), and a demoralized and terrorized population. This is in addition to the incalculable loss of life, hundreds of thousands of war casualties, and the survivors whose medical costs are still mounting to this day. The cost of the war on the Iranian side alone is estimated somewhere between $400 billion and $600 billion—in constant 1986 dollars.

The Iranian calendar begins March 21st and ends March 20th. The purchasing-power-parity (PPP) estimate of Iran's Gross Domestic Product (GDP) in 1980/1981 was $98.8 billion. This estimate is based on official exchange rate of 70.61 Iranian rials for every U.S. dollar, while the PPP estimate for 1985/1986 is $186.8 billion. In 1982/1983, the economy recovered and exhibited an average growth rate of 6.9%, thanks to resumption of oil exports to an acceptable amount, in conjunction with relatively higher oil prices, in the first half of the 1980s. The fortunes of the Iranian Government, however, reversed in 1986/1987 when the price of oil hit rock bottom, prompted by a formidable one-two punch that was jointly delivered by Saddam Hussein and the Saudi Government. This was not only against the political survival of the regime but also against the economic survival of Iran itself. The massive destruction of Iran's oil facilities by the Iraqi forces took care of reduction in *quantity* of oil production, while the self-injurious flooding of oil market by Saudis took care of reduction in *price*. Consequently, Iran's GDP dropped nearly 9%—with a 3.6% negative rate of growth in 1986/1987.

ECONOMIC REFORM AND POSTWAR RECONSTRUCTION (1989–1996)

The Iran–Iraq War ended August 20, 1988, but despite the horrendous devastation, neither Saddam Hussein nor his main backer, the Reagan administration, accomplished their objectives. The impetus for post-war reconstruction led to the first official Five-Year Economic Development Plan (1990/1991–1994/1995) by the Islamic Republic. This coincided with Ayatollah Khomeini's death (June 1989) and the emergence of pragmatic politics and economic reform under Rafsanjani. The PPP estimate of GDP reached $206.8 billion for the 1989/1990 fiscal year, with the real growth rate of 4.2%. Again the oil industry functioned as the leading sector and, given the favorable conditions in global oil market, GDP in 1990/1991 and 1991/1992 showed 11.5% and 8.6% growth, respectively. Real GDP (in constant 1982/1983 prices) and GDP per capita, however, were still below those of the 1977/1978 levels. Despite the robust recovery in the early 1990s, and notwithstanding increases in wages within the industrial sector (11.8% and 22.6%, respectively, in 1989/1990 and 1990/1991), wages and salaries lagged far behind the consumer price index across the economy as a whole. In the early 1990s, the attempt was made to reform the exchange rate of Iranian rial *vis-à-vis* the U.S. dollar by devising a set of multiple exchange rates; one (at 70 rials) for government transactions (e.g., oil export revenue, import of essential goods, and payment of foreign debts), another (at 600 rials) for import of intermediate and capital goods, and still another for the remaining transactions, floating according to foreign exchange market. However, once again, the attempt was made to unify all these rates under a managed floating exchange rate regime in 2002.

The lack of direct foreign investment (particularly in 14 anticipated projects within the petrochemical industry) over the span of the First Five-Year Economic Development Plan was one thing, and a fresh round of sanctions imposed by the Clinton administration in 1995 (followed by Iran and Libya Sanctions Act [ILSA] by U.S. Congress in 1996), quite another. On the domestic front, given the stagnating price of oil in the mid-1990s, Rafsanjani's second term was fraught with bulging foreign debt, on the one hand, and staggering domestic borrowing through the Central Bank, on the other. Thus, by the time Rafsanjani left office, the government was well over $16 billion in foreign debt and about 65 trillion rials in debt with respect to domestic obligation.

POLITICAL REFORM AND HIGH EXPECTATION (1997–2004)

Khatami assumed office under conditions that can best be described as economic disarray. Moreover, he had no economic plan or economic vision of his own. Khatami's platform was the reflection of political reform by default, stemming from nationwide mistrust of the rhetoric and reality of Rafsanjani's period. More specifically, in retrospect, this landslide reversal was a spontaneous repercussion induced by the combination of factors, such as further economic polarization, stagnant economy, and a bulging population, which in due course translated into escalating demand for job creation, particularly within the ranks of (youthful) entrants—who make up more than 70% of new applicants each year. Iran's population (just above 70 million) has more than doubled since the establishment of the Islamic Republic. This presents the government with a formidable economic challenge that predictably may have grave political consequences. It would be understatement if unemployment in Iran were defined as youth unemployment, since more than two-thirds of the population is under 30. Here, the sanguine mood and fatalistic attitude of the early years of the new regime—depicted rather aptly by the Persian adage: "He who grants teeth also provides bread"—has led to a lengthy wave of demographic calamity beyond an immediate solution. The upshot of all this can be captured by looking at the annual population growth of 3.9% based on the 1986/1987 census, up 0.44% from the estimated annual growth of 2.7%, just before the fall of the former regime. The Government, however, has departed from the old posture by adopting some measure of population control, the reflection of which can be discerned from much reduced growth rate of 2.7% and 1.4% for 1991/1992 and 2001/2002, respectively.

Rafsanjani's *ad hoc* neoliberal policies had simply come to run into a break wall as the Iranian *rentier* state was sandwiched between the invisible hand of the global oil market and the visible teeth of U.S. economic sanctions. The Second Five-Year Economic Development Plan period (1995/1996–1999/2000) did not fare well until its very end. The rate of economic growth declined precipitously between 1996 and 1997 by 34%. However, a sudden increase in the price of oil allowed the government to repay more than a quarter of its foreign debt and to arrive at a positive trade balance as well as budget surplus at the end of 1999. During Khatami's first term, even though the average inflation rate declined by nearly 45% relative to Rafsanjani's second term, the average unemployment rate increased by a whopping 80%.

According to Article 44 of Iranian Constitution, the economy consists of three primary sectors—state, cooperative, and private—reflecting three complimentary types of ownership side by side. The state sector, however, still holds the lion's share of all three. Nevertheless, the regime's appeal to globalization, in conjunction with the expectation of full membership in the World Trade Organization (WTO), created quite a challenge *vis-à-vis* the Islamic Republic's original vision. Consequently, Article 44 was amended to make room for the privatization of up to 80% of state assets in 2004. This was anticipated in advance in the Third Five Year Economic Development Plan (2000/2001–2004/ 2005). In 2004 the service sector contributed 48% of GDP, with nearly 44% of labor force, while the industrial sector (including construction, manufacturing, and mining) and the agricultural sector made up 42% and 11% of GDP, with 31% and 33% of labor force, respectively. The division among the sectors and their proportional contribution of labor force remained virtually the same in 2006. In short, this by itself is indicative of the dismal state of Iran's agriculture, in which a third of active labor force produces just one-tenth of the total output. Hence there must be a tremendous amount of underemployment in the countryside. The picture becomes gloomier when one adds the lack of self-sufficiency in the production of food, which in turn compelled the government to dip into its uncertain source of hard currency (i.e., oil revenues) for importation of staple food, such as rice, from abroad. Parenthetically, recent importation of gasoline says a lot about the state of industry—particularly the petroleum industry—in Iran. It is noteworthy that the contribution of agriculture to GDP (8.5%) and its relative employment within the economy (32.1%) have changed little since the final days of the Shah's regime in 1977/1978.

POLITICAL UNCERTAINTY AND ECONOMIC STRANGULATION (2005–PRESENT)

The connotation of economic crisis, particularly in developing economies, is downright confusing, if not entirely prone to misapprehension. Aside from textbook (neoclassical) economics, which appears to have no recollection of economic crisis within its lexicon, the rest of the profession has a tendency to define crisis as, more or less, a continuous state of affairs that eventually turns into economic collapse. Yet, the concept of permanent economic crisis is a contradiction in terms. This rather populist, if not pointless, view of economic crisis stands at odds with the real process and genuine meaning of continuity and break, and thus actual *renewal* of circuit of social capital (not to be confused with the neoconservative fallacy of "trust") associated with macroeconomic reproduction. Iran's macroeconomic performance is not, after all, in crisis at this critical juncture, despite the paradoxical policies of state-supported subsidies and the lack of adequate economic diversification, on the one hand, and the petroleum-based *rentier* character—not to be confused with the orthodox view of rent-seeking—of the Iranian state, on the other. Notwithstanding, there are five popular myths, which, *inter alia*, are frequently invoked by the "expert" and the spectator alike with respect to Iranian economy today.

These five myths are (1) Iran's macroeconomic performance is dismal; (2) Iran's actual inflation is twice the official government figures; (3) Iran's poverty is widespread and rising; (4) Iran's actual unemployment rate is twice the official government figures; (5) Iran's oil industry is in a state of breakdown. True, the Iranian economy has serious structural problems and official statistics are approximate figures, which certainly miss the bulk of disguised unemployment (and underemployment), and which undeniably exists in all economies, let alone in a beleaguered (developing) economy like that of Iran. However, with a simple economic argument (and conventional calculation) misleading conclusions are avoided.

First, over the last decade or so, Iran's macroeconomic performance, in both aggregate and growth (5.8%) terms, has been relatively adequate. Thanks to rising oil prices, which have led to soaring magnitude of differential oil rents since the beginning of the century, Iran paid a substantial repayment of its foreign debt and increased its per capita growth in capital formation in the late 1990s. Second, over the last decade and a half, Iran's price index (CPI) should have risen about 950 times if the inflation rate were twice the official rate; CPI, however, tends to display an increase of merely 42 times, thus upholding the official inflation figure of just under 16% for 2006. Third, measures for inequality and poverty are quite different in that the former is expressed by Gini coefficient and the latter by some designated level of poverty threshold. Over the last dozen years, notwithstanding the oil boom of the 2000s, the level of inequality has remained fairly stable at 0.43—well within the average of Iran's U.N.-designated category.

As for poverty, according to a more stringent U.N. estimate (i.e., at 8800 rials or PPP per person per day of $3.60), 20% of Iranians lived below the poverty line in 2003. According to the World Bank, which uses the proportion of individuals who earn under $2 per day, 7.2% of Iran's labor force was below the poverty line in 2005—lower than China, Egypt, India, Malaysia, Mexico, and Turkey. Based upon $2 poverty baseline, poverty in Iran rose steadily with the start of the Iran–Iraq War, gained momentum as a result of the collapse of oil prices in the mid-1980s, and peaked eventually late in the 1980s—with 40% in urban and 47% in rural areas. It began to decline, by nearly 25%, right after the war and recovery of the oil prices until 1993, before increasing once again as a result of external debt crisis in the mid-1990s. From the mid-1990s to the mid-2000s, the poverty rate in Iran declined steadily to 12.7% (the U.N. criterion of $3.3 per person, per day) and 3.3% (the World Bank's criterion of the percentage of the population living on less than $2 a day), respectively. Therefore, the often-quoted CIA figure of 40% for poverty in Iran is not only out of sync with the estimation of major international institutions but also remains suspect as to the agency's motivation.

Fourth, Iran's actual unemployment is scarcely twice the official rate. Iran's unemployment averaged 15.9%, 9.7%, 9.1%, and 16.2% for the intervals of 1981 to 1988, 1989 to 1992, 1993 to 1996, and 1997 to 2000, respectively. It declined from 16.2% to 14.7% in 2002 and then to 11.2% in 2004. These official rates are not significantly different from those of the World Bank. This is apart from the known fact that such estimates, whether official or independent, would not typically lend themselves to calibrate the amount of "discouraged workers" and/or underemployed. And this condition is not unique to Iran alone. Nevertheless, Iran's unemployment is high by any standard, and its future outlook will likely depend upon the annual flood of some 0.7 to 1 million new entrants into the job market, as long as the latent impact of demography will remain intact. In addition to the state's inability to remedy the problem of chronic unemployment, the country's population explosion beginning in the 1960s and the 1970s is also to blame, having swollen the ranks of Iranians of employment age without commensurate rises in the economy's ability to absorb them. This is in spite of a substantial decline in population growth by 62% (from 3.7% to 1.4%) and reduction in fertility rate by 58% (from 6.2% to 2.6%) since the 1980s. The net result still invokes nearly 4% growth for the labor force in Iran. Therefore, even with a sustained annual growth of 5% to 6%, the Iranian economy will be able to create merely a fraction of employment (0.5 million) needed for keeping the demand on an even keel. As a result, while there is no detectable (actual) economic crisis at the present time, the latent potential for such a crisis exists. The day of reckoning, as is known, is not a question of whether but when.

Finally, Iran's oil industry is certainly under heavy stress as a result of U.S. sanctions and the lack of adequate international investment in exploration, development, and timely secondary and/or tertiary recovery of oil from reservoirs. The value of petroleum exports is nearly 25% of GDP and 50% of government budget in 2005. Iran has 40 producing oilfields (27 onshore and 13 offshore), the majority of which are located in the province of Khuzestan in the southwestern part of the country. The majority of Iran's oilfields exhibit a natural decline rate of just under 10% per year. Timing is often a critical factor, since the loss of pressure and prolonged delay may lead to the loss of ultimate recovery. The oil recovery rate in Iran's oilfields is estimated at about 25% as compared to world's average of 35%. Nevertheless, Iran's oil industry is proven to be resilient, as it survived remarkably through eight years of protracted war in the 1980s. With regard to subsidies, the Iranian economy is caught between the horns of a dilemma. On the one hand, government subsidies (particularly food and energy) serve as a political tools in response to political stability, particularly when the government is threatened by hostile powers. On the other hand, economic subsidies set off priorities that are neither compatible with the goal of capital accumulation nor matched by the requirement of global (economic) institutions. Government subsidies are just above $40 billion annually—nearly 40% of Iran's budget in 2006. The subsidized price of gasoline is the cheapest in the world; even with a price hike of 25% that was implemented in May 2007, it costs about $4.50 to fill up a Honda Civic in Tehran today. In the midst of gasoline rationing (about 26 gallons per month) in midsummer 2007, violence erupted and quickly turned to political protest in the capital. Yet the price of gasoline was kept at about $0.42 per gallon. This is only the telling tip of a story that goes beyond the shortage of refining capacity. The whole story pertains to the dilemma of competing investment priorities downstream as opposed to upstream, in the face of burdensome U.S. sanctions against both downstream and upstream investment in Iran's oil and gas industry. Thus, the question of subsidy and importation of gasoline (and/or food) is not separable from the petroleum industry and the economy as a whole.

Foreign direct investment (FDC) in Iran was estimated at $10.2 billion for 2007, compared with $4.2 in 2005. Total FDC has been $24 billion since 1993. Iran has had an observer status in the World Trade Organization (WTO) since 2005. According to the U.N., Iran is classified as a semi-developed country. In the meantime, the Fourth Five-Year Economic Development Plan (2005/2006–2009/2010) aims at expanding Iran's economic connections with the global economy, in trade as well as in foreign direct investment, despite constant pressure of political isolation, blatant threat of "regime change," and, more importantly, deliberate economic strangulation engineered by the Bush–Cheney administration. This plan, cobbled together toward the end of Khatami's second term, in essence reflects the pragmatic, yet deeply guarded perspectives of the ruling authorities in the Islamic Republic of Iran.

See also Economy, Empirical Assessment of; Economy, Historical Background of; Economy, Informal Sector; and Economy, Private Sector.

Suggested Reading

Alizadeh, P. 2001. *The economy of Iran: the dilemma of an Islamic state* (Ed.). London: I.B. Tauris.

Amirahmadi, H. 1988. War damage and reconstruction in the Islamic Republic of Iran. In *Post-Revolutionary Iran*, eds. H. Amirahmadi, and M. Parvin. Boulder, Co: Westview; 126–149.

Amuzegar, J. 1997. *Iran's economy under the Islamic Republic*, Revised Edition. London: I.B. Tauris.

Assadzadeh, A., and S. Paul. 2004. Poverty, growth, and redistribution: a study of Iran. *Review of Development Economics.* Vol 8.

Bina, C. 1992. Global oil and the oil policies of the Islamic Republic. In *Modern capitalism and Islamic ideology in Iran*, eds. C. Bina and H. Zangeneh. London: Macmillan; 121–158.

Bina, C. 1996. Review of *Freezing assets: The USA and the most effective economic sanction. Iranian Studies*. Vol 29.

Bina, C. 1999. The hot summer of defiance: the student protests for freedom and democracy in Iran. *Journal of Iranian Research and Analysis*. Vol 15.

Bina, C., and B. Yaghmaian. 1988. Import substitution and export promotion within the context of the internationalization of capital. *Review of Radical Political Economics*. Vol 20.

Bina, C., and B. Yaghmaian. 1991. Postwar global accumulation and the transnationalization of capital. *Capital & Class*. No. 43.

Bina, C., and H. Zangeneh, eds. 1992. *Modern capitalism and Islamic ideology in Iran*. London: Macmillan.

Farahbakhsh, A. 2001. "Iranian economy in six snapshots," *Payam-e Emruz (An Economic, Social, and Cultural Monthly)*. No. 23.

Fesharaki, F. 1985. Iran's petroleum policy: how does the oil industry function in revolutionary Iran" in Afshar, H., ed., *A revolution in turmoil*. Albany, NY: SUNY Press; 99–117.

Mahdavy, H. 1970. The patterns and problems of economic development in rentier states: the case of Iran," in Cooke, M. A., ed., *Studies in the Economic History of the Middle East*. London: Oxford University Press; 428–467.

Nomani, F., and S. Behdad. 2006. *Class and labor in Iran: did the revolution matter?* Syracuse, NY: Syracuse University Press.

Pesaran, M. H. 1992. The Iranian foreign exchange policy and the black market for dollars. *International Journal of Middle East Studies*. Vol 24.

Pesaran, M. H. 2000. Economic trends and macroeconomic policies in post-revolutionary Iran, in Alizadeh, P., ed., *The economy of Iran: the dilemmas of an Islamic state*. London: I. B. Tauris; 63–100.

Salehi-Isfahani, D. 2006. Revolution and redistribution in Iran: poverty and inequality 25 years later. Paper, Department of Economics, Virginia Tech.

Zangeneh, H. 1989. Islamic banking: theory and practice in Iran. *Comparative Economic Studies*. 67–84.

Zangeneh, H. 1994. *Islam, Iran, and world stability*. New York: St. Martin's.

CYRUS BINA

✦ EDUCATIONAL SYSTEM

Since the revolution in 1979, the Iranian system of education has improved noticeably in terms of such quantitative factors as literacy rates and the number of students in the system. Nevertheless, the fundamental tenets and characteristics of the education system have not changed: state control, a significant gap between resources and demands, and an everlasting quest to

Chess champion Atusa Pourkashian, center, in the seventh grade, listening with classmates to teacher, 2000. (AP Photo/Hasan Sarbakhshian)

balance tradition and modernity. The secular modernization of the Shah's era has been replaced by the centralized Islamization policies of the Islamic Republic of Iran.

FORMAL PRE-UNIVERSITY EDUCATION

As of 2006, there were 15 million students (out of a total population of 75 million people) in 150,000 segregated schools with one million teachers. The pre-university system is still based on the French model: one year of pre-primary education at the age of five, five years of primary from ages 6 to 11 (compulsory under Article 30 of the Constitution), three years of lower-secondary (Guidance) from 11 to 14, three years of upper-secondary from 14 to 17, followed by one pre-university year for those interested in a university education. Farsi is the only language of instruction at all levels and for all ethnicities. The official length of the academic year for pre-university education is ten months, usually running from September to June. The grading system is out of 20.

The Ministry of Education controls and standardizes the textbooks for all levels. The five years of primary education follow a general curriculum, covering the Persian language, study of the Qur'an, natural science, mathematics, arts, social studies, and physical and health education. A national entrance exam after grade five marks the transition to the next level. The lower-secondary program (28 hours per week) covers new topics, such as foreign and Arabic languages, history, geography, and defense preparation. Religious minority groups such as Sunnis, Christians, Jews, and Zoroastrians have their own courses for religious training. The fundamental objective of the lower-secondary program is to offer a broader and relatively deeper knowledge of subjects, in order to prepare students for their choice of specialization disciplines at upper-secondary level (*Dabirestan*).

Upper-secondary education has both an academic stream and a vocational and technical studies stream. On the basis of their tested capacities and interests, students in the academic stream choose a field of specialization from mathematics and physics, empirical sciences, social sciences, and economics. Out of the required 99 units, 36 are taken in the area of specialization and the rest in general studies. The high school certificate is awarded following an examination that is administered nationally *(diplome motawasseteh)*. The year of pre-university studies is to prepare students for the huge annual National Entrance Exam (*konkoor*), for which there are usually 2.5 million candidates. Male candidates who fail the National Entrance Exam are required to enter military service.

Students in vocational and technical schools (VTS, *madaarese fanni herfei*) may take a five-year program after the lower-secondary level, which leads to an integrated associated degree. They can opt for the pre-university preparatory year after three years. VTS students number 900,000 in 115 schools, including technical, business, agriculture, and other professional programs.

According to governmental statistics, the pupil:teacher ratio is 20.5 at the primary level, 31 at the lower-secondary level, and 22 at the upper-secondary level. There are 13,177 non-public, non-profit schools for which the curriculum and textbooks are controlled by the Ministry of Education.

Teachers for the primary and lower-secondary levels receive two years' training in teachers' training centres (*Daneshsaraye rahnamai*). Upper-secondary school teachers are selected through a national entrance examination. Their four-year training program leads to a bachelor's degree from specific universities called *Tarbiat Moallem* (University for Teacher Education).

Adult and Non-Formal Education

Non-formal adult education is conducted primarily by the Literacy Movement Organization (LMO, *Sazemane nehzate savad amoozi*), which was founded in 1984 to deal with the enormous rate of illiteracy among the Iranian population. The LMO's main objectives are to provide education to adults, to adapt textbooks in line with religious and political values, and to train committed teachers. In 1994 and 1995, 89% of the enrollment included adults with an average age of 29 years, thanks to the universalization of formal mandatory education for children. Literacy in Iran rose from 45% before the revolution to 85.2% in 2005. The adult literacy rate among females is 82.6% and 87.7% among males.

HIGHER EDUCATION

Higher education in Iran is mostly state-run, with 54 universities under the supervision of the Ministry of Sciences, Research, and Technology (MSRT); 42 state medical schools under the administration of the Ministry of Health, Treatment, and Medical Education (MHTME); 60 post-secondary technical institutions; and approximately 200 colleges, institutes of higher learning, and professional schools. Admission to free public universities is conditional on passing the extremely difficult National Entrance Examination. Very limited admission capacity and preferential treatment for veterans and soldiers are among factors that explain why high marks do not guarantee admission and why the rate of "brain drain" is high.

Given the historical political activism of students in Iran and their involvement in different protest movements, the Islamic government strictly controls the administration of universities through laws, policies, and institutions. From April 1980 to the fall of 1983, 200 institutions of higher education were shut down temporarily following the Cultural Revolution, by command of the Higher Council of Cultural Revolution (HCCR). The objective was to restructure the academic content of the curriculum in order to implement the Islamization of knowledge and to erase the impact of westernization and secularization. Some of the most obvious changes were the imposition of *hijab*, creation of Islamic Associations of Students in each university, and sweeping changes in the content of curriculum and manuals. Admission to university programs became subject to ideological and moral screening by state authorities.

Currently, control over programs, nominations, and administration is exercised through various ministries (MSRT, MHTME, Ministry of Education), Bureaus of the Representation of the Leader of Revolution, and the powerful HCCR. Members of the latter are appointed by the Leader of the Revolution. HCCR has extensive strategic, administrative, and political powers and appoints the trustee boards of the universities.

As in Western universities, degrees in higher education have four stages: Associate's degree (*Kardani*) after two years, Bachelor's degree (*Karshenassi*) after four years, Master's degree (*karshenasi arshad*) after two additional years, and doctorate after four additional years. Additional entrance exams are required to pass from Bachelor to Master programs or from Master to Ph.D.

Distance learning (*Payame Noor*, Message of the Light) was established in 1987 and offers higher education programs in 147 centers throughout Iran under the supervision of MSRT. These programs, lasting between five and eight years, cover various fields, such as mathematics and Persian literature, and award Associate's or Bachelor's degrees. They target graduates of high school or participants in continuing education programs. In 1998, 33,418 students (including 19,444 women) were admitted to distance learning in 18 academic disciplines.

The non-public sector of higher education is well-developed in Iran. There are generally two sectors of non-public higher education programs: *Daneshgahe azad eslami* (Free Islamic University, FIU) and private, non-profit universities and institutes of higher education. FIU, founded in 1982, is the first non-public network of higher education and now covers 110 cities throughout the country. It has an annual national entrance examination. There are 34 other non-profit universities and institutes of higher education, such as *Daaneshgaahe Imam sadegh* (University of Imam Sadegh) and *Daneshgahe Mofid* (Mofid University), with a total enrollment of 16,091. Both of these universities, and others of the kind, combine religious and secular topics in an integrated program of Bachelor, M.Sc., or Ph.D. degrees. They have close links to the *Hawzeh elmyyeh* (well-known religious schools in Iran that have historically trained the clerical classes).

In 2005, a total of 2,117,471 students were enrolled in a public or private university, 975,361 of them in public institutions.

In the 1990s, there was a significant increase in the number of students sent abroad for postgraduate study: 3,000 over the period, a 100% increase from the 1980s, when few Iranians could leave the country. The United States, Canada, the United Kingdom, France, and Germany are among the most prevalent destinations.

The key governmental agencies and institutions controlling research and education are the Ministry of Education and the Higher Council of Education (both involved with the pre-university system), the Ministry of Sciences, Research, and Technology (known before 2000 as the Ministry of Culture and Higher Education), the Ministry of Health, Treatment, and Medical Education, the National Council for Scientific and Industrial Research, the Institution for Research and Planning in Higher Education, the Technical and Vocational Training Organization of the Ministry of Labour and Social Affairs, and the Literacy Movement Organization.

Although university professors may be graduates from national or international universities, a *Daneshggahe Tarbiate Modarres* (Professor Training University) was founded after the revolution in the 1980s to train university teachers with academic, moral, and revolutionary commitments.

Despite the fact that half of total university enrollments are in the Engineering and Exact Sciences (in both public and private universities), the Minister of Science, Research, and Technology deplored the state of advanced research in Iran, citing as factors the living conditions of professors, a lack of dynamism in universities, low optimization of information and communication technologies, low investment in scientific development, and the lack of organic development between industries, universities, and financial sectors (partly due to the purely theoretical orientation of many university programs). A U.N. report confirms this diagnosis for 1996, when the percentage of scientists was 0.7 per 1,000 habitants and only 0.48% of GNP was spent on research and development.

The Iranian education system, despite imposing restriction on movements and dress for girls, made impressive progress in female education, with girls constituting 49% of the total student population in the 1990s. In 2000, the rate of enrollment for girls was 97.8% at the primary level, 90.3% at the lower-secondary level, and 69.1% at the upper-secondary level.

A source of concern for the IRI system of education is the balance between quantitative growth and qualitative development. The total number of students at all levels of the pre-university education system is 18 million. It is a demanding task to meet the high demand for education at all levels without sacrificing quality. The growing cost of living pushes teachers to take on extra teaching loads (or diversify their jobs), and a great many high school and university graduates suffer from underemployment. The tension between Western values of education and Islamic values and institutions also makes it challenging to form and educate critical minds and to conduct research and empirical investigation.

Although it is difficult to present a definitive assessment of the post-revolutionary Iranian education system, there are reasons for optimism: the high rate of female education at all levels, the expansion of undergraduate and postgraduate programs, the generalized use of the Internet in universities, and increasing cooperation between the public and private sectors in R&D. It is too early to predict with any precision what trends may develop from current changes.

Suggested Reading

Aziz-zadeh, H. 1994. Iran: system of education. *The International Encyclopedia of Education*. Atlanta: Pergamon Press; 3007–3011.

Bazargan, A. 2000. Internal evaluation as an approach to revitalize university systems: the case of the Islamic Republic of Iran. *Higher Education Policy*. Atlanta: Elsevier Press; 173–180.

Mehralizadeh, Y. 2005. New reforms in the management of the university: transition from centralized to decentralized (university-based management) in Iran. *Higher Education Policy*. Hampshire, UK: Palgrave; 67–82.

Mehran, G. 2003. The paradox of tradition and modernity in female education in the Islamic Republic of Iran. *Comparative Education Review*. Chicago: University of Chicago Press; 269–286.

Mehran, G. 2003. Khatami, political reform and education in Iran. *Comparative Education*. 311–329.

Peckham, J. Jr. 2001. Iran. *World Education Encyclopedia: A Survey of Educational Systems World Wide*. New York: Gael Group & Thomson Learning; 616–625.

Shavarini, M. K. 2006. Wearing the veil to college: the paradox of higher education in the lives of Iranian women. *International Journal of Middle East Studies*. New York: Cambridge University Press; 189–211.

Torbat, A. E. 2002. The brain drain from Iran to the United States. *Middle East Journal*. 272–295.

UNESCO. Education system at the end of the twentieth century in the I.R of Iran. http://www.ibe.unesco.org/International/Ice/natrap/Iran_1.pdf.

ALI DIZBONI

✦ ELECTIONS

Elections in the Islamic Republic of Iran (IRI) are defined differently than in truly democratic societies. In the IRI, elections are legally controlled by the clerical ruling power via two mechanisms. First, the Guardian Council is authorized to screen the candidates before allowing them into a race. (The Guardian Council is composed of six clerics appointed by the supreme leader and six lawyers proposed by the judiciary chief and approved by the Majlis. However, only the clerics have authority to judge and interpret if a law is un-Islamic.) For example, opponents of the *Velayat-e Faqih* (clerical rule) are banned from elections as being unfit to hold office in the Islamic system. Second, all elected officials, including the president, are in a subordinate position to the supreme leader (the *walayat al-'amr* and the leader of the Ummah), who enjoys absolute power in the system. Therefore, elected officials have to obey the supreme leader's commands rather than representing the interests of their constituencies if there is a conflict between the two. According to the Article 57 of the Constitution of the IRI, "The powers of government in the Islamic Republic are vested in the legislature, the judiciary, and the executive powers, functioning under the supervision of the absolute walayat al-'amr and the leadership of the Ummah…." (The Constitution of the Islamic Republic of Iran, modified version in 1967.)

Iranian President Mohammad Khatami at the opening ceremony of Iran's Masjid-Suleiman dam, in Khuzestan province, 2001. (AP Photo/Hasan Sarbakhshian)

Normally, appointed individuals enjoy greater power than elected officials. For example, the legislative branch, which consists of 290 elected members, holds no legal status unless there is a (mainly appointed) Guardian Council (GC). According to Article 93 of the Constitution, "The Islamic Consultative Assembly does not hold any legal status if there is no Guardian Council in existence, except for the purpose of approving the credentials of its members and the election of the six jurists on the Guardian Council." The legislative assembly is deliberately named the "Consultative Assembly" because, in the IRI, this organ cannot make laws without the GC's approval. The GC can vote any law passed by the legislative branch as unconstitutional or un-Islamic. Such an order is articulated based on Ayatollah Ruhollah Khomeini's doctrine of *Velayat-e Faqih*, or Islamic Government.

Khomeini, founder of the IRI, believed that elections should not undermine clerical rule. He wrote that the people must accept the rule of the clerics and follow their decisions as religious duties (see Article 1 of the Constitution). More precisely, the notion of *Velayat-e Faqih* originated in the writings of several Shi'a jurists such as Mulla Ahmad Naraqi, who used the idea to legitimize the absolute rule of Fatali Shah Qajar, and Sheikh Fazlollah Nouri, who strongly opposed constitutional rule (1906) as an anti-religious measure in Iran. Other predecessors of Khomeini include Mirza Hasan Shirazi, Mirza Muhammad Taqi Shriazi, and Kashif al-Ghita.

In his book, *Islamic Government,* Khomeini asserted that "the ulema [clerics] were appointed by the imam for government and for judgment among people, and their position is still preserved for them ... Ulema [plural of 'alim] are the heirs to the prophets ... If knowledgeable and just jurisprudent undertakes the task of forming the government, then he will run the social affairs that the prophet used to run, and it is the duty of the people to listen to him and obey him."

The role of the Guardian Council in elections is very crucial in the IRI. According to Article 99 of the Constitution, the GC has the responsibility of supervising the elections and the direct recourse to popular opinion and referenda. However, referring to Article 98, which gives the right of interpreting the laws to the GC, it has been developed into an unquestionable political tool for keeping the entire electoral system under the control of the conservative clerical rule.

The religious minorities of Zoroastrianism, Christianity, and Judaism are recognized as true religions in Iran, and their adherents have certain rights, including electing their own representatives to the Majlis. Article 64 of the Constitution specifies that "the Zoroastrians and Jews will each elect one representative; Assyrian and Chaldean Christians will jointly elect one representative; and Armenian Christians in the north and those in the south of the country will each elect one representative."

Women are now allowed to participate in the election of the Majlis and the City and Town Councils, but they have been prohibited from running for the presidency and the Assembly of Experts. The percentage of women in the Majlis has varied in different terms between 3% and 5%, but regardless of their numbers, women in most cases have followed the political line of their affiliations rather than showing concern for women's interests. The dominant view toward women in the election process has been tokenism—they can run for office and be elected, but they are not empowered.

Within the above-stated rationale and restrictions, however, elections for the Islamic Consultative Assembly, the President, and the Assembly of Experts have been routinely held in the IRI since the 1979 revolution. A few special elections (referendums) have also been held. Elections for the City and Town Councils, though specified in the Constitution, were delayed until 1999, but since then they have also been held as scheduled.

The first special election (referendum) was held on March 30–31, 1979, to decide the type of regime after the downfall of Monarchism. Voters had one option to choose: the Islamic Republic of Iran, yes or no. The turnout in this referendum was very high, so that 20,440,108 people, or 98.2% of eligible citizens, voted in favor of the IRI.

The second special election was held on August 3, 1979, to elect members of the special Assembly of Experts (AE) to review the draft of the constitutional law. There were a total of 428 candidates for 73 seats. This assembly was held instead of a Constitutional Assembly. In this election 10,784,922 people, or 51.71% of the eligible people, participated in the election.

The third special election (referendum) was held from December 1–3, 1979, to vote for the final draft of the Constitution. In this referendum, 15,690,142 eligible people or 70.42% participated to approve the Constitution. However, it is not clear what percentage of the participants voted in favor of the proposed Constitutional Law.

The first presidential election was held on January 25, 1980, during a period when the national mood was revolutionary. Out of 20,993,643 eligible voters, 14,152,887, or 67.42%, voted; and out of 124 candidates, Abol Hasan Bani Sadr was elected as the first president of the IRI. Bani Sadr was forced to flee into exile in France after two years in office in the midst of the Iran–Iraq War as the conflict between the hardliners (supported by Khomeini) and moderate factions increased.

After the elimination of the "moderate faction," consensus among leaders behind the scenes became both more common and more important than elections in choosing the president. Usually, the various factions would reach agreement on who would be the main candidate, then a few other candidates would accept invitations to enter the race to make the election look real and to pull more people to the ballot boxes.

The first legislative election, the election for the first "Islamic Consultative Assembly" or the Majlis, took place on March 14, 1980. A total of 10,875,969 people or 52.14% of eligible voters turned out to elect 270 parliament members out of 3,694 candidates. The first assembly was rather diverse and included some moderate (liberal) members. Ali Akbar Hashemi Rafsanjani, a close adviser to the Ayatollah Khomeini, was elected as the Speaker of the House.

The second presidential election was held on July 24, 1981. In this election 14,572,803 people, or 64.24% of eligible voters, participated, and Mohammad Ali Rajaei, a conservative hardliner, was elected to the presidency during societal tension, with opponents, particularly the Mojahedeen, supporting Bani Sadr. Rajaei and his prime minister Bahonar, a clergyman, were assassinated two months after the election, and thus Iran entered into its third presidential election in less than three years after the revolution.

The third presidential election took place on October 2, 1981. In this election, 16,847,717 people, or 74.26% of the eligible voters, participated, and

Ayatollah Seyyed Ali Khamenei was elected as the new president with Hussein Mousavi elected by the Majlis as the Prime Minister. This was in the midst of the Iran–Iraq War, and the situation was still revolutionary. President Khamenei represented the conservative Right, and Mousavi was associated with the Hezbollah (the Left).

On December 10, 1982, the first election for the Assembly of Experts (AE) was held, with 18,013,061 people, or 77.38% of the eligible voters, participating to elect 82 assembly members. For every seat, there were only two carefully screened candidates, and all candidates were clergymen.

The second legislative election was held on April 15, 1984. In this election, in which 24,143,498 people, or 64.64% of the eligible voters, participated, 270 Majlis deputies were elected. There were 1,592 candidates in the race, and after the election the second Majlis was dominated by the radical Left, known as Hezbollah. Ali Akbar Hashemi Rafsanjani, who appealed to both the Left and Right factions, was reelected as the Speaker of the House.

The fourth presidential election was held on August 11, 1985, and, as expected, Ali Khamenei was reelected as the fourth president, although he drew 10% fewer voters to ballot boxes this time. A total of 14,238,087 eligible voters, or 54.78%, participated in the 1985 election. Although there were 50 candidates, as in his first term a consensus was reached among political factions over Khamenei's presidency.

The third legislative election was held on April 8, 1988. A total of 16,714,281 people, or 59.72% of eligible voters, cast their votes. A total of 1,999 candidates entered the race for 270 seats in the Majlis. Mehdi Karoubi, then a radical Left clergyman, was elected as the Speaker of the House.

A Referendum for the draft of the new Constitutional Law was also held on the day of the fifth presidential election on July 28, 1989. Official figures show that almost every voter who participated in the presidential election, or 54.51% of eligible voters, also voted in the referendum that ratified the new Constitution. The initial Constitution was modified to a more conservative one that solidified the power of the supreme leader as *absolute authority*, which had been established before the death of Khomeini. Khomeini knew that after his death there would be no single person powerful enough to control all of the factions and secure the stability of the system, and so it was necessary to empower the position of the supreme leader through a legal mechanism. To Khomeini, nothing was more important than the existence of the IRI. He appointed 20 prominent figures from different factions, mainly conservative clerics, to redraw the new Constitution. Another major change in the new Constitution was to remove the position of the prime minister and strengthen the power of the president as the head of executive branch.

Ayatollah Khomeini, the unquestionable supreme leader, died on June 3, 1989. After a brief internal dispute over his successor, the Assembly of Experts elected Ayatollah Ali Khamenei, the president at the time, as the new supreme leader. After the death of Khomeini, traditional conservative clerics gained a stronger position.

The fifth presidential election was held on July 28, 1989, and Ali Akbar Hashemi Rafsanjani, the former Speaker of the House, was elected as the new president. The election was held after the war had ended, and so the new government's principal mission was the reconstruction of society. A total of 16,452 277 (54.59%) of the eligible voters participated in the election. As in previous presidential elections, there was no serious contender, and consensus over Rafsanjani's presidency had been reached among the factions before the election was held. Rafsanjani invited both the Left and the Right to participate in his cabinet, but the Right prevailed.

The election for the second Assembly of Experts was held October 8, 1990. This election had the lowest turnout in the history of the IRI, with only 11,202,613 people, or 37.09% of the eligible voters, participating. In this election, 180 clergymen competed for 83 seats. The society had become indifferent to the election of the AE, in which the campaign competition was not serious. The only known function of this assembly is to reaffirm the leadership of the supreme leader at its annual meeting.

The fourth legislative election took place on April 10, 1992. A total of 18,796,787 people, or 57.81% of eligible voters, participated in this election, in which 3,233 candidates competed for 270 seats. Ali Akbar Rafsanjani, the president, was shifting from a more radical political player to a more pragmatic leader. He realized that the IRI could not continue to function without some changes in both social and economic institutions, but the real changes were left to be done in his second term. The supporters of Rafsanjani, the moderates, held only thirty seats in the fourth Majlis. While the Right had 150 seats, the radical Left and radical Right each had 15 seats, and the rest were either swinging or independent votes.

The sixth presidential election was held on June 11, 1993. The situation was different at this election as Rafsanjani took a moderate position. Ahmad Tavakoli, the candidate of the Right, entered the race to challenge him. Even thought Tavakovi drew 24.3% of the votes, Rafsanjani was still at the peak of his power and the whole system favored him. As expected, he won the election with 62% of the votes. The turnout in this election was rather low—a total of 16,796,787, or 50.66% of the eligible voters, participated. More real social and economic reforms, such as privatization of the economy and more social openness, were on Rafsanjani's agenda in his second term.

Consequently, the state grip on society decreased. Expatriates were encouraged to return to Iran and invest in the economy, and the ruling conservatives used their influence in promoting the privatization of the economy and paid less attention to the consequences of the social reforms Rafsanjani was trying to institute. With these changes, the radical and ideological factions (Left and Right) lost more base supporters because the radical Left and Right were against both privatization and social reforms.

The fifth legislative election was held on March 8, 1996, with a total of 24,682,386 or 71.10% of the eligible voters participating. Competition in this election was high among two main factions—the conservative pro-market economy (about 130 seats) and the pragmatist pro-market economy (about 100 seats). Both the radical Left and radical Right lost their positions of influence and were reduced to about 15 seats each. This election showed the trend of the future—the traditional conservative groups kept their majority in the Majlis, and Ali Akbar Nateq Nouri remained the speaker of the house. Nateq Nouri, a clergyman, represented the bazaar interests and the conservative/traditional clerics. Some individuals, such as Faezeh Rafsanjani, the daughter of the president, who entered the race with reform agendas, were elected by large majorities. Thus, the fifth Majlis became the springboard for the reformists to gain a strong majority for the next presidential election and the sixth Majlis, which became known as the government and Majlis of reforms.

The seventh presidential election of 1997 became a turning point in the history of the IRI. Internal consensus was lost following a disagreement over Rafsanjani's running for a third term. At the end of his second term, he tried to change the constitutional law so that he could run for a third term, but this effort was strongly opposed by the rival conservative group, including Khamenei, who wanted Nateq Nouri to become the next president. Therefore, the election entered into a real competition between the pro- and anti-reform factions, with the radical Right joining conservatives in opposing Rafsanjani. Sensing the mood of society, Rafsanjani joined his former rival groups of the radical Left, forming a reform coalition to oppose the conservatives. The radical Left had fundamentally changed after defeats in several elections, and the new coalition chose Seyyed Mohammad Khatami, a former cabinet member in Rafsanjani's government who had resigned from his post because of objections to government policies. Khatami at the time had been sitting aside, working in a non-political position as the head of the national library.

Khatami was hesitant to accept the nomination, because the ruling system and the supreme leader wanted Nateq Nouri to be the president. Khatami met with the supreme leader and received affirmation to run and his assurance that he was not going to dismiss him if elected.

The people were fed up with the regime and wanted real change. Realizing this fact, the Leftist reform coalition promised drastic change, including rule of law, democratization of the system, free press, and formation of civil society. Up to a week before the election, no one could have predicted victory of Khatami. The conservative faction had great confidence in their ability to win, but they did not recognize the new mood of society. While they continued to stick to the revolutionary slogans, the reform coalition proposed change, which was exactly what the people wanted.

The turnout was the highest in history of the IRI. A total of 29,145,754 people, or 79.93% of the eligible voters participated in the election, and Khatami achieved a landslide victory. Out of every four votes, three were cast for Khatami. Young people and women particularly played determining roles in the election—the youth could not relate themselves to the revolution, and women, who were under the severe pressures of restrictive Islamic laws, welcomed Khatami's promised reforms. This election set a landmark in the modern history of Iran, and the date of the election, the second of Khordad (May 23, 1997), is still associated with reforms and reformists.

The third election of the Assembly of Experts was held in the second year of Khatami's presidency, on October 23, 1998. After the victory of the reform coalition in the presidential election, two factors were playing roles in the political atmosphere of Iran. First, the mood of society was positively in favor of the reformists, and second the conservatives badly lost their confidence. While the radical Left joined the reform coalition and won both the executive and legislative branches, the radical Right went underground and formed a shadow government that began terrorizing society by murdering several prominent political figures and pro-reform writers, known as "chain murders," and published a list of 160 other poets, writers, and political opponents to be murdered soon as enemies of Islam. Khatami stopped them as they were acting within the Intelligence and Information Ministry. The minister Dori Najafabadi, a prominent clergyman, was dismissed, while a group of 19 others, including the vice minister Saeed Imami, were arrested. Imami committed suicide while in jail, and his wife was tortured to confess that she was an agent of Israel.

The reformists needed to win a majority of the seats in the AE to be able to implement their promised reforms. Khatami, however, did not realize this. Instead, he urged the electorate to actively take part in the elections, although he himself did little to ensure the victory of reformist candidates to the body. The conservative right was thus assured of an electoral victory, which it got. In turn, the new AE set out to undermine the reform efforts of the presidents and the larger reform movement, which soon began to grind to a halt.

Despite the reformists' best efforts at voter mobilization, voter turnout was low, with only a total of 17,807,869, or 46.32% of the eligible voters participating. This meant that more than 50% of the supporters of the reforms ignored Khatami's request and did not participate in the election. The reformists could have used this opportunity to trade their votes for better positions in the AE, but unfortunately they did not. By this time, the Guardian Council no longer had its absolute power to limit the number of candidates, and so, unlike the previous election in which the GC had allowed only 180 candidates to enter the race, 396 candidates were allowed to compete for 86 seats. Out of the total, fifteen reformist candidates, mainly lower-rank clergymen, succeeded in entering the AE, and these elected reformist clergymen were among the conservative reformists whose ultimate goal was to retain a more genuine Islamic regime, not to change it into a democratic system.

The first election of the City and Town Councils (CTCs), 20 years after the 1979 revolution in 1999, could be considered one of the achievements of the reformists and a showdown for true elections without the interference of the Guardian Council. City and Town Councils were considered in the Constitutional Law as local authorities, but elections were not held because they represented a potential challenge to the very centralized political system in the IRI. Regarding the CTCs, Article 100 of the Constitution reads as follows:

> In order to expedite social, economic, development, public health, cultural, and educational programs and facilitate other affairs relating to public welfare with the cooperation of the people according to local needs, the administration of each village, division, city, municipality, and province will be supervised by a council to be named the Village, Division, City, Municipality, or Provincial Council. Members of each of these councils will be elected by the people of the locality in question.

The first elections for the CTCs were held on February 26, 1999. A total of 23,668,739 people, or 64.42% of eligible voters, in 65,277 cities, 450 suburban areas, and 270,411 villages participated in these elections. These were the first democratically held elections in the 28 year history of the IRI, and most of the elected officials favored reforms.

The sixth legislative election was held on February 18, 2000, one year after the landslide victory of the reformist candidates in the CTCs and while the executive branch was still moving toward political reforms and social openness. The turnout in the election was also high, with 26,082,157 people, or 64.42% of the eligible voters, participating. For the first time, the number of members in the legislative branch increased from 270 to 290 because the size of the population was now 50% higher than at the beginning of the revolution. According to Article 64 of the Constitution, every ten years 20 members should be added to the total number of members in the legislative branch.

The reformists achieved a huge victory in the 2000 legislative elections. Two-thirds of the elected members were from the reformist coalition; however, only about 100 of these deputies were supportive of a genuine reform of the IRI. The reformists still had no unified definition of reforms and no clear strategy to achieve their objectives. Many of these deputies used the coalition to win and did not truly believe in reforms.

The first action of the Majlis to pass a new law in support of a free press was stopped by a direct order of Khamenei, the supreme leader. This was the first open confrontation between the conservative faction and the reformists. Thereafter, the GC halted almost any reform law passed by the Majlis as being non-Islamic. Even though the conservatives had lost both the executive and legislative branches, and along with them the hearts and minds of the people, constitutionally they still had the upper hand. The supreme leader enjoys absolute power and appoints his allies to key military, judiciary, and security positions.

The sixth Majlis, known as the reform Majlis, ended in a month of sit-ins in protest by 120 reform deputies inside the building after the GC rejected the applications of 80 Majlis deputies for the upcoming election as being "unfit." At this time, Ms. Fatemeh Haghighatjoo, one of the youngest members of the parliament, resigned in protest.

The eighth presidential election was held on June 8, 2001. Several factors need to be considered in this election. First, the conservatives were not yet regrouped to take over the executive branch from the reformists. Second, Khatami was still popular despite his inability to move on the promised reform measures in his first term. Third, supporters of the reforms had no alternative, as the reformists were a coalition rather than solid political parties, and Khatami was the center of this coalition. All things considered, Khatami remained the main candidate of the eighth presidential election. Khatami himself was hesitant to run because he felt he was unable to meet the demands of his supporters.

In the 2001 presidential election, participation dropped 13% compared with Khatami's first term election. Overall, 28,081,930 people, or 66.59% of eligible voters cast their votes, and Khatami won the election with more than 70% of the votes. His second term did not witness any significant reforms but instead was characterized by frustration and disappointments. This was part of the conservatives' strategy—to prove that the reformists were not capable of fulfilling their promises. Lack of achievement decreased popular support for the reformists, and consequently their sense of solidarity was lost.

During his second term, Khatami gradually learned that his reform platform contradicted the existing religiously dominated system. He had to choose between the promised democracy and the existing theocracy. He was not mentally and intellectually ready for such a radical change, and the system was not structurally prepared to accept such transformation easily. Khatami was also not a man of confrontation. Thus, he chose to keep the Islamic system almost unchanged and gradually moved away from his initial plan. He ended his second term with no significant legacy.

The second election of the City and Town Councils was held in 2003 when the reform supporters were deeply upset with the reformist leaders, and this mood was reflected in the election results, which turned another page of Iranian modern history backward. This time, unlike in the first CTC election, disillusioned supporters of the reformists remained indifferent, which allowed the newly constituted conservative groups, named *Osoulgarayan*, that were centered on the radical Right and affiliated with the Revolutionary Guard and war veterans, to win the elections in major cities such as Tehran. The 15 conservative members of the city council in Tehran were elected with only 12% of the votes. The new city council selected Mahmood Ahmadinejad, a radical Right wing member, as the Mayor of Tehran and thus opened the path for him to the presidency. A total of 20,230,898 people, or 49.2% of the eligible voters in 33,774 cities, 138 suburb areas, and 185,045 villages participated in the election.

The seventh legislative election in 2004 was held in an entirely different political atmosphere. The conservative faction of the IRI was now on the offensive. Because the major candidates of the reformists, including 80 members of the sixth Majlis, were prevented from entering the race as "unfits," supporters of the reformists had even less reason to participate in the election, which allowed the conservatives to dominate. Supporters of the conservatives were also ideologically motivated to participate in the election. A total of 23,734,677 people, or 51.21% of the eligible voters, chose to send more than 250 conservative and radical Right candidates to the Majlis. In some cities, two conservative candidates were competing with each other. Many people, especially supporters of the conservatives, felt socially and religiously compelled to participate in the election to protect what they perceived as the correct historical trajectory of the revolution. Through the system of screening the reformist candidates, the conservatives won a great majority in the seventh Majlis. Moderate and conservative reformists who were allowed to run won only 40 seats. The conservatives' victory in the Majlis prepared the road for the radical Right to win the next presidency.

The ninth presidential election in 2005 was held when both the conservatives and reformists had lost their unity and consensus. The conservative

Right (represented by Ali Larijani) faced the radical Right (represented by Ahmadinejad) on one side, and a moderate reformist, Dr. Mustafa Moein, faced conservative reformists such as Mehdi Karoubi on the other side, with pragmatists such as Rafsanjani staying in the center. Despite many attempts, neither conservatives nor reformists could come up with one candidate, and so, for the first time, the presidential election was held with several serious candidates. Consequently, the election went into a second round because no candidate won 50% of the votes. The victory by Ahmadinejad in the first round surprised everyone, including the conservatives such as the supreme leader, who favored Ali Larijani. Yet, Khamenei had no choice but to rally behind Ahmadinejad. The reformists, whose candidate did not advance to the second round, eventually decided to support the pragmatists' candidate, Rafsanjani, to face Ahmadinejad in the second round. Once again, coalitions of conservatives and reformist/pragmatists faced each other. In the election, Rafsanjani, the powerful man of the IRI, was defeated by his rather unknown rival, Ahmadinejad. Like reformist candidates, Rafsanjani publicly claimed that his defeat was the result of fraud and interference of the military forces in the election, but he decided not to pursue the case when he learned that Khamenei had forcefully moved to support Ahmadinejad. In the first round of the ninth presidential election, 29,400,857 people, or 62% of eligible voters, participated; and in the second round 59,958,931 people, or 59.76% of the eligible voters, participated. Rafsanjani drew only 36% of the votes. The defeat of the reformists represented yet another turn backward for Iran in the modern era.

In the 28 years of IRI history, a total of 27 elections, including the third CTC election in 2007, have taken place. The experiences show that elections as a part of a democratic process are firmly controlled by the ruling clerics, with the support of the supreme leader and the Revolutionary Guard. Therefore, one may conclude that the election, as an institution, is at an impasse in Iran and cannot help pressure the clerical rulers to accept a real democracy. Many consider the formation of civil society organizations or reforms from outside the government as the only means of removing the obstacles.

KAZEM ALAMDARI

✦ ETHNIC GROUPS

The Iranian Constitutional Revolution of 1906 ended the millennia-old imperial system and ushered Iran into the modern era. Iranian intellectuals, who contributed to the success of the revolution and authored the constitution of

Persia, then to be named Iran, were greatly influenced by European thinkers and were admirers of the Aryan myth created and evolved by late nineteenth century anthropologists such as Hippolyte Taine, Paul Broca, and Edward B. Tylor. Many anthropologists of the period built their ideas on the theories introduced by the linguists such as Sir William Jones and others—the process which has been termed "the tyranny of linguistics." Thus Europe's creation of the Aryan myth, and the fascination of the Iranian elite with it, shaped and reconstructed the history of the land that is called Iran today. As a result, belonging to the "noble" lineage of Aryans and speaking Persian language became the tokens of "noble" Iranians. By deposing Ahmad Shah, the last king of the Qajar dynasty, and with ascendance of Reza Khan to the throne, all non-Persian speaking Iranians became "the Others."

There are also the non-Persian speaking Others such as Iranian Arabs, Azeri Turks, Balochis, Gilakis, Kurds, Lors, Mazandaranis, and Turkmen who were subjected to the rigorous Persianization measures of Reza Shah and Mohammad Reza Shah—the Pahlavi dynasty. The paradigms set by the Pahlavi dynasty were to define the concept of the nationhood for many Iranian elites, which still continues to linger in the minds of current members of the ruling class and also those Iranians whose assumptions about Iranian identity were framed by the post-Constitutionalist elite.

It seems that there have not been any genotypic research or tests to find out the genetic categories of the present inhabitants of Iran. DNA markers to identify the ancestral history and anthropological origins of the Iranians have not been studied so far. However, there have been population headcounts and housing censuses conducted every ten years in Iran since 1956. The results of the 2006 census are not formally available yet as of this writing, but the published news release of the Statistical Center of Iran (SCI), which appeared in the Iranian media in February 2007, put the country's population at 70,049,262. The accuracy, methodology, and focus and goals of the census can be disputed.

It is reasonable to assume that the ancestors of different ethnic peoples inhabiting the present borders of Iran can be traced to as early as the seventh millennium BC. Living through the ebbs and flows of different kingdoms and empires, at times their sovereignty and domain stretched from Central Asia to the Mediterranean. Yet they have gone through many changes due to the migrations and being overrun by outsiders. Some of the powerful rulers ruling the vast expanse of the land were empowered by the ethnic diversity and religious multiplicity of their peoples from the ancient times until the early years after the Constitutional Revolution of 1906. The very name of *Mamalek-e Mahruse-ye Iran*—delineated borders of Iranian Territories—signifies the collective identity of the peoples living within defined borders. It was only after the creation of the Aryan myth in the West, and the infatuation of Iranian intellectuals of the Constitutional Revolution era with it, that a systematic process of Persianization of different ethnic peoples in Iran was initiated by successive Iranian governments. This has resulted in suppressing the cultures and languages of the various non-Persian ethnic groups living in Iran. Due to the misconceptions about nation and nationality, the Iranian intellectuals of the Constitutional Revolution had no awareness about rights of the ethnic groups. They only saw religious diversity in Iran, and established laws pertaining to the recognized religious groups and their representation in the parliament. Not surprisingly, various ethnic groups such as Arabs and/or Turks were often blamed for the backwardness and miseries befalling Iran. Widespread illiteracy and indoctrination by distorted stories misled many Iranians into believing that Ferdowsi's fictional epic, the *Shahnameh*, written around 1000 AD, is a realistic interpretation of their history. Stereotyping of peoples of various ethnic backgrounds is common, and even some Islamic figures, such as Imam Ali, are at times Persianized in the popular imagination. Members of the Academy of the Persian Language and Literature often try to "purify" the Persian language by purging it from Arabic and other foreign influences, but ultimately most of their efforts have been abortive so far. The harsh approach of the Pahlavi state toward non-Persian ethnic groups, meanwhile, continues under the Islamic Republic.

Suggested Reading

Anderson, B. 1991. *Imagined communities: reflections on the origins and spread of nationalism.* New York: Verso.

Childe, G. V. 1993. *The Aryans: a study of Indo-European origins.* New York: Barnes & Noble.

Dorraj, M. 1990. *From Zarathustra to Khomeini: popularism and dissent in Iran.* Boulder: Lynne Reinner.

Eskandari, I. 1984. *In the darkness of the millennia (DarTariki-ye Hezare-ha).* Paris: Ruzegar-e Now.

Karang, A.-A. 1954. *Tati & Harzani: two dialects of the ancient language of Azerbaijan (Tati va Harzani: Do Lahajeh as Zaban-e Bastan-e Aazerbaijan).* Tabriz: Shafaq Publishing House.

Minovi, M. 1967.*Ferdowsi and his poetry.* Tehran: Anjoman-e Asar-e Melli.

Natali, D. 2005. *The Kurds and the state.* New York: Syracuse University Press.

Poliakov, L. 1974. *Aryan myth: a history of racist and nationalist ideas in Europe.* New York: Barnes and Nobles.

Sultan-Qurraie, H. 2003. *Modern Azeri literature: identity, gender and politics in the poetry of Mo'juz.* Bloomington: Indiana University Ottoman and Turkish Studies Publications.

HADI SULTAN-QURRAIE

✦ EUROPE–IRAN RELATIONS

Europe and Iran have continuously been in contact with one another throughout history; however, most Europeans have only fairly recently become aware of Iran for more than the production of their exquisite rugs. They have come to learn more about Iran's culture, history, and politics. Iranians, on the other hand, have had much more of an ongoing knowledge of Europe. Iranian intellectuals borrowed liberal values and ideals from Europe. This influenced Iran's 1906 Monarchy revolution, which succeeded while part of Europe was still under the tyrannical rule of the Kaisers.

In addition to overcoming the many obstacles that have come between Iran and Europe over the past several centuries, Iran has struggled in recent decades to improve or at least to maintain the relationship with Western Europe and Russia. The period after the Islamic revolution of 1979 can be best characterized as a period of trial and error with countless verbal confrontations, and even short-time deteriorations of relation. On the other hand, relation with the United States, despite a significant positive tendency on people's level on both sides, has overall deteriorated. Particularly since the Clinton Administration, who placed unprecedented pressure both politically and economically on Iran trying to isolate Iran and strain its relationships with other countries.

The government policy of Iranian leaders has been clearly set against the notion of dominance by external powers and against isolation, particularly after the war with Iraq, as they began to realize the importance of establishing regular communication and relationships with those in the outside world; however, practically this has not worked out the way it was intended. Iran's foreign policy is clearly set against formal political or military alliances with countries in the West while still encouraging economic and social development within the country.

Iranian leaders have altered their policy of exporting the revolution after the end of the Iran–Iraq War in 1988 as well as the Persian Gulf War in 1991. As a whole—without judging current President Ahmadinejad's policy—they have been less confrontational toward Western powers because the government of Iran has realized the importance and the necessity of alliances for successful implementation of particular programs. They realized the importance of having a strong ally throughout the war with Iraq (1980–1989), but, due to structural problems, no alliances had been established until today.

During and early after the Islamic Revolution in 1979, the relations between Iran and Western Europe painted a very promising picture. There are three main reasons that contributed to the overall hopeful start. First,

Europe as a whole was very supportive of the Shah and his regime but did not have a high involvement in the political and military affairs of Iran. Their approach towards Iran was largely accommodating and liberal, however Europe did not take the Shah's anti-communist rants in the serious manner as did the United States and several other countries. At the time, Europe was home to a portion of the largest communist parties outside of the Soviet Union. Additionally, France had offered a temporary residence to the Ayatollah Khomeini while his exile terminated in Iraq before eventually returning to Iran. Finally, the Islamic Republic realized that strategically, it would be unable to confront both the United States and Europe at the same time. By realizing this and acting accordingly, Iran has benefited greatly.

Western Europe did not always see the Iranian revolution in such a positive light. European governments saw it more beneficial and profitable to do business with the Shah, one powerful entity, rather than with numerous centers of power and authority all acting in state of turmoil. However, a continuous relationship has also proven to be extremely advantageous to Iranian decision makers as they continue to be the most important energy source to Europe and a major consumer of European commodities. Iran accrued a substantial amount of wealth due to oil income, first as a direct result of the Arab–Israeli war in 1973. During this time period, Iran sold one third of its oil supply to Europe. Under the Shah, this newfound wealth allowed for Iran to supply considerable loans to Great Britain and France, as well as providing for investments in the West German industry.

The pattern of the relation changed soon after the revolution when France, along with other Western European states, failed to fully comprehend the full intensity of the Islamic content for the revolution. Problems between the two regions began to emerge in 1980 when the first Islamic Republic President Banisadr and some other officials who had fled to France together with the leaders of the Mujahidin Khagh Organization (MKO) began to organize resistance movements for the eventual overthrow of the Islamic government. France also offered political asylum to Bakhtiar, the last prime minister of the Shah. Accusations of the Islamic Republic of Iran of being involved and responsible for the terrorist activities occurring in France at the time further complicated the relation. In retaliation, Iran refused to allow 157 French citizens to leave Iran. Eventually, a series of negotiations occurred between the two countries and the individuals were eventually allowed to leave Iran. An additional point of contention between the two regions developed as a result of France providing arms to Baghdad during the eight-year Iran–Iraq War.

In July 1987, both Iran and France had changed their views with regard to one another and decided to make changes. Iran had come to realize that the French did not always conform to the constraints of the U.S. foreign policy, and since Iran also needed Europe's diplomatic support, knowing that France carried considerable weight with the rest of Europe, they knew it was in their best interest to make amends. France also came to realize several important aspects of Iran. The first of which was the fact that the Islamic Republic enjoyed a sort of moral and political support from the Islamic world. Additionally, Iran continued to be viewed as a regional power. France also required the assistance of Iran in order to release hostages that remained in Lebanon. Both countries were willing to entertain the notion of participating in the expensive cost of reconstruction plans at the end of the Iran–Iraq War. Iran in particular realized the importance of French support in this multi-billion dollar project.

The United States and Iran broke off diplomatic relations in the immediate aftermath of the revolution. Europe, on the other hand, sought to keep open the lines of communication and maintain a "Critical Dialogue" with Iran. This window served both sides to talk at different diplomatic levels particularly when there was a change that necessitated revisiting the relation. Consequently and within the framework of the "Critical Dialogue" France and Iran resolved their differences, and several major trade and economic delegations ensued. Many of the agreements reached between the EU and Iran have been considered controversial by the United States, who continued to increase pressure by imposing sanctions against Iran.

While much of Europe has been in a state of turmoil with Iran at one point in time or another, Germany had sustained a relatively stable relationship with Iran up until April 1997. It was at this time that a German court implicated members of the Iranian leadership as having direct involvement in the assassination of three Iranian Kurdish leaders in Berlin. Never in their history had Germany followed any colonial ambition in Iran. This agreeable relationship allowed Germany to become the largest European exporter of goods as well as services to Iran. Germany had also been Iran's largest trade partner with approximately $4 billion in trade surplus per year in the Mid 1990s. Interestingly Germany does not import Iranian Oil for technical reasons. However, the German implication against Iranian leadership caused the relationship to sour quickly. Iran denied the charges and any involvement in the assassination. Generally speaking, the problems that have arisen over the years between Iran and Germany, or between Iran and Europe as a whole, are typically on a level similar to conflicts that can occur between states even with a normal relationship.

Western Europe typically tends to view the Islamic Republic with suspicion and as an oppressive and destabilizing entity; however, Western Europe also realizes that Iran is a major actor in both international and regional politics. Europe tends to try to engage with Iran rather than contain it in the manner the United States employs. Iran, on the other hand, views Europe as a gateway of many areas including acceptability by other nations as well as economic development. Overall, there are great incentives for each side to maintain a working relationship with the other.

There have been some notable changes in Iran–European relations since the terrorist attacks of September 11, 2001. The United States along with European governments have made commitments to help encourage the process of political liberalization throughout the Middle East. The seriousness of terrorist attacks became well known to Europe after the bombings in Madrid in March 2004 and London in July 2005. Historically, Europe has had a policy towards Iran that was based very little on containment. This evolved over the years to the point that containment was no longer the policy initiative.

Commitments on the European Union level after the 9/11 attacks touted the promotion of democracy throughout the Middle East. They agreed that well-governed and democratic states would be the best solution in order to achieve a sense of security. The actual strategy adopted by EU toward the Middle East was somewhere between the two extremes and did not seem to follow a coherent modality. Most scholars are convinced that EU is driven by interest rather than security and this goal necessitated a more pragmatic approach on behalf of EU. Additionally, there are numerous concerns about the actual ability of the EU to be able to react and influence any political trends within the Middle East.

The implication of such a policy proves to be inadequately defined in terms of ways and means to work with Iran given the fact that each European country at any given time might be following a totally different interest in Iran. There are several major policy issues in EU–Iran relations that requires further elaboration. First, their policy of engagement and "Critical Dialogue" faced difficulty, and the negotiations over the issue of Iran's nuclear program pointed to more practical steps rather than mere dialogue. Also the return of the conservatives in the Iranian political spectrum and their ascendancy in the arena of Iranian politics further complicated the situation. While under President Khatami the EU and Iran were approaching a workable solution, suddenly with Ahmadinejad and the Iranian conservative parliament problems started to look insurmountable.

While debates about democratization in the Middle East continued to escalate, Iran took what appeared to be a step back away from this discourse. The time period of June 2005 was when the reformist presidency gave way to one of a more conservative nature. This occurred due to clerics being able to gradually stifle political reforms through a calculated measure in Iranian presidency and parliamentary elections. Additionally, efforts for developing nuclear capacity progressed at an alarming rate within Iran. There have been several notable efforts by the EU to strengthen its engagement with Iran, but almost all ended with no tangible results. Such efforts first came on the heels of the 1997 election of Khatami and again after the September 11 attacks. The first effort to support liberalization with Khatami was deemed largely unsuccessful. The European approach for involvement had two aspects. The first was that Iran had been identified as an area where homegrown reform had occurred, and many believed international efforts could be molded after this. The second aspect was the idea that European engagement would have appeared promising compared to the United States' strategy of isolation and exclusion.

Because the United States garnered such a bad reputation in the eyes of Iranians dating back to 1979, Iran attempted to play off both the United States and the EU at the same time. They also sought to offset tension with the United States by developing relationships with the EU. Improvements in diplomatic relations between the two sides were based largely on upward trends in trade and investment. Europeans viewed Iran as an extremely important source of oil and gas. The EU eventually established themselves as Iran's largest trading partner. In turn, they also started running a growing trade deficit problem with Iran.

Post-9/11 policies of the United States towards Iran were perceived as tightening; however, it appears as if the European determination to implant more systematic engagement with the current president of Iran has only intensified. Issues grew to become more complex and tensions increased. European governments disregarded President George W. Bush's "axis of evil" affirmation and expressed discontent over not having been consulted on the issue. New negotiations between Iran and the EU were initiated in December 2002. By the summer of 2003, many realized negotiations were not proceeding as planned and that the degree of interest had diminished. Tensions over Iran's nuclear capability also increased, with the EU expressing more concern and interest over this issue. They touted their main goal as containing Iran's nuclear activities efforts.

After many negotiations and issues involving Iran and the EU, European intentions continued to remain ambiguous; however, diverse trends were emerging in European policies. Discussions on the nuclear issue were linked to human rights issues. The need for government initiatives were being explored and endorsed by many, with the EU making no indication that they would be willing to consider any large-scale, reform-oriented funding. During the time of the June 2005 elections, European diplomats expressed disappointment that reformists fell short of tempering the toughing of nationalist sentiment. It was also announced after the conclusion of the elections that the EU was extremely critical of the manipulation assumed by the conservative powers.

Depending on the perspective one wishes to adopt, Iran can either be classified as one of European foreign policy's successes or disappointments. There were many discussions on nuclear activities, both in October 2003 and November 2004, that were viewed as evidence of a successful European approach to one of the most serious and yet complex international challenges. On the other hand, the EU was unable to prevent reversals in Iran's internal political reform momentum and the subsequent return to power of conservative authorities.

The European strategy on the human rights issue was founded on the notion that Iran would yield to the pressure exerted by both the EU and United States and human rights improvements would ensure. The positive European influence coupled with the hardlined strategy adopted by the United States was intended to increase the necessity of Iran to acquire other international allegiances. This dynamic did not take effect as it was originally anticipated. After the events of 9/11, the European view on human rights was extinguished and was replaced with the higher priority of securing a deal on the nuclear weapons issue. An additional concern that became problematic was that the EU was not always the main protagonist within all European strategies. Some of the most powerful member states developed initiatives that were not always congruent with the international interests.

The U.S. Administration closely monitored negotiations between Iran, the U.K., France, and Germany. The negotiations included Iran's ending its uranium enrichment plan in exchange for a package of incentives that included economic and political benefits. Additionally, it was also discussed that the efforts to report Iran to the Security Council would be halted. President George W. Bush championed the European initiative while never even remotely giving up his rhetoric that *all options including military attack are on the table*. There was an agreement reached on the temporary suspension of Iran's enrichment between Iran and European negotiators just several days before the IAEA Board of Governor's meeting, but finally the course of action changed. Iran rejected the deal and case was sent to the U.N. Security Council.

Suggested Reading

Crook, J. R. 2005. Iran's nuclear program. *The American Journal of International Law.* 99:270–271.

Tarock, A. 1999. Iran–Western Europe relations on the mend. *British Journal of Middle Eastern Studies.* 26:41–61.

Youngs, R. 2006. *Europe and the Middle East.* Boulder, Co: Lynne Rienner Publishers, Inc.

JALIL ROSHANDEL

F

✦ FAMILY PLANNING

The family planning program in Iran has met with much success in the last decade. However, the gains achieved have only been enjoyed by married couples, while unmarried young men and women still face challenges in accessing necessary contraceptive methods. This continues to result in a variety of health challenges.

One of the gains achieved by the educational arm of the new family planning program is that the average age of marriage for women has increased from 19.7 years in 1976 to 22.4 years in 1996. Recent unofficial statistics have placed the average age of marriage for women at 25. However, qualitative research shows that the first age of intercourse for women is at an average of 15. Therefore, there exists a potential 10-year period in which young women are engaging in sexual activities without access to contraceptives. Though strict Islamist interpretations of *shari`a* law provides for heavy punishment for premarital sex, an increasing youth demographic (70% under the age of 30), an increasingly educated youth (due to the Islamic Republic's free education policies), and an increasing unemployment rate (most recently at 45% for young people under the age of 35), all combine to provide young adults more opportunities for mixed-gender social interaction. This can, in turn, lead to sexual encounters. The Islamic Republic must recognize the unmet need of many young people for family planning, and must consider opening up its family planning to all citizens, married or single.

History of Family Planning in Iran Since 1979

The success of the family planning program in Iran is evidenced by the fact that it has been hailed as a role model for other countries in the Middle East by organizations such as the United Nations Fund for Population Advancement (UNFPA). It has been greatly successful in reducing the number of children that women bear from over 6 per woman in the mid 1980s to 2.1 in 2000. Additionally, the contraceptive prevalence rate rose from 37% in 1976 to about 75% in the year 2000. This included a rise in rural areas from 20% in 1976 to 72% in 2000, and in urban areas from 54% to 82%. This success, however, has come at a great cost to the government. Prior to 1989, there had been no specific budget line for family planning activities in Iran. Between 1991 and 1992, approximately 13 billion rials had been allocated to the program. By 1993, the budget had grown to 16.8 billion rials. In 2000, the Ministry of Health and Medical Education provided 75% of all family planning services.

Many of the efforts toward improving the family planning program in Iran have taken place in the last two decades. Immediately following the revolution, much of the family planning system that was under the old regime was disintegrated. The new government adopted a policy advocating early marriage and large families, reducing the minimum legal age for marriage to 9 years old for girls and 12 years old for boys. In addition to this pronatalist position of the government, the war with Iraq fueled the desire for a growth rate, as Ayatollah Khomeini pushed to bolster the ranks of "soldiers for Islam," aiming for "an army of 20 million." Additionally, the previous family planning system was denounced as part of the Shah's Westernization efforts. During this period, the rate of children per women jumped from 6.3 in 1976 to 7.0 in 1986.

Even though contraceptive use (as long as it did not hurt the mother or child) was not illegal, did not include abortion, and was often not opposed by married women or their husbands, many suppliers of contraceptives were closed. Those that were not closed quickly ran out of contraceptive supplies and replacements were not procured, leading to shortages. IUD and sterilization methods were officially suspended until 1980, when Dr. M. R. Moatamedi requested and received a *fatwa* from Imam Khomeini, allowing sterilization methods to be used with the consent of the couple as long as it did not expose them to harm. However, the issue of sterilization was still under much debate after this *fatwa* and was therefore not made available. Imam Khomeini later issued a statement saying that any devices that did not harm women physically or make them sterile were permissible (1985). The universal rationing system that was introduced as a means to equal access to basic necessities also encouraged higher fertility. The rationing system included everything from property ownership to basic food items to modern consumer goods, and all items were distributed on a per capita basis—larger families were entitled to a better share of both basic commodities and modern consumer items; families with more than five children were given a free plot of land.

It was not until December 1989 and early 1990 that the government officially changed its position regarding family planning, although beginning in 1988, free contraceptives were available through the primary health care system (however, only to married couples). The new plan was deemed the National Birth Control Policy and included an intensive campaign to persuade the public of the need for family planning through newspaper reports, television spots, and Friday prayer speeches. This was supported by a three-day Seminar on Population and Development held in Mashad in September 1988, which announced that the population growth rate was too high, and the *fatwa* regarding family planning was reiterated; in December 1988, the high Judicial Council declared that "there is no Islamic barrier to family planning."

By 1986, the Iranian population had reached nearly 50 million, an increase of 14 million in the time span of a decade. The family planning program had three declared goals: encouraging women to space their pregnancies three to four years apart, discouraging pregnancy among women younger than 18 and older than 35, and limiting family size to three children.

In 1990 the Birth Limitation Council was created by the Council of Ministers. The council was given the duty to increase contraceptive prevalence among married women and to decrease the total fertility rate, birth rate, and the population growth rate. This meant a mass campaign of education programs (including the construction of billboards throughout the country with slogans such as "*bache kamtar—zendegi behtar*" or "fewer children—better life"), increased access to contraceptives, a wider variety of contraceptives, and researching on aspects of family planning services. In 1991, a separate Directorship of Population and Family Planning was established to oversee family planning service delivery within the primary healthcare network. The system included all forms of modern contraceptives supplied free of charge to married couples only.

In 1993, a Family Planning Bill removed most of the economic incentives for having large families. Many of the allowances to large families were canceled, as well as several benefits for children, which began to provide for the first three children in a family only. Other aspects of the 1993 Family Planning Bill included measures such as guaranteed time off for maternity leave for female workers and other privileges in the labor law, cutting the subsidies for daycare for female employees, and cutting subsidies for health insurance premiums on fourth or higher ordered children. As part of the second social, economic, and cultural plan of the Iranian government (1994–1999), the family planning program was fully integrated into the primary health care system.

In addition to typical modern methods of birth control, Iran also allows for both tubal ligation and vasectomies, as well as abortion in the most serious of cases to save a woman's life (while abortion is not covered under the family planning system, post-abortion care is provided by the primary healthcare system; however abortions, like contraceptives, are available to married women only). In 1992, the pill was the most frequently used modern method (64%), followed by the IUD in urban areas (21%) and tubectomy in rural areas (18%). In 1992 57% of modern contraceptives were supplied through public hospitals, health centers, health houses, and pharmacies. The remainder was supplied by the public sector. However, in 1996, 30% of pill users did not know how to use it correctly. Failure of the contraceptive in use was the most commonly cited reason for unwanted pregnancies of the 5.2% of married women between the ages of 15 and 49 who were pregnant in 2000, showing that there is still some educational work concerning contraceptive use that needs to be undertaken by the government.

There is no doubt about the success of the Family Planning program in Iran. There is, however, some doubt that the government will be able to continue to afford such an extensive program. This is questioned because within the next 10 years the number of reproductive-aged women will grow by more than 20%. Iran however, has been hailed as progressive in their family planning system, particularly for their region of the world. The Middle East's only condom factory operates in Iran, they are in the process of expanding their services to couples with emergency contraceptive needs, and while abortion is illegal, post-abortion care is provided as part of the primary health care system.

UNMET NEEDS

While Iran could be applauded for its efforts in the family planning arena, the many unmet needs of an increasing portion of Iran's population can also be acknowledged. Officially, statistics show that only about 7.6% of all married women have an unmet need for family planning in Iran, however my qualitative research shows that this number is higher than official statistics indicate (because many unmarried young women are hesitant to come forward about the experiences with unmet needs out of fear of stigmatization and punishment from the morality police or their family members). That is, they would prefer to avoid pregnancy but are not using any form of family planning. This unmet need is said to be often higher in rural areas, though it can be seen as specific to certain provinces as well. Such provinces as Sistan and Balouchestan have a total unmet need of 24.9%, Hormozgan 20.1%, and Kohgilooyeh 15.5%. Studies have also shown that the primary reason for not using contraceptive methods is pregnancy, the second reason being health concerns about contraceptives and side effects, including fear of disease. The third reason of nonuse cited was the opposition of husbands or other relatives. Many suggestions have been made for government policies to be designed to focus on these unmet areas. In addition to this, the counseling of men is also seen as a beneficial change to the program, as male disapproval in the family is a high factor for unmet need. On the other hand, those couples that do use contraception largely include males in the process. Studies have found, however, that 59% of Iranian couples that practice family planning rely on methods that require men's direct involvement: "male methods" (withdrawal, male sterilization, and condom use) account for 36% of all methods used, and female sterilization (which by law requires the husband's consent) is used by 23% of couples.

Many believe that the success of the family planning program in Iran is a cause for celebration and pride and that the many achievements of family planning providers and educators must be recognized and upheld. However, there is a rapidly growing segment of Iran's population, the young adults who were born during the pronatalist years and are now coming of age, and they are in need of access to information, family planning services, and contraceptives. In the coming years, as young people continue to engage in premarital sexual activity, some see that the family planning program in Iran must be modified to address their needs in order to face the potential reproductive and sexual health challenges that lay ahead.

Suggested Reading

Abbasi-Shavazi, M. J. 2001. The fertility revolution in Iran. *Population and Societies*. No. 373.

Abbasi-Shavazi, M. J., A. Mchryar, G. Jones, and P. McDonald. 2002. Revolution, war and modernization: population policy and fertility change in Iran. *Journal of Population Research.*

Aghajanian, A. 1994. Family planning and contraceptive use in Iran, 1967–1992. *International Family Planning Perspectives*. Vol. 20, No. 2.

Aghajanian, A., and A. H. Merhyar. 1999. Fertility, contraceptive use and family planning program activity in the islamic republic of Iran." *International Family Planning Perspectives*. Vol. 25, No. 2.

Ahmadi, A., and J. Iranmahboob. 2005. Unmet need for family planning in Iran." XXV IUSSP International Population Conference. Tours, France. July 18–23.

Boonstra, H. 2001. The Guttmacher Report on Public Policy. Vol. 4, No. 6 *Islam, Women and Family Planning: A Primer*.

Law of May 23, 1993 pertaining to population and family planning. National Report on Population, the Islamic Republic of Iran, Tehran, Iran, Government of Iran, 1994.

Roudi-Fahimi, F. Iran's Family planning Program: Responding to a Nation's Needs. Population Reference Bureau. MENA Policy Brief.

Roudi-Fahimi, F., and M. El-Adawy. 2005. Men and family planning in Iran. XXVth IUSSP International Population Conference. Tours, France. July 18–23.

PARDIS MAHDAVI

✦ FOREIGN DIRECT INVESTMENT

Foreign direct investment (FDI) is defined as an investment involving a long-term commitment, interest, and control by a resident/entity in one country (investor/ enterprise) in another entity in a different country (host). It implies a significant degree of influence in the management of the enterprise. It requires a minimum of 10% ownership of the enterprise by the foreign entity.

BACKGROUND

After WWII, less developed countries (LDCs) received foreign development aid from friendly developed countries as well as from multinational banks such as the World Bank and the International Monetary Fund (IMF). Also, those countries that were considered "creditworthy" secured financial resources from European–American financial institutions in commercially profitable projects. However, these became an albatross for their economies. They acquired short-term high-interest rate loans for investment in development projects that were either not viable or, if viable, were mismanaged. That is, foreign exchange proceeds of these projects were used for other purposes rather than saved for repayments of foreign obligations. As a consequence, these loans were refinanced with higher–interest rate short-term loans and, therefore, LDCs' foreign debts mushroomed. In the mid-1970s, the problem of Latin American countries' foreign debts became large and prohibitive to the extent that they exceeded their total exports (Sachs, 1985).

Consequently, political risk assessment became a significant factor in decisions about foreign direct investment. One source of risk is policy-based and stems from potential expropriation, foreign exchange control, policy-induced risk, systematic risk, default and repudiation of foreign debt, restriction in production and exportation, confiscation with or without compensation, and the existence of government-extended sanctioned monopolies that make competition impossible. Another source of risk stems primarily from instability, inconsistency and discontinuity, class or ethnic conflict, revolution, ideological confrontation, real or potential internal and external wars, and the political environment of the host nations.

The very first factor that a corporation considers is general instability risk, which includes the prospect of a revolution, subversion, turmoil, and external aggression. According to Franklin Rook, if the answers to these questions lead to a decision that the country is unstable or chaotic, the process stops. No further consideration is given to other risk factors such as nationalization, intervention, price control, restriction on reparation of dividend, royalty, etc.

Political risk, especially after the Iranian revolution and the demise of Shah Mohammad Reza Pahlavi in 1979, has become important enough to lead multinational enterprises to recruit and hire political risk analysts, or use the services of enterprises that specialize in political risk assessment throughout the world. Political risk assessment has became so indispensable to MNCs that they hire former high-ranking state department officials, congressmen, and senators as well as academicians to perform political risk (in capital theory terminology, alpha risk, non-business risk, unsystematic risk) analysis in addition to fact-finding trips and exchange of information. It became important enough to result in the establishment of national and international agencies such as the Overseas Private Insurance Corporation (OPIC), the Multilateral Investment Guarantee Agency of the World Bank, and the U.S. Agency for International Development (USAID), which issue insurance policies to investors. These polices are issued against adverse consequences of revolution, unrest, uprising, insurrection, and policy-induced damages.

Iran and FDI

Against this worldwide background, the Islamic Revolution of 1979, which was based on populist and left-wing rhetoric, took place. They had warned that foreign direct investment would compromise Iran's national sovereignty and security. As a result, they initially enunciated and codified policies in the Constitution and trade laws that were anti-trade and anti-foreign direct investment in Iran. Seeds of isolationism and protectionism from the advanced industrial world, especially the United States, were sowed. The revolution set as its goals a cleansing of the country from the visages of imperialism that had crept into the Iranian socioeconomic and political life and to sever any relationship that was not deemed to be in the "national interest" of Iran. They declared that socioeconomic and political configuration of the country must be made Islamic and independent of the decadent world capitalists and socialist systems. The turn of events, especially the hostage crisis, brought Iran and the United States to a costly confrontation that is still continuing. This confrontation resulted in economic sanctions, which are still in place and spreading to a wider world community.

The fact that a trade embargo was imposed on Iran was probably "a blessing in disguise" for Iranian ideological standings. Initially, commercial policies of the revolutionary regime and the goals of the embargo were compatible. That is, Iranians were not eager to do much business with the West and were more interested to trade with the developing countries—an ideologically convenient tendency. So, the fact that an embargo was enforced, Iran's ideological proclivities not withstanding, was considered a proof of the imperialist conspiracy against the revolution.

However, the country has turned a corner somewhat and the leadership of the Islamic Republic have softened their rhetoric *vis-à-vis* foreign trade and foreign direct investment. It has actively pursued foreign direct investment since the early 1990s, despite the Western, mainly U.S. efforts to frustrate their pursuit. Iran passed a new law in 2002, the Law on Attraction and Protection of Foreign Investment, establishing a clear legal framework for FDI prospects.

Under the new law the government is obligated to insure the security of any investment against any non-commercial adverse consequence such as appropriation, nationalization, or confiscation. It also allows for repatriation of profits. This is a definite turning point in Iran's modus operandi since the establishment of the regime. Nevertheless, as Table 3 shows, all the efforts have not changed the picture in any significant way. Inflows of FDI into Iran relative to Turkey or developing countries or the world are minuscule. Iran's 2001 to 2003 ranking of inward FDI Performance Index, a measure of the extent to which a host country receives FDI, is 136, right after Haiti and Zimbabwe. Efforts such as the gathering of potential investors in Tehran on October 20, 1999 to evaluate and bid on 100 mining and 15 exploration projects totaling $10 billion, have been less than fruitful for a promising country such as Iran with vast natural resources and a sophisticated labor force. According to the IMF country report, "between 1993 and October 1997, 50 projects, totaling U.S. $722 million, were approved [by Iranian government]; however, actual investment inflows amounted to a total of U.S. $40 million."

Table 3 Inward Foreign Direct Investment (U.S.$ millions)

	1990–2000 Average	2003	2004	2005	2006
Iran	4	390	282	360	901
Turkey	791	1,758	2,883	9,803	20,120
Developing countries	130,722	178,699	283,030	314,316	379,070
World	495,399	564,078	742,143	945,795	1,305,852
Iran/Turkey	0.00506	0.22184	0.09781	0.03672	0.04478
Iran/developing countries	0.00003	0.00218	0.00100	0.00115	0.00238
Iran/world	0.00001	0.00069	0.00038	0.00038	0.00069

Source: World Investment Report 2007, *UNCTAD*.

The Islamic Republic of Iran has shown to have a slow learning curve in economic management. Even though they have been trying very hard to attract foreign direct investment in Iran, so far they have been less than successful. The Iranian leaders have been quite successful in instilling uncertainty and the prospect of economic and political instability in the minds of potential foreign and domestic investors, which frustrates their goal of attracting much needed resources and, most importantly, technical know-how.

Suggested Reading

Cataquet, H. 1988. Country risk assessment: where to invest your money. *National Business Quarterly*. pp. 26–35.

Dadkhah, K., and H. Zangeneh. 1998. International economic sanctions are not zero-sum games: there are only losers. *CIRA Bulletin*. 14:24–29. A complete version of this is also published in the *Iranian Journal of Trade Studies Quarterly*. 2:1–14.

Dadkhah, K., and H. Zangeneh. 2001. Liberalization of foreign trade: an imperative for the health and growth of the Iranian economy. *Journal of Iranian Research and Analysis*. 17:64–86.

Desta, A. 1993. *International political risk assessment for foreign direct investment and international lending decisions*. Ginn Press.

Foreign Investment Promotion and Protection Act (FIPPA). http://www.mefa.gov.ir/laws/investment_law_eng.asp.

Goodman, S. H. 1981. Corporate attitude, assessing country risk. *Euromoney*. p. 111.

Greene, M. R. 1974. The management of political risk. *Best's Review: Property/Liability Edition*. p. 71.

IMF Staff Country Report. No. 98/27, p. 19.

Robinson, J. N. 1994. Is it possible to assess country risk? *The Banker*. pp. 71–79.

Root, F. R. 1995. *Entry strategies for international markets*. Lexington Books. p. 155.

Sachs, J. D. 1985. External debt and macroeconomic performance in Latin America and Asia. *Brookings Paper on Economic Activity 2*. Washington, DC: 523–553.

Weston, F. V., and B. W. Sorge. *International management finance*. Homewood, IL: Irwin. p. 60.

World Investment Report, United Nations Conference on Trade and Development, various issues.

Zangeneh, H. 1997. International trade in Iran: an appraisal. *Research in Middle East Economics*. 2:165–191.

Zangeneh, H. 2001. An analysis of the domestic and international economy of Iran. In *Iran encountering globalization*, ed. A. Mohammedi. pp. 105–133.

HAMID ZANGENEH

G

✦ GILAKIS AND GILAN

The Iranian province of Gilan stretches along the Caspian Sea to the west of Mazandaran Province. Ardabil Province is to the west of Gilan, Qazvin and Zanjan Provinces are on the south. Gilan includes the northwestern end of Alborz chain and the Western part of the Caspian lowlands. Because of its topographic position, Gilan belongs to the exceptionally humid "Hyrcanian" climate. The climatic privilege of Gilan explains its luxuriant natural vegetation. Rasht is the central city of the province and Bandar-e Anzali its major port on the Caspian. Gilan is believed to be one of the most populated provinces of Iran, with the population close to 2.5 million. Although the main agricultural crop of Gilan is rice, the region traditionally relied on silk production, later complemented by the introduction of tea cultivation.

The people of Gilan, the Gilaks, have always taken pride in their national heroes throughout history. They take pride in their Deylamite warriors and the defeat of Abbasid Caliph's army by Mardavij, the founder of Ziyarid rule. In modern history, Mirza Kuchak Khan's Jangali movement is glorified by Gilaks and by other Iranians alike. Mirza Kuchak Khan's establishment of the Republic of Gilan and his resistance against the British and the central government from June 1920 through September 1921 has been admired by all Iranians—an admirable event of pride for the people of Gilan. Gilaki, classified as Indo–Iranian, is the language spoken by most Gilaks. Other Iranian languages, such as Kurdish and Tati, are spoken in Gilan as well. However, the languages spoken in Gilan are losing ground in many cities due to heavy immigration of people from Azerbaijan.

HADI SULTAN-QURRAIE

✦ GLOBALIZATION, ECONOMIC ANALYSIS OF

The Iranian economy has gone through three stages of development since the Constitutional Revolution (1906–1911). First is the period that may be referred to as early "primary accumulation," a pre-capitalist stage in which separation of producer from the means of production leads to an unlimited reservoir of wage labor and allows for urbanization and development of capitalism proper. In Iran, this was both the cause and the consequence of the Constitutional Revolution, which carried on essentially in a *sui generis* manner, halfway through the Reza Shah period (1925–1941). Reza Shah understood that the key to modernization is replacement of the religious and social norms of traditional society with twentieth-century institutions. But he himself—far from objectives of the Constitutional Revolution—was the creation of a British coup d'état (1921) that also established him as an absolute monarch until his forced departure, subsequent to the British and Russian invasion, in 1941. The most important development project in Reza Shah's era was the construction of Trans–Persian Railway. Development of modern manufacturing plants and light industry was also significant in his period, culminating in some 350 modern plants by 1941.

The second period is the transition era to what is known as the capitalist mode of production, with the countryside still under sway of the landlords. This period extends through World War II, well beyond the Mossadegh period (1951–1953), and up until the so-called White Revolution—a series of reforms imposed by the Kennedy administration on the then Shah of Iran (Mohammad Reza Pahlavi) in the early 1960s. This era is the precursor to the creation of an *internal* market for *import-substitution* industrialization and, simultaneously, potential penetration of international capital (and world market) in agriculture and industry in Iran. Given the early 1960s reforms, Iran's economy had become a *de facto* part of the world market which, following the globalization of oil in the 1970s, attained further mutuality with the world economy beyond the now defunct Pahlavi regime.

Today, under the Islamic Republic, notwithstanding obstructions resulting from U.S. sanctions, the Iranian economy is much more integrated in the global economy than anytime during the former regime under *Pax Americana*.

One of the consequences of this is a classic double-edged sword of departure from domestic agriculture toward industry—through the medium of the global market—and consequently relying on the importation of food from abroad. The upshot of this policy is the creation of dispossessed and bulging urban unemployment and unproductive and impoverished rural population.

Accepting that the development of capitalism emerges both intranationally and internationally, it is imperative to study the nature and historical significance of these contradictory yet reinforcing realms in terms of (1) the transformation of nation-states with dominant pre-capitalist structures, (2) the further development of advanced capitalist economies, and (3) the integration (and certainly uneven unification) of global socioeconomic structure as a whole. These three interrelated trajectories are both conceptual and historically evolutionary, and, as such, may lay the cornerstone of epochal significance of today's globalization. It is in this context that, for instance, several decades of import-substitution industrialization (ISI) and/or export-led development in the so-called Third World would find contextual relevance and material significance eventually for the transnationalization of capital and eventual globalization.

Finally, globalization refers to a macro socioeconomic configuration that encompasses an intertwined, systematic, and stage-by-stage integration of the world economy, polity, and social structure. It represents a newly emerged historical stage beyond the conventional international trade and transnational capital movements. Globalization, so defined, thus counters the existing local, regional, national, legal, and presumably cultural boundaries that hitherto have been dividing the material, ideological, and social transformation of our epoch under the hegemony of global social capital. It is in this context that the transnationalization of the three basic forms of capital (via the circuit of social capital) obtains material force beyond the sphere of transnational circulation and provides us with a stage theory appropriate for globalization and accumulation of capital in terms of an aggregate category. Hence, in its transnational jurisdiction, social capital (not to be confused with its orthodox rendition by liberals and neoconservatives) goes beyond individual markets, individual industries, and individual countries. The renewal of the circuit of social capital manifests the constant technological revolution and thus cheapening of the labor power across the boundaries of nation-states.

There are two dimensions to the question of globalization in Iran. First is the globalization of oil, a commodity the production and export of which are vital for foreign exchange earning, capital formation, and thus economic growth in Iran. Second is the *epochal* meaning of globalization for the world as a whole and its exacting repercussions for Iran.

Oil is indeed the very first economic sector that completed its globalization in the perplexing decade of the 1970s. The oil crisis of 1973 and 1974 was a genuine avenue of change that turned into actualization against the International Petroleum Cartel (secret arrangement forged, in 1928, at the Achnacarry) by the independent oil producers and OPEC from *within* the industry. It was an implosion that reverberated throughout, from North Africa, the Persian Gulf, Indonesia, and Latin America to the oilfields of the oldest producers, the United States. The result appeared as a convoluted departure to the confused public or identical reconfiguration to self-proclaimed oil experts and monopoly buffs in both academic and media circles. The truth is far from all of these populist propositions. The crisis eventually led to the rationalization of U.S. oilfields, decartelization of world oil, formation of differential oil rents, and development of spot and futures markets for all crude oil across the globe. Consequently, speaking of independence from the Middle East oil by exploring more oil, say, from the high-cost non-OPEC sources (including U.S. domestic) is invalid. This claim, *inter alia*, is based on the misleading proposition that OPEC is a cartel and that differential oil rents are monopoly.

Hence, two crucial points are in order. First, the imposition of economic sanctions against Iran's oil and gas industry is unwise, as the long-term effects of this policy will eventually catch up with the global supply that is in dire need of shorter lead time for further exploration and development of oil. The bravado value of these sanctions may enhance the sentimental feeling of U.S. control but their latent boomerang would cause a real shortage and thus material insecurity globally, beyond the United States. This is the curse of globalization of oil against U.S. policy. Second, U.S. sanctions have an overwhelming effect on Iran's oil and gas industry. This means that from the upstream to downstream operations, Iran's economic needs are *mutual* with the transnational capital for capital accumulation. The Iranian economy relies on the oil revenue for the lion's share of the government budget and significant share of GDP, and market volatility and fluctuation of oil prices literally wreak havoc with the annual budget, demand for imports, rate of capital formation, and national economic development planning. This is a distinct character of an oil *rentier-state* and thus a *rentier economy* amidst the high stage of globalization. The globalization of oil and formation of differential oil rents as sources of oil revenue are but a backdrop that is out of the control of the Iranian Government. This is the curse of globalization of oil against the Islamic Republic.

The *tendency* towards globalization is as old as proliferating capitalism itself. Yet, to be able to separate a mere tendency (i.e., its potential) from its fully developed actualized stage (i.e., as an epoch) one must recognize, by analogy, a difference between a human embryo and a grown-up human body and mind. Therefore, those on the left and right are equally incorrect. The common denominator of the left and the right thus appears to hinge upon their respective ahistorical (and non-evolutionary) attitude.

Notwithstanding the cumulative sanctions to date, particularly the newly devised unilateral economic and political sanctions by the Bush–Cheney administration, the authenticity of interdependence and globalization is clear. Here the run away proliferation of capital accumulation and institutionalization of nearly all markets beyond the border of nation-states create a boomerang and injurious effect on both sides of the aisle. In other words, the global economy has entered into an epoch in which it operates like a knitted sweater vulnerable to possible unraveling by a thread or two. This hearkens to the long-standing debate on U.S.-sanctioned "neoliberal policy" and misunderstanding over identifying *globalization* with *Americanization*. To be sure, today's globalization is an objective (structural) fact that causes "plant closings" and other dislocations. Therefore, globalization cannot be reduced to a mere U.S. neoliberal policy.

Suggested Reading

Alerassool, M. 1993. *Freezing assets: the USA and the most effective economic sanction.* New York: St. Martin's.

Bina, C. 1988. Internationalization of the oil industry: simple oil shocks or structural crisis? *Review: A Journal of Fernand Braudel Center.* Vol. 11.

Bina, C. 1989. Competition, control and price formation in the international energy industry. *Energy Economics.* Vol. 11.

Bina, C. 1992. Global oil and inviability of the pax Americana. *Economic and Political Weekly.* Vol. 27.

Bina, C. 1992. Global oil and the oil policies of the Islamic Republic, in Bina, C., and H. Zangeneh, eds., *Modern capitalism and Islamic ideology in Iran.* London: Macmillan; 121–158.

Bina, C. 1993. The rhetoric of oil and the dilemma of war and American hegemony. *Arab Studies Quarterly.* Vol. 15.

Bina, C. 1994. Towards a new world order: U.S. hegemony, client-states and Islamic alternative," in Mutalib, H., and T. Hashimi, eds., *Islam, Muslims and the modern state.* London: Macmillan; 3–30.

Bina, C. 1995. On sand castles and sand-castle conjectures: a rejoinder. *Arab Studies Quarterly.* Vol. 17.

Bina, C. 1997. Globalization: the epochal imperatives and developmental tendencies, in Gupta, D., ed., *The political economy of globalization.* Boston, Mass: Gluwer Academic Press; 41–48.

Bina, C. 2004. The American tragedy: the quagmire of war, rhetoric of oil, and the conundrum of hegemony. *Journal of Iranian Research & Analysis.* Vol. 20.

Bina, C. 2006. The globalization of oil: a prelude to a critical political economy. *International Journal of Political Economy.* Vol. 35.

Bina, C. 2007. America's bleeding 'cakewalk' (the 4th anniversary of the Iraq War issue). *EPS Quarterly*. Vol. 19.

Bina, C., and B. Yaghmaian. 1988. Import substitution and export promotion within the context of the internationalization of capital. *Review of Radical Political Economics*. Vol. 20.

Bina, C., and B. Yaghmaian. 1991. Postwar global accumulation and the transnationalization of capital. *Capital & Clas*. No. 43.

Bina, C., and M. Vo. 2007. OPEC in the epoch of globalization: an event study of global oil prices. *Global Economy Journal*. Vol. 7.

Campbell, K. 2007. Is Iran facing an economic crisis?" *The U.S. Institute of Peace Briefing*. United States Institute of Peace.

Dorraj, M. 2007. The secular mirage: modernity, the postmodern turn, and religious revivalism. *Journal of Globalization for the Common Good*.

Economist.com. *Country Briefings: Iran*, October 9, 2007: http://www.economist.com/countries/Iran/profile.cfm?folder=Profile- (retrieved: 10/9/2007).

The Looming Oil Crisis in Iran. *The Financial Express*: http://www.financialexpress.com/print.php?content_id=162022 (retrieved: 4/30/07).

Myers, S. L., and M. Mazzetti. 2007. U.S. finding says Iran halted nuclear arms effort in 2003. *The New York Times*. December 4 (Front Page; two separate articles by two separate authors sharing the same headline).

Nakhjavani, A. 2003 [1382 H.S.]. *Iranian Economic Problems*. Tehran: Iranian Center for Education and Industrial Research, in Persian.

National Security Archive, Electronic Briefing No. 28. *The Secret CIA History of Iran 1953 Coup*. Washington, DC: George Washington University. http://www.gwu.edu/~nsarchiv/NSAEBB/NSAEBB28/index.html#documents (retrieved: 3/9/ 2007).

The World Bank. *Iran: Country Brief*. September 2006: http://go.worldbank.org/1QTWSY93G0 (retrieved: 11/5/2007).

The World Bank. April 2007. *World Development Indicators Database*.

CYRUS BINA

H

♦ HEALTH CARE

The World Health Organization has ranked Iran's health level as 93rd in the world. However, the health status of Iranians has been improving over the past two decades due to an extension of public health preventative services and the establishment of an extensive Primary Health Care network (PHC). Iran has become a role model in the Middle East in terms of equitable health care, and the PHC has received much attention in recent years. According to the post-revolutionary Iranian Constitution (Article 29), the government of the Islamic Republic of Iran (IRI) is required to extend a form of social security to every citizen that, in part, consists of health and medical treatment and care services. This health system, formulated in 1979, has several principles of priority at the heart of its program including: priority of rural and underprivileged areas, priority of high-risk groups, priority of general practice over specialized medical care, outpatient over inpatient care, integration of services, decentralization of services, and the formation of self-sufficient regional and local facilities. A "Master Health Plan" that was drawn up during the 1980s and serves as the basis for the Primary Health Care network (PHC) indicates the exact sites of establishment for rural and urban facilities in each district. It also includes a formula that incorporates the relationship between the population in different areas and the type of services required by each, to project an estimate of human resource requirements.

This "Master Health Plan," which was adopted in the 1980s and lasted from 1983 to 2000, gave priority to basic curative and preventative services, focusing on the population groups at highest risk and in deprived areas. In early 1983, an Expanded Program on Immunization (EPI) began as an independent and vertical project in Iran, and it is gradually being integrated into the PHC network. Complete immunization on a child's first birthday in rural areas, with PHC services, now stands at 44.1%, and urban areas other than Tehran (34.9%) at 28.1%. This high coverage of rural areas is attributed to the active approach of the immunizers. In October of 1985, there was a proposal to integrate the medical education and health services, which led to the Ministry of Health being replaced by the Ministry of Health and Medical Education (MOHME).

In 1994, the Islamic Consultative Assembly passed the State Medical Services Public Insurance Act and the Medical Services Insurance Organization (MSIO) was subsequently created in 1995. By the year 2000, the PHC of Iran was considered the leading strategy for attaining health for all.

Structure

According to the census of the Statistical Centre of Iran in 2003, 730 medical establishments with a total of 110,797 beds existed in Iran. This included 488 facilities (77,300 beds) run by MOHME and 120 (11,301 beds) facilities run by other organizations, such as the Social Security Organization of Iran (SSO). In addition, 73% of all Iranian workers have SSO coverage. In 2004, there were 0.5 physicians per 1000 people in Iran.

All Iranians are eligible for the community-based preventative, public health, and limited curative health services of the PHC network, which reaches about 90% of the population. In addition, formal sector workers and dependents have mandatory curative coverage through the SSO, while armed forces and their dependents rely on the Armed Forces Medical Service Organization. Those still left without coverage are eligible for the MSIO, which comprises four distinct groups: government employees, rural households, the self-employed, and "others" (such as students). MSIO is compulsory for all government employees, and individuals are eligible for immediate benefits once enrolled (except for the self-employed, who have a three-month waiting period before the individual is covered for inpatient care). In 1997, 23.4 million people were covered through SSO, mostly in the urban areas; 29.1 million were covered through MSIO (mostly government employees, farmers, students); 3.1 million were covered by other institutions such as the Imam Khomeini Foundation; 5.4 million were not covered by any form of insurance.

The PHC network includes the benefits of immunizations for children and pregnant women, pre- and postnatal care, growth monitoring until the age of 5, promotion of nutrition and breast feeding, control of diarrheal diseases and acute respiratory infections, environmental health, water and sanitation, control of endemic diseases such as malaria, surveillance of communicable diseases, provision of basic curative services, and school health promotion. These services have no cost-sharing or premium, as they are fully paid through budget allocations. MSIO, SSO, and the Military Insurance provide comprehensive curative benefits. The SSO has no cost-sharing for services at SSO facilities, but 10% of inpatient care and 20% of outpatient care for services that are non-SSO facility-oriented cost share are covered. The MSIO has a copayment system of 25% for outpatient and 10% for inpatient services, except for rural households which face a copayment of 25% for inpatient care.

The primary health care system of Iran consists of a rural and an urban branch, with 85% of the rural and 60% of the urban population covered by the government's PHC network. As the cities are also served by the private sector, 96%–99% of the population has access to healthcare. Some rural areas have been a cause of problems due to nomadism, peri-urban areas of migrant settlement, and difficulty in recruiting community health workers (called *behvarzes*). The center of the primary healthcare network is the behvarz, or health house, which is run by community health workers (behvarzes) who develop intimate relationships with their communities, after a two year course of training.

Coverage in the rural areas consists of a network of Rural Heath Centers (RHCs) and Health Houses (HHs), manned by two health workers (behvarzes). One or two doctors are assigned for a two-year period, supported by technicians and nursing aids, to the RHCs. The HHs are supported with a 74-item list of supplies, and usually linked by telephone to the RHCs. As far as transportation for medical emergencies, the HHs are supplied with a motorcycle and the RHCs are provided with a car as means of transportation. Each RHC is responsible for supporting up to 5 or 6 HHs. Management support is provided by District Health Centers (DHCs), which are the lowest independent unit in the health system's management hierarchy. There are 220 DHCs that are responsible for supporting, supervising and monitoring the PHC network.

Urban areas are mostly populated with Urban Health Centers (UHCs), with only a few HHs. Rather than developing more urban Health Houses, the government decided to implement a program that recruits women health volunteers to work with the UHCs as members of the community outreach support team. In Tehran, there are roughly 40,000 women involved in this role. Currently, no new facilities are planned; rather the government is focusing on consolidating its PHC system, ensuring the physical assets remain in good condition, and replacing old equipment and stock.

Overall, since 1986, urban health centers have almost doubled, from 1,220 to 2,242. Rural health centers have also grown, from 1,200 to 2,400. Health houses have seen a dramatic increase, from 1,800 to 16,261.

The main flaws criticized in the system include: the prevalence of indifference by hospitals to the network, the lack of support for the Health Houses by the Rural Health Centers, lack of proper work place and facilities, the passive delivery methods of the Urban Health Centers (in particular in regard to vaccinations), the fact that the networks need to rely on a case-by-case basis external assistance—particularly in the form of materials—that must be received from abroad, and the problem of PHCs acting outside of the role of curative services. The PHC has also been criticized for having too centralized of an organization system, having the funding being too complex and not transparent, containing a system of reimbursing to medical care providers that is inefficient and counter to more modern systems, and that policy makers lack the critical information needed for decision-making. However, the government and PHC show a strong commitment to addressing all of these criticisms and to finding a way to smooth out the breaks in communication between the various health centers and health houses.

The IRI currently spends 5.7% of its GSP on health, 40% of which is from public sources. As of 2000, Iran had 0.8 physicians and 1.6 hospital beds per thousand populations, but this is rapidly changing. Training for health professionals is free at state universities, and thus Iran is producing between 4,000 to 5,000 new physicians every year. These physicians, along with the many public health professionals and community health workers who are being trained in increasing numbers, have all made a commitment to promoting equitable access to health care and in improving the already strong PHC in the IRI.

Suggested Reading

Islamic Republic of Iran. 1999. Health financing reform in Iran: principles and possible next steps. http://www.who.int/nha/docs/en/Health_financing_reform_Iran_ principles_next_steps.pdf, p. 5.

Nasseri, K., et al. 1991. Primary health care and immunization in Iran. *Public Health.* 105:229–38.

Powell, A. 2003. Iranian primary care produces big results. *Harvard Gazette.* January 23.

Shadpour, K. 2000. Primary healthcare networks in the Islamic Republic of Iran. *Eastern Mediterranean Health Journal.* Vol. 6.

World Bank. 2004. Iran national health accounts. http://www.who.int/nha/docs/en/ Iran_NHA_report_english.pdf.

World Bank. 2006. Country brief: Iran. September 2006. http://web.worldbank.org/ WBSITE/EXTERNAL/COUNTRIES/MENAEXT/IRANEXTN/0,menuPK:312966~ pagePK:141132~piPK:141107~theSitePK:312943,00.html.

PARDIS MAHDAVI

✦ HUMAN RIGHTS

The human rights situation in Iran since the 1979 Islamic Revolution and its aftermath has been described as problematic at best and dismal at worst. The revolutionary leaders and Islamic Republic governments have increasingly engaged in repressive policies reminiscent of the Shah's rule. Human rights violations under the Islamic Republic can be attributed to political, legal, and cultural sources. To secure their power base, the clerical elite have created a hierarchical structure of power that has denied equal opportunity to the individuals in the society. They have also maintained a social control of sorts that has trampled upon the human rights of the opposition forces, especially when such forces have posed a direct threat to the vested interests of the Islamic Republic.

The authoritarian, theocratic state has consistently precluded the formation of any "power blocs" or "alternative political force" among women, labor unions, students, intellectuals, professionals, and ethnic or religious minorities. Beyond political explanations, human rights violations can be traced back to the Islamic Republic's legal system. Islamic law has been widely used as a device to camouflage the clerical establishment's pervasive political powers. Similarly, a closer examination of the causes of gender-biased abuses, in both legal and economic terms, points to the country's deeply entrenched patriarchal cultural system and social practices.

THE POLITICS OF HUMAN RIGHTS

The Islamic Revolution has relied on several quasi-official and parallel institutions (e.g., the *Basiji*) in crushing opposition forces arising from civil society and other democratic and social movements. Under the control of the Office of the Supreme Leader, such groups have confronted student protests and progressive sociocultural elites. They have also disrupted academic and intellectual forums frequently. On several occasions, the *Basiji* have committed violent crackdowns on activists celebrating International Women's Day in Tehran. Similar attacks have been organized against reformist academics and journalists, creating an atmosphere of intimidation and fear.

The clerics have also established their monopoly over the crucial state institutions, such as the judiciary, the revolutionary guards and the Pasdaran, national broadcasting media, and the quasi-governmental organizations known as *bunyad-e mostazaffin* ("foundations for the oppressed"). During the 1980s, the war against moral and economic corruption (*mufsid fil-arz*, or corruption on earth) involved brutal punishment prescribed by revolutionary tribunals. During this time, a prison system emerged in which tutelage and torture was concurrent. In Evin prison's workshop, for example, the prisoners chanted slogans while working or changing shifts, and posters exhorted prisoners to change their ways. Political prisoners continued to receive unfair trials before special courts, such as the Special Court for the Clergy, which fell far short of international standards. Amnesty International has regularly called upon the Iranian government to ensure impartial and thorough investigations into allegations of torture, disappearances, and extrajudicial executions.

In the early years of the revolution, concepts of Islamic government (*velayate-e-faqih* (rule by the jurisconsult) and the primacy of Islamic law were enshrined in Iran's constitution. These changes gave the clerics ultimate authority in managing and guiding the state. Under the de facto leadership of Ayattollah Khomeini, the revolutionary government of Mehdi Bazargan struggled during a chaotic and troubling era. In July 1988, Ayatollah Khomeini ordered the mass execution of political prisoners, many of whom were members of the leftist parties that belonged to a very wide spectrum of communism.

To maintain stability and security, the Iranian state has had to come to grips with several critical issues, including tensions over ethnic minorities (especially the Kurds), Iran–U.S. relations, the Iran–Iraq War, the antigovernment guerrilla forces, and the Salman Rushdie affair. In 1989 Khomeini issued a death *fatwa* (religious edict) against Rushdie because his novel, *The Satanic Verses*, derided Muslims' sacred values. The ensuing Iranian governments, however, never enforced the death *fatwa*.

Following Khomeini's death in 1989, factional infighting and competition permeated all aspects of the political process. Through a national referendum in 1989, the post of prime minister was abolished and was replaced with a popularly elected president as head of the government. The president, therefore, did not need to be approved by the Majlis, the sole chamber of parliament. At the time, this was taken to mean that the *velayate-e faqih* would no longer dominate the political sphere. Consequently, the president emerged as the most powerful figure of the state.

Iran remained officially neutral in the first Persian Gulf War of 1991. The Islamic Republic's relations with most Arab states remained poor, and the prospects of improving ties with the United States were dim. In September 1992, four Kurdish opposition leaders in Berlin, at the Mykonos Café, were assassinated. The German media published legal findings demonstrating the involvement of Ali Fallahian, then Iranian Minister of Intelligence in these terrorist acts. In March 1996, a German court issued an arrest warrant for Ali Fallahian for his role in the Mykonos case. In April 1997, the court asserted that the government of Iran had pursued a deliberate policy of eliminating the regime's opponents living outside Iran, including the opposition Kurdish

Democratic Party of Iran (KDPI). The judge implicated the most senior levels of the Iranian government in the Mykonos murders.

During the 1980s, political liberalization in Iran came to a standstill. The press law, passed in 1985 and still in effect, allows the Ministry of Culture and Islamic Guidance to ban any publication that insults leading religious elites. The courts have closed many periodicals. Under the press law, the government repeatedly charged journalists with espionage for activities that were routine practices in journalism. The works of the best-known Iranian film directors, including Bahram Beizai and Mohsen Makhmalbaf, were frequently censored.

In 1994 public discontent over economic and political conditions resulted in riots in several Iranian cities. Violent confrontations between demonstrators and security forces were reported in Tehran, Tabriz, Zahedan, Qazvin, and Najafabad. Officially sponsored vigilantism became widespread in 1995 as Hezbollah directed its attacks against people critical of state corruption, such as Abdol-Karim Soroush. Domestic human rights organizations—including the Parliamentary Human Rights Committee, the Organization for Defending Victims of Violence, and the Human Rights Commission—were not allowed to operate effectively.

In the March 1996 parliamentary elections, the Council of Guardians excluded nearly half of the more than 5,000 candidates for parliament on the basis of discriminatory and arbitrary criteria. This practice obstructed access to the political process and citizens' freedom of choice. In the same month, Maurice Copithorne, the U.N. human rights rapporteur, argued that the social climate in Iran had become intolerable and that the regime harassed and violated the rights of Baha'is as a religious minority and continued to assassinate dissidents living abroad.

The Rise and Fall of Reform (1997–2005)

In a landslide victory on May 23, 1997, Mohammad Khatami was elected Iran's new president. Khatami, himself a cleric with close ties to the religious establishment, became known for his pragmatism. He had served as the minister of culture and Islamic guidance from 1982 to 1992 but was forced to resign when conservatives criticized his somewhat permissive policies on issues such as allowing limited access to television satellite dishes. Khatami's overwhelming support from both the youth and the women demonstrated his success at winning the trust of a generation that had not been born at the time of the revolution. Furthermore, despite the fact that no general consensus on the meaning and feasibility of civil society emerged, there seemingly was a general agreement that civil society would solve many of the country's social and political problems.

Khatami's legacy, however, was often overshadowed by the intense power struggles between those who demanded change and those who defended the status quo—loosely, Iran's reformists and hardline conservatives. Nowhere were such power struggles more obvious than over cultural politics—that is, the real struggle was over whose vision of an Islamic society would prevail. The central conflict that characterized Khatami's years was the perceived incompatibility between global and local paradigms. Prominent Iranian intellectuals and journalists began to challenge the underlying concepts of Islamic governance. In April 2000, many newspapers were closed down and many journalists and editors were imprisoned, while editors and publishers were regularly called before what became known as the Press Court.

During Khatami's presidency, the judiciary, which is accountable to the Supreme Leader Ali Khamenei rather than the elected president, was at the center of many human rights violations. Many abuses were carried out by the so-called parallel institutions (nahad-e movazi)—these are the plainclothes intelligence agents and paramilitary groups that violently attack peaceful protests, students, writers, and reformist politicians. These institutions also refer to the illegal and secret prisons and interrogation centers run by intelligence services. Groups such as Ansar-e Hizbollah and the Basij, who are under the control of the Office of the Supreme Leader, are examples of such organizations.

The operation of these "parallel institutions" alongside the government institutions demonstrated the lack of any control over them by the executive branch. The serial murder case of secular dissidents after President Khatami's election in 1997 illustrated the extent of the struggle between the moderates and the hardliners. The security agents murdered five prominent dissidents. The killings were carried out on November 22, 1998, with the stabbing of Dariush Forouhar and his wife Parvaneh, who ran a small opposition party. In the following weeks, secular and outspoken writers Majid Sharif, Mohammad Jafar Pouyandeh, and Mohammad Mokhtari disappeared and later were found murdered with their bodies dumped in the outskirts of Tehran. The closed trials of these serial murderers, which occurred during December 2000–January 2001, led to controversial verdicts. On January 27, 2001, a judge handed down the sentences. Several "rogue" agents from the intelligence ministry were sentenced to death or life imprisonment.

Amid this controversy and public outrage, the outspoken dissident journalist Akbar Ganji published a book and several essays alleging former President Akbar Hashemi Rafsanjani was linked to the murders. Ganji also told a revolutionary court that senior figures of the Islamic Republic, including former Intelligence Minister Ali Fallahian and a senior judge, Gholam-Hossein Mohseni Ejei, were directly involved in these serial killings. Because of these critical views of the government, Ganji spent more than five years in prison. He went on a hunger strike to focus the world's attention on the widespread human rights violations in Iran. The worldwide protests, both in Iran and abroad, eventually led to his release in 2006.

Amnesty International has consistently reminded the Iranian government of its specific obligations under Article 19 of the International Covenant on Civil and Political Rights (ICCPR) to protect the right to freedom of expression. Political prisoners in Iran have frequently gone on hunger strikes to protest their inhuman treatment and have demanded an inspection of prisons by the Amnesty International. Activists have noted that Iran has adopted a tactic of housing political prisoners together with common criminals in an attempt to demonize them and break down their morale.

In early December 2000, a lawyer for the families of Mokhtari and Pouyandeh, Nasser Zarafshan, was jailed after he pointed to other disappearances and slayings, while claiming that the assassinations had been ordered by religious decree. On July 15, 2002, Mr. Zarafshan was sentenced to 5 years imprisonment by the Military Court of Tehran. He is currently serving time in Evin prison.

The victory of Mahmood Ahmadinejad in the 2005 presidential elections returned Islamic populism to Iranian politics. Despite their irregularities, elections demonstrated that Iranian people had lost their faith not only in the Khatami's government but also in elections more generally. This accounts for the boycott of the 2005 elections by many Iranians—a boycott that made possible the victory of Ahmadinejad.

During his tenure as Tehran's mayor, Ahmadinejad reversed many of the changes enacted by previous moderate and reformist mayors, putting serious religious emphasis on the activities of the cultural centers founded by previous mayors. It is also said that Ahmadinejad separated elevators for men and women in the municipality offices. Hardliners under President Ahmadinejad have insisted on enforcing Iran's strict Islamic dress code, which obliges Iranian women to wear proper *hijab*. There have been some reports of imposing a single university dress code on women, while not allowing perfumes and cosmetics to be used on university campuses.

Ahmadinejad, however, appointed a woman as Vice President. Fatemeh Javadi was appointed as Vice President and Head of the Environment Protection Organization. Javadi's appointment indicated that Ahmadinejad is following the footsteps of his predecessor. Ahmadinejad faced several gender-related questions at the dawn of his presidency, but perhaps none more important than the following: (1) can a women's role in society, in general, and in the public sphere, in particular, be curtailed? And (2) will the legitimacy of women's rights as universally recognized human rights be denied? Ahmadinejad is unlikely to undo social reforms and rollback gains women have achieved in recent years, but he is supported by conservative clerical rulers who oppose globalizing dynamics surrounding Iranian society and favor a degree of cultural conformity. Fearing that their Islamic interests and values would be compromised or undermined, the Islamic Republic's leaders, such as Ahmadinejad, will most likely tighten their grip on society.

THE LEGAL SYSTEM AND WOMEN'S RIGHTS

The Islamic Republic replaced the secular legal code with an Islamic constitution that has had negative consequences for women's rights. According to the 2003 Nobel Peace Prize winner, Shirin Ebadi, men can have four wives and divorce a wife without a cause, while women have no such rights. After divorce, the son belongs to his mother until the age of 2 and the daughter until the age of 7. Women need their husband's permission to travel abroad. Islamic dress code (headscarf-*hijab*) and segregation are enforced in public places. According to the country's election laws, the Guardian Council must pre-qualify candidates for the Majlis (parliament). All of the 89 women who sought approval from the Guardian Council to run for 2005 Presidential elections were rejected.

The constitution of the Islamic Republic contains a penal code that prescribes several kinds of punishment: *hodud*, *qasas*, *diyat*, *ta'zirat*, and prohibitive punishments. In the case of *hodud* (punishment prescribed in religious law), in several cases the testimony of two just women equals that of one just man. Article 74 (adultery) of the penal code reads: whether punishable by flogging or stoning, may be proven by the testimony of four just men or that of three just men and two just women. With regard to *qasas* (retribution), Article 237 indicates that evidence for second degree murder or manslaughter shall consist in the testimony of two just men, or that of one just man and two just women.

In the first two years of Khatami's presidency, Iranian parliament enacted several laws significant to women, including a provision for readjusting the value of the *mahr* (monetary sum the husband pledges to his wife in the marriage contract, which is due to her in full upon demand in keeping with inflation). A law was also passed that permitted women civil servants to retire after 20 years' service. Some five thousand women were given a chance to run for 220,000 local council seats in cities, towns, and villages across the country. Nearly 300 women were elected to the local city councils. In some cities, women gained the majority of votes. Among the 15 members of the Tehran city council were three women, including Jameileh Kadivar. In the legal sphere, in 1998, seven women were given licenses to open and head notary offices, a job devoted exclusively to men and clerics previously.

Many non-governmental organizations (NGOs) have actively promoted women's rights in both rural and urban areas. The Iranian Islamic Women's Institute, headed by Azam Taleghani, is one such NGO. Its aim is to improve women's status by providing literacy classes, informing women of their rights, offering them free legal advice, and bolstering their financial independence with training in diverse activities, including carpet weaving, pottery works, and sewing. Secular women have created solidarity networks for mutual assistance. Lawyers and jurists provide legal advice as to how to fight back. In their informal groups, they organize debates on such topics as *hijab*, motherhood, employment, feminism, and activism. Increasingly Iranian feminists, both Islamic and secular, have resisted conservative religious forces and have negotiated and reconstructed their position in society since the 1979 Islamic revolution.

Decades of ideological and political mobilization by the Islamic Republic to forge a collectivist identity and force it on Iranian women have proved counterproductive. Many Iranian women attempt to strike a balance between the extremes of Western individualism and Islamic collectivism. Increasingly, Iranian women have become less concerned with political power, revolution, and ideology. They are more concerned with the control of their lives within political, social, and economic institutions, regardless of the ideological configurations of these institutions.

Khatami's administration proved incapable of curbing the security apparatus, as the latter continued to act independently of the executive branch. In 2003, Zahra Kazemi, an Iranian–Canadian photojournalist, died while in custody in Tehran. Forensic reports showed that Kazemi died of a brain hemorrhage. No serious attempt has since been made by the judiciary to identify or prosecute those responsible for Kazemi's death.

Similarly, legal reform was blocked by the Majlis on a few occasions. Khatami withdrew bills that proposed extending the powers of the President and prohibited the Guardians' Council from disqualifying parliamentary candidates. The seventh parliament rejected the previous parliament's passage of a bill granting women inheritance rights equal to men's. In August 2005, the Guardian Council rejected a proposal to make Iran a party to the U.N. Convention on the Elimination of All Forms of Discrimination Against Women (CEDAW).

Given that geopolitical realities often tend to trump human rights considerations, the future prospects of much improvement in Iran's human rights situation remains dubious for the foreseeable future. Absent a direct link to

Iran's internal reforms and the protection of basic freedoms of the Iranian people, the Western leverage on Iran appears limited. Unless the state of human rights in Iran occupies a key part of negotiations between Iran, the European Union, and the United States, no sustainable improvements in human rights conditions could be achieved over the long run.

Suggested Reading

Abrahamian, E. 1999. *Tortured confessions: prisons and public recantations in modern Iran.* Berkeley: University of California Press.

Afkhami, M., and E. Friedl, eds. 1994. *In the eye of the storm: women in post-revolutionary Iran.* Syracuse, NY: Syracuse University Press.

Afshari, R. 2001. *Human rights in Iran: the abuse of cultural relativism.* Philadelphia: University of Pennsylvania Press.

Amnesty International. 2005. *Amnesty International Report of 2005: the state of the world's human rights.* New York: Amnesty International.

Esfandiari, H. 2001. "The politics of the 'women's question' in the Islamic Republic, 1979–1999." In *Iran at the crossroads,* eds. J. L. Esposito and R. K. Ramazan. New York: Palgrave, pp. 75–92.

Human Rights Watch. 2005. *World Report 2005: events of 2004,* New York: Human Rights Watch.

Kamrava, M. 2001. "The civil society discourse in Iran." *British Journal of Middle Eastern Studies,* Vol. 28, No. 2, November, pp. 165–185.

Kian-Thiebaut, A. 2002. "Women and the making of civil society in post-Islamist Iran." In *Twenty Years of Islamic Revolution: Political and Social Transition in Iran Since 1979,* ed. E. Hooglund. Syracuse, NY: Syracuse University Press, pp. 56–73.

Mahdi, A. A. 2003. "Iranian women: between Islamicization and globalization." In *Iran encountering globalization: problems and prospects,* ed. Ali Mohammadi. New York: Routledge Curzon, pp. 47–72.

Mayer, A. E. 1991. *Islam and human rights: tradition and politics.* Boulder, Westview Press.

Moallem, M. 2005. *Between warrior brother and veiled sister: Islamic fundamentalism and the politics of patriarchy in Iran.* Berkeley: University of California Press.

Monshipouri, M. 1998. *Islamism, secularism, and human rights in the Middle East.* Boulder, CO: Lynne Rienner Publishers.

MAHMOOD MONSHIPOURI

✦ INDUSTRIAL DEVELOPMENT

For centuries the Iranian economy was based on agriculture and trade. With the notable exception of the carpet industry, some food processing, and a small jewelry industry, this remained the case up until the early 1900s. Apart from oil, modern industry in Iran dates from the mid-1930s, when Reza Shah launched a vigorous program of industrial investment as part of his program of modernizing the country.

Except for a few private textile mills in Isfahan, the industries started in the 1930s were almost all government-owned. While industrialization did not occur on the scale of Ataturk's Turkey, some progress was made. This included the beginnings of what are today the three major factory industries in the country—textiles, sugar, and cement. An integrated steel mill of 60,000 tons capacity was begun but not finished (because the war interrupted shipments from Germany). A few of these plants did reasonably well, but many began to decay immediately upon completion because of shortages of technical personnel, managerial inexperience, poor location, and wartime problems with raw materials and replacement parts.

By 1946 when studies for the First Plan were begun, the government owned and operated 34 industrial and mining establishments and 39 tea factories and rice mills. Unfortunately, by the 1950s, few of the government's plants were well-run, and the only profitable ones were those enjoying a monopoly (e.g., sugar and tobacco).

Working on the assembly line at the Iran Khodro car manufacturing company on the outskirts of Tehran, 2007. Fuel rationing forced Iran's largest car maker, Iran Khodro, to scale down the manufacture of gasoline-powered cars and increase production of dual-fuel cars that also run on natural gas as part of Iranian government's attempt to reduce the billions of dollars it spends each year to import gasoline. (AP Photo/Hasan Sarbakhshian)

Although Iran's industrial development before World War II was modest and confined almost exclusively to state-run enterprises, the post-war period saw an impressive flowering of private entrepreneurship. This stemmed from the demand from the government's generally high level of infrastructure investment, the ready availability of foreign exchange to finance the import of capital goods, the development of arrangements for extending public funds to assist private projects, and the emergence of a substantial number of industrial entrepreneurs. These were men who had either accumulated funds through foreign trade, had shifted their energies and family funds out of an increasingly uncertain and unprofitable land-lordism, or who had been recruited to industry by an engineering education.

The growth was especially marked after 1956; the next four years saw private industrial investment climb rapidly from around $60 million per year to an estimated $120 million. This was not an orderly and soundly based expansion. Instead, the boom was partly the product of an extremely liberal policy of industrial credit, a policy administered by the Ministry of Industries and Mines entirely outside the Second Seven-Year Plan. By the end of the Second Plan in

September 1962, industrial production had rapidly expanded to account for 13% to 14% of domestic production.

The First Plan did not contribute all that much to the country's industrialization, due to its interruption by the oil nationalization crisis. The entire $15 million spent on industry went into a half-dozen government factories, most of which had been started before the Plan started. The Second Plan was still limited almost exclusively to investment in government-owned plants but was much more ambitious than the first. Like its predecessor, the Second Plan consisted purely of financial allocations. It did not contain any physical targets or any statements of the philosophy underlying the allocations. Nevertheless, the Plan's approach to industrialization seems to have been guided by five unwritten objectives:

1. To assure the availability of essential consumer goods, free of the disruptions caused by international events. This policy found expression in the "Article of the Plan" law, where the government stated its intention of producing "public necessities within the country."
2. To lay the basis for a greatly broadened pattern of industrialization by starting the domestic production of iron and steel.
3. To assure the availability of cement, perhaps the most important construction material for civil works.
4. To demonstrate to private investors the feasibility of certain industrial and mining projects by making initial investments in industries not previously carried on in the country. This policy underlay the proposed Plan Organization projects in paper, polyvinyl chloride, olive oil extraction, a few canneries, some of the mining projects, and the cane sugar experiment in Khuzestan.
5. To assist private investment by giving suggestions, technical assistance and credit, or credit guarantees. To exercise these functions, Plan Organization was authorized to establish a bank or similar specialized agency.

The process of import substitution (production for the domestic market of goods previously imported) began, in earnest, in the 1960s, and was initially confined to consumer goods. Protective measures for the domestic market were the chief stimulus, as firms were expected to eventually expand into import substitution of intermediate and capital goods. At least ten distinctive features characterized the sector's subsequent growth during this period.

1. Industrialization proceeded at an extremely rapid pace and in a wide variety of industries.

2. Manufacturing (primarily of food processing, textiles, footwear, and similar industries) and capital goods industries began immediately following the growth of light consumer goods.

3. Investment in intermediate products industries was concentrated in steel, fertilizers, chemicals and transport equipment. Capital goods expansion was primarily in construction materials and electrical equipment.

4. The normal time lag usually experienced in moving from light to heavy industry was drastically shortened.

5. Almost all industrial growth was oriented for the domestic market as a process of pure import substitution. Most industries were started in response to already existing or anticipated demands on products previously imported.

6. Industries were given generous incentives by the government. These consisted of tariff protection or import prohibitions.

7. Both domestic and foreign private capital participated in the industrialization, with a domestic entrepreneurial class evolving out of the import trade business.

8. The demand for labor increased selectively. Although there were large masses underemployed in the rural areas, shortages of skilled and semiskilled labor resulted from the industrialization process.

9. While a policy of geographical decentralization was pursued by the government, industry became increasingly concentrated in Tehran.

10. Although most of the industrial growth took place in the private sector, the government continued to exercise a major influence on investment and output. Some projects such as in petrochemicals were government-owned, as was the integrated steel mill in Isfahan.

During the 1960s it appears that, as a proportion of total industry sales, domestic production increased most rapidly in the consumer durable area. The domestic production of capital goods also expanded rapidly during this period with Iranian firms gaining an additional 25% of the domestic market in this area. Domestically produced electrical equipment, for example, accounted for fewer than 5% of domestic sales in 1960, but by 1969, its share had increased to almost 40% (of an expanded market). Vehicle assembly was another area in which rapid growth took place. By 1969 domestic firms supplied over 70% of the market compared with only 40% in 1960.

The expansion of domestic output of intermediate goods was much more uneven with production of products such as paper, printing, rubber, and chemicals increasing very rapidly with only limited expansion in metal products and nonmetallic minerals. As noted earlier, imports of capital goods, such as machinery, were very significant. By the end of the 1960s, imports of these goods still accounted for over 90% of the domestic market, amounting to about 25% of the country's total imports.

Apparently, the degree of interdependence and reliance of various sectors of the economy upon each other and not on the foreign sources of intermediate goods declined during the period under consideration. This occurred at the same time the manufacturing firms enjoying the protected home market became less competitive in world markets. At least this is the picture one obtains by comparing the country's input-output tables over time. In 1962, for example, sales from the manufacturing sector were about 31% of the entire sector's sales. However, by 1970 this ratio had fallen to only 19%. Although direct comparisons with other countries are difficult, 19% is quite a low percentage, by any measure, and is indicative of the economy's weak linkages.

By the mid 1970s, it was clear that Iranian industry could not justify the priority treatment it was enjoying in terms of investment. By 1975, it was still generating only 18% of the GDP. In the years following the 1973/1974 oil boom, industry failed to respond significantly to the surge in domestic demand. The proportion of imports in the aggregate supply of goods rose from 20.6% in 1973 to 26.9% in 1975, and the trend continued until the time of the revolution. Meanwhile, the effect of rising demand on non-oil exports was predictably detrimental, and these were lower in 1975 than in the two previous years.

Thus the pattern of import substitution industrialization, initiated in Iran, not only presented a seriously distorted way of development, high social cost, unemployment, underemployment of resources, inequitable distribution of income and wealth, and relatively neglected agricultural and handicraft industries, but also involved problems associated with the building of over-capacity in key industries such as petrochemicals, fertilizers, steel, and refineries. The limited size of the internal market coupled with the skewed income distribution pattern in the country further impeded the full utilization of productive capacity already built or the planned capacity being contemplated in the various development plans. The consequences of import substitution industrialization were the high costs of production, a decrease in quality of products because of the heavily protected domestic industry, and perpetual dependence on world markets, both to build new production capacities and to maintain existing capacities.

On a speculative note, a number of observers have commented from time to time that the system of industrial controls, licensing, tariffs, etc. was set up so that the Shah's family and close business associates would have an easy source of monopoly profits and political influence. While there is little doubt that abuses along these lines did occur, it is unlikely that most of the industrial regulations and the whole strategy itself was created with this purpose in mind. A careful reading of the industrial history of this period shows that, in many respects, Iran's import substitution strategy was similar to that taking place in a number of other countries. A more accurate description of the country's industrialization strategy is that it evolved first by necessity out of the economic crises of the early 1960s and later largely by whim and emulation of other countries.

Still, no sector of the Iranian economy under the Shah's regime came under more blistering attacks from the opposition and the victorious revolutionaries than the industrial (mainly the manufacturing) sector. The standard indictment was that Iran's pre-1979 industrialization was pushed forward without due regard to either domestic resource endowments and capabilities, or society's basic needs. As a result, industry allegedly failed to meet the country's basic requirements. Excessive protectionism, unwise availability of tax exemptions and easy credit, inappropriate use of foreign technology, and expertise and the reliance of domestic enterprises on foreign technicians, raw materials, and processed goods were said to create a system of assembly plant operation and fragile "dependent capitalism" at the mercy of external crisis. In short, industry was blamed for failing to meet agriculture's needs for heavy machinery, the oil sector's requirements for exploration and refining, and even its own needs for spare parts and raw materials.

From its inception, the Islamic Republic was bent on radically altering the Shah's industrialization drive. But unlike other major sectors, industry was beset by many incapacitating problems of its own, which defied political or ideological solution. In the wake of the revolution, manufacturing enterprises experienced an accelerated decline in capacity utilization, due mostly to disruption of supplies and a drop in sales. Essential problems involved private industrial enterprises whose owners or managers had left the country; colossal debt owed by these companies to the faltering banking system; labor agitation, confusion regarding ownership and administration of abandoned units; constant threats by new managers to shut down operations and dismiss workers unless assisted by the government; and the intrusion of Islamic *komitehs* in the enterprises decision-making process.

The Islamic republic's short-term industrial policy placed its main emphasis on two principles: encouraging industrial activities with the quickest, high-value possibilities; and supporting enterprises with the highest domestic content and least dependence on foreign exchange. The overriding long-term criteria were industrial self-sufficiency and independence and the redirection of the industrial sector toward the implementation of the Constitution's clause 43, requiring the government to ensure the provision of food, clothing, and housing needs.

A bill for the Protection and Development of Iranian Industries passed by the Revolutionary Council in July 1979 had the following five diversified objectives: determination of workers' pay according to Islamic tenets; deliverance of Iran from foreign economic dependence; the expropriation of properties belonging to agents of the previous autocratic regime; the avoidance of state domination over the economy; and protection of the private sector against unfair foreign competition.

The 1979 legislation divided existing industrial enterprises in Iran into four categories: basic and strategic industries (including oil, gas, railways, fisheries, electric utilities, automobile manufacturing, shipbuilding, aviation, and basic metals); mining and industrial units belonging to individuals deemed to have been acquired or expanded by illegal or illegitimate means; factories, firms, or enterprises which owed the banks more then the value of their assets; and fourthly, enterprises not classified under the previous three categories.

The first category enterprises were to be placed under public ownership and operation; their legitimate owners were to be compensated for the net worth of their holdings. Some 200 firms and units under the second category were to be confiscated and transferred to the government. Another 200 or so enterprises under the third category were to be placed under the (nationalized) banks' trusteeship, and to be run, or liquidated, on behalf of their public or private creditors. Enterprises not included in the above categories were recognized as legitimate private enterprises protected by law.

To date, manufacturing activity under the Islamic Republic has been carried out, supervised, and regulated by several different agencies, institutions, and owner/manager establishments in a complex (not always coordinated) fashion. In 1981, the Ministry of Industries and Mines was divided into two new ministries: Industries, and Mines and Metals. In 1982, a separate Ministry of Heavy Industries was established. These three ministries have been in charge of the direction and supervision of medium and large scale enterprises. The Ministry of Industries is broadly responsible for industrial development and policy coordination. It is in charge of issuing required licenses for the establishment or expansion of eligible projects; it makes industrial surveys and through the National Iranian Industries Organization (NIIO), it oversees a large number of nationalized firms.

As might be expected the high degree of change and uncertainty associated with the post-revolutionary period has resulted in a mixed performance. In the years immediately following the revolution, the manufacturing sector experienced some expected ups and downs, but for much of the decade, the sector went through a period of lack of direction, neglect, decay, and poor performance. Throughout the 1980s, the manufacturing subsector showed intervals of sporadic recovery, but generally declining capacity utilization. Technological obsolescence and deteriorating international competitiveness followed heavy domestic protection and exchange overvaluation. Growing state ownership, production, and regulation combined with institutional weakness and legal confusion resulted in a dwindling interest and participation on the part of private entrepreneurs.

Throughout most of the post-revolution period, the Iranian manufacturing sector has experienced years of negative growth, low capacity utilization, small scale operations, aging technology, overstaffing inexperienced management, lack of easy access to raw materials and parts, high cost of transport and warehousing, the replacement of efficiency criteria by ideological considerations, excessive price and exchange rate regulations, addictive and unhealthy protection against foreign competition, and the politico-economic crowding out of the private sector.

External factors and structural handicaps—including exchange overvaluation and ineffective customs duties—have also played their part in keeping growth down. By the 1990s, it was clear that a new policy towards the industrial sector was essential for the country's economic health. Public ownership and management of non-strategic sectors are to be gradually relinquished to the private sector. Private investment in the manufacturing and construction sectors is actively encouraged. However, import substitution still seems to be favored over export orientation.

The true weakness of Iran's manufacturing process, however, continues to lie in its overdependence on oil revenues for the purchase of imported inputs; in its neglect of employment generation; and its nearly exclusive concentration on production for a soft home market. The sector has not played a significant role in job creation. The result has been to force workers into low productivity or technically stagnant areas such as services and small industries.

Because of widespread industrial inefficiency and lack of job creation, the government has, since 1990, embarked on a new liberalization and privatization policy. In the manufacturing sector, for example, price controls have been removed from a host of "non-essential" manufactured products, and the cost-plus approach to pricing domestic and imported products has ended. This move has been followed by the lifting of quantitative restrictions on exports and imports.

Under the privatization drive several significant measures have been put into effect. Some industrial enterprises have been returned to their original owners. Former industrialists have been encouraged to return to Iran and reclaim their expropriated property through the judicial system. The government has also declared its intention to gradually divest hundreds of large-scale industrial enterprises under its ownership or supervision or owned by nationalized banks.

Suggested Reading

Karshenas, M. 1990. *Oil, state and industrialization in Iran*. Cambridge: Cambridge University Press.

Looney, R. 1982. *Economic origins of the Iranian Revolution*. New York: Pergamon Press.

ROBERT E. LOONEY

✦ INTELLECTUALS

Similar to many other developing countries, Iran has had a long tradition of intellectual political activism, dating back to the late nineteenth century. Inspired by the political ideals of the West, by the contradictory forces of tradition and modernity, and spurred into action by hopes of fostering economic progress and political development in Iran, Iranian intellectuals played important roles in the Constitutional Revolution of 1905–1911, the era of Reza Shah and his son Mohammad Reza Pahlavi, the Islamic Revolution of 1978–1979, and in the post-revolutionary period. Either through compulsion or on their own, Iranian intellectuals have reflected the popular and/or the political mood and tenor of the times in which they have found themselves—constitutionalism in the late 1800s and the early 1900s, statism and statist growth in the 1920s to the 1940s, radicalism in the 1960s and the 1970s, revolutionary Islam in the 1970s and the 1980s, and various shades of postmodernism and what might be termed "post-Islamism" from the 1980s on.

During the life of the Islamic Republic so far, Iranian intellectuals may be divided into four broad and often interchangeable categories. By far one of the most important groups, and one of the earliest, may be classified as "Islamic revolutionaries," who were inspired by the ideals of the late Ali Shariati (1933–1977) and Ayatollah Morteza Motahhari (1920–1979). Often considered the ideologues of the Islamic Revolution, Shariati and Motahhari, and before them the author and cultural critic Jalal Ale-Ahmad (1923–1969), sought to modernize and revolutionize Islam at once, turn it from what they claimed had become a tool of oppression of the masses and popular superstition into the blueprint for liberation and progress, which was its original intent. Islam is deeply compatible with science, they maintained, and its

Abbas Abdi and Hossein Ali Qazian, right in background, sit for the second hearing on a controversial survey about Iran–U.S. relations during their trial in Tehran, 2002. Qazian and colleagues Abbas Abdi and Behrouz Geranpayeh were arrested in October and November 2002 after conducting a survey that showed strong public support for dialogue with the United States. The poll angered Iran's hardline clerics who had ruled that relations with Washington were treasonous. (AP Photo/ Hasan Sarbakhshian)

proper interpretation, as practiced by the Prophet Muhammad and by other early Islamic—and especially Shi'a—personages, allows for an end to the Islamic community's political oppression, its economic exploitation and backwardness, and its cultural alienation. Islam needs to renew itself by rediscovering its original message, embracing its liberating essence, and recapturing its dynamic spirit. Only then, claimed Shariati, will true Islam once again be reestablished. For his part, Motahhari, less of an activist and more of a scholar compared to Shariati, sought to show the deep compatibility of Islam with science and progress.

The ideas of Shariati and Motahhari inspired millions of young Iranians and emerged as the dominant ideals of the Islamic Revolution, even after such dynamic, revolutionary interpretations of Islam fell out of favor with the more conservative and traditional heirs of the revolutionary movement in the early to mid-1980s. Gradually, however, as the terror of post-revolutionary consolidation gave way to the economic and industrial reconstruction of the late 1980s, and as profound changes began to occur to the country's polity—with the end of the Iran–Iraq War in 1988, the passing of Ayatollah Khomeini in 1989, major constitutional revisions in the same year, and the routinization of charismatic authority—a new generation of Islamic thinkers began to make their presence felt. This post-revolutionary group of religious thinkers was inspired by hopes of not necessarily revolutionizing Islam, but rather alleviating its potential for excesses and by reforming its extremism. Islam, they claimed, had become overly radicalized, its ideological fervor blinding it to its inherent democratic tendencies, and, in the process, it had become a mere tool for justifying political centralization and autocracy. Islam needed to be reformed; more specifically, it needed a new framework for original interpretation, *ijtihad*.

By far the most prominent of this group of "religious reformist" intellectuals is Abdolkarim Soroush (b. 1945), who, among other things, calls for a separation of religion as a guide for man's divine ascent versus religion as a historically encumbered set of rites and rituals. A prolific author and thinker, Soroush has been subject to frequent harassment by the authorities and divides his time between Iran and various Western countries. Also important in this group are Hojjatoleslam Mohsen Kadivar (b. 1959), whose writings center on the historic misinterpretations of Islamic precepts and notions, and Hojjatoleslam Mohammad Mojtahed Shabestari (b. 1936), who maintains that Islam has become a victim to "official" interpretations by the state and, instead, must be rediscovered through the science of hermeneutics.

A small number of contemporary Iranian intellectuals disagree with the religious reformists' claim that Islam has been misinterpreted and needs to be reformed. Although they do not necessarily endorse the many excesses of the Islamic Republican state, they do, nevertheless, generally refrain from openly criticizing it. Instead, they see in Islam a powerful remedy to the ills of contemporary society, an anchor against the uncertainties and unpleasant side effects of modernity. By far the most prominent of these thinkers is Reza Davari Ardekani (b. 1933), a philosophy professor at the University of Tehran, many of whose ideas can be traced back to his old mentor, Professor Ahmad Fardid (1939–1994), who also taught philosophy at the University of Tehran. Although Fardid was avowedly secular, he was in many ways considered the father of postmodernist thought in Iran.

A fourth group of contemporary Iranian intellectuals are secular-modernist thinkers, in whose worldview religion does not have a central place but who are instead inspired by the ideals of liberal democracy, globalization, and modernity. For these intellectuals, Iran's salvation lies not in religion's dominance over public life—religion, they maintain, must be respected as a private matter—but rather in its embracing of the tenets of modernity in politics, economy, and culture. One of the most articulate and prolific of these secular-modernist intellectuals is Ramin Jahanbegloo (b. 1961). Other notable figures include Daryush Ashouri (b. 1938), Jamshid Behnam (b. 1928), Daryush Shayegan (b. 1935), and Musa Ghaninezhad (b. 1951).

Throughout contemporary Iranian history, the country's intellectuals have operated in less than hospitable political environments. The post-revolutionary period is no exception, and the political harassment, and often even imprisonment, of intellectual figures is common. Very few of the intellectuals named here have managed to escape the wrath of the Islamic Republic. The political context within which intellectual endeavors occur is bound to influence their outcome. Which intellectual trend will emerge as dominant, and what future direction each will take, remains to be seen, victim, in large measure, to the travails of the country's politics.

Suggested Reading

Boroujerdi, M. 1996. *Iranian intellectuals and the West: the tormented triumph of nativism.* Syracuse, NY: Syracuse University Press.

Gheissari, A. 1998. *Iranian intellectuals in the twentieth century.* Austin, Tex: University of Texas Press.

Mirsepassi, A. 2000. *Intellectual discourse and the politics of modernization: negotiating modernity in Iran.* Cambridge: Cambridge University Press.

Shayegan, D. 1992. *Cultural schizophrenia: Islamic societies confronting the West.* Syracuse, NY: Syracuse University Press.

MEHRAN KAMRAVA

✦ INTERNATIONAL ORGANIZATIONS

The World Bank is a multilateral development institution whose stated purpose is to assist developing member countries in furthering their economic and social progress. It comprises two legally and financially distinct bodies: the International Bank for Reconstruction and Development (IBRD), established in 1945, and the International Development Association (IDA), established in 1960. Their functions are to lend funds, provide economic advice and technical assistance, and to act as a catalyst to investment by others. Affiliated organizations are the International Finance Corporation (IFC), established in 1956, often referred to as the leading private sector aid agency in the world, and the Multilateral Investment Guarantee Agency (MIGA), established in 1988, which aims to protect direct foreign investors from noncommercial risk.

World Bank activity in Iran began in 1946 when it began playing an important role in assisting the country's initial efforts at economic planning. This culminated in a seven-year plan for "Iran's Reconstruction and Development." Iran was one of the original IBRD members; Abol Hassan Ebtehaj represented Iran at the 1944 Bretton Woods conference that created the World Bank and the IMF. He had been the Governor of the Bank Melli for many years and was destined to become one of the most successful Managing Directors of the Iranian Plan Organization.

Iran was a major World Bank client during the 1960s but halted its borrowing practices in 1975 as oil price increases provided the government with adequate funding for its development programs. After 1979, the Islamic government maintained its distance from the World Bank until after the end of the Iran–Iraq War. In 1991, however, it returned to the Bank for an initial $250 million loan for emergency earthquake relief. The Bank's return coincided as well with a brief détente with Washington.

From July 1993 to May 2000 the Group of Seven advanced countries (G-7) worked together to stop lending to Iran. Apparently, that consensus unraveled when some members—notably European ones—began supporting reengagement with Iran. Some of this reengagement was due to their expressed view that engaging with Iran's reforms would support them in their efforts against Iran's hardliners.

Resumed lending coincided with the revival of the government's large reconstruction effort. In May 2000, the 24-member board voted overwhelmingly in favor of the two loans, which totaled $232 million. The United States cast the only vote against the loans while France and Canada were the only abstentions. In part, the U.S. position was dictated by the fact that, by law, its representative to the Bank must vote against the loans for any government on the State Department's list of state sponsors of terrorism.

Worries were expressed by some directors that momentum for economic reform was weakening in Iran. The Bank said it would be at least six to nine months before any further loans for Iran were considered, and that would happen only if efforts at reform yielded results. In addition, many directors at the meeting spoke against what they called the politicization of the Bank and noted that loans should be granted on economic criteria only. The loan was viewed favorably, some directors said, because financing the Tehran sewerage system and primary health care addressed human needs. The loans were also seen as helping the reform efforts of President Mohammad Khatami against conservative elements. Lending continued, and over the next several years major loans had been granted for a series of major projects: the Primary Health Care and Nutrition Project, Environmental Management, Emergency Earthquake Reconstruction projects (following the Qazwin and Bam earthquakes), Ahwaz and Shiraz Water and Sanitation, Urban Upgrading and Housing Reform, Northern Cities Water and Sanitation, and Alaborz Integrated Land and Water Management.

Despite the importance of these projects, the Bank's major contribution to Iranian economic development has been in its advice to the Iranian authorities. The framework for the Bank's current consultations began in May 2001 when a two-year Interim Assistance Strategy (IAS) was approved by the Board of Directors. The Bank's approach was two-pronged: (1) policy dialogue on the reform program through non-lending services; and (2) targeted lending in key social and environmental areas consistent with the Third Five-Year Development Plan

(FYDP) objectives. During the IAS period, the World Bank undertook a series of economic studies in support of the government's reform efforts. These included a study on the reform of the Energy Pricing System, a Trade and Foreign Exchange System Reform Study, a Public Expenditure Review, and a Country Economic Memorandum (CEM), as well as other sectoral studies. In addition, policy reviews were prepared for urban water, housing, agriculture, air pollution control, the pension system, and social safety nets.

The Bank and a number of Iranian Reformers, both inside and outside of government, saw the World Bank playing a large role in assisting the government implement its third Five-Year Development Plan (2001–2005). The Plan aimed at a growth rate of 6% per annum during the Plan period. To achieve its objectives of rising economic growth potential, increasing the living standards of the population, and reducing unemployment, the Plan envisaged a wide range of structural reforms aimed at a balanced and gradual transition to a market economy. The Plan gave special emphasis to areas where the World Bank has special expertise—agricultural and rural development, and housing. In addition, both these sectors had not only potential for growth, but also for job creation and poverty alleviation given their higher labor intensity—particularly of unskilled and poor workers. The Plan also gave particular priority to the environment, inducing managing air and water pollution and the preservation of natural resources—again all areas the World Bank has strong expertise.

In short, the Bank saw its lending as largely focused on priority areas of the Plan such as low-income housing, sewerage, urban upgrading and community-based infrastructure, and employment creation schemes for the poor. These are areas that are least constrained by policy distortions being addressed, are most resilient to a potential country's economic and social risks, and, at the same time, have a quick impact on improving the situation of the poor and the environment and enhance resource management.

Following the completion of the third FYDP the Bank began work on a new four-year Country Assistance Strategy (CAS). The overarching aim of the new CAS was to assist the government in implanting the structural reform agenda, supporting the transformation of the economy, promoting high and sustainable growth, and creating employment opportunities. The CAS placed the emphasis on poverty alleviation and capacity building for a knowledge-based economy. It envisaged a lending program in water and sanitation, urban transport, agriculture, community development, and education and vocational training. The analytical and advisory program proposed to include public finance, financial and public sector reform, and human capital development, in addition to ongoing work on growth diagnostics as well as public expenditure and pension strategies. The CAS also seeks to align its policy recommendations with the government's priorities and the objectives of the Fourth FYDP. To support Iran's reform efforts, the World Bank is intensifying its assistance for capacity building in the formulation, sequencing, and implementation of economic and social policies.

Several of the World Bank group's member banks have also been active in Iran. The International Finance Corporation's (IFC) support of the World Bank's program for Iran has focused on selected investments as well as technical assistance and advisory services. IFC's activities will support the private sector supply response that Iran needs to achieve higher and sustained growth and accelerate job creation. IFC will support the establishment of a modern, open and competitive financial sector, a cornerstone for private sector development. As of January 31, 2006, IFC's committed portfolio in Iran was $29 million, primarily in the financial sector.

Iran became a full member of another World Bank group member, the Multilateral Investment Guarantee Agency (MIGA), in December 2003. In May 2005, MIGA issued $122 million guaranteed coverage for a joint venture petrochemical project, its first coverage ever for a project in Iran. At present MIGA is considering several arrangements to provide coverage for both inward and outward investment. There appears to be significant potential demand for MIGA guarantees among Iranian investors venturing abroad. As the Iranian government and Iranian companies become more aware of MIGA's potential value-added services in South–South transactions, MIGA may see more requests for coverage, especially for transactions with neighboring countries like Afghanistan and Iraq.

As of January 31, 2006, Iran received 54 World Bank loans totaling $3163 million net of cancellations and terminations of which $1989 had been disbursed. The ongoing portfolio consists of nine loans in the total amount of $1355 million of which $1167 million remained undisbursed.

The International Monetary Fund (IMF) is an international organization of 184 member countries and was founded at the same Bretton Woods Conference (1944) as the World Bank (Iran does not yet belong to the third Bretton Woods Institution, the World Trade Organization). It was established to promote international monetary cooperation, ensure foreign exchange stability and orderly exchange arrangements, foster economic growth and higher levels of employment, and provide temporary financial assistance to countries to help ease balance of payments adjustment.

Iran holds one of the 24 seats on the IMF Executive Board. It has never applied for an IMF loan in the past three decades and, therefore, has not been influenced or affected by its political structure. Iran's cooperation with the IMF is a successful example in terms of international relations. However, Iran does not hold any seat on the IMF Board of Directors.

Iran became a member of the IMF on December 29, 1945 with a paid-in quota of $25 million. Iran's quota in the early 2000s had increased to $1497.2 million. The Islamic Republic is also the head of the Iran Group which consists of Pakistan, Afghanistan, Algeria, Ghana, Morocco, and Tunisia.

The Iranian economy has evolved through four main phases since 1945, with each period defining in large part its relationship to the IMF. The first phase after the Second World War was characterized by a reduction in foreign trade, lower oil income, and economic adjustment problems associated with post-war transition. During this period it was eligible to make use of Fund resources to support its currency and assure exchange rate stability.

The second phase started after the dramatic increase in oil prices in 1973/1974. During this period Iran ran a large balance of payment surpluses and was able to be a net lender to the Fund. In 1974/1975 Iran provided the Fund with a loan of $580 million, followed by one of $410 million in 1975/1976. These funds went largely to 19 oil importing countries enabling them to finance in part their higher oil import bills.

The third phase started at the time of the Islamic Revolution, a turning point for IMF–Iran relations. While relations were strained at times, they remained ongoing with Iran, obtaining advice from the IMF in the form of economic reports plus participation of the Central Bank personnel in the training courses offered by the IMF. The fourth phase (1990–) was the starting point for sending the first group of economic experts for economic counseling in Iran. In recent years, Iran and the fund have worked closely together on issues such as money laundering and combating terrorist financing.

In 2004, Iran accepted the obligations of Article VIII, Sections, 2, 3, and 4 of the IMF Articles of Agreement. In doing so, Iran agreed to refrain from imposing restrictions on the making of payments and transfers for current international transactions, or from engaging in discriminatory currency arrangements or multiple currency practices, except with IMF approval. By accepting the obligations of Article VIII, Iran gives confidence to the international community that it will pursue economic policies that will make restrictions on the making of payments and transfers for current international transactions unnecessary and will contribute to multilateral payments system free of restrictions.

Suggested Reading

Iran medium term framework for transition: converting oil wealth to development. 2003. Washington: World Bank, April 30.

ROBERT E. LOONEY

✦ INTERNET

The Internet captures the contradictions, paradoxes, and the dynamism of Iranian society better than any other phenomenon in today's Iran. Iran was the second country in the Middle East (Israel was the first) to be connected to the Internet. In spite of its short history, the Internet has had phenomenal growth in Iran. The rise of what we might call the Internet culture is an important development with significant economic, social, and political implications. The Internet culture here encompasses not only new technologies, but also lifestyle changes, media habits, new forms of socialization and associations, changes in organizational structures and reach, and new tools and forms of governance.

The Internet made its debut in Iran in January of 1993 with an email communication between the Institute for Studies in Theoretical Physics and Mathematics in Tehran and the University of Vienna. The earliest forms of the networking capabilities and connectivity set the path for the development of the Internet as a domain of academic activities. At the same time, national academic networks played a major role in establishing domestic Internet connections. The academic nature of the Internet as a phenomenon and the state's interests in promoting scientific and technological developments in the aftermath of the Iran–Iraq War during the "reconstruction era" meant that the state did not take steps to stifle the conditions for its growth. Moreover, the state sought to deploy the Internet as a tool for a more efficient communication

Iranians work at an Internet cafe in Tehran, 2006. (AP Photo/Hasan Sarbakhshian)

amongst various organizations and entities. Additionally, a lack of sophisticated internal networking capabilities initially meant that it was connectivity to the outside world that made the Internet viable in Iran. This was yet another reason that the state could not be a strong factor in the development of the Internet in Iran. These conditions provided the context for the development of an independent telecom sector that later became productive and proliferated into a commercially viable IT (information technologies) industry.

The number of Internet users rose from less than 100,000 to a recent estimate of 11 million (as of March of 2007). That number is expected to grow even higher with the addition of broadband and fiber optics capabilities in some areas. There are presently around 1400 Internet Service Providers (ISPs) in Iran, which have formed an association of ISPs. Among the factors that have fueled the demand for access to the Internet are the entrepreneurial drives that created "coffee nets" (Internet cafés), numbering 1500 in Tehran alone. Persian was the fourth most common language used for blogs (weblogs) until recently. There are reportedly more than a 100,000 Persian blogs active presently. The state's policy of "higher education for the masses" has led to the proliferation of academic centers across the country and to a high literacy rate (above 80%). The rising number of students and academic settings with access to the Internet has helped the spread of the Internet culture. In a country where 70% of the population is under the age of 30, and where more than 67% of the population lives in urban areas, the Internet is likely to grow at an even faster pace.

Even a cursory online examination of the Internet in Iran reveals not only a dynamic IT sector, but also the strong presence of the Internet in various spheres. One may conveniently classify a range of Internet-related practices, structures, and content as the academic, technical, governmental, cultural, and political spheres. Since the academic sphere is the most familiar, attention here will be paid to the other spheres.

A glimpse of the IT companies, their products and services, and the proliferating news and information centers about IT in Iran could be provided by an examination of the following entities. ITI, Information Technology of Iran, which claims to be the first portal in Iran dedicated to information technologies, provides a range of information to its readers under the subheadings of news, articles, and interviews. In addition to gathering information on IT-related entities, it produces news and analysis on IT in Iran. Sanaray Corporation, which boasts to be "the independent port to the Persian software industry," is a consortium of Iranian software companies established in 1998. Registered software companies, numbering 50 shareholders presently, make up this consortium. Although it maintains "close contacts" with entities such as the Supreme Council of Information and

Communication Technology (SCICT), the High Council of Informatics (HCI), and the Ministry of Information and Communication Technology (MICT), Sanaray is a private company that works in consultation with the government to implement national IT policies. The Iranian Association of Internet Service Providers offers a range of information and news about ISPs in Tehran and in provinces throughout the country. Pars Online is the largest ISP operating in Iran, offering companies and individuals various products and services (e.g., dialup, broadband, networking, data). Neda (or Neda Rayaneh) is another important ISP in Iran. The four-layer architecture of Internet services in Iran, according to a Sanaray's report, includes Internet Connection Providers (whose role is to purchase Internet connections in large volumes from international vendors), second-tier providers (e.g., ISPs, Internet Data Centers, Public Access Providers), coffee-nets and game-nets, and users (home, business, and government). A list of relevant websites for these entities is provided in the Suggested Reading section for this entry.

In the governmental sphere, one may point to the government's efforts in utilizing the Internet for its various activities and projects. The notion of "e-government" has been embraced as a motto since the mid 1990s. While only 10% of governmental organizations had Internet access by 1995, there are presently very few governmental organizations without Internet access or some form of online presence.

Selected List of Entities and Organizations with Internet Access and Online Presence
✦

NON-MINISTERIAL GOVERNMENTAL ENTITIES

Management and Planning Organization: http://www.mporg.ir
Iran Academy of Sciences: http://www.ias.ac.ir
Iran Drug Control Headquarters: http://www.dchq.ir/html/index.php

NON-GOVERNMENTAL PUBLIC ENTITIES

Iranian Red Crescent: http://www.rcs.ir/fa/index.php
Tehran Municipality: http://www.tehran.ir
Astan Quds Razavi: http://www.aqrazavi.org

MINISTERIAL ENTITIES AND THEIR AFFILIATED ORGANIZATIONS

Ministry of Information and Communication Technology:
   http://www.ict.gov.ir

Ministry of Commerce: http://www.moc.gov.ir

Telecommunication Company of Iran: http://www.irantelecom.ir

NON-PROFIT PRIVATE ENTITIES

Iran Chamber of Commerce, Industries and Mines:
http://www.iccim.org/persian/RDefault.aspx?nid=34

The Islamic Propagation Office of the Islamic Seminary of Qom:
http://www.balagh.net/english/index.htm

Medical Council of Iran: http://www.irimc.org/News/Default.aspx

FOR-PROFIT PRIVATE ENTITIES

Eghtesad Novin Bank: http://www.enbank.ir/MainF.asp

Parsian Bank: http://www.parsian-bank.com/farsi/home_f.php

Pasargad Bank: http://fa.bankpasargad.ir

A recent sample list of Internet addresses for major governmental organizations and entities inside Iran circulating on a listserv included over 200 such addresses. It is clear that the Iranian government has been pursuing its intentions of implementing e-government. The state's official policy of promoting IT is reflected in the declaration of "National Information and Communication Technology Agenda," known as TAKFA. This ambitious agenda, adopted on July 2, 2002, calls for the utilization of IT in the creation of an "information society." A review of the executive summary of TAKFA, posted on the website for High Council of Informatics (*Shoraye-e Alee E'tela Rasanee*), reveals the extent to which the state views IT as a tool for development. It states, "Regarding the Millennium Development Goals and the WSIS, Geneva, Declaration and Action Plan adopted by all members of the United Nations, our aim is to realize the prerequisites for an Information Society and a knowledge-based Economy in which ICT is an Enabler Technology." The document goes even further to claim one of the aims of the TAKFA is to transform the "digital divide" into a "digital opportunity" (http://www.takfa.ir/Portal/Home/www.takfa.ir). In short, the Islamic Republic has adopted ambitious strategic plans for IT. Although the present implementations are impressive, it remains to be seen to what extent the state is able to carry out its goal of creating a "knowledge-based" economy.

In the cultural sphere, the Internet has become an important factor in several ways. The Internet has enabled the youth to find forms of socializing that might not be permissible otherwise. Online communities (e.g., http://www.orkut.com; http://www.gazzag.com) and chat rooms have provided the youth a space in which the official culture of the Islamic Republic might be sidestepped. Blogs, as online personal diaries and journals, address a range of issues from the mundane, the personal, and the ordinary to the taboo subjects of various kinds. From online literary competitions to online rock music festivals and competitions, the Internet has enabled the dissemination of cultural forms and contents that might otherwise remain underground. Forms of popular culture that remain outside the acknowledged boundaries of Iranian youth culture have found the Internet as their only viable stage (e.g., heavy metal bands such as *Ahoora*, rappers such as *Hichkas*). Online magazines have also enabled Iranian youth to bypass state restrictions on partaking in global youth cultures (e.g., http://www.tehranavenue.com). Internet cafés have become elements of an alternative public sphere.

Although the Internet has been a part of various spheres in the Iranian society, it is in the political domain that it has attracted the most attention. The importance of the Internet to Iranian politics was evident during the 2005 presidential election when all the candidates maintained websites that promoted their platforms. In a sign of the growing importance of the Internet in Iran, President Mahmoud Ahmadinejad launched his own weblog (http://www.ahmadinejad.ir) in June of 2006. One commentator even compared blogs to the audio cassettes that helped bring about the Islamic Republic. Weblogs are often characterized as the space of dissent. As the number of politically inclined Persian-language weblogs has increased, the state's actions toward the weblogs seem to indicate that the state also views blogs as politically significant. And as the state limits the range of oppositional opinions expressed in the print press by closing newspapers, many reform-minded and influential journalists have turned to the Internet and to weblogs to continue their work. Some bloggers prefer to remain anonymous. Many others have decided to use their names. The state's response has varied from the filtering of websites to jailing bloggers for crossing the infamous "red line." Reporters without Borders designated Iran in 2005 as one of the 15 countries it deemed as "the enemy of the Internet."

Restricting the Internet on a wide scale, however, is a challenging task for the state for a number of reasons. First, the Internet is a technology that defies hierarchical control and capture and enables evasion. Second, the Iranian state does not have the technical resources and expertise needed for such a task. Third, the state's policies of education for the masses and promoting information and communication technologies tend to work against its desire to control the means of communication in this environment. Finally, the state does not wish to use draconian measures on a wider scale fearing political repercussions.

In summary, the remarkable Internet culture that has developed in the past decade cannot simply be ignored or eradicated. The rapid growth of the Internet in all of its manifestations took conservative elements of the Islamic Republic off-guard partly because they did not initially appreciate its complexity and significance. If it does not take more drastic measures, it is because the state is aware of the political risks involved. For a population that is mostly young, urban, and literate, the Internet has become a part of their everyday life. For some, it has become an alternative form of expression. For others, the Internet has afforded them membership in the global youth culture. Many use the Internet to engage in new forms of socialization that take place outside the sphere of the official culture. For many families the Internet has provided new ways to maintain contact with their loved ones who live abroad (e.g., webcams, e-mails, affordable Internet-based phones, photo sharing). Finally, the Internet has allowed new forms of political expression and political mobilization. These are only the most visible examples of the ways in which the Internet culture has introduced transformations in the Iranian society that might prove irreversible.

Suggested Reading
Alavi, N. 2005. *We are Iran: the Persian blogs*. Brooklyn, NY: Soft Skull Press.
Rahimi, B. 2008. The politics of the Internet in Iran, in Semati, M., ed. *Media, culture, and society in Iran: living with globalization and the Islamic state*. London: Routledge.
http://www.ict.gov.ir
http://www.irantelecom.ir
http://www.isp.ir
http://www.itiran.com
http://www.neda.net
http://www.parsonline.com
http://www.sanaray.com
http://www.takfa.ir

MEHDI SEMATI

✦ IRAN–IRAQ WAR

The Iran–Iraq War started on September 22, 1980, and ended on August 20, 1988, with Iran's adoption of UNSCR Resolution 598 on July 20, 1987. It was thus the longest conventional war in the twentieth century. The strategic campaigns during the war, referred to as *defahe moghaddas* ("holy defense") and *jangeh tahmili* ("the forced war") in Iran and *Saddam's Qadisiyya* in

According to a claim by an Iranian opposition group, the bodies of Iraqi prisoners
of war are seen after execution by the Revolutionary Guard, 1981, in Bostan, Iran,
after they refused to chant slogans praising Iranian spiritual leader Ayatollah
Khomeini. (AP Photo)

Ba'thist Iraq, can be structured along three periods. First, the period of the Iraqi
offensive from September 1980 until March 1982, when the Islamic Republic
launched "Operation Undeniable Victory," which shifted the strategic balance
in favor of Iran and led to the recapture of the city of Khorramshahr in May
1982. Second, the "war of attrition" between early 1984 and mid-1987, which
refers to Iranian and Iraqi attacks on international shipping in the Persian Gulf
(the "tanker war") and Iraqi attacks on civilian population centers in Iran (the
"war of the cities"). And finally, the termination of the war from mid-1987
onward, that is, during a period when Iraq made excessive use of chemical
weapons and after Iraqi forces recaptured the Al-Faw peninsula on April 18,
1988, Shalamche on May 25, 1988, the oil-rich Majnoon islands on June 25,
1988, and after they reentered Iranian territory with the help of the Mojahe-
din-e Khalq (MKO) organization between July 22 and July 29, 1988.

In terms of political violence, human losses, and material destruction, the
First Persian Gulf War was the most devastating in the modern history of
West Asia. Never before had there been bloodshed on such a scale, and not

since the First World War and Vietnam had there been a comparable systematic use of chemical weapons on the warfront. On the Iranian side, according to Hadi Qalamnevis, Director General of the Statistics and Information Department at the Islamic Revolution Martyrs Foundation, 204,795 people lost their lives, including 188,015 military and 16,780 civilians. Earlier estimates by Mohsen Rafiqdust, the former head of the Iranian Revolutionary Guard Force, had stated that 400,000 were wounded during the war. According to Iranian health officials, 60,000 Iranians were exposed to Iraqi chemical weapon attacks. In an off-the-record interview with this author, a Senior Iranian Foreign Ministry official stated that 60,000 Iranians were killed by chemical weapons attacks, with more than 300,000 suffering from related syndromes (124,000 with more than 25% exposure, 200,000 under 25%, 120,000 minimal contamination, and 600 with 80% and higher who are close to death). In addition, more than 15,000 war veterans suffering from chemical weapons syndromes reportedly died in the 12 years after the end of the Iran–Iraq War, according to Abbas Khani, the head of Iran's Legal Office of War Veterans. Overall, it is estimated that 370,000 people were killed on both sides during the war, with an additional number of approximately 700,000 people maimed and injured. In terms of material losses, Iranian government estimates indicate that the war caused $440 billion in direct losses to the Iranian economy, with another $490 billion categorized as indirect losses. According to additional sources, it is estimated that the costs amount to aggregated direct and indirect costs of $627 billion to Iran and $561 billion to Iraq, with the total costs exceeding the overall oil revenues of the two states in the twentieth century.

The causes of the Iraqi invasion of Iran continue to be controversial. Whilst in terms of international law, the question of who started the war was settled belatedly by the U.N. report of December 9, 1991 (S/23273)—which only after Iraq's invasion of Kuwait refers to "Iraq's *aggression* against Iran," although the overall picture is far more complex. Three arguments dominate the mainstream discourse: first, Saddam Hussein seized the favorable international moment that was conducive to a military attack against the newly established Islamic state in Iran (the "realist," power politics argument); second, the Iran–Iraq War was inevitable due to the "historic" enmity between the two states (the "orientalist" argument); and third, the Ba'thist state felt threatened by the spillover of the Islamic revolution and decided to preempt further Shia uprisings in Najaf, Karbala, Samarra, Kazimiyah, and Baghdad as a means to contain a Shia resurgence in the greater west Asian area (the "balance of power" argument). The latter aspect was rather more central to Saddam Hussein's efforts to justify the invasion. From that perspective, by interfering in the internal affairs of Iraq, Iran had broken the terms of the Algiers Agreement of 1975. The agreement delineated the Shatt-al Arab along the thalweg and called for mutual non-intervention in the internal affairs of the two countries. Moreover, Saddam Hussein pointed out that the delineation of the Shatt al-Arab in favor of Iran itself was forced upon the country during a period of Iranian supremacy and after the shah's long-lasting covert war against the Iraqi government (via the Iraqi–Kurds) sponsored by the United States and Israel. Taken together with what was considered to be the continued Iranian occupation of the three Persian Gulf islands (the Greater and Lesser Tunbs and Abu Musa) and the "Persianization" (*tafris*) of the southwestern Iranian border province of Khuzestan—which continued to be referred to as "occupied Arabistan" by Iraqi Ba'thist officials—Saddam Hussein believed to have a solid case to portray the invasion as a just cause.

The Iran–Iraq War was precipitated by the Islamic revolution in Iran and cannot be satisfactorily discussed in isolation of this event. It has become a truism that the rhetoric of the Iranian revolutionaries turned neighboring Iraq into the primary agent of protests outside of Iran. At least three factors supported that development: The country's majority Shia population was marginalized by the governing Arab nationalist regime; Ayatollah Khomeini had developed a close association with the Iraqi *marja'e taghlid* (source of emulation) Ayatollah Seyyed Mohammad Baqir al-Sadr during his exile in Najaf; and third (and related to the former point), once in power, the revolutionary movement could employ the Shia clerical network spawning from Qom and Mashhad in Iran to Karbala and Najaf in Iraq to coordinate mutual activities. Organized Shia opposition in Iraq was spearheaded by the *Hizb al Da'wah al-Islamiyyah* (The Party of the Islamic Call), which had been engaged in anti-governmental campaigns since the party's establishment in the late 1960s. *Al-Dawah*'s efforts were joined by new parties such as the *al-Mujahidun* (holy warriors) formed by Shiite religious intellectuals in 1979 and later by the Supreme Council for Islamic Revolution in Iraq (SCIRI) led by Ayatollah Baqir al-Hakim. During 1978 and 1979 serious rioting spearheaded by the *al-Dawah* party turned into an assassination campaign against Ba'thist government officials, including a bomb attack against Tariq Aziz. The Iraqi state responded by decapitating the Shiite movements and eroding their power base: After announcing in March 1980 that membership of the *al-Dawah* party was punishable by death, the government moved on to execute Ayatollah Baqir al-Sadr and his sister Bint-al Huda. Another senior Shia cleric, Ayatollah Abu al-Qasim al-Khoi, was put under house arrest, and during 1980 alone an estimated 40,000 Iraqi–Iranians were forcibly expelled to their country of origin.

How did the Ba'thist state legitimize these actions and the war itself prop-agandistically? First, the challenge of "the Persians" was projected back to the reign of the Persian king Cyrus, who gave refuge to the Jews when they were persecuted by the Babylonian king Nebuchadnezzar in the sixth century BC. The myth was invented that there has been a perennial conflict between Arabs and Persians, and that Iranians had a history of collusion with "Zionist" and "imperialist" forces against the "Arab nation." This was the central argu-ment of two books published in the early 1980s: *Al-Madaris al-Yahudiyya wa-l-Iraniyya fi-l-'Iraq* (Jewish and Iranian schools in Iraq) by Fadil al-Barrak and *Al-Harb al-sirriyya, khafaya al-dawr al-Isra'ili fi harb al-khalij* (The secret war: The mysterious role of Israel in the [First] Gulf War) by Sa'd al-Bazzaz. The former deals with the "destructive" and "dangerous" impact of Jewish and Iranian schools on Iraqi society, whereas the latter outlines how Israel and Iran conspired to combat Iraq, with special reference to the destruction of the nuclear reactor in Osirak by the Israeli Air Force in June 1981. Describing Iranians as *ajam*, an inferior people within the dominance of Islam, which was deemed to be first and foremost an Arab domain, the Ba'thist state also disse-minated overtly racist propaganda, exemplified by pamphlets such as Khairal-lah Talfah's, *Three Whom God Should Not Have Created: Persians, Jews and Flies*, serials entitled *Judhur al-'ada al-Farsi li-l-umma al-'Arabiyya* (The roots of Per-sian hostility toward the Arab nation), and proverbs such as *Ma hann a'jami 'ala 'Arabi* (An *ajam* or Persian will not have mercy on an Arab). According to Ba'thist state propaganda, hatred towards Arabs was an integral part of the de-structive mentality of Persians (*aqliyya takhribiyya*), which was deemed an unchangeable racial attribute that had not changed since the days when Islam came into the Sassanian empire in the seventh century AD.

Second, the Ba'thist state countered Iran's revolutionary ideology and the political religious appeal of Ayatollah Khomeini by reverting to Islamic sym-bols and imagery. Central to this task was the decision to officially refer to the Iran–Iraq War as *Saddam's Qadisiyya* or *Qadisiyyat Saddam*, projecting two cen-tral institutions of Ba'thist Arab nationalism: the romantic mystification of the leadership ideal on the one hand and suspicion and antagonism towards Iranians on the other. The phrase, which was to be used in any official Iraqi correspondence, likened the war to the battle of *Qadisiyya* in 637 AD. During that battle the armies of Sassanian Iran led by General Rustum which were fighting as a Zoroastrian–Persian force were defeated by a Muslim army under the command of Saad bin Abi Waqqas. The defeat led to the capture of the Sassanian capital Ctesiphon (its ruins are near Baghdad), causing the ending of Sassanian suzerainty in Iraq and opening up ancient Iran for the ensuing process of spreading Islam. Iraqi intelligence documents captured after the

Second Persian Gulf war compiled by the Iraq Research and Documentation Program at Harvard University suggest that Saddam Hussein's identification with a comparable historical role and the regime's anti-Iranian disposition were indeed systematic. Whilst most of the documents refer to the Iran–Iraq War as *Qadisiyyat Saddam*, Iranians are consistently referred to in derogatory terms as the "Zionist Persians," *al- 'adu al-ajami* (the illiterate or foreign enemy), *al- 'adu al-Irani* (the Iranian enemy), or *majus* (fire worshippers).

It has been a central argument of recent research on the Iran–Iraq War that the Ba'thist state could not have acted on its war plans without its real and perceived confirmation by regional and global actors.

The Gulf monarchies had already reacted positively to the tactical moderation of Iraqi behavior in the period after the signing of the Algiers agreement in 1975. Diplomacy followed suit: In February 1979, Saudi Arabia and Iraq signed a security agreement which committed Iraq to defend the former in the case of war. The agreement was accompanied by high level diplomatic exchanges between the two countries and Iraq and Rais al-Khaimah, Oman, and Kuwait. Apart from Dubai and Sharjah, which continued to have cordial relations with the Islamic Republic, the other sheikhdoms were either directly or indirectly involved in the Iraqi war effort, especially after the failure of the Iraqi *Blitz* and the Iranian counteroffensive into Iraqi territory in 1982. Several measures were taken: Saudi Arabia and Kuwait agreed to forward the profits of oil production in the Khafji oil field, located in the neutral zone between Saudi Arabia and Kuwait, to the Iraqi government; the two countries provided Iraq with loans ranging from an estimated $35 billion to $50 billion, most of them not necessarily meant to be repaid; and both countries opened up their ports for the shipment of products bound to the Iraqi market and the selling of oil on behalf of the Iraqi government. During the "tanker war" period intensifying in 1984 and the "war of the cities" beginning in the spring of 1985, Kuwait supported Saddam Hussein directly by transhipping arms and supplies via its port overland to Iraq. There was also direct military engagement exemplified by the shooting down of an Iranian fighter jet in violation of Saudi controlled airspace in June 1984. The sketch of regional collusion with Iraq provided here should not mislead, however—the support was not unequivocal. Concurrent with the support of Egypt, Jordan, Saudi Arabia, and Kuwait to Iraq and the support of Libya and Syria to Iran, the regional states were continuously engaged in containing the economic calamities and military spillover of the war. Apart from sustained efforts to appease Iran, the Gulf sheikhdoms also refrained from formalizing their relationship with Saddam Hussein. After all, the six states of the Persian Gulf established the Gulf Cooperation Council (GCC) leaving both Iran *and* Iraq out.

The first international reaction to the conflict is emblematic of the pattern of behavior that followed: After six days of hostilities, on September 28, 1980, the U.N. Security Council unanimously adopted Resolution 479, calling for an immediate cessation of hostilities without, however, naming Iraq as the invading force, or calling for the country's withdrawal from Iranian territory (the call to return to internationally recognized boundaries came only after Iranian advances into Iraqi territory as a result of the counteroffensive in mid 1982). In essence, then, Resolution 479 and the final Resolution 598 adopted after nearly eight years of fighting were similar with regard to the question of who started the war. Both failed to name Iraq as the invading party.

It is well established in the literature about the war that from the outset the U.S. government provided Iraq with intelligence information about Iranian force deployments and movements from the U.S. Airborne Warning and Control System (AWACS) that had been stationed in Saudi Arabia and was operated by the Pentagon. After the ending of the "Hostage crisis," the change of U.S. administrations from Carter to Reagan, and Iranian advances on the battlefield, intelligence sharing was complemented with diplomatic, financial, and military cooperation. On the diplomatic front, the United States followed an active policy of reconciliation with Iraq, removing the country from the State Departments list of "state sponsors of terrorism" in February 1982, followed by the official resumption of diplomatic ties in November 1984. Economic support ranged from authorization of dual use equipment, such as the sale of helicopters which were capable of being converted to military use, and generous loans provided by the U.S. Export–Import Bank (Eximbank) and other financial institutions. In a speech presented to the U.S. House of Representatives by Henry Gonzalez (Democrat–Texas) on July 27, 1992, it was outlined that "[b]etween 1983 and the invasion of Kuwait in 1990, Iraq received $5 billion in CCC [US Department of Agriculture's Commodity Credit Corporation] guarantees that allowed them to purchase United States agricultural products on credit." In October of the same year, the U.S. Committee on Banking, Housing, and Urban Affairs held hearings which were later confirmed by the "Riegle Report," confirming that the United States had not only exported agricultural products but also "chemical, biological, nuclear, and missile-system equipment to Iraq that was converted to military use in Iraq's chemical, biological, and nuclear weapons program," which were in turn also used against U.S. soldiers in the Second Persian Gulf War.

On May 25, 1994, the aforementioned investigation conducted by Senator Riegle showed that the U.S. government approved sales of a wide range of chemical and biological materials to Iraq, including components of mustard gas, anthrax, Clostridium Botulinum, Histoplasma Capsulatum, Brucella Melitensis, and Clostridium Perfringens. The official "tilt" towards Iraq was defined in a State Department Information Memorandum dated October 7, 1983, concluding that the "policy of strict neutrality has already been modified, except for arms sales, since Iran's forces crossed into Iraq in the summer of 1982," adding that the "steps we have taken toward the conflict since then have progressively favoured Iraq."

Moreover, in a State Department memo to then Secretary of State Shultz in November 1983, it was confirmed that the United States knew "that Iraq has acquired a CW [chemical weapons] production capability, primarily from Western firms, including possibly a U.S. foreign subsidiary" and that it appears that Iraq uses chemical weapons almost on a daily basis. Further intelligence suggested that "as long ago as July 1982, Iraq used tear gas and skin irritants against invading [sic] Iranian forces quite effectively" and that "in October 1982, unspecified foreign officers fired lethal chemical weapons at the orders of Saddam during battles in the Mandali area."

Before Donald Rumsfeld returned to Baghdad in late March 1984 for a second official visit, the United States, for the first time during the war, had publicly condemned the use of chemical weapons. Yet, whilst acknowledging that the "United States has concluded that the available evidence substantiates Iran's charges that Iraq has used chemical weapons," the press statement also condemned the Iranian insistence on the removal of the Ba'thist regime. The U.S. government thus named Iran as the invading force, declaring that it "finds the present Iranian regime's intransigent refusal to deviate from its avowed objective of eliminating the legitimate government of neighbouring Iraq to be inconsistent with the accepted norms of behavior among nations and the moral and religious basis which it claims."

The support to Saddam Hussein also extended into diplomatic cover in the United Nations. When the Iranian government submitted a draft resolution asking for U.N. condemnation of the chemical warfare by Iraq, the U.S. delegate was instructed to lobby for a general motion of "no decision" on the resolution. At a meeting between the Iraqi interest section head Nizar Hamdoon and then Deputy Assistant Secretary of State James Placke on March 29, 1984, the former spelled out what the Iraqi government expected from the U.N. resolution. Hamdoon stressed that his country favored a Security Council presidential statement to a resolution, reference to former resolutions on the war, progress toward termination of the conflict, and no mentioning of responsibility regarding the employment of chemical weapons. One day after the meeting, the Security Council issued a presidential statement, condemning the use of chemical weapons without naming Iraq as the offending party. A State Department memorandum from March 30, 1984, acknowledged the successful diplomatic "spin" in support of Iraq, noting that the "statement ... contains all three elements Hamdoon wanted."

The actions during the latter half of the war, such as the U.S. attacks on Iranian oil platforms during the "tanker war" period, and the accidental shooting down of an Iranian Air Bus aircraft by the USS Vincennes, which killed 290 civilians, only reconfirmed the Iraqi position. The Iraqi regime even got away with an apology and payment of $27.3 million for hitting the USS Stark, which killed thirty-seven U.S. navy personnel and wounded twenty-one. The support for Saddam Hussein did not preclude, however, deals with the Iranian government. After all, it was not knowledge about Iraqi war crimes that proved disastrous for the Reagan administration but the much publicized Iran–Contra Affair. Yet there is no escaping the fact that from the perspective of Saddam Hussein the international context before and after the invasion of Iran must have appeared quite reassuring, indeed. Ultimately, it contributed to Saddam Hussein's ability to claim the right to go to war (*jus ad bellum*), and to avoid the right conduct of the war itself (*jus in bello*). It was this international constellation that implicitly empowered the Ba'thist state to pursue the "Anfal" campaign against Iraq's Kurdish population and Iranian army units operating in the area, culminating in the gassing of the Northern Iraqi town of Halabja which killed at least 4,000 to 5,000 people in March 1988. The international community did not only not intervene previously, the newly declassified documents sketched above provide enough evidence to presume confidently that it provided the Iraqi regime with the means to implement its policies.

Suggested Reading

Adib-Moghaddam, A. 2006. *The international politics of the Persian Gulf: a cultural genealogy*. London: Routledge.

Chubin, S., and C. Tripp. 1988. *Iran and Iraq at war*. London: I. B. Tauris.

Ehteshami, A., and G. Nonneman. 1991. *War and peace in the Gulf: domestic politics and regional relations into the 1990s*. Reading, UK: Ithaca Press.

Khadduri, M. 1988. *The Gulf War: the origins and implications of the Iraq-Iran conflict*. Oxford: Oxford University Press.

Potter, L. G., and G. G. Sick, eds. 2004. *Iran, Iraq, and the legacies of war*. London: Palgrave.

Rajaee, F., ed. 1997. *Iranian perspectives of the Iran-Iraq War*. Gainesville, Fla: University Press of Florida.

ARSHIN ADIB-MOGHADDAM

J

◆ JEWISH COMMUNITY

The Jews of Iran see themselves as denizens of Iranian territory for 2,700 years. Throughout their history, the Iranian Jews have coped with significant challenges, especially during the Safavid era (1501–1722) and under the Qajar rulers (1796–1925). Nevertheless, Iran's Jews are connected to Iran through history and territory and also as speakers of the Persian language.

The years of the Pahlavi dynasty, however—especially the reign of Muhammad Reza Shah (1941–1979)—are often considered a "Golden Age" for Iranian Jewry. The Iranian Jewish community thrived economically under the Shah's reform plan, the "White Revolution" (1963–1979). The White Revolution's rapid modernization provided exceptional opportunities for the Jewish community in Iran.

On the eve of the Islamic Revolution in 1978, the Jewish community in Iran numbered around 80,000, with 60,000 living in the capital, Tehran. The Constitutional Revolution (1906), the change of laws in Iran, the temporary abolishment of the Shi'a concept of religious impurity of non-Muslims (*nejasat*), and ensuing social changes all came together to surmount the obstacles to social mobility of the Jews and to enhance their assimilation in the Iranian society.

Although the Jews constituted less than a quarter of a percent of the total Iranian population of 35 million at that time, their economic, professional, and cultural impact on the country prior to the 1978–1979 revolution was significant. During this period, the majority of the Jewish population in Iran

An Iranian Jew pours wine during the Passover holiday in Tehran, 2008.
(AP photo/Hasan Sarbakhshian)

was middle class or upper middle class. There were Jewish schools, active social and cultural organizations, and about 30 synagogues in Tehran alone. Under the Pahlavi rule, many Jews left the Jewish neighborhoods (*mahallah*) and moved to integrated neighborhoods.

THE ISLAMIC REVOLUTION

With the outbreak of opposition to the Shah in the autumn of 1977, what had been considered the strengths of the Jewish community quickly transformed into its principal weaknesses: their socioeconomic status, close identification with the Shah and his policies, and ties to Israel and the United States. The Jewish community was viewed by the protestors as an ally to the Shah and part of the ruling establishment, and was seen by some in the revolutionary movement as an enemy of the revolution.

Expressions of anti-Jewish animosity soon intensified. In Tehran, pamphlets were circulated threatening to take revenge upon the Jews for plundering Iran's treasures. Slogans scribbled on the walls of synagogues and Jewish institutions carried anti-Jewish messages. Some extremists began ostracizing their Jewish neighbors and exhorted the authorities to liquidate their property.

A growing sense of unease about the evolving direction of the revolution led some in the Jewish community to declare November 6, 1978, as a day of fasting and prayer for peace for Iran and its Jewish community. However, there were Jews who participated in the revolution, joining hundreds of thousands of Muslim demonstrators who filled the streets of Tehran in organized groups. They held placards expressing opposition to the regime and shouted anti-Shah slogans.

During the revolution itself, a wave of anti-Israel sentiment swept over Iran, impacting the Jewish community. For example, *Keyhan*, at the time Iran's highest circulation daily newspaper, stated in its June 12, 1979, edition that Israeli commando troops had taken part in the "Black Friday" massacre of September 8, 1978, in which government troops had killed a number of demonstrators. The newspaper further maintained that Israel had recruited a group of Iranian Jews for the specific purpose of suppressing the demonstrators.

But at the same time, Jews were optimistic about the regime change. When Ayatollah Khomeini returned to Iran on February 1, 1979, five thousand Jews, led by Iranian Chief Rabbi Yedidya Shofet, were among those welcoming him. Some of them held pictures of Khomeini and signs proclaiming: "Jews and Muslims are brothers."

On May 14, 1979, five days after the execution of the former Jewish community leader Habībullah Elqānyān, who was accused of Zionist espionage and activities, a delegation of Jewish leaders set out for Qom to meet with Khomeini, who allayed their fears with the following words:

> We make a distinction between the Jewish community and the Zionists—and we know that these are two different things. We are against [the Zionists] because they are not Jews, but politicians ... but as for the Jewish community and the rest of the [minority] communities in Iran—they are members of this nation. Islam will treat them in the same manner as it does with all other layers of society.

Since the establishment of the Islamic Republic, the regime has officially distinguished between Iranian Jews, considered loyal citizens, and Zionists, toward whom the regime has not concealed its hostility. Zionist activity was made a crime, punishable by severe penalties.

This development served as a catalyst for changes in internal Jewish communal affairs. At the end of March 1978, a new generation of progressive Jewish Iranian intellectuals supplanted the old Jewish council, *Anjumān-i Kalīmīan* (Jewish Association), with the founding of the anti-Zionist radical *Jāme-yi Rowshanfikrān-i Yahūd-i Irān* (The Organization of Iranian Jewish

Intellectuals), whose platform included full support of the Islamic Revolution of 1979, religious and cultural revival, and community protection. Since its founding this organization has struggled to preserve the community from disintegration. This organization started publishing in the month of Tammuz (the tenth month in the Hebrew calendar) 1979 a weekly entitled *Tammuz*.

On February 27, 1979, the Organization of Iranian Jewish Intellectuals (OIJI) issued a public statement that expressed the "full identification of Iranian Jews" with the goals of the Islamic Revolution, lauded the Palestine Liberation Organization's struggle to "liberate Palestine," and harshly attacked Zionism and the Israeli government. The OIJI recognized the State of Israel's right to exist but condemned its Zionist nature. In its 28-article bylaws, the OIJI states as one of its goals: "to wage war on imperialism and on all forms of colonialism, including a war on Zionism and an exposure of its conspiracy with world imperialism, and a war on all forms of racial discrimination, racism, and anti-Semitism." The organization, in accordance with the policy set forth in its bylaws and in the articles published in its weekly, sought to maintain a Jewish, leftist, anti-Zionist, and pro-revolutionary tone. The issues of *Tammuz* also contained articles that promoted Jewish self-defense and condemned the anti-Jewish incitement and statements that were then poisoning the country's social atmosphere.

In the aftermath of the revolution, the private wealth of a number of Jews was confiscated on a large scale, including many cinemas, hotels, factories, luxurious residences, and other real estate. The value of the Jewish properties confiscated in Iran is estimated to be more than a billion dollars. For example, the 27-year-old hotel owner Ebrāhim Berukīm was executed in late July 1980. Berukīm was one of the few Jews who were executed during 1978–1980 in charges of Zionist activities, cooperation with the Shah's regime, and connection with Israel. Other Jews were suspected of being pro-Shah and were jailed, while some of them managed to leave Iran.

The revolutionary extremism aroused fears among Iranian Jews and caused about two thirds of the community to leave Iran. The emigrants included the majority of the community's leaders, philanthropists, and professionals. According to estimates, 30,000–40,000 Iranian Jews immigrated to the United States, 20,000 to Israel, and 10,000 to Europe, notably the United Kingdom, France, Germany, Italy, and Switzerland. At present, there are about 150,000 Jews in Israel who identify themselves as Iranian descendants—about 54,000 of them were born in Iran, and the rest were born of Iranian parents. Of those Iranian Jews who made their way to the United States, around 25,000 live in California (20,000 in Los Angeles alone) and

8,000 live in the New York area. Today, the number of Jews still residing in Iran is estimated from as low as 17,000 to as high as 30,000.

JEWISH LIFE IN IRAN

Official recognition of minorities is rooted in the Iranian constitution: Zoroastrian, Jewish, and Christian Iranians are the only recognized religious minorities who, within the limits of the law, are free to perform the religious rites and ceremonies and to act according to their own canon in matters of personal affairs and religious education. As stated in the constitution of the Islamic Republic: "Zoroastrian, Jewish, and Christian Iranians are the only recognized religious minorities, who, within the limits of the law, are free to perform their religious rites and ceremonies, and to act according to their own canon in matters of personal affairs and religious education" (Article 13); "the government of the Islamic Republic of Iran and all Muslims are duty-bound to treat non-Muslims in conformity with ethical norms and the principles of Islamic justice and equity, and to respect their human rights. This principle applies to all who refrain from engaging in conspiracy or activity against Islam and the Islamic Republic of Iran" (Article 14). Within this framework, the Jewish minority was guaranteed permanent representation in the Iranian parliament: "The Zoroastrians and Jews will each elect one representative" (Article 64). The constitution also dictates that the Islamic Republican government and Iranian Muslims must treat non-Muslims according to Muslim principles of ethics and justice.

Since 2000, the Tehran Jewish Council publishes a periodical by the name *Ofoq-e Binā*. The content of this publication resembles that of *Tammuz*. The Tehran Jewish Committee operates a website: http://www.iranjewish.com. The Jews are represented in the *Majles* by the Moris Mo'tamed who tries to protect their rights. The precise number of the Jews currently living in Iran is unknown. The figure is thought to be in the vicinity of 25,000. This number includes 3,000 Jews in Shiraz and 1,500 in Isfahan. Other cities and settlements in Iran such as Hamadan, Kermanshah, Kashan, Sanandaj, and many other cities, once populated by thousands of Jews, either have one or two Jewish families or none.

In practice, Jewish freedom of worship has not been curtailed in a meaningful way, and to this day Jewish holidays receive coverage in the media. Each year, local television stations broadcast programs on Jewish holidays, especially Passover, when the state media carries the blessings of the Jewish community head and *Majles* representative. The community has continued administering its own schools, synagogues, and other institutions, including

Jewish hospitals, nursing homes, cemeteries, and libraries. For example, Tehran has 11 functioning synagogues, many of them with Hebrew schools. In Jewish schools, special textbooks are used to teach the Jewish pupils in elementary schools about the Jewish religion: "Ketāb-e Ta'alimāt-e Dīnī-ye Kalīmyān" (the book of the religious instructions of the Jews, 5 vols.). Tehran has two kosher restaurants, a Jewish hospital, an old-age home, a cemetery, and a Jewish library with 20,000 titles.

Despite the apparent discriminatory laws and attitudes toward the Jews in Iran, the Jews enjoy a relatively peaceful and comfortable life. The economic condition of the Jews is reported to be relatively satisfactory. Generally, Jews who have chosen to stay in Iran say that they are content and have no desire to leave their homeland. However, the remaining community faces several problems, among them is the shortage of suitable Jewish spouses. The remaining Jews have tried to compensate for their diminishing numbers by adopting a new religious fervor. Just as it radically transformed Muslim society, the revolution changed the Jewish community. Families that had been secular in the 1970s started keeping kosher and strictly observing rules regarding Shabbat (Sabbath). The synagogue became the focal point of their social lives. Iranian Jews testify that they socialize far less with Muslims now than before the revolution. As a whole, they occupy their own separate space within the rigid confines of the Islamic republic, a protected yet precarious niche.

Iranian Jews have some freedoms that Muslims do not have. Jewish women, like Muslim women, are required by law to keep their heads covered. However most wear a simple scarf in place of the more restrictive chador. Unlike Muslims, Jews are allowed to use alcohol for religious purposes. Some Hebrew schools are coeducational, and men and women dance with each other at weddings, practices strictly forbidden for Muslims.

However, discrimination against minorities still exists. In a speech in the *Majles* on December 24, 2000, the Jewish representative Maurice Mo'tamed lashed out at the widespread discrimination against non-Muslims in Iran. He pointed to discrimination in academic education, in government recruitment and job promotion (although many Jews hold jobs in government ministries or within state-owned firms, they say they are unlikely to rise to top positions), in criminal law, and restrictions on Hebrew instruction. All these, he said go "against the noble goals of the Islamic Revolution" and certainly had grave impact on Jewish community. Until February 2002, Article 30 of the Criminal Code dealing with homicide and involuntary manslaughter (the *diyah*) did not equally apply to Muslims and non-Muslims.

ATTITUDES TOWARD JEWS

The Islamic regime's relatively tolerant approach is noticeable on the surface, but a closer scrutiny reveals that matters are often more complex. Anti-Jewish sentiments abound among segments of the population and occasionally find expression in official statements. The distinction between Jews, Israel, and Zionism is often blurred.

Today, Jews participate in Iranian civic and political life. Many Jews join the Iranian masses in protesting the State of Israel on the annual "Qods Day" (Jerusalem Day), and during the Iran–Iraq War (1980–1988) Iranian Jews supported the war effort by donating ambulances and surplus goods as well as making hospital visits. Sometimes this support was rejected because of the concept of *nejasat*. Some Jewish youth even took part in the fighting and were wounded in combat. The Jews of Iran were equally targeted by the Iraqi war machine as their Muslim neighbors.

Anti-Semitism, however, remains. In March 1999, 13 Jews from Shiraz and Isfahan were arrested on charges of spying for Israel, and they were convicted in July 2000. By February 2003 all of them had been released, but the arrests planted fear in the heart of the Jewish community, bringing its loyalty under question. This affair has been suggested to reflect the pervasive internal power struggle between the conservative and the reformist camps during Khatami's presidency, and it purportedly was intended to put the former president Khatemi between the hammer and the anvil.

In recent years, Iran has become a major center for disseminating radical views regarding anti-Semitism and the Holocaust. For instance, at times officials linked with the Islamic Republic promote ideas found in *The Protocols of the Elders of Zion*. Anti-Semitic books, slogans, cartoons, television shows, and films have penetrated Iranian popular culture. In some official publications, the Jews in modern history are referred to very briefly, and there is little mention of their culture, history, or their achievements in the Iranian textbooks. On the eve of the Jewish holiday of Purim in 2008, a news column was published in *Farda* newspaper that presented the Jewish holiday as a celebration of the genocide of Iranian citizens during the Torah time.

In January 2006, in response to President Mahmoud Ahmadinejad's critical tone and frequent inflammatory statements regarding the Holocaust, Haroun Yashaya'i, the head of Iran's Jewish community, sent a letter to Ahmadinejad complaining about his Holocaust denial comments. Yashaya'i said the remarks have shocked the international community and struck fear within Iran's small Jewish community. He described the Holocaust as one of the twentieth century's "most obvious and saddest events" and asked: "How is it possible to ignore all the undeniable evidence existing for the killing and exile of the Jews in Europe during World War II?"

Despite these difficulties, most of the remaining Jews of Iran feel an unbreakable bond to their homeland and continue to live there by choice. Some visit Israel, however, but return to Iran. Judaism is part of their identity, but it does not contradict their Iranian identity nor their view of Iran as their home. They neither lament their fate nor yearn to leave Iran. They do not feel the need to apologize for the fact that they live in Iran, and they see no reason to reconcile a contradiction where they see none.

In the summer of 2007, members of the Iranian Jewish community residing in the United States offered $60,000 to any Iranian-Jewish family willing to immigrate to Israel. The proposal was strongly spurned by those Jews who prefer to stay in Iran. On July 10, 2007, on the official website of the community, a statement was posted saying: "Iranian Jews identity is not exchangeable for money." By December 2007, only forty Jews had accepted the offer and immigrated to Israel. Iran is still the home to the largest Jewish community in the Middle East, outside Israel.

Suggested Reading and Viewing

Bahgat, G. 2005. The Islamic Republic and the Jewish state. *Israel Affairs*. 11:3.

Choksy, J. 2006. Despite Shāhs and Mollās: minority sociopolitics in premodern and modern Iran. *JAH*. 40/2.

Farahani, R. 2005. *Jews of Iran*. Film.

Golshani, V. S. 2008. Iran: Jewish life under Islamic rule. *New Society: Harvard College Student Middle East Journal*. January 29. http://newsocietyjournal.com/2008/01/29/ iran-jewish-life-under-islamic-rule.

Greenberger, R. R. 2006. How Jew-friendly Persia became anti-Semitic Iran. *Moment*. 31:6.

Hakakian, R. 2004. *Journey from the land of no*. New York: Three Rivers Press.

Menashri, D. 2002. "The Pahlavi monarchy and the Islamic revolution," in Sarshar, Houman, ed. *Esther's children: a portrait of Iranian Jews*. Philadelphia: Jewish Publication Society.

Rahimiyan, O. R. 2008. "Jewish community: life in Iran." *ShiurTimes*. 2:15.

Rahimiyan, O. R. "Modern history of Iranian Jews." My Jewish Learning, http:// myjewishlearning.com/history_community/Jewish_World_Today/JewishDiasporaTO/ MizrachiJews/Iran.htm

Sanasarian, E. 2000. *Religious minorities in Iran*. Cambridge: Cambridge University Press.

Satrapi, M. 2003. *Persepolis: the story of a childhood*. New York: Pantheon Books.

Soroudi, S. 1981. "Jews in Islamic Iran." *Jewish Quarterly*. 21.

ORLY RAHIMIYAN

✦ JUDICIARY

The Iranian modern judiciary was established by Ali Akbar Davar (1886–1937). He was the Minister of Justice between 1927 and 1932. In the beginning of the twentieth century, the traditional Islamic jurisprudence (*fiqh*) was not able to cope with the new needs of Iranian society. Other than theoretical and practical inadequacies, the struggle between *shari'a* and state courts usually could not be easily settled. In pursuing judicial reform, Iranian elites were looking directly at the judicial and legal achievements of Western civilization. As a result, Iran's judicial system between 1927 and 1979, modeled after that of Europeans, was based on a hierarchy of courts ranging from the district courts on the lowest level, up to the Supreme Court, i.e., the court of final appeal. One of the most important goals of judicial reform in this period involved the correction of the judicial procedures.

Dāvar presented 120 drafts on judicial affairs to the parliament. The shah, his court, and the majority of the members of parliament completely supported him. Most of the laws codified during this period were directed to increase the power of the state in the judicial process. For example, most of the changes in the Civil Code that allowed greater jurisdiction to lower courts increased the powers of state attorneys and prosecutors. To further limit the power of the clerics, the judiciary under Reza Shah's rule undertook a codification of the laws that created a body of secular law, applied and interpreted by a secular judiciary outside the control of the religious establishment. Among the codes constituting the new secular law were the Civil Code, enacted between 1927 and 1932, the General Accounting Act (1934–1935), a milestone in financial administration, a new tax law, and a civil service code. Articles 75 and 76 of the Constitution gave Dāvar the opportunity to upgrade the position of the Supreme Court. This court was the highest court in appealing procedure. Dāvar increased the number of primary, appellate, and cassation courts and established itinerant appellate courts and limited reconciliation courts. Hence, there was more access to justice.

The Islamic revolutionary regime after 1979 pursued three tasks regarding the judiciary: purging those judiciary officials and judges who had close ties with the monarchy; establishing revolutionary courts to try high ranking official of the Old Regime; and bringing thousands of clerics who have been claiming the judgeship seat for centuries to the Islamic judiciary. After 1981 and the consolidation of the Islamic regime, judicial authority was constitutionally vested in the Supreme Judiciary Council; this was a group with responsibility for supervising the enforcement of all Islamic laws and for establishing judicial and legal policies. Focusing on the authority of the judge in the court, lawyers were literally pushed out of the judicial system.

The structure and functions of the judiciary in the post-revolutionary era are detailed in Articles 156 to 174 of the 1979 Constitution. According to Article 157, the highest judicial power was a council known as the Supreme Judicial Council, later abolished due to revision of the Constitution in 1989. This council had five members, including the head of the Supreme Court, the Prosecutor General, and three judges possessing the degree of *ejtehād* (expert in Islamic law), to be chosen by all the judges of the country. The democratic feature of this body was not functional in an authoritarian regime and was stopped by the revised edition of the Constitution of 1979, which put an appointed official in the office of head of the judiciary. The occupier of this position should be a *mujtahed* (Islamic jurist), but previous judgeship is not a must. The Ministry of Justice has merely been an administrative body, which provides the logistics for the judiciary. The Minister of Justice is chosen by the Prime Minister (and later the President) from among those proposed to him by the Head of the Judiciary (Article 160 of 1989 Constitution). The function of the Minister of Justice is a liaison between the judiciary on one hand and the executive and legislative body in administrative matters on the other. Another change in the revised Constitution regarding the judiciary was to transfer all the responsibilities of the Supreme Council of the Judiciary and the Head of the Supreme Court (suggesting amnesty to the leader, membership in provisional council of leadership and presidency) to the head of the judiciary.

The Council for Revision of the Constitution abolished the five-member Judicial Supreme Council, three of whom were elected by the judges, as the highest authority in the Islamic Republic, and replaced it with a head of the judiciary appointed by the leader (Article 157). This action destroyed the collective leadership of the judiciary. Consequently, the partially elective nature of the judicial authority was denied. The Minister of Justice is also to be chosen by the President from "among those proposed to the President by the Head of the Judiciary" (Article 160), and hence the Parliament and the President as elected bodies have almost no say in choosing the Minister of Justice. There is an inconsistency between the duties and power of this position in the Constitution. It is the head of the judiciary who appoints the head of the Supreme Court and the Public Prosecutor–General; in the Constitution of 1979, they were appointed by the Leader. According to Article 164, the head of the judiciary can remove judges after consultation with the chief of the Supreme Court and the Prosecutor General.

The establishment of the office of the head of judiciary in the post Khomeini era, considered in the revision of the Constitution in 1989, was partly modeled after the office of the *qāzi al-quzāt* which was created in the latter part of the eighth century. The traditional view on the judicial organization would not tolerate a council to direct and manage the judiciary; for hundreds of years the Iranian judiciary had been headed by an individual at the top. The holder of this office in the Constitution, like *qāzi al-quzāt*, is merely the highest judicial officer with important administrative functions. He is not an independent judicial professional. From a practical point of view, the idea was a modern one of centralization: one head for the judiciary power to match the one head for the executive power, which resulted in the abolition of the office of prime minister. This development in the Constitution of 1989 centralized all powers of the regular judiciary in one person appointed by the leader. The Leader keeps his power to prosecute and punish dissident clerics through the Special Court of Clergy, which is organizationally independent from the judiciary.

The most important reform to the Iranian judiciary during Mohammad Yazdi's term was executing the General Courts Law of 1994. This court structure was modeled after the court structure of Islamic lands during centuries of Islamic civilization. During those centuries, the judge who was supposed to be just (*ādel*) was the only actor in the court. The procedure did not guarantee justice, but rather, a non-verifiable and non-measurable characteristic of the judge, i.e., his fairness. The judge would be considered just and fair unless proven otherwise, which proved an almost impossible task. His verdict was final, and there was no appeal jurisdiction. From an Islamist point of view, the revival of the jurist justice in the form of General Courts was a way to revive Islamic civilization and Islamic judiciary.

Every power in the judiciary in this period was concentrated in the Head of Judiciary and, through him, in the hands of the Leader. As such, the judicial system has lacked political independence, especially since according to the Constitution (Article 164) members of the judiciary, including its highest judge, could be removed from office by the Leader. According to Article 156 of the 1989 Constitution, the Iranian judiciary is formally independent. All high-ranking officials of the judiciary are directly and indirectly appointed by the Leader (Article 157 of the 1989 Constitution), without any formal input from the elected President or the Parliament. The minister of justice is chosen by the President from among candidates nominated by the head of the judiciary (Article 160 of the 1989 Constitution).

The Parliament is not allowed to draft judicial laws (Article 158 of the 1989 Constitution). The Parliament does not have any powers of oversight over the judiciary, and all judicial policies are dictated by the Leader; judges are regularly removed from their posts, or transferred and redesignated without their consent when their decrees in political matters do not sit well with high-ranking members of the establishment. This non-elected state body has a number of political functions, such as representing the council for the Revision of the Constitution (Article 177), determining membership of its head in the country's National Security Council, and membership of its representatives in the Press and Political Parties Commissions. The judiciary, designated as the enforcer of the ideological cause of the Islamic regime in the preamble of the Constitution, cannot be, and is not, neutral in political tensions.

See also Legal System.

Suggested Reading

Āqeli, B. 1990. Dāvar va ʾAdlieh (Dāvar and the Judiciary). Tehran: ʾElmi.

Mohammadi, M. 2006. Judicial reform and reorganization in 20th century Iran. Ph.D. dissertation. Stony Brook University.

Zerang, M. 2002. *Tahavvol-e Nezām-e Qazā'i in Iran (The development in Iran's judiciary system)*, Vol. I & II. Tehran: Markaz-e Asnād-e Enqelāb-e Eslāmi,

MAJID MOHAMMADI

K

✦ KHAMENEI (KHAMENE'I), AYATOLLAH SEYYED ALI HOSSEINI (1939–)

Early Life and Education

Ayatollah (Ay.) Seyyed Ali Hosseini Khamenei (Ali Khamene'i is a closer transliteration of خامنهای علی) is the *Vali-ye Faqih* (Guardian Religious Jurist) of Iran. He is commonly referred to as the Rahbar (Leader) or Rahbar-e Moazzam (Exalted, Honorable, Leader) in Iran, but not as the "Supreme Leader," a designation used commonly in the West and corresponding to his actual current leadership position.

He was born on July 17, 1939 (Tir 24, 1318 AH) in the holy city of Mashhad (Meshed), Khorasan, the site of the shrine of Imam Reza (Ridha), the eighth and only one of the twelve Shiite Imams interred in Iran. His father, Seyyed Javad, was a cleric of Azeri background, with modest economic means and eight children. As the second son, Khamenei recounts: "Sometimes for supper we had nothing but bread with some raisins, which our mother had somehow improvised.... Our house ... consisted of a single room and a gloomy basement. When visitors came to see my father as the local cleric to consult about their problems, the family had to move into the basement while the visit went on.... Years later some charitable persons bought the small, empty lot adjacent to our house, so we were able to build two more rooms!" As a "Seyyed" (descendant of the descendants of Imam Ali), the current Leader's reported genealogy combines three of ethnicities of Iran: Arab, Azeri, and Persian. He has four sons and two daughters.

Ayatollah Ali Khamenei, left, walks with President Mohammad Khatami to visit Khatami's new cabinet in Tehran, 2001. (AP Photo)

His education began at the age of four with tutoring by his father and attending, with his elder brother Mohammad, a *maktab* (a traditional primary school teaching the alphabet and reading of the Qur'an by a mid- to low-level cleric and common before modernization of the educational system by Reza Shah). Later, mostly at Dar al-Ta'leem Diyanat, Soleiman Khan, and Nawwab religious schools, he completed the intermediate level curricula including logic, philosophy, and Islamic jurisprudence in about five and a half years as a student of Ayatollahs Mirza Jawad Tehrani and Sheikh Reza Aysi. At the age of thirteen he attended a lecture and was greatly impressed by Seyyed Mojtaba Nawwab Safavi, the leader of Fedaiyan-e Islam, an Iranian group influenced by the Islamic revolutionary ideas and activism of Hasan al-Banna and the Muslim Brotherhood in Egypt. Nawwab Safavi, later executed by the Shah's regime, also influenced Ayatollah Rouhollah Khomeini in his early clerical career and writings.

At the age of eighteen, Seyyed Ali started taking courses in "sat'h" (based on reading texts) and "dars-e kharej" (beyond reading texts) with such scholars and tutors as Haj Sheikh Hashem Qazvini and Ay. Ali Hosseini Milani. In 1957 he left Iran for pilgrimage to the shrines of Iraq. Although impressed by courses of such ayatollahs as Mohsen Hakim, Mohammad Shahrudi, Baqer Zanjani, and Seyyed Yahya Yazdi in Najaf seminary, he had to return to Iran in 1958 at the behest of his father to pursue his higher religious education in the holy city of Qom with such ayatollahs as Hossein Borujerdi (the sole marja' in Iran for a number of years prior to his death in 1962), Khomeini, Morteza Yazdi, and (Allamah) Mohammad Tabatabai. In 1964 he returned to Mashhad to take care of his father, who had become blind in one eye and unable to read well, and his family, but he continued his studies until 1968 with such resident scholars as Ayatollah Milani to complete his advanced-level jurisprudence. Meanwhile, he had already been arrested and detained by the SAVAK for a short period in Birjand, Khorasan, in 1963, subsequent to the first wave of religious revolts against the regime, and started teaching religious subjects to seminary students, Nahaj-ul-Balaghah (Statements of Imam Ali) at mosques, and lecturing at universities in 1964.

Ayatollah Khamenei is now widely recognized not only as a *marja* (source of emulation) and the preeminent political leader of Iran but also one the most important *marja*s (*maraje'*) and "Grand"Ayatollahs among the Shiites in Lebanon, Iraq, Bahrain, Afghanistan, Pakistan, and elsewhere. His initial appointment as Vali-ye Faqih, however, elicited controversy and various degrees of opposition from a number of traditional Ayatollahs who had either been against Velayat-e Faqih since its inception, but had kept a low profile while Khomeini was alive, or opposed to Khamenei's succession. Since Khamenei was not a recognized *marja* when Khomeini died in 1989, a new amendment to the constitution was proposed to authorize an individual of his qualifications to become the Vali, and the Assembly of Experts elected him on a temporary basis until the amendment was ratified. In 1994 the Society of Seminary Teachers of Qom proclaimed Khamenei as a new *marja* after the death of Ay. Mohammad Ali Araki. However, (Grand) Ays. Mohammad Shirazi, Hossein Ali Montazer Najafabadi (dismissed from his position as successor by Ay. Khomeini), Hassan Tabatabai Qomi, and Yasobeddin Rastegari objected. At least one of these opponents preferred a college of Velayat. To abate the controversy, Khamenei accepted *marjaiyyat* only for Shiites outside Iran.

Selected Publications of Ayatollah Khamenei
✦

Ay. Khamenei has written many books and tracts. They consist of original works in Arabic and Persian and four translations. The Arabic book listed first may have served as his resalah (treatise). It was originally written in two volumes and later combined into one. It is available in Arabic, Dari, and Persian.

ARABIC

Ajawbat al-Istifta'at [Replies to Inquiries]. Beirut: Rabitat al-Thiqat val-Alaqat al-Islamiyyah, 1999.

DARI

Al-Osul al-Arba'ah fi Elm al-Rejal [The Four Principles (Books) in Knowledge of Distinguished Men (Narrators of Traditions)]. Beirut: Dar al-Thaqalain, 1994.

Fi Rehab al-Mawaqef al-Karimah wa al-Mashahid al-Sharifah: Mansek al-Hajj [Concerning Revered Sites and Noble Martyrs' Shrines: Rites of Pilgrimage to Mecca]. Damascus: Daftar Maqm Moazzam Rahbari dar Sour-riyeh, n.d.

Al-Khotut al-Ammah lel-Fekr al-islami [General Lines of Islamic Thought]. Beirut: Markaz Baqiyyat Allah al-A'zam, 1996.

PERSIAN

Hokumat dar Islam [Government in Islam]. Tehran: Sazman Sanaye' Melli Iran, 1983.

Az Jarfaye Namaz [On Profundity of Prayer]. Tehran: Daftar Nashr Farhang Islami, 1990.

Bazgasht beh Nahgulbelaghah [Return to Nahgulbelaghah]. Tehran: Sazman Nahjulbelaghah, 1993.

Zarurat-e Tahavvol-e Hawzeh Ha-ye Elmiyyeh [The Necessity of Reorganizing Religious Seminaries]. Tehran: Sazman Tablighati Ostan Tehran, 1984.

Mashruiyyat-e Ahkam-e Ateshbas dar Islam [Legitimacy of the rules of Armistice in Islam]. Tehran: Sazman Aghidati Artesh Jomhury Eslami, 1990.

V(W)elayat [Guardianship]. Tehran: Markaz Chapp va Nashr Sazman Tablight Eslami, 1991.

OTHERS

Islamic Thought in the Quran: An Outline

Unity and Political Parties

A Discourse on Patience

The Islamic Seminary of Mashhad: A General Report

Imam Al-Sadiq (AS)

Arts: Personal Views

Understanding Religion Properly

Struggles of Shiite Imams (AS)

The Necessity of Returning to the Quran

The Essence of God's Unity

Imam Reza (AS) and His Appointment as Crown Prince

TRANSLATIONS (FROM ARABIC INTO PERSIAN)

The Future in Islamic Lands, by Seyyed Qutb

Muslims in the Liberation Movement of India, by Abdulmu'nim Namri Nassri

An Indictment against the Western Civilization, by Seyyed Qutb

Peace Treaty of Imam Hassan (AS), by Razi Al Yaseen

Political Activities and Positions

Khamenei was arrested and imprisoned several times for his pro-Khomeini and Islamic revolutionary activities during the Shah's regime: twice in 1963 as a result of the first wave of Islamic revolts, in 1964 for two months of solitary confinement, in 1967, in 1975, and, finally, in 1976 for two and a half years of confinement in exile. He was released shortly before the revolution.

Khamenei Mini-Chronology
✦

1979	Revolutionary Council member
1980	Islamic Republican Party founding member
	Deputy Minister of Defense
	Supervisor of Islamic Revolutionary Guard
	Imam of Tehran's congregational prayers
	Elected to the Majlis
1981	Khomeini's representative to the High Defense Council
1982	Chairman, High Council of Revolutionary Cultural Affairs
	Object of an assassination attempt through a bomb hidden inside a recorder and placed on the rostrum in Abuzar Mosque in Tehran, reportedly by Mojahedin Khalq members, which exploded very close to his body but damaged only his right hand permanently because he had moved slightly to the left during his speech.
1982–1990	President of the Islamic Republic
1986	President, Expediency Council
1990	Chairman, Committee for Constitutional Revision
1990–present	Leader

LEADERSHIP STYLE AND POLICIES

Khamenei succeeded Khomeini at the end of the first turbulent decade of the IRI's history. Revolutionary dislocation and eight years of the disastrous Iran–Iraq War had left Iran internationally isolated, its infrastructure substantially deteriorated, such cities as Khorramshahr and Abadan largely destroyed, the arsenal of weapons thoroughly depleted, and the economy in dire straights and chafing under heavy debt. In light of these conditions and the initial controversy surrounding Khamenei's succession, his legitimacy was considered shaky, his power insignificant, and the survival of the Islamic Republic doubtful by most opposition groups and Western analysts.

It is too early to know whether *velayat-e faqih* is sufficiently institutionalized to survive Khamenei for a historically significant period. But his position as the leader, arbiter, and balancer of contending political forces and the stability of the Islamic regime are clearly more firmly established than in 1989, as Iran has since experienced many peaceful elections, its economic and social systems have made substantial progress, its defense forces and weapons systems are considerably stronger and more advanced, and it is now widely acknowledged as a major regional power. These developments are to a great extent attributable to his leadership style and policies, despite major supportive roles played by such leaders as Ays. Ali Akbar Hashemi Rafsanjani—current President of the Expediency Council, Vice Chair of the Assembly of Experts, and former Speaker of the Majlis and President of the IRI—Ali Akbar Meshkini—Chair of the Assembly of Experts and of Society of Seminary Teachers of Qom—other members of this society, and many non-clerical leaders and technocrats. As is the case with top leaders of most pluralistic political systems, however, he still remains partly hostage to some of his more extreme supporters.

Khamenei clearly does not have the kind of charisma possessed by Khomeini, but he is considerably more astute, pragmatic, willing to consult before making decisions, responsive to trends in the political system and society, and prone to engage in innovation in and adaptation through *ijtihad*. While Iran is still plagued by serious difficulties in such areas as bureaucratic inefficiency and corruption, inadequate economic development, problematic judicial process, and arbitrary exclusion by the Guardian Council of candidates for elections, the following concrete policy decisions are instructive:

1. Khamenei replaced Khomeini's policy of encouraging fertility with a highly effective family planning program consisting of public education, family counseling, and monthly distribution of millions of condoms and pills at the government's expense through a network of

health clinics established in cities, towns, and villages across the country. It has been rated by the U.N. as the best of its kind in the Third World.

2. He has been instrumental in improving women's status and rights despite persistent resistance by conservative religious leaders who have so far managed to block some of the proposed reforms, e.g., a law passed by the Majlis substantially expanding women's highly restricted right to divorce, which is pending submission to the Expediency Council for decision. After maintaining that "Islam does not see any difference between a man and a woman, their sex difference has no relevance," he challenged an established tradition:

> Of course, some of the requirements that are known to be established in *fiqh*, such as for those religious judges, are susceptible to flaws. We cannot certify that being a man is a requirement for being a religious judge. Perhaps in some matters it is fundamentally a woman who must issue a fatwa. There are some issues that you and I as men are not capable of comprehending … (Session 124 of Dars-e Kharej)

3. In contrast to Khomeini and Shah Mohammad Reza Pahlavi who regularly extended their hand to be kissed by Iranians of all stripes visiting them, Khamenei, in line with the behavior of the early leaders of Islam, has discouraged this practice. He also lives modestly despite his status and has complained about the amount of material wealth accumulated by some of the cleric-politicians.

4. Khamenei has also been instrumental in discontinuing the practices of *qameh zani*, bloodletting by cutting the skin of the forehead with strait poniard, and self-flagellation with chains during commemoration ceremonies and passion plays of *ashura*, the anniversary of tenth day of the killing of Imam Hossein (Hussein, Husain) in Karbala. These practices, however, continue among the devout Iraqi Shiites.

5. He has expressed great respect for scholars and scientists, supported investment in science and technology to develop the country's infrastructure, and has been a pioneering Muslim religious leader in allowing stem cell research and therapeutic cloning. He has emphasized the significance of nuclear energy for civilian purposes since "oil and gas reserves cannot last forever." He has also issued a fatwa stating that the production and use of nuclear weapons are forbidden in Islam.

6. Khamenei has also promoted economic privatization. In 2004, Article 44 of the constitution, requiring that the basic infrastructure of the country be managed by the state, was repealed. In 2007 he suggested

on several occasions that officials expedite privatization and recommended that the Ministry of Justice establish special courts to protect ownership rights to provide incentive for private investment.

7. In response to those who have expressed concern with Shiite Iran's influence or promoted sectarian conflict between the Shiites and the Sunnis in the Middle East, Khamenei has argued that the Iranian revolution was an Islamic, not a Shiite, one and its primary banner remains the Qur'an. This argument deserve serious examination in light of the influence of Hasan al-Banna, Seyyed Qutb (one of whose books was translated by Ali Khamenei and published in Iran in 1980), and the Muslim Brotherhood of Sunni Egypt on the ideologies of Nawwab Safavi, Khomeini, and Khamenei, the only revolutionaries among the relatively quietist Iranian clergy of the time.

8. Khamenei unequivocally condemned the September 11, 2001 attack and its instigators specifically and all terrorism in the world, including Israel. Iranians subsequently held several nights of candlelight vigil for the victims in the United States.

9. He has accused Western governments of hypocrisy about human rights because of their imposition of and support for despots and oppression of the peoples of the Third World. He argues that human rights, including the right to welfare, are fundamental to Islam and maintains that since the American government has committed many crimes it is not capable of judging human rights in Iran.

10. Khamenei is an ardent supporter of the right of the Palestinians to armed resistance against Israel, but has shown flexibility in accepting a just solution of their disputes with the Israelis in the future. He has also indicated that Iran will not be bullied into surrendering its right to produce nuclear energy and would retaliate and try to stop energy shipments from the Persian Gulf if attacked by the United States.

Suggested Reading

http://www.khamenei.ir/EN/Biography/index.jsp (See also the Persian version).

http://www.leader.ir/langs/EN/index.php?p=bio.

Iran Chamber Society. 2007. Ayatollah Seyyed Ali Khamenei. *Historic Personalities*. February 18.

Wright, R. 2000. *The last great revolution: turmoil and transformation in Iran*. New York: Alfred A. Knopf.

GHOLAM HOSSEIN RAZI

✦ KHATAMI, SEYED MOHAMMAD (1943–)

Seyed Mohammad Khatami, two-term Iranian president, was born on September 29, 1943, in the city of Ardekan, near Yazd. His mother, Sakineh Ziai Khatami, and his father, Ayatollah Ruhollah Khatami, belonged to the middle classes and were well-respected members of their community. At age nineteen, Khatami went to study religion at the Qom Theological Seminary, but three years later he left to study philosophy at the University of Isfahan. It was here where as a member of the Islamic Students Organization he began his political activities alongside Ayatollah Khomeini's son, Ahmad Khomeini. A few years later, he earned his Master of Arts in Educational Sciences from Tehran University. After completing his traditional education, he returned to the Qom Theological Seminary for further religious training and more in-depth studies regarding *ijtihad* and reinterpretation of Islam.

At the time of the 1978–1979 revolution, Khatami was Director of the Hamburg Islamic Center in Germany. He soon returned to Iran and, as a member of the new revolutionary political system, he began to serve in a variety of political positions. These included, among others, as Member of Parliament, Director of the War Information Headquarters, Minister of Culture,

Iranian president Mohammad Khatami at the opening ceremony of Iran's Masjid-Suleiman dam, in Khuzestan province, 2001. (AP Photo/Hasan Sarbakhshian)

Chair of the Central Council of the Association of Combatant Clerics, and from 1992 until being elected President, as the head of the National Library.

In 1997, Khatami was elected president of Iran and emerged as a symbol of what came to be known as the "reform movement." His election came as somewhat of a shock to the political system, especially in the more conservative quarters, which neither anticipated Khatami's surprising, landslide victory nor welcomed the new president's reformist initiatives. Khatami's election campaign and his presidency were both premised on two assumptions: the essential compatibility of Islam with civil society; and the importance of engaging in a dialogue of civilizations. Both of these premises generated considerable support and enthusiasm among many Iranian urban middle classes who saw in Khatami a welcome departure from the austere revolutionary character of the earlier years.

In many ways, Khatami's first year in office can be considered a milestone in the life of the Islamic Republic. Press and publishing restrictions were eased, and many of the other pervasive social and cultural restrictions, such as dress code and music, were relaxed. Khatami also made significant strides toward repairing some of Iran's strained relations with other Middle Eastern powers, especially with the conservative states of the Persian Gulf, and Iran's relations with the European Union were also improved. Some initiatives were also taken to improve relations with the United States, although ultimately neither Iran nor the United States was willing to take substantive steps necessary to normalize relations.

Khatami, and the many public intellectuals to whose voices he gave expression, sought to reform the revolutionary system from within, and in the process they gave rise to multiple, entrenched sources of opposition and resentment. Immediately prior to the 1997 election, Iran had witnessed a flowering of intellectual activity that culminated in substantial expansion in publication of books, journals, and newspapers. This trend continued and intensified throughout Khatami's two terms, the frequent harassment and imprisonment of writers and public intellectuals notwithstanding.

Despite significant changes in the larger atmosphere and context of Iranian politics during his presidency, Khatami encountered significant difficulties in carrying out his reformist agendas. His popularity among the urban middle classes, reaffirmed through his landslide re-election to the presidency in 2001, turned out to be insufficient to enable the president to make good on many of the promises of reform and liberalization that were generally ascribed to him by Iranians at large. Khatami had popularity, and enjoyed particular support among the youth, technocrats, and professionals, but most levers of power remained firmly in the hands of his conservative opponents, some of the more notable of whom included Supreme Leader Khamenei, influential members of the Assembly of Experts, the Guardians Council, the judiciary, and the Islamic Revolutionary Guards Corp (IRGC). Before long, by the middle of his second term, the conservative forces had effectively stymied many of Khatami's reform initiatives, and his presidency began to lose luster among his throng of supporters. To the urban electorate he was seen as a source of disappointment, of promises unfulfilled, and expectations frustrated. Painfully aware of the frustrated expectation of his presidency, near the end of his term in office, Khatami released a booklet called "A Letter for Tomorrow" in which he promised to reveal the reasons for his failures at a later date. In 2005, having served the constitutionally maximum two terms in office, Khatami left the presidency.

Khatami's significance goes beyond what he did while he was in office. He was—and continues to be—part of what came to be known as Iranian "religious intellectuals," a crop of thinkers seeking to foster a dynamic *ijtihad* (independent reasoning) of Islam. A creative use of ijtihad would allow religious intellectuals to address some of the most pressing issues of contemporary society, issues such as democracy, the nature of the relationship between reason and faith, religious hermeneutics, the rights of minorities, the responsibilities of the faithful, and the like. The writings of the former president place him squarely within the reformist tradition of Muslim thinkers and intellectuals. Hence, the relatively open atmosphere that his presidency created helped to foster the flourishing of intellectual activism.

Out of office, Khatami has taken a relatively low-key position, delivering occasional lectures and assuming the role of an opposition figure. Given his relatively young age and fond memories of his presidency, especially in comparison with the tumultuous policies of President Ahmadinejad, Khatami may still make a comeback in Iranian politics and, at least for the foreseeable future, will continue to be an important figure in the political life of the Islamic Republic.

Suggested Reading

Brumberg, D. 2001. *Reinventing Khomeini: the struggle for reform in Iran.* Chicago: University of Chicago Press.

Ehsani, K., and M. Saghafi. 2004. The new landscape of Iranian politics. *Middle East Report.* 233: 16–23.

Kamrava, M., ed. 2006. *The new voices of Islam: rethinking politics and modernity,* Berkeley: University of California Press.

Khatami, M. 1997. *Hope and challenge: the Iranian president speaks.* Translated by Parvis Morewedge and Kent P. Jackson. Binghamton: SUNY Press.

Mehran, G. 2003. Khatami, political reform and education in Iran. *Comparative Education.* 39: 311–329.

Moslem, M. 2002. *Factional politics in post-Khomeini Iran.* Syracuse, NY: Syracuse University Press.

MEHRAN KAMRAVA

Ayatollah Ruhollah Khomeini speaks in 1979 at a news conference following morning prayers. (AP Photo)

✦ KHOMEINI, RUHOLLAH (1902–1989)

Ruhollah Mustafavi, better known as Ruhollah Musavi Khomeini, will be remembered as one of the giants of the twentieth century, along with such other historic figures as Lenin (1870–1924), Stalin (1879–1953), Mao (1893–1976), and Churchill (1874–1965). His name is synonymous with the reemergence of religion in public life, and he is the engine behind the reversal of the process of secularization. But he is a much more complex figure than just being a political leader or even a revolutionary. Charismatic, with penetrating eyes, he is a man of multiple faces who brought Iranians home from almost a century of pseudo-modernization and Westernization.

The last child of an obscure cleric in the small town of Khomein in southwest Iran, Ruhollah Khomeini lived for most of the twentieth century. He was born in 1902 and died, still in full power, in 1989, as the leader of the first classic but non-Western revolution. He joined the clerical rank at an early age, and despite the magnitude of his earthly success and power, he lived a modest life of a mystic, philosopher, jurist, and a scholar throughout his life. His lifestyle notwithstanding, in the last decade of his life he was the supreme power-yielder in Iran, and according to many, he ruled with an iron fist. This kind of complexity is extremely difficult to convey, making it almost impossible to emphasize the importance of a single aspect of Khomeini's life, career, character, or scholarship.

Many, including some of his fellow clerics, think that Khomeini's actions and ideas changed and evolved as he got closer to power. For example, some suggest that in Khomeini's life, four stages can be identified. The first is the Khomeini of Qom, where he lived from 1921 until he was exiled in 1964, as a scholar and the voice of dissidence. Although he lived the life of a teacher and a scholar within the seminaries in Qom, he maintained two faces. As long as the prominent leader of the clerical establishment, Ayatollah Burujerdi

(d. 1961) was alive, he agreed with the quietist attitude that was prevalent, and in his writings even accepted the existing parliamentary constitution. Nevertheless, he was critical of the people, whether in power or not, who did not adhere to indigenous norms, particularly the laws of Islam. Whenever he found the opportunity to safely express himself, he did so, as is evidenced by his first comprehensive book on political and social issues, *The Revealing of the Secret*, published in 1943. In this book, he not only criticized the deposed Reza Shah (who ruled from 1921–1941), but also those voices of religious reformism that, he claimed, had attacked Shi'ism and its tenets. Indeed, the aforementioned book was a verbatim refutation of a short tract published a few months earlier called *The Secret of a Thousand Years*, authored by Ali Akbar Hakamizadeh, a close associate of Ahmad Kasravi, the avid advocate of secular reforms at the time.

After Burujerdi's death, Khomeini showed ambitions of wanting to secure a leadership position for himself, and he adopted an oppositional role to the government as a way of attaining this goal. He became vocal in his activities, and, under the rubric of the White Revolution (1962–1963), he opposed the pseudo-modernization of Mohammad Reza Shah (who ruled from 1941–1979). Khomeini's actions did not lead to his political success, but instead led to his exile from Iran in 1964.

Khomeini's second stage occurred while a political exile in Najaf. Although officially in exile, he assumed the role of a scholar, gradually gaining leadership in opposition to the Shah, which was gaining widespread popularity within most segments of the Iranian population. Already a recognized cleric in the Shi'ia hierarchy, the Khomeini of Najaf (1964–1978) continued with his scholarship but took a more active role in the fate of the Muslim world. What later proved to be a major incident was his delivery of a series of lectures in 1970 on Islamic government, later published as a treatise calling for an Islamic revolution and the formation of a government under the guardianship of a jurisconsult (*faqih*). He apparently responded to accusations by secular and leftist Iranians that Islam has no theory of state or no position on government and politics. He wrote in easy Persian prose, more or less free from the scholarly jargons of traditional Muslim jurists, calling for a revolution, claiming that Islam has the answer, and asserting that the proper government is the rule of Islamic law under the supervision and guardianship of trustworthy jurists.

When the revolutionary wave took over Iran in 1978, it shook the regime of the Pahlavi dynasty. Khomeini was forced out of Iraq and took up residence in a Parisian suburb until his victorious return to Iran in January 1979. Paris proved to be an ideal temporary residence for several reasons. He had access to world media and was surrounded by Iranian revolutionaries of all varieties, each gaining confidence and trust in him as a leader. In fact, he was granted the title of Imam (something new in Shi'ism, where this title is the prerogative of the twelve infallible leaders), and was recognized as the leader of the revolution. While in Paris, he endorsed a republican form of government for the future of Iran and supported the views of the largely liberal-democratic revolutionary elite that had gathered around him. Khomeini even went so far as to endorse the first draft of the constitution that was to create a republic in Iran. Most Iranians saw him as a hero of freedom and the voice of anti-imperialism.

With his return to Iran, Khomeini moved toward the establishment of an absolute "Islamic" rule under control of a jurist, and he took every opportunity to institutionalize such a system. His increasing sense of security in power enabled him to strengthen the position of the jurist to the point that he expounded this position as absolute in 1988. Before his death, Khomeini elevated the position of the jurist as "absolute," facilitating the emergence of autocratic tendencies within the system. Thus, this account considers Khomeini as a power-oriented person who increased his authority as he found himself at the center of politics in Iran. While this seems to be a plausible portrayal of Khomeini, the danger is that it may reduce this complex figure to a political being who only responded to power.

A better approach to capturing Khomeini's world is to concentrate on his two roles—one as a Muslim scholar, and the other as a political activist. The first Khomeini is a figure for the elites, and the second is for the masses. The first was a humble scholar whose central ideas relate to man as a creature devoted to the worship of God. Such a person would be oblivious to all worldly events, including the great political, economic, social, and cultural forces that occur around him. Indeed this Khomeini rarely saw the enormous forces that he had unleashed. Note, for example, the incident during his victorious return from a long exile to Iran: He knew that he had permanently destroyed both the present regime and the monarchy, and when asked what he felt regarding his return home he simply declared, "Nothing!" His answer perplexed many Iranians but can be understood as normal for a philosopher and a disciple of the seventeenth-century Iranian philosopher, Sadr al-Din al-Shirazi (Mulla Sadra 1571–1640), the last great Muslim philosopher and the founder of the school of transcendental theosophy.

At the same time, he was preoccupied with ethics throughout his life, wrote mystical poems, and as a jurist he transformed jurisprudence in Shi'a Islam. Therefore, one must wonder how he combined these four seemingly contradictory trends? But the brilliance of Khomeini lay in his ability to combine the four disciplines of *Fiqh* (jurisprudence), *'Erfan* (mysticism), *Akhlaq* (ethics), and *Falsafe* (philosophy) in Muslim tradition.

Khomeini's scholarly works include treatises in all these areas. Indeed, his first work, *Mesbah al-Hedayeh* (The Light of Guidance), ca. 1929/1930, is a work combining ethics and mysticism. His early teaching career was all about ethics, morality, and later philosophy. However, his philosophy was in the tradition of neo-Platonism, or what in Muslim tradition is called transcendent philosophy, because he thought the highest form of intellectual exercise was contemplating God's attributes. In his mind, God is the beginning, end, appearance, and essence. Whatever exists, even each individual, is nothing but a sign both from and of God. If God is all there is, and whatever appears is simply His manifestation, then humanity is part of a bigger scheme of orderly and good things. In other words, everything on earth emanates from God. The destiny of humanity dictates a harmonious life with the natural order of things. Such a life is possible because God has bestowed the desire for perfection and the power of reasoning within humanity. The main purpose of all revelations has been to elevate humanity to its highest possible stature, and Islam is no exception. Whether writing philosophy, poetry, or even jurisprudence, this idea is the overarching notion in the works of the scholar Khomeini.

However, Khomeini has another face. On one level, he was considered an arbiter and a guardian of the most authentic Muslim tradition in Iranian context. On another, he was the most important spokesperson of revolutionary and political Islam at the end of the twentieth century. That may explain why the most traditionalist and the most radical Islam-minded Iranians supported and followed him. He represented what his followers perceived as the truth of religion and was a man whose desires became law. In this capacity, Khomeini was also the voice of traditionalism and Islamism, and he could easily navigate the sophisticated clerical system of Shi'ism, where a labyrinth of ranks, titles, and rituals determined each clerical rank's order. In this capacity, he represents the truth of revolution and religion, and he became the embodiment of an oriental despot. This character is the "Khomeini of the masses," who appeals to passion and the will to power. As a man of enormous conviction and relentless principle, Khomeini would either remain silent, or if he entered the scene, he would remain truthful to his views. For the first half of his life, Khomeini kept silent and acted as a teacher and scholar.

The main reason for his initial silence was that he knew how the hierarchy within the Shi'i clerics functioned and never violated any of the protocols. For example, as long as Ayatollah Mohammad Hossein Tabatabei Burujerdi (d. 1961) was alive, Khomeini remained silent, even if he disagreed with him, out of deference. After Burujerdi, Khomeini felt his turn had come to assume leadership of the Muslims in Iran. This coincided with the agrarian, economic, and social reforms in Iran, which the opposition branded as a project of

Americanization. Thus, Khomeini defined his new leadership in terms of opposing the existing order and advocating an order based on Islam. At that point, his casting of the Pahlavi regime as the instrument of American dominance in the region brought him publicity and popularity but also imprisonment and exile. In June 1963, he was arrested and incarcerated in Tehran. He was released after nine months, but upon his return to Qom he resumed his vocal opposition to the reforms of the regime, guaranteeing his own arrest and exile from the country in November 1964 until January 1979 when he returned as the leader of the Islamic Revolution that ended the monarchy in Iran.

During his years in exile he remained active and vocal. He was helped most by the fact that he was a natural master of timing and language. He knew when to speak and had an enormous power of silence. His interactions with his fellow men relied on his interpretation of the truth, which concentrated on the notion of the ideal leader having absolute authority over the life and property of the people at large. While Khomeini of the elite clearly stated that God's message is beyond human grasp, as a general leader, he suggested that there are people who can grasp God's wishes, wills, and commands. He presented this conviction in the theory of "the Guardianship of the Jurisconsult." This idea has its root in a series of lectures Khomeini delivered in Najaf, between January 20 and February 6, 1970, on the theory and implementation of an Islamic government.

At this point, Khomeini began to partake in the revolutionary discourse of the day. There was a competition to capture the minds of the youth about the future. The Left presented a Marxist alternative to the existing monarchy, but more alarming was the so-called "Islamist-Marxist," the People's Mojahedins, who presented a Marxist narrative of Islam. In fact, a contemporary historian and member of the clergy who devoted his life to the study of Islamic discourse said that Khomeini's lectures were a response to the claim that Iranian youth were inflicted with un-Islamic views. Apparently, in the late 1960s, a group of activist clergies, whose members became the prominent leaders of the revolution, sent a report to Najaf, alarming Khomeini about the rapid progress of Marxist ideas among the Muslim youth. As a response, Khomeini delivered a series of lectures in an easy syntax so that the youth and those unfamiliar with Islamic discourse and the nuances of Islamic jurisprudence would understand them. This was to be an alternative government to the existing monarchy.

His theory of government is based on Islamic law, which was the reason it became obligatory for all to follow (since the Qur'an commands Muslims to "obey God, obey His Prophet and those who are in authority amongst you" [Qur'an 4:59]). Most Muslims developed the notion of Caliphdom, and the minority Shi'is developed the notion of Imamate, stipulating that the formation of government was the prerogative of an Imam designated by God. Since Khomeini argued for the rule of the jurisconsults, in some ways, his theory represented an innovation in the history of Shi'i political thought. Instead of an infallible Imam, henceforth, Khomeini declared that it was possible for any jurisconsult to take charge, provided he was capable; but more importantly, provided he was righteous and well-versed with Shi'i law.

Khomeini died a natural death while still in power, a very rare occurrence anywhere in the Muslim world. Ironically, his formula of "Islamic Republic, not One Word more and not One Word Less" has caused great amount of debate since his death. While his legacy remains strong, there are many who challenge the extent of the power of the jurist. The republican aspect is alive and well as the republic, and there is no balance established yet. Khomeini's theory, in the parlance of Muslim jurisprudence, was *"Ijtihadi Ekhtelafi"* (reasoning of one scholar and an area of contention), thus another strong scholar may abrogate it just easily as it was instituted, but for now it provides the parameter of political discourse in Iran.

Suggested Reading

Davani, A. 1981. *Nahzat-e Rohaniyun-e Iran.* (The movement of the clerics of Iran), 11 volumes. Tehran: Bonyad-e Imam Reza.

Khomeini, R. *Sahifeye Noor* (The book of light), 21 volumes. Tehran: Vezarat-e Ershad Eslami.

Millani, M. 1994. *The making of Iran's Islamic revolution: from monarchy to Islamic republic.* Boulder, Co: Westview Press, Second Edition.

Moin, B. 2000. *Khomeini, life of the Ayatollah.* New York: St. Martin Press.

Rajaee, F. 1983. *Islamic values and world view: Khomeyni on man the state and international politics.* Lanham Md: University Press of America.

FARHANG RAJAEE

✦ KURDS

The Iranian Kurds, who like most other Iranian nationalities are of Indo–European origin, account for roughly 6 to 7 million of Iran's 70 million population. Although the number of Turkish and Iraqi Kurds is increasing, demographers project that the increase in Iran's Kurdish population will remain minimal through 2050. Kurds in Iran have become urbanized at a rapid rate. However, tribal affiliations and tribal organizations have remained quite strong throughout the rapid urbanization of the Kurdish society. Kurdish belongs to the Iranic branch of the Indo–European family of languages. As such, it is more akin to Persian than Arabic and Turkish. There is no Kurdish *lingua franca*. However, one should not overemphasize the differences among various Kurdish vernaculars, as they are all related to each other. In Iran, the main Kurdish dialect is Sorani, which is widely used in such major cities as Mahabad, Saqqez, Sanandaj, and Marivan. Kurds in Kermanshah use Kirmanshahi, which is similar to Lori, an Iranian language spoken by the Lors, who live primarily in the neighboring province of Loristan. The Kurds living around Paveh and several other towns near the Iran–Iraq border use Hawrami (Gurani). In general, language remains the most significant barometer of Kurdish identity in today's Iran.

Three-fifths of the Kurds are Sunni Muslims. However, 1.5 million Iranian Kurds are Shi'ia Muslims, many of whom live in major cities of Kermanshah and Hamadan as well as in the Khorasan region. In addition, there are also Kurdish followers of the various Sufi orders as well as very small communities of Christian Kurds.

The Iranian Kurds joined the rest of their compatriots in supporting the 1978–1979 revolution in the country. The downfall of the Pahlavi monarchy offered the Kurds an opportunity to push for sociocultural autonomy long demanded by the Kurdish Democratic Party of Iran (KDPI). In March 1979, the Iranian government conducted a referendum asking the voters to choose between two alternative forms of government: monarchy and the Islamic republic. The secular KDPI boycotted the referendum because it only offered two choices to the voters. Given the profound antipathy towards the fallen monarchical regime at that time, it was evident that the majority of voters would opt for the choice of the Islamic republic. The Kurds thus lost their first political battle with the country's new revolutionary regimes.

The Kurds then shifted the focus of their political struggle to affect the draft of Iran's new constitution. Although the draft of the constitution contained democratic provisions to defend the rights of all Iranians, the Kurds felt that it did not address their autonomy demands. Moreover, when the revolution's leader Ayatollah Khomeini ordered the establishment of an Assembly of Experts to review the proposed draft of the constitution, Kurdish nationalists were excluded from this body. Khomeini and his supporters feared that the foundation of their preferred system of government would be weakened if ethnic secular nationalist demands were accommodated in the country's new constitution.

Tension between the Islamic authorities and the Kurds eventually manifested itself in a series of armed clashes between the KDPI and the newly formed Islamic Revolutionary Guards. The dispatch of Sheikh Sadegh

Khalkhali as the chief revolutionary judge to the Kurdish regions further exacerbated the conflict between the Kurds and the Iranian authorities. In a series of impromptu trials, Khalkhali condemned scores of Kurdish nationalists to death. Continuing military confrontations between the Kurds and government forces led to the banning of the KDPI in autumn 1979. However, this did not discourage Ghassemlou from continuing his dialogue with the Iranian government, but Ghassemlou's diplomatic approach did cause fissures within the KDPI. The ensuing power struggle among the party's different factions came to a head during the KDPI's Eighth Congress in 1988, resulting in the expulsion of 15 top members of the party's Executive Committee. The expelled members then announced the establishment of the Kurdish Democratic Party of Iran—Revolutionary Leadership. However, this breakaway party failed to develop into a broad-based popular organization and soon ceased to function effectively.

The KDPI was dealt another major blow when Ghassemlou was assassinated on July 13, 1989 while meeting with the representatives of the Iranian government in Vienna. Both the KDPI and independent sources blamed the agents of the Iranian government for carrying out the assassination. Sadegh Sharafkandi succeeded Ghassemlou as the KDPI's new Secretary General. In a scene similar to Ghassemlou's assassination, Sharafkandi was gunned down in the Mykonos restaurant in Berlin in 1992. On April 10, 1997, a German court handed down a decision that implicated the highest officials of the Iranian government, including the Supreme Guide Ayatollah Khamenei and the then-president Ali Akbar Hashemi Rafsanjani, in masterminding Sharafkandi's assassination. These two assassinations, especially that of Ghassemlou, dealt a heavy blow to the strength of the KDPI inside Iran. Ghassemlou was an adept politician who had extensive contacts with a large cross-section of Iranian society.

The misfortunes of the KDPI, both before and after Ghassemlou's assassination, allowed another Kurdish movement, the Revolutionary Organization of the Kurdish Toilers of Iran (Komala), to emerge as the main contender for Kurdish aspirations in Iran. Komala claimed to be a revolutionary Marxist–Leninist party and saw the success of the Kurdish struggle within the context of a Marxist revolution in Iran. However, a faction within the Komala's leadership soon broke away and created the Workers' Communist Party of Iran. Most of the remaining members of the Komala eventually returned to the KDPI. Today, the Komala is a shell of its earlier years, and its organizational effectiveness inside Iran is questionable. The Workers' Communist Party has also splintered into two subgroups. It is, however, doubtful that this rigidly doctrinaire party has any firm base inside Iranian Kurdistan.

The election of the reformist candidate Mohammad Khatami as Iran's president in May 1997 generated a great deal of enthusiasm in the country, and the Kurds were cautiously optimistic about the prospects of change under the Khatami administration. But Khatami was never able to overcome his conservative opponents. In Kurdistan, many officials who had identified with Khatami's programs were forced out of office or arrested by security agencies. Throughout Khatami's presidency, city council elections were nullified by his entrenched opponents, and the credentials of either pro-reform or independent Kurdish candidates were routinely rejected by the country's powerful Council of Guardians whose members were generally hostile to the nascent reform movement.

Furthermore, some Kurds remained suspicious of several reformists in Khatami's camp because of their earlier participation in the suppression of Kurdish uprisings. For example, Hamid Reza Jalaipour, a significant architect of the reform movement and one of its prominent theoreticians, had spent 10 years in the province of Kurdistan fighting Kurdish autonomy demands. As a commander of a Revolutionary Guard unit in the early years of the revolution who later served as the Governor of Naqdeh and Mahabad and Deputy Governor General for Political Affairs in Kurdistan, Jalaipour was directly or indirectly responsible for some of the worst revolutionary excesses in the region.

A notable feature of the campaigns during Iran's 2005 presidential election was the open discussion of the nationality issues by some of the aspirants for the presidential office. This marked the first time since the establishment of the Islamic Republic that ethnic and nationality issues were recognized as part of public policy debate, and several candidates openly sought the votes of Iranian nationalities. Mostafa Moin, the torchbearer for the reformist camp, made special efforts to woo non-Persian voters and turned Iran's multinational character into an important part of his campaign platform. Moin criticized both those who ignored Iran's multinational character and those who sought to divide the country on ethnic, linguistic, and religious grounds. Recognizing discrimination as politically destabilizing, Moin stated that his administration would represent all nationalities. Echoing Khatami's campaign slogan, Moin also made "Iran for all Iranians" the centerpiece of his presidential campaign. In addition to Moin, several reformist personalities and writers opined that without recognizing the rights of Iranian nationalities, democracy would not take root in Iran. In the same vein, many reformists welcomed Jalal Talebani's election as the first Kurdish president of Iraq, and Iranian Kurds celebrated Talebani's victory as the natural progression of recognition of nationality rights in the region.

The reformists were soundly defeated in the first round of presidential balloting. Mahmoud Ahmadinejad, the eventual winner of Iran's ninth presidential election, campaigned on the platform of socioeconomic justice and Islamic values. His main target was the country's lower classes whose economic conditions had deteriorated under the reformist Khatami administration. Although Ahmadinejad did not make the issue of nationality rights part of his campaign platform, he was certainly not an unknown figure among the Kurds. In the early years of the revolution, Ahmadinejad was assigned to the Ramazan base of the Revolutionary Guards with responsibility for military operations in western Iran. He later served in other capacities, including a stint as a principal advisor to the Governor General of Kurdistan. Given the negative memories of Revolutionary Guards activities in Kurdistan since 1979, it was not surprising that the Iranian Kurds participated minimally in the country's 2005 presidential election. Between the two finalists in the second round of the election, Ahmadinejad received 17,248,782 votes while his opponent, Hashemi Rafsanjani, garnered 10,460,701 votes. According to Iran's Ministry of Interior, 62.66% of eligible voters participated in the election, with the highest turnout (80.43%) in the Ilam Province and the lowest rate of participation (37.37%) in the province of Kurdistan. West Azerbaijan, which includes Mahabad and Urumiyeh, two cities with a large Kurdish population, recorded the second lowest voter participation rate (44.02%) in the entire country. In other words, the Iranian Kurds expressed their dissatisfaction by boycotting the ninth presidential election in large numbers.

Moreover, the military confrontation between the Kurds and the Iranian government forces has intensified since mid-2005. For example, Iranian forces and the forces of the Kurdish Independent Life Party (Pjak), an offshoot of the Turkish-based Workers' Party of Kurdistan (PKK), have engaged in low-level military confrontations inside Iran. The Iranian authorities have accused the United States of arming and financing Pjak as part of Washington's policy of destabilizing the Islamic Republic. The involvement of outside groups in Kurdish affairs in Iran has added an unpredictable twist to the war of attrition in Iranian Kurdistan. For example, the KDPI has accused Pjak of undermining the legitimate struggle of the Iranian Kurds by its adventurist tactics.

Perhaps the most significant development in the post-Khatami Iranian Kurdistan has been the grassroots uprising in several Kurdish cities throughout the country since mid-2005. On July 11, 2005, Shavaneh Qaderi, a young Kurdish activist from Mahabad, was shot to death and pictures of his body were posted on a number of websites. Major demonstrations were held throughout Kurdistan demanding punishment for security forces responsible for Qaderi's killing, and this has become a catalyst for sporadic demonstrations that have been held elsewhere, including among Kurdish university students in Tehran, in support of broader Kurdish rights.

There has also been a resurgence of civil society Iranian Kurdistan, and a number of reformist Kurdish groups and organizations have found a way to work within the confines of the Iranian political system. This trend is reflected in a myriad of magazines and newspapers that are published by the Iranian Kurdish intelligentsia. For example the weekly magazine *Sirwan*, which has a large circulation in Kurdistan, publishes sophisticated analytical articles that are vastly superior to the vacuous sloganeering one finds in most of the Kurdish exile publications. Likewise, the biweekly *Hawar* covers internal developments in Kurdistan in an objective and highly informative manner that one does not find by reading Kurdish publications in Europe and North America. However, the Kurdish publications inside Iran operate under financial and political duress, and their long-term viability remains precarious. Although some Iranian Kurdish organizations operate their own websites, the number of domestically operated Kurdish websites has declined since 2005. For example, *asokurd.com*, the best online source about developments in Iranian Kurdistan, is no longer operational. In short, internal sources provide a far more nuanced picture of the complexities of inter- and intraethnic relations in Iranian Kurdistan than do the exile publications.

Suggested Reading
Entessar, N. 1992. *Kurdish ethnonationalism*. Boulder, Co: Lynne Rienner Publishers.
Koohi-Kamali, F. 2003. *The political development of the Kurds in Iran: pastoral nationalism*. New York: Palgrave Macmillan.
Natali, D. 2005. *The Kurds and the state: evolving national identity in Iraq, Turkey, and Iran*. Syracuse, NY: Syracuse University Press.
Vali, A., ed. 2003. *Essays on the origin of Kurdish nationalism*. Costa Mesa, Calif.: Mazda Publishers.

NADER ENTESSAR